ARCHITECTURAL AGENTS

ARCHITECTURAL AGENTS

The Delusional, Abusive, Addictive Lives of Buildings

Annabel Jane Wharton

UNIVERSITY OF MINNESOTA PRESS
MINNEAPOLIS • LONDON

The University of Minnesota Press gratefully acknowledges financial assistance for the publication of this book from the Department of Art, Art History and Visual Studies, Trinity College of Arts and Sciences, Duke University.

All photographs and illustrations are by the author, unless credited otherwise.

Published by the University of Minnesota Press
111 Third Avenue South, Suite 290
Minneapolis, MN 55401–2520
http://www.upress.umn.edu

Library of Congress Cataloging-in-Publication Data
Wharton, Annabel Jane.
Architectural agents : the delusional, abusive, addictive lives of buildings / Annabel Jane Wharton.
Includes bibliographical references and index.
ISBN 978-0-8166-9338-2 (hc : alk. paper)
ISBN 978-0-8166-9339-9 (pb : alk. paper)
1. Architecture. 2. Architecture—Human factors. I. Title.
NA2540.W475 2015
720.1—dc23
2014032695

Printed in the United States of America on acid-free paper

20 19 18 17 16 15 10 9 8 7 6 5 4 3 2 1

Dedicated to

Tessa Annabel and Vesper James Ramsdell,

who animate every space that they occupy

Contents

Acknowledgments ix

Introduction *Architectural Agency* xiii

PART I. DEATH

1 Murder 3

2 Spoils 31

PART II. DISEASE

3 Amnesia 59

4 Urban Toxicity 85

PART III. ADDICTION

5 Gambling 119

6 Digital Play 151

Conclusion *Buildings/Things, Bodies/Texts, History/Theory* 185

Notes 221

Bibliography 253

Index 283

Acknowledgments

Everywhere I worked on this book I benefited enormously from the knowledge and generosity of those who lived there. Most providentially at home, as has been the case for nearly a quarter of a century, my partner, Professor Kalman Bland, read and reread what I wrote, always with remarkable equanimity and new insight. Abroad, colleagues and friends shaped my experiences of the local and, consequently, my thoughts on it. This is particularly true of Jerusalem. Dear friends Dr. Rajai Dajani and Fadwa Dajani, Rami Dajani, and Hidaya Dajani introduced me to remarkable places in Jerusalem and Ramallah. Dr. Yoram Tsafrir provided me the experiences of recent archaeological undertakings and small Palestinian eateries. Dr. Sy Gitin, director of the Albright Institute, Dr. Khader Salameh, director of the Islamic Museum, and Dr. Thomas Neu, Middle East Representative of American Near East Refugee Aid, offered me access to otherwise impenetrable spaces. I very much appreciated my frank discussions with James S. Snyder, the Anne and Jerome Fisher Director of the Israel Museum. I also received collegial help from Avner Amiri, architect and restoration expert, with whom I collaborated in a study of the fabric of the American Colony in Jerusalem; Paul Vester, president of the board of directors of the American Colony; Michael Schwartz, current overseeing architect of the American Colony Hotel; and the late Val Vester, who generously shared with me both memories and a prepublication manuscript of her "Family Album: A Brief History of the American Colony." I am also indebted to Professor Oleg Grabar who in Princeton revealed to me some of the secrets of institutions in Jerusalem.

I am very grateful to the archivists who have made the work that I did in their archives pleasurable as well as productive: Lee Hiltzik, archivist at the Rockefeller Archives in Tarrytown, New York; Michael K. Carter, the head of the Cloisters Library and Archive; the staff of the Philadelphia Museum of Art Archive who made available to me the George Grey Barnard Papers; Rachel Lev, American Colony archivist; Dr. Barbara Bair of the Manuscripts Division of the Library of Congress; Peter Michel, director of Special Collections at the University of Nevada, Las Vegas; Arieh Rochman-Halperin, head archivist at the Rockefeller Museum in Jerusalem; and Mary Jo Mandula, vice president and general manager of the Tribune Properties, who was in charge of the archival files of the Tribune Tower in Chicago when I consulted them.

I am also deeply indebted to those who generously contributed to my field research in Las Vegas. I benefited from discussion with Sara Gorgon, public relations manager for MGM Resorts International, and particularly from the insights into casino programming and decoration offered by Roger Thomas, executive vice president of design for Wynn Resorts. My daughter, Andrea Epstein, offered me her invaluable take on Vegas during our visits together to the Strip. In Santiago de Compostela, Esperanza Senande, director of marketing of the Hostal de los Reyes Católicos, provided historical information as well as access to the inner workings of the building.

In the unfamiliar territories of addiction and gaming, I am particularly grateful for the help of my Duke University colleagues: Professor Timothy J. Strauman, professor of psychology and neuroscience, and Dr. Robert H. Shipley, director of the Duke Medical Center QuitSmart program, with whom I have discussed the chemistry and habits of obsessive behavior. I realized a new obstacle to interdisciplinary work in the process of producing this text: the rapidity of publication in the sciences and its slowness in the humanities ensures that the science cited in humanities books is always out of date. The same is true of digital media developments. Professors Julian Lombardi, Mark McCahill, Victoria Szabo, and Mark Olson softened the impact of my immersion in the digital world. I also benefited greatly from the assiduous and capable work of my research assistant, Allison Clark. We learn from all of our students, but I was taught a great deal by those attending my graduate seminars on Spatial Practices, particularly Bobo Bose-Kolanu, Maria Doerfler, Sonia Hazard, and John Vincler, and Live Images, especially Lidia Klein and Ainehi Edoro. I also received excellent training in three-dimensional digital image construction from two of our undergraduates, Charles Sparkman and Michal Koszycki.

The presentation of parts of this text as works-in-progress in different venues much improved them. I received useful comments on the Hospital de los Reyes Católicos in Professor Anthony Cutler's seminar on sacred space at the Pennsylvania State University. I thank him and Professor Charlotte Houghton for arranging my visit there in September 2006. The hospital was also the subject of a plenary paper for the Patristic, Medieval, and Renaissance Studies Conference at the University of Villanova, presented in October 2006. I am grateful to Kevin Hughes for his comments as well as his invitation and hospitality. An initial rendering of the Rockefeller Museum material was presented at the invitation of Miriam Elman and Madelaine Adelman in a conference on "Jerusalem Across the Disciplines" at Arizona State University in Tempe in February 2007. A preliminary version of the Cloisters Museum argument was presented at the generous invitation of Professor Julia Foulkes at a Rockefeller Archive Center workshop titled "The Arts in Place" in April 2007. Material on the American Colony was first presented in 2008 at Bar-Ilan University, where it received a productively hostile reception. My analysis of *Assassin's Creed* as an expression of the picturesque was initially offered in a College Art Association session on "The Politics of the Panoramic" in February 2012. I am grateful to the session organizer, Professor Alan Wallach, and other members of the panel and audience for their useful comments on the material. I am also indebted to Professor Ra'anan Boustan for inviting me to present a foray into thing theory in a colloquium on "Relics and Other Sacred Objects" at the University of Texas at Austin in 2012. The material on Protestant missionaries to Palestine was introduced in a symposium at Yad Ben Zvi in Jerusalem, also in 2012. There I got to know Professors Ora Limor and Elhanan Reiner, with whom I subsequently corresponded about Zion. Discussion should always be such fun and disagreements so comradely and productive.

I am very grateful to the careful reading of the manuscript given to me by Professor Terry Smith. Those criticisms made it a much better work. I also want to thank Pieter Martin of the University of Minnesota Press for his expeditiousness, craft, and collegiality, and Sheila Dillon, chair of my department, for her support of the project's publication.

As is apparent from these acknowledgments, this text has been long in the making. Some part of the delay was due to the diversionary delights and obligations of grandparenting. Though our granddaughter may have slowed its writing, *Architectural Agents* is all the better for the joie de vivre with which she infected its author. This volume is lovingly dedicated to Tessa Annabel Ramsdell and her new brother, Vesper James.

Introduction

Architectural Agency

> I will show you how the building is given form and substance by analogy with the members and form of man. . . . I will [then] show you [that] the building is truly a living man. You will see what it must eat in order to live, exactly as it is with man. It sickens and dies or sometimes is cured of its sickness by a good doctor. Sometimes, like man, it becomes ill again because it neglected its health. Many times, through [the care] of a good doctor, it returns to health and lives a long while and finally dies in its own time. There are some that are never ill and then at the end die [suddenly]; others are killed by other people for one reason or another. . . . Through corruption, the body of the building rots like that of a man. Through excess it is ruined and dies like a man.
>
> —Antonio di Piero Averlino (Filareti),
> *Treatise on Architecture,* ca. 1465

> It was as if, after its successive extensions, the colossus had been seized with shame and repugnance for the murky neighborhood in which it had first sprung up and which it had later massacred, and had just turned its back on it, leaving the mud of the narrow streets behind it, presenting its upstart face to the sunny thoroughfare of the new Paris. Now, as it was represented in the picture on the advertisements, it had grown bigger and bigger, like the ogre in the fairytale whose shoulders threatened to break through the clouds.
>
> —Description of the department store in Émile Zola,
> *The Ladies' Paradise,* 1883

Agency

Places, like people, are usually more engaging and less dangerous the better we know them. Part of that understanding involves the recognition of their effects, their agency. "Agent" and "agency" are derived from the Latin verb *agree,* "to set in motion"; its present participle, *agens, agentis,* used as an adjective, means "effective." In philosophy and in common language, the term "agent" is embedded in complex concepts of human morality, intentionality, and individual autonomy.[1] But in law and business the meaning of "agent" is less freighted. There, applied not only to persons but also to corporations, "agent" loses most of its ethical baggage: "A person [the agent] employed by another [the principal] to act for him."[2] In chemistry, as in law, no intentions are ascribed to agency; an agent is a substance, not a person, that has a physical, chemical, or medicinal effect on proximate things.

As in chemistry, "agent" is used in this book to name nonhuman entities—spatial objects—that have an effect on their animate environments, independent of intention. The agent here, as in business, may also have been assigned tasks by its principal (architect, patron, or owner), though if and how those tasks might be carried out can never be contractually binding. That is, a principal might intend a building to behave in a certain way on her behalf, but the structure's actual performance in the world can never be fully controlled. As the French sociologist Pierre Bourdieu observed, "Each agent, wittingly or unwittingly, willy nilly, is a producer and reproducer of objective meaning."[3] However, here, in contrast to business, the architectural agent is particular, individual, and ethical. "By means of microscopic observation and astronomical projection the lotus flower can become the foundation for an entire theory of the universe and an agent whereby we may perceive Truth."[4] In this text "agent" retains an ethical valence similar to that of the lotus in Yukio Mishima's short story.

The assumption is often made that agency also involves consciousness.[5] Although buildings in novels, like the department store in Zola's *Ladies' Paradise,* may have consciousness, buildings in the landscape do not. But consciousness is not an essential attribute of agency. Human agents, who we all acknowledge to have consciousness, often enough act unconsciously. Drunk drivers are, for example, particularly dangerous agents in a state of unconsciousness. Moreover, in many instances, human actions are demonstrably not the result of rational reflection, but rather a conditioned or mechanical response to physical, social, or personal circumstances—freezing temperatures, conformity, addiction, and the like.[6] Some human agents serving certain institutions and corporations may also frequently act without conscience, if not without consciousness.

The law certainly doesn't require consciousness of the recipients of its protection—as the ascription of legal rights to the unborn and the long dead demonstrate. Indeed, the most developed arguments for agency without consciousness are legal ones. In England, at least from the twelfth through mid-nineteenth centuries, things, including buildings, were held liable as agents for the human deaths that they caused under the law of *deodands.* A *deodand,* though literally "a thing given to God," was actually forfeit not to God but to the king and commonly levied as a fine, equivalent to the thing's worth.[7] The fine was paid into the royal purse by the object's owner or, if there was no owner, by the township in which the death occurred. For example, in 1322, a coroner's jury considered the case of a certain woman, Sarah Woodward, from the town of Radstone.

> They say that the said Sarah was lodged in a frail and dilapidated house, and on the preceding Sunday it fell in upon her by misadventure, and she died forthwith. They also say that no one was guilty of her death in any way. The fallen wood and stones are appraised at twelve pence, for which Radstone will account.[8]

The house and no one else killed Sarah. And even the house was assessed only for the stones and wood that did her in.

The deodand was common in medieval legal proceedings. Before the recognition of mitigating circumstances and degrees of murder and manslaughter, causing the death of a person was a capital offense. At that time the deodand may well have functioned as a legal ploy by which the liability for a death might be assessed in a just manner. Although the deodand seems to have almost disappeared in England by the eighteenth century, the law was revived in the nineteenth century. With industrialization the deodand was redeployed as a means of levying penalties for the many deaths caused by mechanical devices, particularly locomotives.[9] Legislation was passed to protect industrial interests, and the deodand was eliminated by an act of Parliament in 1846. Premodern intuitions about the animation of things allowed those things a semblance of the moral agency associated with culpability. With the rational repression of that intuition in modernity, the legal system required revision.

In the late twentieth and early twenty-first centuries, the law seems to be moving again in the direction of recognizing things as agents. In law, agents have long been exempted from self-consciousness (responsibility) in acting on behalf of a principal.[10] Now the corporation, a nonhuman agent, patently without consciousness (or conscience), has been awarded the legal status of personhood.[11] Officers of the corporation sought legal recognition of its agency not for the sake of justness but for profit. Indeed, in common understanding, the corporation is regarded at best as amoral and at worst as immoral. Most egregiously, the U.S. Supreme Court has recognized the corporation as an agent with First Amendment free-speech rights and hence the privilege to intervene in politics through the campaign funding of those candidates for elected office who will work in its interest. There are even those who argue that corporations are not only agents, but moral agents or agents with intentions.[12] Recognizing a corporation as a moral agent seems utterly obscene, perhaps because, if corporations do have intentions, they are so unrelentingly venal.

Juristically less successful, but ethically more compelling, are efforts to extend legal standing to the things closest in their responsiveness to human beings—that is, animals and machines. A particularly persuasive legal argument has also been offered to extend standing to natural things.[13] Many of the arguments for the legal standing of rivers and trees can also be made for buildings. Like some rivers or trees, some buildings have a legally recognized worth independent of their use value. Like some rivers or trees, some buildings have authoritative public bodies, like the National Trust for Historic Preservation and the Society for the Preservation of Historical Buildings, prepared to review actions inconsistent with their well-being. What rivers and trees lack now, but what has been argued that they should have, are executors empowered to institute legal actions on their behalf—on the model of executors who act for minors or for comatose persons. Such rights might with equal legitimacy be claimed on behalf of buildings. Of course, it is unlikely that either trees or buildings will attain legal standing anytime soon.

The ascription of agency to a building calls attention to three underemphasized aspects of architecture: its commodity-resistant particularity, its text-resistant materiality, and its phenomenology-resistant history.

1. Uniqueness. All the sites discussed in this text—from the Cloisters to Mount Zion—are obviously sui generis. Granting uniqueness to major structures with knowable histories is easy; allowing uniqueness to nondescript spaces might seem more problematic. Nevertheless, the specificity of location and particularity of use make each built space singular. The distinctive spatial difference of even the humblest place is noticeable when an attempt is made to eliminate it. One fictional example makes this point albeit with parodic excess. In Neal Stephenson's *Snow Crash,* the female protagonist's mother works for what remains of the federal government. Her office is "a large room with computer workstations placed across it in a grid."

> At one time the workstations were partitioned, but partitions have been removed. Now there are just workstations and chairs. Not even any desktops. . . . [T]here's the question of interchangeability. Fed workers, like military people, are intended to be interchangeable parts. What happens if your workstation should break down? You're going to sit there and twiddle your thumbs until it gets fixed? No siree, you're going to move to a spare workstation and get to work on that. And you don't have that flexibility if you've got half a ton of personal stuff cached inside of a desk. . . . All workstations are the same. You come in in the morning, pick one at random, sit down, and get to work. You could try to favor a particular station, try to sit there every day, but it would be noticed. Generally you pick the unoccupied workstation that's closest to the door. That way, whoever came in earliest sits closest, whoever came in latest is way in the back, for the rest of the day it's obvious at a glance

> who's on the ball in this office and who is—as they whisper to each other in the bathrooms—having problems.[14]

In Fedland, the successful elimination of human difference is recognized as being dependent on the erasure of spatial distinctions. The dystopic quality of the narrative issues from the viciousness required to commoditize spaces as well as humans. The suppressed desire of the workers to identify their own place signifies the particular spatial agency of even the least distinctive sites.

According to the *Oxford Dictionary of Economics,* "commodity" is defined as "a standardized good, which is traded in bulk and whose units are interchangeable."[15] Soy beans and crude oil are commodities; the histories that each bean and drop once had are irrecoverably lost in the process of their commoditization. Commodities are utterly fungible. Buildings, each of which is unique because of its history, form, and/or location, are not.

2. Embodiedness. Buildings' bodies are poked and prodded in this book.[16] Their accretive capacities are investigated in the Las Vegas Strip and Mount Zion; the health of their circulatory systems is examined in the casino and the Palestine Archaeological Museum. Even the building's fabric and its ornament are considered in the discussion of the Cloisters and the Tribune Tower. Ernest Richmond, a British architect working in Mandate Jerusalem, knew the importance of a structure's outer membrane. "All skin decays, but so long as there is life in the body which it covers its tissues are continually renewed. So long as the Dome of the Rock remains a live building—a building that is to say which is an integral part in the life that surrounds it—so long as it fulfills the functions it has fulfilled for 1,200 years, so long must its skin be continually renewed."[17] Richmond's observations of an old building assume its bodiliness.

That buildings have bodies is also apparent in the way we judge them according to the length of their lives. It is presupposed that young structures should look and behave youthfully; old structures are allowed their decay. Buildings that don't act their age are disorienting. Zola describes such a building in his novel *Pot Luck.*

> To put his friend at ease, Campardon showed him round the apartment. First of all, there was the big white-and-gold drawing room, elaborately decorated with imitation moldings. This was situated between a little green parlor, which had been turned into a study, and the bedroom, which they could not enter but whose narrow shape and mauve wallpaper the architect described. When he took him into the dining-room, all in imitation wood, with its strange mixture of beading and panels, Octave, enchanted, exclaimed: "It's very handsome!"

> There were two great cracks running right through the paneling on the ceiling, and in one corner the paint had peeled off and was showing the plaster.
>
> "Yes, it certainly creates an effect," said the architect slowly, with his eyes riveted to the ceiling. "You see, these kinds of houses are built for effect. The walls, though, aren't very solid. The house was only built twelve years ago, and they're already cracking. They build the frontage in very fine stone, with all sorts of sculpture, give the staircase three coats of varnish, and touch up the rooms with gilt and paint; that's what impresses people and inspires respect."[18]

It might also be noted that the bodily symptoms of aging in both humans and buildings may be treated cosmetically—in neither case with much success.

In this book, the embodiedness of buildings acts as a foil to their textualization. Certainly, as bodies, buildings can be disciplined by texts—building codes and zoning laws, marketing lists and real estate brochures, popular and scholarly critiques. Buildings can also be described and investigated by texts, as I hope this volume demonstrates. But buildings always exceed texts. Buildings, like bodies, cannot be reduced to texts. The theoretician and architect Bernard Tschumi observed, "There are numerous ways to equate architecture with language. Yet such equations often amount to a reduction and an exclusion."[19] "Always," however, should be substituted for Tschumi's "often."

3. Historicity. In *Poltergeist,* the classic horror film written by Stephen Spielberg, the concealed history of the site of a suburban house is the cause of its destruction.[20] The greedy property speculator who developed the housing tract built it on a cemetery from which headstones but not bodies had been removed. Immoral histories, left unrecovered and hidden behind conveniently invented narratives, tend to fester. Buildings, by the traces of their endurance, may well provide evidence for their own recuperative history. As the Hostal de los Reyes Católicos and the American Colony demonstrate, a building's unique body provides the observer with an archive of the particular pasts, good and bad, in which it participated. A site's agency is only accessible after a serious assessment of the lies told about it in its past as well as in its present. The ethical lessons of a building are deeply historical.

If the uniqueness of a building works to preserve its history, its history resists a building's absorption into phenomenological thinking. Phenomenology, by its name, promises to take physical phenomena seriously. Indeed, Maurice Merleau-Ponty, one of phenomenology's greatest practitioners, suggests that that material reality enjoys some independence of its human interpreters: "The world is there before any possible analysis of mine. . . . When I begin to reflect my reflection bears upon an unreflective experience."[21] But as noted in the *Stanford Encyclopedia of*

Philosophy, "Phenomenology is the study of structures of consciousness as experienced from the first-person point of view."[22] A critique of Eliade and Heidegger in the conclusion finds that phenomenology is more likely to kill objects than to animate them.

My arguments for the bodily agency of buildings, in contrast to those made for corporations by the Supreme Court, are not presented to promote those sites' profitability. The case made for agency in this book is social and political, not legal or economic. Nor are my arguments offered as a medievalist's nostalgic appeal for the reenchantment of the world.[23] Nothing in my propositions should raise expectations that relics will again consistently work miracles or that sacred spaces will regularly stage epiphanies. Things and places work differently in different cultures and at different times. Indeed, the sample cases in this volume are presented to argue that the power of sites lies in the specificity of their location in the physical and social landscape and in the distinctive marks that they make on their settings. Now, as in the past, buildings may be immobile, but they are by no means passive. Our *habitus*—the way we live in the world—is certainly informed by our relations with other human beings.[24] But spatial objects also model our lives. Some structures, like Bentham's infamous Panopticon, are insidiously manipulative.[25] But most buildings, like most people, can both confirm our familiar patterns of behavior and modify them. We build a classroom to accommodate a certain kind of learning; the classroom in turn molds the kind of learning that we do or even that we can imagine. Modifications in the room might lead to innovations in teaching practices. Buildings, in this sense, certainly have social agency. Indeed, the acts of buildings may be compared with the acts of their human counterparts insofar as those acts are similarly overdetermined—that is, fraught with more conditions in their social circumstances or individual histories than are necessary to account for the ways in which they work.

Agency Avoidance

The ascription of agency to buildings is largely avoided in the literature of architectural history. Perhaps it has been too readily dismissed as simple anthropomorphizing. Certainly this book flirts with the pathetic fallacy. John Ruskin invented the phrase "pathetic fallacy" as a label for the literary ascription of human capacities to nonhuman things or ideas.[26] My formulation, "this text flirts," causes Ruskin to roll over in his grave. But Ruskin is not aggravated either by my text's purportedly immodest behavior or by the apparent absurdity of the trope that a book desires love. His disdain is incurred by my having ascribed human capacities to a book to make such a trivial point. This instance of the pathetic (empathetic) fallacy is bad not because it is untruthful (a book obviously does not have the capacity for romance), but because its pathos has no emotional credibility. For Ruskin, the phrase reveals its author's lack of an elevated sensibility. If a writer's passion is true and her object worthy, anthropomorphizing is, for Ruskin, not a literary error but a legitimate mode of expression. In a lecture of 1857, he uses it himself to express his disgust at elaborate apparel of the sort worn by some members of his audience:

> If, for a moment, the spirits of Truth and of Terror, which walk invisibly among the masques of the earth, would lift the dimness from our erring thoughts, and show us how—inasmuch as the sums exhausted for that magnificence would have given back the failing breath to many an unsheltered outcast on moor and street—they who wear it have literally entered into partnership with Death; and dressed themselves in his spoils.[27]

Anthropomorphizing is not wrong—it is not a pathetic fallacy—if it is used appropriately to make a morally important point. In any case, by ascribing agency to sites, I certainly describe buildings as acting, sometimes in the same ways that humans act. But I try hard to avoid suggesting either that those structures act with intention or that their actions are without human consequences.

In contemporary writing on architecture, the attribution of agency to buildings is, outside fiction, rare. In the humanities, the agency of built space is often presumed but rarely argued. For instance, Jane Jacobs's epochal *Death and Life of Great American Cities* insistently (and justifiably) anthropomorphizes the city not just in the title of her book but also in its contents. In discussing the "unslumming" of urban space, Jacobs describes a city's ability to grow its own middle class; and in commenting on building complexes, she recognizes "the tendency for massive single elements in cities to cast a deadening influence."[28] Two astute but very different projects, Terry Smith's *Architecture of Aftermath* and Robert Bevan's *Destruction of Memory,* focus on the deaths of buildings but treat the social effect of their loss not their suffering.[29] In his *Edifice Complex,* Sudjic Deyan evokes authoritarian buildings through his powerful descriptions of their effects. From Hitler's Chancellery to Reagan's presidential library, Sudjic compellingly reveals the bad acts of buildings.[30] The "edifice complex" that is subject of the book is not, however, the psychological state of buildings but that of their monomaniacal patrons. When the architectural body is addressed directly in the humanities, it tends to be bracketed as metaphorical. For example, Neil Harris, in his engaging volume *Building Lives,* expects his title to be understood as a figure of speech: "The sustaining assumption for what follows is a simple, not to say a simple-minded device. To see what might happen by treating buildings as if they formed some kind of special species, a hybrid class whose character, identity, survival, interaction with humans, and, above all, whose defined life stages merited systematic examination. Of course, this is a conceit."[31]

The same merely metaphoric understanding of buildings as embodied agents occurs in scientific and social scientific discussions of architecture. For example, "sick buildings"—buildings that make those who occupy them ill—are at the moment a hot topic. But in those studies on the subject that I have read, "sick" applies only analogically to the offending structure. As the author of *Sick Buildings*, Thad Godish, noted, "The term 'sick building'... implies that a building is sick. Being nonhuman, of course, a building can only be sick in a metaphorical sense."[32] Similarly, in the growing field of biomimetics, buildings are the displaced subject in investigations of the human environment. Architecture is accorded no agency. One of the leaders in the field, Petra Gruber, writes: "The basic assumption of the research is that the study of the overlapping fields of biology and architecture will show innovative potential for architectural solutions."[33] Architecture is passive in this formulation. It is the recipient of knowledge, not its generator. No claim is made that the observation of architecture might provide biologists with a better understanding of the environment. More cognizant of the acting body of a building is current work in the field of cultural geography. In a 2012 essay, Donald McNeill and Kim McNamara, for instance, articulated some of the rewards of considering the duration of buildings in a brief review of the status of architectural biography in their field.[34] Nevertheless, in the field of art and architecture, biography still is reserved for humans—as exemplified by an engaging book entitled *Biographies and Space: Placing the Subject in Art and Architecture*.[35]

Architectural Agents investigates the ontological status of buildings as embodied agents more persistently than these previous studies. It certainly recognizes both the controls on buildings imposed by their topographies and the effects that human producers have on their architectural products. But it also makes the case that buildings exert a force on the world independent of human intention or even human consciousness. A biographical treatment has advantages for the building. More about a structure is learned by considering the whole of its history. Architectural historians have been inclined to focus on a building's origin and its ur-form. But as is the case with humans, an evaluation of the youth of a building is more accurate when its old age is taken into account. A reconstruction of the duration of a structure requires more careful observation of its old body, obliging the researcher to appreciate the irregularities of its fabric and the inconsistencies of its program.

A biographical treatment of a building also has advantages for the observer. In the posthistorical present, the past is increasingly ignored.[36] Reviewing the full life span of a structure provides witness to its various social and cultural pasts, offering a more textured understanding of its temporal location. Probing a building's duration also uncovers the false histories that have been fabricated for it. Several of the structures discussed in this text have been embedded in fictional pasts as part of their economic or political manipulation. Investigating a structure's representation as well as its fabric unmasks the venal or ideological functions for which a structure has been appropriated. In any case, by recognizing what in the past a structure has endured or perpetrated, the observer also has a firmer basis for an empathetic or critical response to its present condition.

Content

We are more aware of the corruption of our political system when its protection of powerful interests enables the deaths of innocents.[37] We are commonly more aware of our bodies and their various parts when they aren't working properly. Architectural bodies are also particularly conspicuous in their malfeasance or in their suffering. Consequently, pathological sites make the case for the embodied agency of buildings more readily than healthy ones. Further, those who acknowledge the pain of buildings may avoid the bad consequences of ignoring it. As Elaine Scarry, a critic and historian of literature, observes:

> The difficulty of articulating physical pain permits political and perceptual complications of the most serious kind. The failure to express pain—whether the failure to objectify its attributes or instead the failure, once those attributes are objectified, to refer them to their original site in the human body—will always work to allow its appropriation and conflation with debased forms of power; conversely, the successful expression of pain will always work to expose and make impossible that appropriation and conflation.[38]

All architectural pathologies have their particular economies, usually rapacious, and politics, commonly despotic. The bulk of this book records biographies of problematic spaces and offers diagnoses of dangerous places.[39] The three parts of its core are composed of paired structures or sites. One member of each set is located in Jerusalem. Jerusalem has arguably suffered longer and more spectacularly from chronic violence than any other continuously inhabited city in the world. Violence begets violence. Jerusalem is historically one of the planet's most pathological spaces. The recurrent consideration of Jerusalem provides the basis for assessing the pathology of an urban space as well as the health of particular buildings, a theme that is more fully developed in several chapters, particularly that on Las Vegas.

Although the selection of sample cases might appear to be arbitrary, they were chosen to exemplify architectural agency through a specific set of spatial pathologies. Built spaces everywhere suffer from similar symptoms. The lessons learned from the sites treated in this text are applicable elsewhere.

Each brace of buildings probes a distinct spatial pathology: violent death, disease, and addiction. Part I considers various forms of physical violence done by buildings through assessments of two museums. A museum appears to be the most benign of buildings—its cultural benefits are certainly broadly acknowledged. If the dark sides of two of the world's most magical spaces (the Cloisters Museum in New York and the Palestine Archaeological Museum in Jerusalem) can be revealed, the argument for the pathological agency of buildings is well begun. Visitors are aware of what a museum brings to a culture but tend to overlook what it has taken away. To redress this omission, the making of one museum is treated here as a murder case. The Cloisters, funded by John D. Rockefeller Jr. and opened in 1938, is a synthetic whole constructed from the transplanted parts of old European buildings. Some of the mutilated bodies left behind survived, though scars still attest to the removal of their vital parts. Others did not. The investigation focuses on how the museum's artworks present evidence of the history of their fragmentation. It also examines the collusion of both the market and contemporary urban incoherence in the alibis of those suspected of the crime.

Although they look very different, the Palestine Archaeological Museum in Jerusalem and the Cloisters are siblings, sharing both the year of their openings and their patron. The Jerusalem museum is a grand, Orientalizing, beaux-arts structure, magnificently located near Damascus Gate overlooking the Old City and the Mount of Olives. Like many great archaeological museums, it is a product of imperialism and a showcase of the effects of empire. Built during the British Mandate, its collections came to include the world's largest archive of Dead Sea Scrolls. Now the museum itself is the object of conquest. Rendered comatose, the museum is eviscerated; its precious contents are a form of modern *spolia. Spolia* is now usually deployed as a benign art-historical term for the reuse of architectural fragments. It has lost its classical reference to the plunder taken from a slaughtered enemy's body. This chapter reminds its readers of a fact that the ancients never forgot: the public spectacle of *spolia* demands death. In the early twenty-first century, the denuded corpses are emptied buildings.

Part II observes the effects of disease on a building's agency. Ferdinand and Isabella's great hospital in Santiago was an ex-voto promised to the Apostle James in 1492 in return for his aid in the conquest of Granada, the last Muslim power in the Iberian Peninsula. Built with blood money, the hospital was the progeny of the Counter-Reformation and Inquisition. After World War II, as a complement to the reinvention of the medieval pan-European pilgrimage to Santiago de Compostela, Francisco Franco, the fascist dictator of Spain, converted the early modern hospital into a five-star hotel. The conversion had two purposes. One function was economic. The hotel was an important part of a larger project to attract urgently needed hard currency to Spain through tourism. Another objective was ideological. Tourism was critical to the project of remaking the international image of the repressive fascist regime. The Hospital/Hostal de los Reyes Católicos was forced from its origins to perform primarily for the promotion of the state under the guise of succoring those within its walls. The building's chronic deceit, imposed first by inquisitional Catholicism and later by fascism, is encoded in the manipulation of its history. Repressive politics once made the building an agent of suffering. Now it is the duplicitous agent of excess.

Santiago de Compostela briefly benefited from distant conflict; Jerusalem has chronically suffered from severe local violence. Chapter 4 investigates the effects of an urban illness on a healthy building. Analysis focuses on a particular mid-nineteenth-century affliction: the Protestant occupation of the Holy City. A building that acts as a foil to infectious Protestantism is the Palestinian house of Rabbah Effendi al-Husseini, located in one of the first neighborhoods built outside the walls of the Old City in the 1860s. Over the course of the late nineteenth and twentieth centuries, the function of the home shifted from that of a private dwelling, to the setting of a messianic Christian commune, and finally into the five-star American Colony Hotel. The American Colony Hotel has remained immune from the contagions of Jerusalem—including that now identified in medical literature as the Jerusalem Syndrome—by sustaining the well-remembered past rather than masking it: the history of the building is carefully maintained as the model for how it continues to perform hospitably in a deeply inhospitable city.

No contemporary discussion of place and agency would be complete without an assessment of digital spaces. Part III probes the potential addictiveness of cyberspace by investigating the devices that produce it and the physical settings in which those instruments perform. An introductory definition of addiction sustains the discussions of chapter 5 on the Las Vegas Strip and chapter 6 on computer play. The Strip's agency is characterized as that of an urban cyborg for two purposes. First, the megaresort casino of the Strip is very much the aberrant offspring of an abnormal urban setting. Second, although a great deal has been written about the history of Las Vegas, the current critical assessment of architecture's contribution to the dramatic changes of the Strip is inadequate. A few suggestions are offered here as to how to resee the Las Vegas that has emerged since Venturi, Brown, and Izenour published their canonical appraisal of the city, *Learning from Las Vegas,* in 1972. A final section examines the casino and its slot machines as cues for addiction.

The digitalization of the casino's game space segues into the pathologies of video game spaces and virtual worlds of the final chapter.

Defined space is essential to play. Chapter 6 analyzes the contribution of virtual architectonics to addictive play through a consideration of paradigmatic products of three digital genres. The video game (*Assassin's Creed,* which is set partially in Jerusalem) depends on spatial articulation for its violent narrative. The persuasiveness of the game's spatiality depends not on illusion, as has often been assumed in game critics' discussions and scholarly debates, but rather on the politically weighted visual conventions it deploys. The massively multiplayer online role-playing game or MMORPG (*World of Warcraft*), with its beautifully passive simulated spaces, provokes the aggressive possession that grounds the game's reactionary economy. An immersive world (*Second Life*) is not a game, but a playground. If escape by diversion is the primary reward of the digital game, the virtual world offers greater possibilities of creative and political engagement. There have been several versions of Jerusalem's Dome of the Rock in *Second Life,* including one produced by the Israeli Ministry of Tourism. Each looks and acts differently. The chapter concludes with a comparative analysis of the distinctively addictive architectonics of slot machines, video games, and immersive worlds.

The conclusion of the book puts architectural agency into its broader theoretical context. Theory has always functioned for me in the same way as an archive: a place where assumptions are overturned and unexpected rewards are discovered. Working on this project, however, I was particularly aware of theory as a hindrance to understanding as well as a provocation to thinking. Thing theory, apparently one of the most promising of the theoretical means by which the lives of objects might be legitimated, proves remarkably counterproductive. With the help of the odd collection of shards built into the Tribune Tower in Chicago, I argue that literary and phenomenological approaches to the agency of objects are less useful to the present project than socio-anthropological understandings of powerful things. Committedly material and historical approaches offer more productive models for rethinking architectural agency. I also suggest that even the most useful and sophisticated theoretical treatments of space can be nuanced through the recognition of buildings as agents.

Architectural historians have found phenomenological conceptions of space useful as a means of escaping both old-fashioned positivism and postmodern relativism. Despite compelling critiques from within religious studies, the work of Mircea Eliade is still embraced by some architectural historians. Structured around Zion, the second half of the conclusion makes the argument that phenomenological readings of a place undermine the site's authority rather than augmenting it. As with things, those theoretical approaches that privilege the physicality of the place and, consequently, its historical specificity offer a better basis for conceptualizing its status as a body and thereby as an agent. The introduction of ahistorical and disembodied digital spaces to the argument serves two analytical purposes. First, it engages architecture in current discussions of the posthuman erosion of the boundary between technology and the body. Second, the limits to spatial agency that disembodiedness and ahistoricity impose on virtual places confirm the centrality of the body and history to the performance of material structures. Architectural historians increasingly make use of theory. The most ambitious objective of the conclusion is to suggest that that theory, to do any good for a building or its users, must engage its archive and its archaeology.

PART I

DEATH

1

MURDER

> Museum and mausoleum are connected by more than phonetic association. Museums are the family sepulchres of works of art.
>
> —Theodor Adorno, "Valéry Proust Museum"

> Do you know what houses you are compelled to live in? There is scarcely one of them that had not been defiled by crime, blood and infamy before it was brought to its present site. The Palace was constructed out of bits and pieces from the ruins of buildings that had been the scenes of bloody conspiracies and revolutions. To collect his materials, Patera went right back to ancient times. Fragments of the Escorial, the Bastille and Roman arenas were used; his agents stole blocks of masonry from the Tower of London, the Hradschin in Prague, the Vatican and the Kremlin and had them transported here.
>
> —Hercules Bell's Proclamation to the People of Pearl, from Alfred Kubin, *The Other Side*

Murder

Though terrorism now invokes greater outrage, murder is still a serious allegation. In formal language "murder" is reserved as a descriptor of a criminal act with a human victim. In most U.S. states' legal systems, murder comes in two degrees. First-degree murder is willful and premeditated. Felony homicide—a killing that takes place during the commission of a crime such as robbery—is regarded as first-degree murder in many jurisdictions. Second-degree murder is that which is not planned in advance. Lesser infractions are voluntary manslaughter, which is basically second-degree murder committed with mitigating passion, and involuntary manslaughter, which is homicide committed without intent but with reckless disregard. Humans killed in a state-sanctioned war or sent to the gas chamber by a court of law are not murdered.

In the Old Icelandic law that affected Anglo-Saxon legal order, the term "murder" was applied more narrowly than it is now. "It is prescribed that if a man murders a man, the penalty is outlawry. And it is murder if a man hides it or conceals the corpse or does not admit it."[1] Murder's application was restricted to clandestine homicides: killings accomplished secretly or in the night, involving anonymity and the concealment of the corpse. The perpetrator was outside the protection of the law.[2] Those who killed in plain sight, acknowledged their killing publicly, and properly attended to the corpse might treat their crime as a debt discharged by the payment of *wergild,* the price of individuals determined by their social status. Although "murder" has long lost such specificity, the ancient residue of hidden malevolence still clings to it.

In informal language of the early twenty-first century, as apparent from the blogosphere, the word "murder" retains its old venom but is employed much more broadly. Women who have legal abortions, judges who pass a death sentence, and presidents who initiate unprovoked invasions of sovereign nations are identified as murderers. Murder is even applied to the killing of animals. It is deployed by those incensed by deaths of animals staged for human entertainment—notably bulls and foxes. Scientists responsible for the deaths of lab animals—notably rodents and primates—are named murderers. More commonly, animals classified by bloggers as murder victims are present or potential friends—particularly pets, dolphins, and whales. State supreme court justices might even be analogized to brutal serial killers. In a blog titled "Is Denver's Animal Murder Act Constitutional?" Mike writes: "Yes, the Colorado Supreme Court held that the city can, consistent with due process, kill your dog before giving you a hearing. Who knew Hannibal Lecter wore a robe?"[3] Even those who kill cute animals to eat may be called murderers.[4] Animals that were born to be commodities—cattle, pigs, sheep—are slaughtered, not murdered, even in the uncivil discourse of the blogosphere.

Buildings are rarely accused of murder. However, in those cases where the act of a building's destruction is brutal, undeserved, and concealed, that structure might be productively considered as murder's victim. Where that act is also premeditated, intentional, and occurs during the commission of a theft, its perpetrator might be considered particularly culpable.

The American artist and art dealer George Grey Barnard (1863–1938) was a collector and sculptor from childhood, developing his skills for both vocations from the age of eight as a taxidermist. He describes his exhibition of Midwestern fauna:

> I painted in the backgrounds and arranged the foliage as naturally as I could. The first specimens were stuffed, as I had seen a few such mounts done, with tow or wool, but I soon discovered that this gave the specimen an unnatural appearance. A bird skin, as you may know, stretches; it has hollows under it and—what most people don't know—other spots on which there are no feathers. To stuff such a skin

> was bound to give the bird a distorted look. So I began modeling the bodies in clay or plaster or wax—whatever I had handy—and then pulling the skin back over that.[5]

By the age of twelve, Barnard had a collection of over 1,200 specimens. How these specimens were obtained is not described.[6] Presumably it involved immolation. His museum of medieval sculpture in New York City, the Cloisters, four decades later, also required sacrifice.

Cloister

The monastery exiles the monk from the world. The sixth-century Rule of Saint Benedict provided the model for later western monastic charters. It lists seventy-three good works expected of monks, among them a number of familiar maxims: not to kill, not to steal, not to bear false witness, to love one's neighbor as one's self, to honor all men, to relieve the poor, to clothe the naked, to honor the older, to love the younger. These regulations are not to be acted out in the broader community, however; they are restricted to the confines of the monastery: "The workshop in which we perform all these works with diligence is the enclosure *[claustra]* of the monastery."[7] Indeed, knowledge as well as experience of the external world is banned. "Let no one presume to relate to another what he hath seen or heard outside of the monastery, because it is most hurtful. But if anyone presumes to do so, let him undergo the penalty of the rule. In like manner let him be punished who shall presume to go beyond the enclosure *[claustra]* of the monastery, or anywhere else, or to do anything, however little, without the order of the abbot." The monastery expells the world and banishes its bad practices. "Coarse jests and idle words or speech provoking laughter, we condemn everywhere to eternal exclusion *[clausura]*; and for such speech we do not permit the disciple to open his lips."[8]

By the eleventh century, *claustrum* (enclosure, site of exclusion) had become the name for the courtyard at the core of the monastic complex as well as for the monastery as a whole (Figure 1.1).[9] The *claustrum* (Old French and later Middle English, *cloistre*; in modern English, "cloister") singularly represented the isolation of the monk at the same time that it defined the hub of monastic activity.[10] By the late twelfth century, the cloister so fully embodied the precepts of monastic life that it functioned as a mnemonic device for their recitation.[11] The form and location of the cloister were remarkably stable: a square or oblong open space with a fountain framed by covered arcades, set on the warm side of the church and surrounded by institutional precincts (dormitory, refectory, chapter house or meeting hall, library). The cloister provided the organizational principle of the complex. Like the peristyle

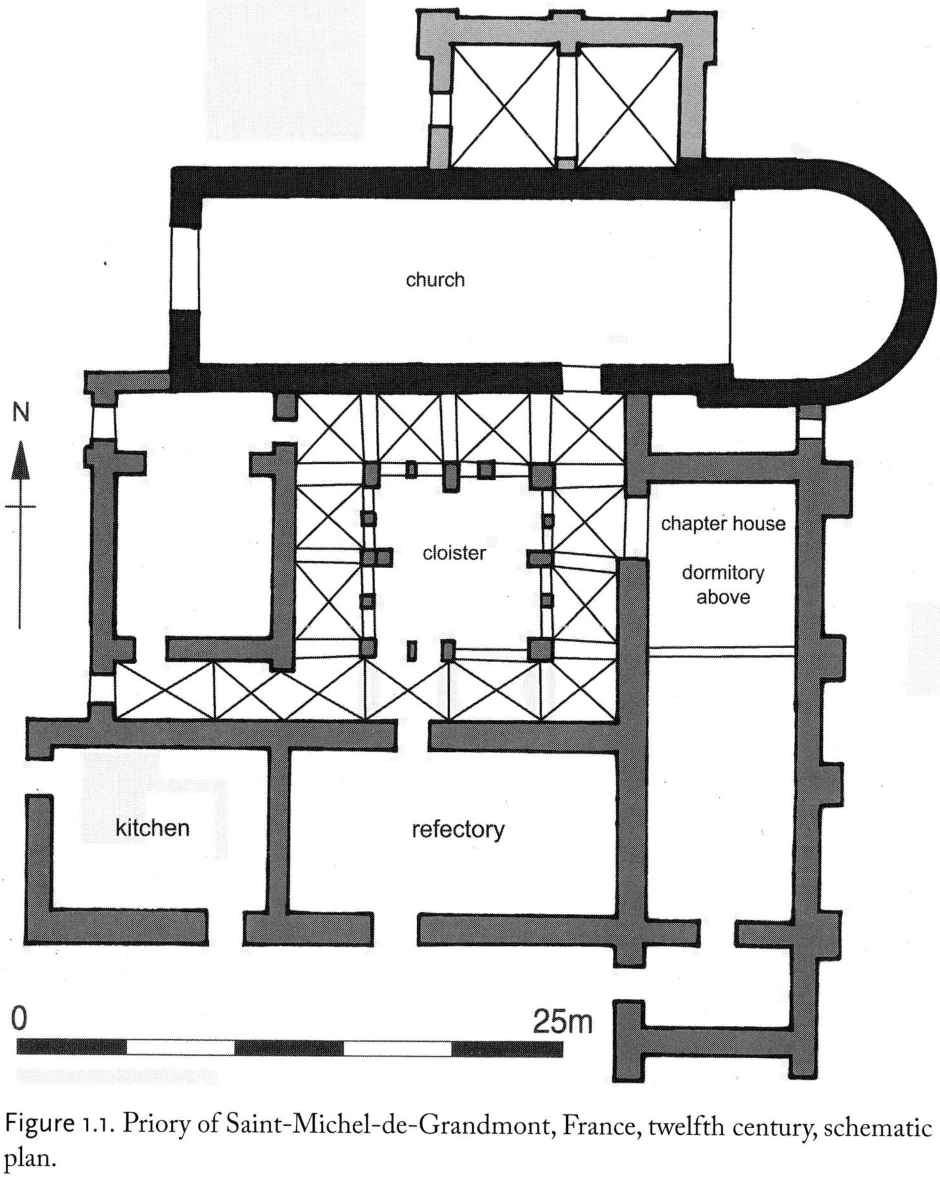

Figure 1.1. Priory of Saint-Michel-de-Grandmont, France, twelfth century, schematic plan.

of a private Roman villa, it delivered light and air to the chambers surrounding it.[12] The cloister was the monastery's lung.

Most of the spaces adjoining the cloister had dedicated functions but a wide variety of forms. For example, the church, whatever its size or arrangement, was, according to Saint Benedict, meant to serve one function—that of prayer: "Let the place of prayer *[oratorium]* be what it is called, and let nothing else be done or stored there."[13] Cloisters, in contrast, were conventional in their plan but heterogeneous in their functions: prayer and liturgical processions, reading and contemplation, as well as gardening, ablutions, laundry washing and drying, disciplinary beatings, head shaving, even legal proceedings.[14] In a setting of silence, the cloister was commonly the prescribed place to talk on those specified occasions when conversation with someone other than God was allowed.[15]

For monasteries from the late eleventh through the early thirteenth centuries, the adornment of the cloister with lavish figural and ornamental capitals is, first of all, an indication of the privileged status of the place. Here, often in contrast to the church, the relation of the observer to the object was intimate. The capitals are set on short columns not far above eye level. They demand attention by the immediacy of their placement and the virtuosity of their execution. A variety of subjects is represented in these cloister sculptures—from apostles and scenes from the life of Jesus to nude dancing women and fornicating animals. These plastic forms must have served some of their medieval viewers as memory aids and moral lessons. Modern scholars have read them as didactic, dogmatic, allegorical, analogical, liturgical, and aesthetic (Figure 1.2).[16] No doubt cloister decoration functioned in all these ways at some time or another. But perhaps more basically, the diversity of subjects represented within the cloisters was both a response to the broad assortment of activities staged there and a compensation for the loss of those activities that were excluded.

The Cloisters Museum in New York City, an appendage of the Metropolitan Museum of Art, is appropriately named after the medieval spaces that form the core of its exhibition.[17] Occupying the heights on the east side of the Hudson in northern Manhattan, it is a bastion of the Middle Ages in one of the world's great modern cities. Sited in seclusion overlooking the Hudson, a distant view disguises the museum as a monastery (Figure 1.3).[18] The earliest monks sought solitude by moving away from populated areas into the desert; isolation depended on the inhospitable character of their habitation.[19] Later in the West, the immense landholdings of a great foundation endowed its seclusion. Like the powerful abbeys of the European past, the Cloisters is afforded its spectacular setting through gifts of a wealthy patron. John D. Rockefeller Jr. bought the Billings mansion and its grounds as Fort Tryon Park and the site of the museum. On the model of Central Park, he had the

Figure 1.2. Abbey of Saint-Michel-de-Cuxa, France, cloister capital, fornicating beasts.

Figure 1.3. New York, the Cloisters Museum, view from the south. Courtesy of the Cloisters.

Olmsted Brothers remodel the suburban property as pastoral. Rockefeller also contributed to the Arcadian character of the larger setting by buying bits of land on the New Jersey bank of the Hudson, opposite the site of the Cloisters, for the Palisades Parkway. The Cloisters, in its publications, misrepresents Rockefeller's intentions by claiming that these parcels were purchased for the sake of providing the museum with an appropriate vista. Its website, for example, asserts that he donated "seven hundred acres of additional land to the state of New Jersey across the Hudson River *to ensure that the view from The Cloisters remain unsullied.*"[20] Rather, Rockefeller had been quietly acquiring land for a parkway along the top rim of the Palisades on the west side of the Hudson since about 1906, long before the Cloisters was envisioned.[21] These parcels of land he gave to the Palisades Park Commission in 1933. Rockefeller was, in any case, responsible for the unnatural naturalness of the Cloisters's setting at the edge of a great metropolis.

From a distance, the massive vertical tower with its asymmetrical base of recumbent geometric volumes invokes an ancient abbey. The illusion is only partially dispelled by proximity; even up close the building remains ambivalent in its historical claims. The equivocation of the structure is figured both in its collection and in its design. Many of the objects on display were once parts of earlier buildings; several are reinstalled as building parts. At the physical core of the Cloisters are seven more-or-less whole structures: four monastic cloisters, two chapels, and one chapter house, all built between the eleventh and fifteenth centuries in rural France and Spain and rebuilt in the twentieth century in New York City (Figure 1.4). The visitor moves through open and closed, old and new spaces. After ascending the barrel-vaulted staircase to the domed rotunda where she pays her admission, the visitor enters the austere Romanesque Hall, whose modern masonry walls are perforated with ancient portals. The Romanesque Hall serves as the twentieth-century antechamber to medieval structures: Fuentidueña Chapel (ca. 1160) from near Segovia and the cloister (before 1260) of the Monastery of Saint-Guilhem-le-Désert near Montpellier on one side, Langon Chapel (founded in 1126) from Bordeaux at the end, and, on the other side, Cuxa Cloister (12th c.). Cuxa Cloister is a perfect rectangle somewhat bigger than a basketball court.[22] The cloister's magical arcades of pink Perpignan marble open the somber interior to the brilliant outdoors, just as they once did at the Benedictine Abbey of Saint-Michel in southern France (Figure 1.5 and Figure 1.6).[23]

Initially, the museum's planners dithered between incorporating these parts of truly ancient structures into a faux-medieval replica or into a modern building.[24] Rockefeller briefly envisioned a version of Kenilworth Castle on the site. Joseph Breck, curator of decorative arts, working with Rockefeller and Rockefeller's architect, Charles Collens, sought a more appropriate monastic model. Breck admired

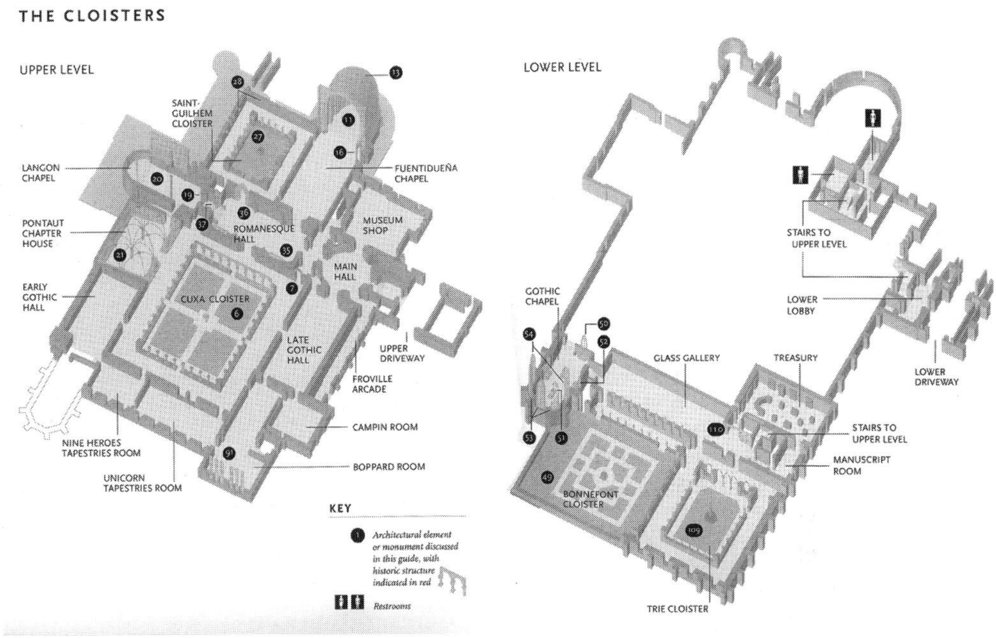

Figure 1.4. New York, the Cloisters, plan. From Barnet and Wu, *The Cloisters,* 20–21. Courtesy of the Cloisters.

the domestic tranquility provided to medieval objects by a medievalizing setting. "The Cloisters is a shrine, where mediaeval art is not so much on exhibition as at home."[25] In response to receiving a set of preliminary sketches, Breck wrote to Collens:

> I enjoyed very much looking over your delightful and suggestive sketches for the Cloisters. Scheme 2 and scheme 3 seem to me the most promising, as examples (1) of the neutral museum plan and (2) of the historical precedent plan. Of the two, I think I prefer the latter; it provides an appropriate and natural setting for the ecclesiastical art which forms the greater part of the collections at the Cloisters, and makes it possible to secure a unity of impression throughout that is impossible in the neutral museum plan. There are difficulties of course. The presence of three cloisters rather implies a larger church than is desirable, but I think this difficulty can be met by assuming that the monastery has been added on to from time to time, while retaining the original small church. . . . I enclose a drawing which I have made, showing a variant of scheme 3, based on the priory of Grandmont. [See Figure 1.1] . . . The second drawing I am enclosing is a variant of scheme 2—

Figure 1.5. New York, the Cloisters, view of the Cuxa Cloister.

Figure 1.6. Abbey of Saint-Michel-de-Cuxa, France, general view of the cloister.

> a neutral museum plan; this takes care of our three cloisters, provides good exhibition galleries, and several small chapels which could be developed in various Romanesque and Gothic styles.[26]

Breck's notion of replication was remarkably literal. In a report on the progress of the museum's design, he deplored the plan's departures from its premodern archetype.

> It is the desire, I understand, of Mr. Rockefeller and of the Museum that the new building should be mediaeval in style. This part of the program has been carried out to the extent of using mediaeval architectural detail in the elevations, but the plan itself departs very widely from mediaeval precedent . . . to reassemble parts of mediaeval plans without due consideration of their logical place in such plans and to combine with these entirely novel elements is almost certain to create a theatrical effect, a "sham Gothic," that is surely out of place in a museum intended to further the better understanding and appreciation of medieval art.[27]

In this report, Breck argued that the museum should follow the plan of a Cistercian monastery, proposing that an expert in the history of medieval architecture be appointed as an advisor to the project. He identified Professor Kenneth Conant of Harvard University for the position.[28] Conant, well known for his imaginative reconstructions of important medieval buildings that were subsequently often misread as archaeologically impeccable renderings, was an excellent choice to oversee the design of a medieval clone.[29] Collens, in a report on his Rockefeller-financed study trip to France, even suggested that ancient stone be used to construct the new museum.

> I am inclined to think that it would not cost any more to purchase in France a few old buildings and have the stone shipped by water to the site on the Hudson. It would thereby be possible to build up walls which would have all the charm of the original work. . . . There are certainly enough abandoned buildings near the seashore to make it possible to buy up a lot of this material and send it by sea direct to the site. This applies also to the roof material. To make the roofs of these cloisters and buildings harmonize with the old work it would be possible to buy up a number of tile abroad and have them shipped with the stone to this country. When you see old roofs being replaced by new red tile all over the south of France, one realizes that there is a large amount of old tile that could be had for the taking. There is a firm in Boston called E. Stanley Wires Company who match these old tile very well and make an excellent substitute, but if the actual tile could be had, it would of course have just so much more artistic value as the old tile is covered with lichen, is weathered and has an appearance which is hard to duplicate in new work.[30]

Collens was not about to repeat Viollet-le-Duc's historical error at Carcassonne of roofing a southern French medieval complex in slate rather than red tile. A twenty-first-century reader may find Collens's relationship to vernacular buildings of the past oddly invidious. The notion of buying old structures cheaply in impoverished interwar France in order to dismantle them as a source of building materials may, in view of the current concerns with architectural preservation, be troubling. Collens was apparently oblivious to such scruples. Also peculiar was Collens's driving desire for the already old, for an instantaneous spectacle of venerability. Every structure grows old differently. The demand for immediate antiquity seems to resist the possibility of the building's own natural aging.

James Rorimer, a connoisseur trained in Paris and Cambridge, Massachusetts, worked at the Metropolitan Museum from the time of his graduation from Harvard in 1927. He was associate curator for medieval art at the time of Breck's sudden and unexpected death while on a skiing trip in Switzerland in 1933.[31] He inherited the Cloisters project. Rorimer despised replicas—they too closely resembled fakes. His version of the Cloisters was a museum, not a monastery. Stone was cleaved from quarries in Connecticut, not from old buildings in France.[32] Only one of its parts reproduces a specific model. Rorimer describes that bit with some embarrassment: "The Gothic Chapel incorporates within its design features suggested by a small chapel in the church of Saint-Nazaire at Carcassonne and the church at Monsempron. This modern setting has been more completely developed than elsewhere in the Cloisters, in order to create an effective background for the objects exhibited."[33] The odd circumlocution for a modern imitation of an ancient space ("more completely developed") reveals the author's anxiety about introducing faux medieval structures amid those claiming authenticity. But if Rorimer's Cloisters does not attempt the reproduction of a medieval monastery, neither does it refuse a generic medieval character.

Medievalizing in appearance, the Cloisters is very much a modern museum project. It is didactic. Labels convey an empirical understanding of the objects to which they are attached. It is historical. The collection's order is broadly chronological. The visitor is gently prodded to visit the Romanesque before the Gothic by circulation signs and the audio guide. A note on a preliminary sketch, presumably by Collens, indicates that this conventional ordering was in place from the beginning: "The rooms are arranged that starting with Romanesque they terminated in Late Gothic."[34] But the Cloister's noncontemporary spaces present some resistance to a time line. In other twentieth-century museums designed with beaux-arts amplitude and symmetry, such as the classicizing National Gallery in Washington, D.C. (John Russell Pope, 1938–41), or the neo-Islamic Rockefeller Museum in Jerusalem (Austen St. Barbe Harrison, 1930–38), artworks may be didactically ordered in an easily legible, chronological, and national order. Further, despite the historical reference of their exteriors, the interior spaces of these other structures have an anonymity that offers no competition to the works of art exhibited within them. In contrast, the display spaces of the Cloisters are individual and corporeal. The ligatures and supplements constructed around its ancient imported structures tie them together but do not compromise their particularity. In contrast to the isolation of artworks in the neutral boxes of the conventional museum gallery, many of the artifacts of the Cloisters are fully integrated into the spaces they inhabit. The galleries are not neutral zones in which any object might appear, but rooms that, by their plans, proportions, apertures, appurtenances, coffering, vaulting, and paving, complement the medieval works that occupy them.

The museum's medieval and medievalizing spaces are filled with precious and beautiful objects of premodern cult and court. The building's cores as well as its contents are recycled shards of medieval Christianity. These architectural and artistic remnants collude in the simulation of intactness. They succeed in persuading most of their viewers that they are complete.[35] Why are these fragments pretending to be whole? They only conform to the desire of the patron who made their life in the museum possible. John D. Rockefeller Jr., a man whose actions were remarkably consistent with his religious and ethical commitments, expressed his hopes for the Cloisters at the museum's opening ceremonies on May 10, 1938:

> With the changes that time has brought, the wholesome and profitable use of leisure, now so startlingly prevalent, is one of the great *problems* of the day. In its solution the cultural and uplifting value of beauty, whether apprehended with eye or ear, is playing an increasingly important part. . . . May it not well be that The Cloisters in their new environment, surrounded by nature at her best, will become another stimulating center for the profitable use of leisure? If that should prove to be true, if what has been created here helps to interpret beauty as one of the great spiritual and inspirational forces of life, having the power to transform drab duty into radiant living; if those who come under the influence of this place go out to face life with new courage and restored faith because of the peace, the calm, the loveliness they have found here; if the many who thirst for beauty are refreshed and gladdened as they drink deeply from this well of beauty, those who have builded here will not have built in vain.[36]

Dissonant to an early twenty-first-century American audience is Rockefeller's early twentieth-century comment that leisure is a "problem" and that art offers its "profitable" solution. Rockefeller's pronouncement on the Cloisters as the site of producing "profitable" leisure was made two days after the southern conservative opposition to the Fair Labor Standards Act of 1938 collapsed.[37] The congressional passage of legislation stipulating a forty-hour week for the American worker was, after years of struggle, finally assured.[38] At last leisure was a possibility for workers as well as for professionals. That the laboring classes might put their new freedom to radical political use was a widespread middle- and upper-class anxiety. Art and athletics appeared to be possible alternatives to radical activism.

Rockefeller based his belief that art might provide a productive means of filling the void of nonwork time on his own experience. How art was profitable for Rockefeller is evident from a letter, written a decade earlier, reasking his father for a loan for the purchase of Chinese porcelains from the Morgan collection after his first request for the money was rejected.

> I have never squandered money on horses, yachts, automobiles or other foolish extravagances. A fondness for these porcelains is my only hobby—the only thing on

> which I have cared to spend money. I have found their study a great recreation and diversion, and I have become very fond of them. This hobby, while a costly one, is quiet and unostentatious and not sensational. I am sure that if I had the actual cash on hand, you would encourage rather than discourage my development of so innocent and educative an interest. The money put into these porcelains is not lost or squandered. It is all there, and while not income-producing, I have every reason to believe that even at a forced sale I could get within ten per cent of what these things would cost, while a sale under ordinary circumstances would certainly realize their full cost value, and as the years go by, more. . . . Is it unwise for me to gratify a desire for beautiful things, which will be a constant joy to my friends and to my children as they grow to appreciate them, as well as to myself, when it is done in so quiet and unostentatious a manner? Much as I want to do this thing—and I think you do not realize how much I should like to do it, for you do not know the beauty and charm of these works of art—I want more to do what you fully approve, so I have ventured to write this long letter, hoping that perhaps this fuller statement of the situation may lead you to see it in a somewhat different light.[39]

John D. Rockefeller Sr., in the end, made the loan for the purchase of the collection; later he converted the loan into a gift to his son.

Art offers a good investment and an unostentatious source of recreation. Time engaged in the presence of beauty and charm is innocent and instructive. Rockefeller's engagement in the acquisition and contemplation of Chinese porcelains was apparently a deeply satisfying diversion in the life of this hard-working billionaire. Chinese porcelains were not the only art forms of interest to Rockefeller. He was equally committed to the highly crafted art of the Middle Ages. Rockefeller's pleasure was derived from art as an expression of consummate and disciplined skill rather than individual genius. He never was able fully to appreciate contemporary avant-garde art.[40] Attention to the work of the great artisan provided a means of escaping, at least momentarily, from one's own labor. The Cloisters was intended to function as a safe haven of peace and beauty, removed from the violence and ugliness of the modern city. Its loveliness and calm refill the depleted soul; its beauty reaffirms the wholeness of life. The urban worker—white collar or blue—might find the museum a source of spiritual and physical restoration.

The Cloisters presents art as a foil to the always unfinished and incomplete practice of the urban everyday. The Cloisters offers a model for an integrated self; its performance of coherence is an illusion that diverts the observer's attention from the arbitrary incoherence of lived experience. The Cloisters is a kind of spectacle: to do the job its patron demanded, the Cloisters's organic presentation serves to mask the fragmentary character of its objects.[41] If the Cloisters allowed the works in its collection to reveal themselves as shards, the museum's affect would be opposite of that intended by its benefactor. Instead of offering consolation and distraction, it would present confirmation of the brutality and disorder that characterize modern urban life.

Fragments

The histories of the Cloisters's acquisition of its Florentine Annunciation panel and one of the museum's principal cloisters—from Saint-Michel-de-Cuxa—suggest something of the violent character of art collecting and the losses that it entails.[42]

A late twelfth-century marble relief of the Annunciation, about the size of Leonardo da Vinci's *Mona Lisa,* stands against the back wall of the Saint-Guilhem-le-Désert Cloister (Figure 1.7).[43] It has all the gravitas of Walt Disney's *Snow White*; it also has that film's strong narrative impact (Figure 1.8). Two toonish figures confront one another from within the security of their own arched compartments. Architectural motifs, decorative banding, and low-relief background vine scrolls enliven the ground of the panel without diverting the observer's attention from the central message of God's incarnation.[44] The panel is the visual equivalent of an effective modern billboard—it conveys its story with highly crafted simplicity.

The bottom right corner of the slab is missing. Though the break does not disrupt the panel's report of the Annunciation, it records the piece's suffering during its forced migration from its place of origin to its present location. Two remarkable accounts of the history of the Annunciation piece by Thomas Hoving, former director of the Metropolitan Museum of Art, document its loss. The first, published in the institution's *Bulletin,* provides a perfect example of academic art-historical writing, a tour de force of connoisseurship and archival research. The account manifests the author's forensic genius without mentioning it.[45] The Annunciation was made for the pulpit of San Piero Scheraggio, an important church at the administrative center of medieval Florence. The church was partially destroyed in 1410, and by the sixteenth century what was left of the basilica had been fully incorporated into the Uffizi. In the eighteenth century San Piero's pulpit was partially reconstructed in San Leonardo in Arcetri, a small church near the Fortezza di Belvedere on the periphery of Florence.[46] The pulpit is assembled from six marble reliefs illustrating the life of Jesus but missing one of cycle's main scenes—the Annunciation.[47] The Cloisters's Annunciation, sharing as it does the style, technique, material, and dimensions of the other members of the group, is compellingly identified as its missing member. Hoving reconstructs its role in the Incarnation narrative of the original pulpit. Sometime after 1410, the Annunciation was estranged from its sibling panels. Now it is permanently separated.

Figure 1.7. New York, the Cloisters, marble relief of the Annunciation, Cloisters collection, 60.140. Courtesy of the Cloisters.

Figure 1.8. Walt Disney's *Snow White and the Seven Dwarfs*, lithograph (1937). Copyright Walt Disney.

The second account of the marble Annunciation appears in Hoving's novelistic chronicle of his capture of the breathtaking Bury St. Edmunds altar cross, one of the Cloisters's great trophies.[48] The tale of the acquisition of the Annunciation panel is offered as a canapé to whet the reader's appetite for the book's main course. This narrative reverses the first: the author displaces the object as the subject of the story. Hoving's own effort in the acquisition provides the plot. In a script that all aspiring museum curators should read, Hoving candidly describes his introduction to the Annunciation through a letter and photographs sent by a dealer to the Metropolitan, his initial assessment of the quality of the piece, his archival stalking and discovery of its origins, his meeting with the panel and its possessor in Genoa, his negotiations over its price, and his collusion with its illegal exportation to Switzerland for purchase by the Cloisters. Once upon a time the Annunciation marble contributed to the thick texture of meaning produced in an ecclesiastical setting by an aggregate of spatialized ritual forms: visual, auditory, olfactory. Now all that is left of its affective past is its label. The Annunciation slab has suffered dislocation, damage, and theft; it has lost all hope of restitution. As complete as the museum makes it seem, it is only a fragment.

The histories of the other medieval parts of the Cloisters are variants of the story of the Annunciation panel. The cloisters that form the core of the museum were gathered in the southeast of France by the American sculptor mentioned at the beginning of this chapter, George Grey Barnard.[49] In 1902, Barnard was selected to execute a monumental program of sculpture for the capitol of Pennsylvania.[50] He established his workshop in Paris but found himself without the promised funds for his ambitious sculptural ensemble. He financed his continued work on the project by profitably speculating in medieval monuments.[51] Even after funding for the Harrisburg production in Paris rematerialized, Barnard continued his investment in medieval artworks. His unsold pieces were shipped to New York only days before new national legislation forbidding the export of France's patrimony was passed on December 31, 1913. This law was at least in part a response to Barnard's own wholesale export of French monuments; it turned his treasure into contraband, frustrating his efforts to carry off further artifacts.[52]

Those medieval monuments that Barnard managed to export he subsequently reconstructed as a mock ecclesiastical complex on his own Washington Heights property, near the present site of the Cloisters. In 1914, he opened his collection as "the Cloisters" to an admission-paying public who were attended in their tour by custodians dressed as monks.[53] Lewis Mumford, the distinguished urbanist, described this Cloisters as "the most perfect museum in the city."[54] Barnard's Cloisters was not just a museum, however. It was also a gallery in which works for sale were exhibited. In 1917, Barnard was bargaining with the Philadelphia Museum of Art, as evident from correspondence in his archive there.[55] He also engaged in negotiations with representatives of John D. Rockefeller Jr., who wished to make a gift of the collection to the public through the Metropolitan Museum. Barnard's mode of haggling is revealed in the Rockefeller Archive's collection of his annoying letters, like that of May 11, 1925:

> There is a movement on foot to buy the cloisters as a monument to the City of New York, thus insuring them "pour tous jours." This however does not stop my offers to Museums to sell any part of objects. If your Museum desires to purchase the St. Guilhem cloisters, and will put in writing the price they will give for it I promise to consider it, but only however after offering it at my original price given to you in option. A wealthy amateur said (2 years ago) he would pay this sum if ever I wanted to break up the cloisters. . . . As to other objects in my collection there are a few I cannot sell at the prices given in the Inventory as the 12th Century Virgin & Child, stone. Of course the Metropolitan is free to buy what they desire, as I have notified other museums.

> Thanking you for your kindness and *wonder* why we were all put to such labor and I to great *hardships* and loss in calling *off 4 Museums* "who had come to New York to purchase" in order to give a new option to Mr. R. de. F. at $700,000 I having refused the 500 and yet when all was done only 500 was offered.[56]

Later in 1925, after a great deal of haggling, Barnard sold his collection and his property to John D. Rockefeller Jr.[57] Rockefeller then presented the medieval objects to the Metropolitan Museum of Art. He also provided for a new museum. The land that he had bought earlier he presented to New York City for Fort Tryon Park, supplemented with monies for the building, landscaping, and maintenance of both the museum and the park. Barnard continued to nag Rockefeller into purchasing further works.[58] Typical is a letter of 1927:

> This is the reason why I am writing you—I have in the studios the greatest collection of Romanesque XII Century sculpture ever assembled. No other equal to it will ever be made. This collection (ten years in the making) added to the Cloisters, would complete a unique and great history of the art and chisel of the middle ages.
>
> Can you, who saved the Cloisters let pass this opportunity to give New York and America a heroic history of Christian art?
>
> I should like you to see before it is too late, the great capitals, many superior to any capitals in St. Germain de Pres, Paris. I have found nothing to equal them in the churches of Paris. Then the great XII Century wall fountain, six small musician kings, the early XII Century red marble cloister, the four sides, every piece absolutely ancient; the capitals, columns, foundations, arches, perfect, dug from the earth two years ago.
>
> If you are not interested, feeling you have done all you should do, no answer is necessary; I shall feel I have brought my best fight to build a complete history of Gothic in the New World, and sign an option with the Philadelphia Museum for the sale to them of my entire collection of December 1st.[59]

Barnard's letters, if not his self-promotional press interviews, reveal that he was interested in the public good only when it proved profitable to himself.

Possessing someone else's inheritance is ethically awkward. Indeed, a sense of moral anxiety is conveyed by the explanations Barnard offered for his acquisition of European monuments. As soon as controversy about his collection of French medieval monuments arose, the market disappears from Barnard's public discussion of his assets. He represents his desire for medieval sculpture as issuing from a love of Art, not a desire for money. In 1913, his justification appeared in the *New York Times* with the headline "G. G. Barnard Plans Art School Here."[60] He claimed that the medieval sculptures he had collected were intended to serve as models for his students. An art school never materialized. Such rationalizations for the large-scale removal of old buildings and sculptures from their original sites reappear in scholarly literature, suggesting that art historians as well as collectors might feel a little guilty. For example, J. L. Schrader, a curator at the Cloisters, reproduced the collector's justifications uncritically in 1979: "Barnard repeatedly explained that one of his original intentions, aside from acquainting Americans with medieval art, had been to introduce young American sculptors to what he called 'the patient Gothic chisel.'"[61] Or again, in the most recent guidebook produced for the Cloisters: "Barnard's interest in acquiring medieval sculpture stemmed from his frustrated attempts to introduce his students at New York's Art Students' League . . . to the beauty of medieval stone carving."[62] So far as I can ascertain, Barnard only taught at the Art Students' League *before* he began his collection of medieval artifacts.[63]

The unease caused by depriving others of their patrimony was also expressed in another, subtler form. In 1941, James Rorimer, not only codesigner of the Cloisters but also later director of the Metropolitan Museum of Art, published an admirable book titled *Medieval Monuments at the Cloisters: As They Were and As They Are.*[64] The text reports, briefly and articulately, on the histories of the construction and destruction of selected monuments in the Cloisters's collection. But the book's triumph rests in its photographs. Paired images contrast the messy sites in France from which objects were taken with their present clean and orderly place in the New York museum. The volume was revised and republished in 1972.[65] Rorimer describes Cuxa Cloister, a privileged part of the museum's collection:

> The cloister was built in the twelfth century at a time when the abbey was celebrated throughout western Europe. . . . In 1654 the monastery was sacked by the troops of a local count; in 1793, three years after the decree of the "Civil Constitution of the Clergy," the French Revolution brought ruthless plundering and pillaging; finally the monastery was sold in parts to three inhabitants of the region. . . . Sometime before 1875 a number of the fragments from Cuxa . . . were placed by Pierre Yon Vernière . . . in his garden at Aniane near Montpellier. Vernière was the first person in modern times to appreciate this material and the first of the several collectors who made possible The Cloisters as it is today. By 1906 these carvings had been brought to Paris by a noted antiquarian who supplied American collectors with many of their bits of mediaeval architecture. George Grey Barnard, the American sculptor, . . . acquired Vernière's Cuxa material.[66]

Rorimer's brief history suggests that the monastery was a ruin already in the seventeenth century, but the Cuxa cloister was intact well into the nineteenth century.[67]

Though secularized after the French Revolution, the cloister seems to have survived until its owner sold it in lots in the 1840s. The local archaeological association could not compete with the art market. When the cloister was dismantled, its capitals were bought as artworks, not defaced or destroyed. Also absent from the narrative is the record of Barnard's own ten-day trip to Prades in 1907. There in the monastery's vicinity, he sought to purchase as many remaining cloister fragments as he could identify. His efforts to obtain possession of one large lot, reused in the privately owned public baths of Prades, were frustrated by Emmanuel Sans, the departmental architect of the Commission of Historical Monuments. The ensuing scandal contributed to the introduction of the cultural patrimony legislation of 1913. In the end, Barnard got away from France with only half of the cloister. Also absent from Rorimer's text is any mention of the fate of those sculptures left behind. These remained in place locally; they were collected and restored to their original site beginning in 1949.[68] Saint-Michel-de-Cuxa is now again a functioning Benedictine monastery. It has a Facebook page. Its generous cloister is restored, but most of its arcade and its medieval fountain are missing (Barnard sold the fountain to the Philadelphia Museum). The monastery is alive, but its body's amputations are conspicuous.

In Rorimer's descriptions of the collection, the abuse of the monuments in the deep past is described as violent, the result of religious and political intolerance. The dispersal of the monuments' pieces by the art market in the nineteenth and twentieth centuries is treated as redemptive, the consequence of art appreciation. Collectors are represented as the agents of a dead building's revival, not scavengers effecting its final dismemberment. Most of the documentary photographs in the book sustain the author's implicit argument that collectors and the Cloisters saved medieval monuments from utter ruination. A few of Rorimer's photographs, however, contradict the redemptive premise of the book. Views of the monastery of Notre-Dame-de-Pontaut before (1930) and after (1935) the chapter house was removed, for example, offer poignant proof of the predatory effects of art entrepreneurs (Figure 1.9). A humble cluster of historic structures has been crudely disemboweled, leaving a gaping hole at its center. In the 1972 edition of the book, the photograph of the painful gap left by the chapter house's expatriation is replaced with a less excruciating image of the site before its mutilation (Figure 1.10). Again, the photographs of the Cistercian abbey of Bonnefont-en-Comminges witness the predations of the nineteenth century, not the remote past. Bonnefont's cloister was fundamentally intact until 1807. Throughout the nineteenth century, most of its parts were reused locally.[69] The removal of the capitals meant that the site could never be reconstituted. Now the monastery's sadly desolate remains are found only with some difficulty (Figure 1.11 and Figure 1.12).

A. The Exterior of the Chapter House at Pontaut (1930)

B. The Chapter House Set Up near Paris (1932)

C. Pontaut After the Chapter House Was Removed (1935)

Figure 1.9. Pontaut Chapter House, comparative photographs from Rorimer, *Medieval Monuments at the Cloisters* (1941).

16 The exterior of the chapter house of the abbey of Notre-Dame-de-Pontaut (1930)

17 The chapter house from Pontaut set up near Paris (1932)

18 Pontaut before the removal of the chapter house (center)

Figure 1.10. Pontaut Chapter House, comparative photographs from Rorimer, *Medieval Monuments at the Cloisters*, rev. ed. (1972).

Rorimer and others recycled parts of *Medieval Monuments at the Cloisters: As They Were and As They Are.* Some of the images and bits of the text from his 1941 volume appeared in more popular and available publications; their reuse is found, for example, in the 2012 edition of the guidebook for the Cloisters.[70] In all of these later contexts, the original message is also reproduced: the Cloisters's medieval monuments were dismantled for their own good.

> Taking as a center of operation the site of some ruined abbey or church, [Barnard] would visit the neighboring farms, for he had many times noticed that peasants would use the debris to serve for one utilitarian purpose or another. He found that a pigsty would yield the slab of a crusader's tomb, or an attic some long forgotten statue that had at one time graced an altar or church portal.[71]

Had Barnard not bought their parts and exported them to the United States, it is implied, these works of art would have been lost forever in rural pigsties. However, had those medieval objects that now find themselves in New York remained in their native lands, they might have been able to find their ways home. Were it not for the art market, Bonnefont, like Cuxa and Saint-Guilhem-le-Désert, might well now look less like a ruin and more like a monastery.[72]

Vindications for the removal of ancient monuments from France and Spain cover up more than they reveal. Identifying the museum's pieces as salvage, just like Barnard's claim to use them for the betterment of students, obscures the role of money in their acquisition. Barnard was a shady entrepreneur speculating in medieval objects for his own profit.[73] Rorimer and Hoving were enlightened, aesthetic entrepreneurs, appropriating beautiful things to increase the status of their collection. Both contributed to the robustness of the twentieth-century art market. In the market, money is the great equalizer. Money's fungibility permeates the market's vendibles, converting them into commodities and eroding the particularity that comes from their pasts. The operations of the market obscure its objects' histories.[74] As the traffic in archaeological objects demonstrates, the market often eliminates a work's past in the process of cloaking its theft.[75] Hoving's story of the Annunciation panel from Florence suggests how the market obscures the history of a work at the same time that it provides the curator with the celebrity of a famous detective in that history's reconstruction.

The story of the wreck of the body of which the fragment was once a part tends to be neglected in the histories of art. Why is the violence that makes a fragment overlooked? Perhaps because wholeness is an existential oddity: the fragment's promise of a lost completeness engages the observer's attention exclusively in its reconstruction. Or perhaps because the fragmentary is utterly familiar: the fragment

Figure 1.11. Abbey of Bonnefont-en-Comminges, France, general view from the east.

is so thoroughly naturalized by everyday experience, by dreams, and by texts that its original wholeness is not missed.[76] Or perhaps because the loss is so perfectly masked by the magic of the museum: we are habituated to the museum as a place where objects are presented as things-in-themselves. Certainly the museum and the market contribute to the alchemy that converts medieval artifacts from craft works with significant practical utility for a local community to artworks that succeed in their new role as Art only insofar as they resist utility. The works exhibited in the Cloisters have been wrested from one physical and historical context for a new and alien purpose in another. On display are objects that only became Art in modernity. The medieval artifact might be beautiful or grotesque, sophisticated or crude, pious or impious, but in contrast to a modern artwork, it was never intended to be self-referential—it was never exclusively about either its author or its own objecthood. A medieval work inevitably served a broader social function. The objects that fill the Cloisters have lost their originating purpose; they miss their initiating vocations. A Mondrian can act in much the same way in the Museum of Modern

Figure 1.12. New York, the Cloisters, the "Bonnefont" Cloister. The same comparison is made in Rorimer, *Medieval Monuments at the Cloisters,* Plates XIA and XIIA.

Art as it once did in the living room of the patron for whom it was made; a processional cross is not allowed to behave in the museum as it did in a church.

The sense of loss felt in the Cloisters has sources other than the works' nostalgia for their old tasks. Many of the objects in the museum are deprived of more than the functions for which they were made. They have been deprived of their own vital parts—lost segments and absent landscapes. The Cloisters muffles the mourning of its fragments by masking their loss and presenting them as whole. Their narrative and physical context—with placards and audio tours, tiled roofs and herb gardens—make them seem at home in the museum. The violence done to them is disguised by their present tranquility. Even if they were to return home, they would now be made to perform in Europe in much the same way that they act in New York. There, as here, their primary audience would be tourists.[77] Certainly, were they repatriated, they might help resurrect sites long dead. However, buildings would be resuscitated as part of a primarily economic, not a primarily spiritual, enterprise.

With the return of its pieces, the Abbey of Bonnefont might be reborn as a destination, but it would attract sightseers, not pilgrims.

So what do we lose by experiencing these fragments in New York at the Cloisters rather than where they were once whole? Certainly not authenticity. It is more difficult to distinguish the old from the new, the true stone from the cast cement, the real vault from the faux arch in many of the rebuilt "historical" structures of Europe than in an American museum. Certainly not a space more perfectly contemplative. It is much easier to reflect on the past in the Cloisters, with its meditative quiet, than it is during the tedious group lecture tours that seem to be the only means that a visitor has of seeing the restored French monasteries of Fontfroid or Canigou. But there, despite the annoying handouts and odd obliviousness to the fabric, a sense of the medieval habitus lingers. The Cloisters provides no evidence for the ways in which the cloister might glue monastic life and buildings together. The visitor has no sense of how the bulky, monster-infested capitals of Cuxa complemented the raw construction of the Romanesque church to which it was originally attached, or how the slender columns from the "Bonnefont" cloister conformed to the refined proportions and finish of its Gothic Cistercian chapel. The sense of a monument's cultural consistency is lost, even as some didactic understanding of historical and stylistic progress is gained. In their originating sites, the objects, however worn and broken, would not be fragments.

2

SPOILS

> In the heroic ages no victory was considered complete unless the conquerors could succeed in stripping the bodies of the slain, the spoils thus obtained being viewed (like scalps among the North American Indians) as the only unquestionable evidence of successful valor. . . . Spoils collected on the battle field . . . were employed to decorate the temples of the gods, triumphal arches, porticoes, and other places of public resort . . . but those which were gained by individual prowess were considered the undoubted property of the successful combatant, and were exhibited in the most conspicuous part of his dwelling.
>
> —William Ramsey, "Spolia," *Dictionary of Greek and Roman Antiquites,* 1875

> I was again impressed . . . with the beauty of the building, the excellence of its provisions for exhibition, technological activities and scholarly research, as well as with the quality and wealth of the objects exhibited or available for exhibition. It is sad indeed to see so brilliant an institution lifeless. . . . What a challenging job it would be to bring this institution back to life were the means and the person available.
>
> —Carl Kraeling, letter to John D. Rockefeller Jr., April 21, 1951, Rockefeller Foundation Archives

Spolia

The Cloisters Museum in New York provides a scene for the investigation of crimes committed at a distance, revealing evidence of the venal destruction of monuments for the sake of money and status. The victims are the buildings, maimed or murdered for their parts. The culprits are traffickers in ancient works; their accomplices are curators and art historians. A second museum offers an investigator a different victim—the museum itself. It also presents another villain—the state.

Museums have always been expressions of economic excess, but they have expended that surfeit for different purposes at different times.[1] In the early modern West they originated as private spaces designated by the very wealthy for the exhibition of singularity. Maps, exotic fauna, and oddities in nature as well as highly crafted objects were collected and displayed.[2] In the nineteenth and early twentieth centuries, museums, like universities, became more rigorously disciplinary, presenting a scientific and systematic ordering of knowledge. Major collections were purified and devoted solely to Art or to Science. State art and archaeological museums were public spaces for the display of the aesthetically important artifacts not only of their own nation, but also of the cultures of those over which they exerted economic or political control. Museums remain the great repositories of the spoils of empire building.[3]

Certainly states have always appropriated the precious artifacts of those they conquer and displayed them as proof of their superiority. Ancient descriptions of conquest often culminate in the public execution of the enemy and the exhibition of *spolia.* Josephus's account of Titus's triumphal procession after his defeat of the Jewish Revolt in 70 CE climaxes with the beheading of its leaders in Rome, the dedication of trophies to the Palatine gods, and the display of the spoils from the Jerusalem Temple in the Temple of Peace constructed for their exhibition (Josephus, *Jewish Wars,* 7.5.6–7). The ancients never forgot that gore was essential to the aura of *spolia.* But now *spolia* no longer commemorates violence—armor stripped from the corpses of soldiers and staged to honor the prowess of those who vanquished them. *Spolia* is now benign, a word used by art historians to name the reuse of old architectural or sculptural elements in new contexts.[4]

The display of rare artifacts remains the privileged function of museums, though memorialization (holocaust, presidents, sports) has gained new prominence. The great public museums, repositories of precious and beautiful objects, persist as stalwart bastions of a high modernist commitment to great art. Certainly in the early twenty-first century, museums function progressively as destinations for entertainment and consumption. They also behave ever more like the corporations upon which they increasingly depend for their support. Nevertheless, the museum's trusted commitment to great works and their display still tends to obscure its other roles. Most visitors imagine that the narrative presented by the museum is true history. But in all phases of its development, the museum's architecture, no less than its collection, has performed the authority of its patron. It is always a place for the representation of particular versions of history. Chapter 1 considered fictions related by the Cloisters. In this chapter another museum tells a very different kind of story, a story in which the museum and its collections painfully recall the ancient understanding of *spolia.*

Archaeology

The Palestine Archaeological Museum, which opened to the public in 1938, perfectly exemplifies the modern museum in its civic presence and in its disciplinary order.[5] Its collection was magnificent. Artworks and artifacts from the Bronze Age through the Hellenistic, Roman, Byzantine, Islamic, and Crusader periods remain on permanent display. Exceptional secular objects, like the voluptuous eighth-century sculpture from the Umayyad palace at Khirbet al-Mafjar, are juxtaposed with works from intensely religious contexts—rich sculptural pieces from Al-Aksa Mosque and the Church of the Holy Sepulchre.[6] The museum is world class.

The Palestine Archaeological Museum was part of an encyclopedic project imagined by an academic, James Breasted, realized with monies from an oil magnate, John D. Rockefeller Jr., and sanctioned by the state, the British Mandate Authority.[7] Documents in the Rockefeller Archive Center indicate that the museum's producers were committed to providing a cultural history of Palestine from the Stone Age to 1700 for three purposes: the edification of the local population and tourists, the preservation of archaeological artifacts, and the promotion of scientific research. The museum succeeded in the early twentieth century because its mission was embraced by those in control. The museum fails in the early twenty-first century because that mission is no longer of interest to those who possess it.

James Henry Breasted (1865–1935), a small-town Midwesterner, aspired to the ministry. Upon learning Hebrew as part of his education for the pulpit, he discovered that the King James Bible was hopelessly flawed: "I could never be satisfied to preach on the basis of texts I know to be full of mistranslations," he told his mother in announcing his career shift to Semitic languages.[8] His obsession with biblical texts and their Near Eastern origins entangled him in inscriptions and archaeology. Breasted's understanding of history and language study as science was cutting edge—honed by graduate study in Berlin and expanded to embrace material culture through fieldwork in Egypt.[9] He sought to catalog all surviving epigraphic evidence in the Near East in order to track with empirical precision the evolution of Western civilization.

At the University of Chicago (founded by Rockefeller and structured by William Rainey Harper, another professor of Semitic languages), Breasted became the first professor of Egyptology appointed in the United States. There, again with Rockefeller's support, he developed the Oriental Institute.[10] The Oriental Institute began life as a research center but grew a museum function with the accumulation of Breasted's archaeological acquisitions. He planned, with a commitment from John D. Rockefeller Jr., a magnificent sister institution for Cairo—an enormous beaux-arts, neo-Egyptian complex that included a separate, lavishly appointed research building with offices for visiting scholars and the latest scientific equipment.[11] In the end, Rockefeller's $10 million gift was not accepted. The proposed site—Qasr al-Nil (or Fortress/Palace on the Nile), located next to the old Egyptian Museum and adjacent to Tahrir Square at the center of modernizing Cairo—was, at the time, occupied by a British barracks.[12] Though initially interested in divesting itself of this property, the British reversed their position in reaction to increasing political unrest in Egypt. (The strategic importance of the location was still very much in evidence during the Arab Spring, 2011.) British troops at Qasr al-Nil were finally evicted in 1953 with the Egyptian Revolution only to be replaced by another group of foreigners: in 1958 Gamal Abdel Nasser opened the Nile Hilton on the site.[13] There was a further cause for the gift's refusal: the project came with too many strings attached.[14] The new museum was to absorb all the great archaeological collections of Egypt under a wholly Western administration—the proposal was an institutional affront to Egyptian nationalism.[15]

Jerusalem was identified as an alternative location from which the Near East's contribution to Western civilization might be studied, classified, and displayed. Palestine's archaeological finds were less spectacular than those of Egypt—ossuaries can't compete with mummies, and pottery doesn't compare with monumental stone sculpture. Nevertheless, the artifacts of Palestine had the singular advantage of an intimate association with scripture. Biblical archaeology was, at the time, a growth industry.[16] Objects uncovered in the search for the historical truth of the Bible demanded public presentation. Protestants—missionaries and explorers prominent among them—multiplied in the Holy Land from the middle of the nineteenth century through the early twentieth.[17] As argued more substantively in chapter 4, converting, mapping, and excavating were closely related enterprises.[18] In early twentieth-century Palestine, proselytes were remarkably rare, but biblically rich archaeological sites were remarkably common. Jerusalem had other advantages. It was not only the city where Jesus walked but also one that the West controlled. Jerusalem's mandated British authority was another of its great attractions for Rockefeller—a Western government could be trusted with the administration of a cultural institution in a way that an Oriental government could not.

Rockefeller clearly articulated the convenience and financial benefit of dealing with the British:

> I talked with Dr. Breasted last night about the Jerusalem museum project. He told me that the English appointee who is in charge of the antiquity matters in Palestine represents a wholly to be relied upon group and that if we were interested to make possible the construction of the museum, we would not need to assume any responsibility for the development of a plan of organization or maintenance, but could simply make a gift outright with the assurance that whatever was agreed upon would be carried out. This alters the situation to the extent that it would reduce to a purely financial question the problems involved.[19]

Raymond B. Fosdick, Rockefeller's brilliant and humane advisor on philanthropic as well as legal matters, recognized that the Egyptians would be affronted by the patron's greater confidence in British administration.[20] While the letter of gift was being drafted, Fosdick wrote to Thomas M. Debevoise, John D. Rockefeller Jr.'s senior counsel:

> I do not think that Mr. Rockefeller's letter of gift ought to be made public by Lord Plumer because its terms are so much more liberal than the terms which we offered the Egyptian Government. If the Egyptian project should ever be revived, the contents of this letter might prove embarrassing.[21]

In addition to Western control, the British offered in Jerusalem a perfect piece of immediately available real estate for the project—a privileged property, known as Karm el-Sheikh, just outside the northeast corner of the Old City. The museum occupies the same site from which the crusaders breached the wall and began their bloody slaughter of Jerusalemites in 1099. The property had been in the possession of the distinguished Khalidi family for at least two hundred years (Figure 2.1.A).[22] Prominent in the early photographs of the place is a pine tree, which had been brought as a seedling from Hebron; it was one of the tallest trees in Palestine at the time. It survived until 1988. Lord Plumer, high commissioner of the British Mandate of Palestine between 1925 and 1928, expresses his commitment to the museum project in the guise of a property description:

> The ideal site ... near Herod's Gate and the principal Schools of Archaeology, and facing one of the most picturesque parts of the old walls with outlook to the Mount of Olives and over Gethsemane to the hills of Moab, is fortunately available for purchase and is not likely to be disposed of pending arrangements for its expropriation by Government. I may tell you confidentially, for Mr. Rockefeller's information, that I have already represented to the Secretary of State in London the necessity to acquire this site without delay even though there is little likelihood that the Palestine Government will be able in the immediate future to provide funds for building a museum.[23]

All these considerations are embedded in the gift letter of October 11, 1927, written by John D. Rockefeller Jr. to the high commissioner of the British Mandate for Palestine:

> My dear Lord Plumer:
>
> I am informed by Professor James H. Breasted, of the Oriental Institute of the University of Chicago, that the Palestine Government is engaged in a project for the construction of an archaeological museum, to be built and maintained in accordance with the following plans:

1. That the building site known as the "Karm-el-Sheikh" situated at the northeast corner of the wall of Jerusalem, and containing about eight acres will be contributed by the Palestine Government as the site for the Museum building.

2. That the adjoining municipal incineration plant will be permanently removed from the immediate vicinity.

3. That the terrain adjacent to the "Karm-el-Sheikh" site will be included in what is known as the Jerusalem "town planning scheme."

4. That the collections in the new Museum will include all material throwing light on the past of man in Palestine; that natural resources and materials pertaining to natural science would therefore be included only in so far as they concern the human career in the past: in short that the Museum is to be an archaeological institution, not a museum of natural science.

5. That the responsibility for the erection of the Museum will be assumed by the Palestine Government, and that its future administration will likewise be carried on by the Palestine Government in such advisory relations with an International Advisory Committee as the Palestine Government may deem feasible.

In support of this proposition as outlined above, I am glad to pledge whatever may be necessary up to two million dollars toward the cost of building, equipping and endowing the Museum, the last payment to be made not later than January 1, 1931, on which date any uncalled for balance of the maximum amount mentioned above will lapse.

With all best wishes for the success of this very interesting project, I am

Yours very truly, John D. Rockefeller, Jr.[24]

The British provided the architect as well as the land. The museum was designed by Austen St. Barbe Harrison, the chief architect in the Department of Public Works in the British Mandate Administration in Palestine between 1923 and 1937.[25] Like a number of other Western architects working in Palestine from the later nineteenth through the early twentieth centuries, Harrison favored an Islamic-vernacular/modern building style. His version of this Western understanding of the East was remarkably successful, perhaps because it was grounded in a serious study of Byzantine and early Islamic architecture at the British School in Athens. He also employed local artisans, local materials, and local construction techniques. Though its plan is imperiously beaux-arts (grandly large and bilaterally symmetrical), on site the building makes a less authoritarian, more irregular appearance with low volumes massed around the entrance tower (Figure 2.2 and Figure 2.3).[26] The fabric of the building is limestone quarried from the Jericho road; in contrast to buildings of Jerusalem now, the ashlar masonry was not just skin deep. The interior

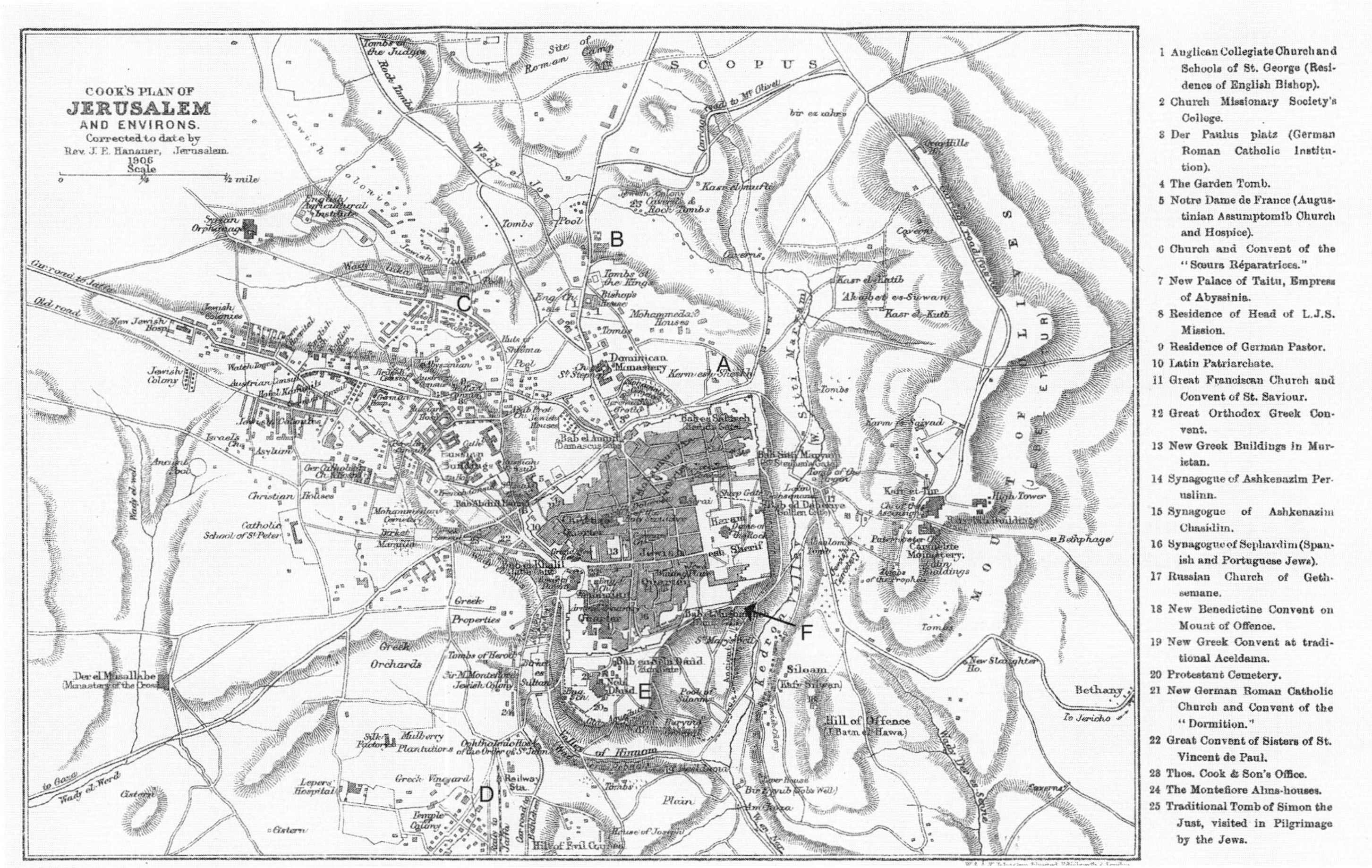

Figure 2.1. Jerusalem, Cook's 1904 map of Jerusalem. Author's collection. A = Palestine Archaeological Museum; B = American Colony; C = Me'ah She'arim; D = German Colony; E = Mount Zion; F = City of David.

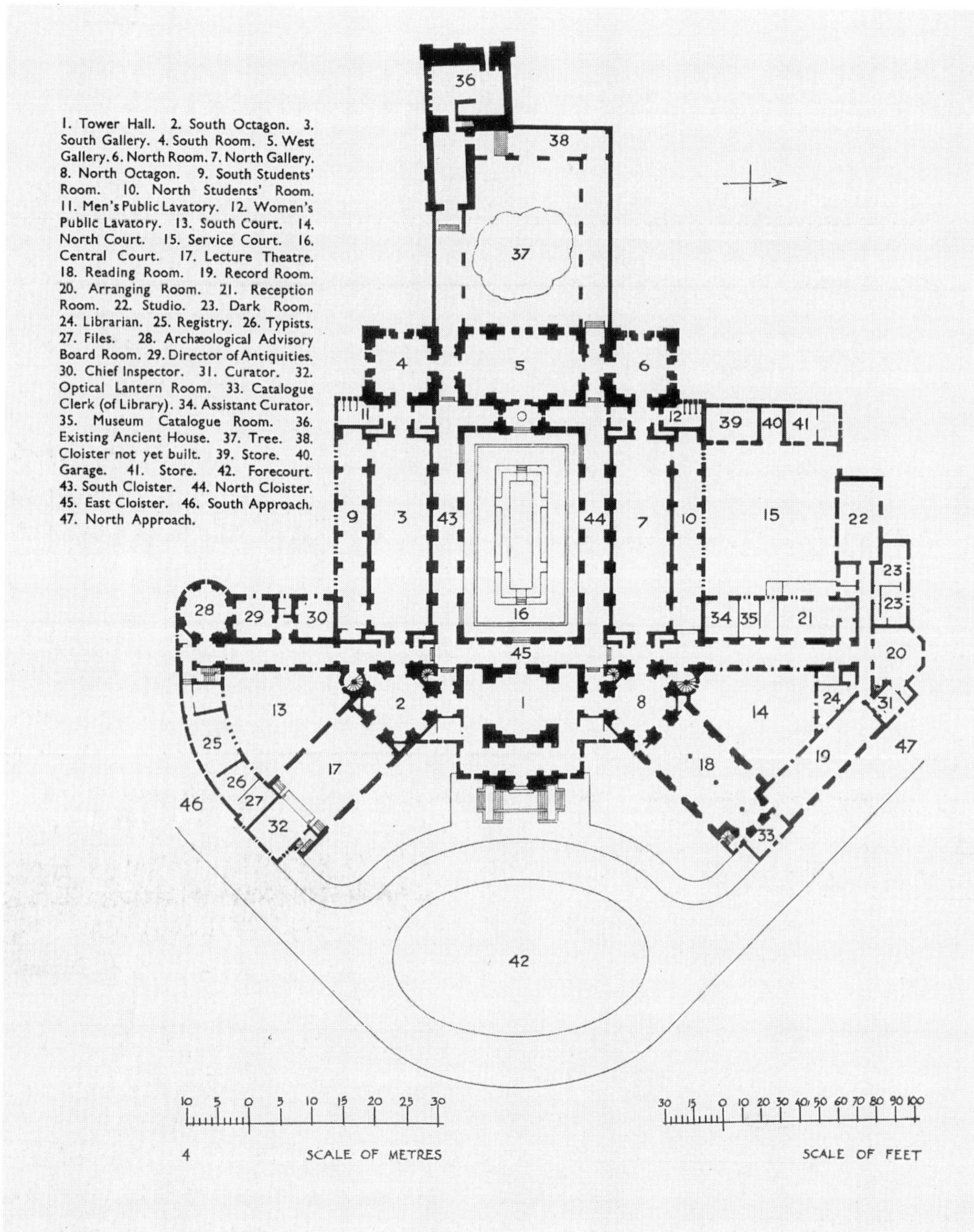

Figure 2.2. Jerusalem, Palestine Archaeological Museum, plan. From "The Palestine Archaeological Museum."

Figure 2.3. Jerusalem, Palestine Archaeological Museum, view of the Central Court.

walls are plastered and whitewashed, with revealed stone arches and moldings confirming the structure's substantiality. At the core of the plan is a long courtyard bisected by a narrow pool with fountains at either end, inspired by the Patio de la Acequia in the Generalife in the Alhambra, one of the great sites of Islamic architecture.[27] The museum's public display spaces are ceremonially proportioned and ordered, with processional galleries punctuated by more intimate domed bays (Figure 2.4). It is a very nice place to visit.

Earlier, at the beginning of the British Mandate, Patrick Geddes, the distinguished Scottish town planner, proposed a museum for Jerusalem. A comparison between the museum outlined by Geddes and that constructed by Breasted, Rockefeller, and Harrison indicates both the changed place of archaeology in the West's understanding of the East and a dramatic shift in political perspective. Geddes described his ideal institution:

> Begin then with early Man—Paleolithic, Neolithic and Bronze—and these presented, as far as may be, by local antiquities. But also supplemented and expanded by good reproductions, figures, friezes etc. as well as by labels and by illustrated guide books. In such a way we come to the Pre-Israelite peoples in Palestine. Thence on one hand to specific Hebrew history, and on the other to the presentment of the great succession of historic cultures, which have surrounded and in various measures affected, both Hebrews and Palestine generally. Begin then with a large Museum Hall for Egypt. . . . The simple visitor should thus see as he entered a good relief model of the whole Egyptian region, with [a] realistic Nile flowing from its reservoirs in the Great Lakes to its outlet on the Sea. Here recall the magnificent realism of the models and panoramas so characteristic of the Paris Exhibition of 1900. . . . How attractive will be a series of good Relief Models of Jerusalem, illustrating, as far as may be, the extent and character of the city from its earliest Jebusite days, to its glories under David, it greatness under Solomon, and so on throughout its checkered history.[28]

Geddes projected a nineteenth-century concept of the museum into the twentieth. In 1917 the imagined display began with Egypt and culminated in the reigns of David and Solomon. The Old Testament dominated the historical narrative of the projected display. That narrative was to be illustrated with a few "antiquities" and by many models, panoramas, and relief maps, like those found in the great international exhibitions of the nineteenth century. As an aside, it may be noted that Geddes's proposal for a celebration of Israelite Jerusalem is now realized in the Museum of the History of Jerusalem lodged prominently in the Citadel by Jaffa Gate. The narrative presented in that museum's exhibition is remarkably nineteenth century

Figure 2.4. Jerusalem, Palestine Archaeological Museum, view of the North Gallery.

in both its colonialist content and its media. The acclamation of the Israelites' accomplishments is conveyed by means of an elaborate display of models, maps, tableaux, and a few artifacts and replicas, enhanced now with computer imaging. The Pre-Israelite, Byzantine, Arab, Turkish, and British histories of the city are minimally referenced. The archaeology of the Citadel itself, the site of the museum, is oddly blurred, with little reference to the substantial additions made to it by the Ayyubids, Mamluks, Ottomans, and British.[29]

By the 1930s, the Palestine Archaeological Museum had a very different, thoroughly twentieth-century story to tell. John Henry Iliffe, its first curator, describes the order of display:

> The Exhibition Galleries, which are on one floor only, are designed to admit of simple circulation in a clockwise direction.... [From the South Octagon, where Egyptian and North Mesopotamian sculptures and inscriptions in stone of the Late Bronze and Iron I Ages are on display] the visitor passes into the South Gallery, containing the exhibition of Stone and Bronze Ages.... Beyond this is the South Room, where are exhibited sculptures of the Hellenistic and Roman periods with some smaller objects. From here one will pass successively into the West Hall, designed for Inscriptions and Epigraphic material of all kinds, the North Gallery, and the North Octagon, which will contain the remainder of the chronological series of objects illustrating the Iron Age and subsequent periods down to the year A.D. 1700. Thus the exhibition galleries, when completely arranged, will offer a chronological synopsis of the cultural history of Man in Palestine, from his beginnings in the Stone Age (a period to which Palestine has lately contributed material of the first importance) down to A.D. 1700.[30]

Certainly for many visitors in the 1930s, the new Palestine Archaeological Museum remained a monumental confirmation of the historical truth of religion, as is apparent in the response, both popular and elite, at its opening. John D. Rockefeller Jr. commented, "That the Museum may prove of great use to scholars and that it may be a powerful factor in the promotion of a deeper and fuller knowledge of what the Holy Land means to Christendom, is my earnest hope."[31] James G. McDonald, who in the spring of 1938 became chairman of President Roosevelt's Advisory Committee on Political Refugees and later served as U.S. representative and ambassador to Israel between 1948 and 1951, wrote, "Not only the people of the Middle East but from all over the world are, and will for a very long time be, your debtors for this unique institution which supplements the biblical teachings about the Holy Land as nothing else could possibly do."[32] An anonymous contributor to the *Boston Transcript* similarly observed that the new museum will "beautify Jerusalem ... [as well as] fill an important need not only of archaeology but of religion. It will help to separate the true from the false in the way of sacred relics and reminders in and about a city which is holy to three religions. . . . Mr. Rockefeller does an excellent thing for science, for sacred history, in providing for such a museum in Jerusalem."[33]

Despite the common assumption that a museum in Jerusalem must document religion, the order of things in the Palestine Archaeological Museum explained the origins of Western civilization rather than the glories of a particular Semitic tribe or the truth of Protestant Christianity. The museum frames that narrative scientifically. For Breasted, archaeology's purpose was not to provide proof of the Bible's authority, but to penetrate the obscurity of man's shift from barbarism to civilization and to document that development empirically:

> Between the historians and the natural scientists there has been a "great gulf set," with the result that we now have on the one hand the paleontologist with his picture of the dawn-man enveloped in clouds of archaic savagery, and on the other hand the historian with his reconstruction of the career of civilized man in Europe. Between these two stand we orientalists endeavoring to bridge the gap. . . . *The task of salvaging and studying this evidence* [of the advance of civilization] *and of recovering the story which it reveals—that is the greatest task of the humanist today.*[34]

For Breasted, the place to locate the critical "bridge" between Africa and Eurasia in man's cultural trajectory was the Near East, site of the Egypto-Babylonian culture from which civilization was diffused to the rest of the Old World. "The Old World is . . . made up of two continents, Africa and Eurasia; . . . the earliest civilizations arose and spread on both sides of the intercontinental bridge between them."[35] The permanent exhibition at the Palestine Archaeological Museum is organized to convey to the public the lessons learned by archaeologists about the origins of "civilized" (i.e., Western) man from artifacts excavated from the cradle of higher culture. That which is absent from the exhibition's narrative is central to its understanding. The Jews are no longer the culmination of the story, just a minor part of the script. The local modern is also excised; according to this account the culmination of civilization happened elsewhere. The vacuum is filled by the tourist who, in the absence of competition, readily identifies himself and his culture as the climax of this material and epigraphic account of man's ascent to civilization.

The Islamic form of the museum is an index of the displacement of the Jews as the principal subject of narration. The building's figural decoration further confirms the agenda manifested in the organization of its collection. In the spandrels of the lateral arcades of the central court there are ten low-relief figures executed by the well-known English artist Eric Gill. These plaques personify the ten civilizations that affected the culture of the region: Egyptian, Mesopotamian, Phoenician, Canaanite, Hebrew, Greek, Roman, Byzantine, Islamic, and Crusader.[36] The series appears in chronological sequence. No one of these cultures is particularly privileged. Jewish history and its cognate, biblical history, have lost their cultural dominance.

The impression of the diminished place of Judaism in the archaeological history of Palestine is reinforced by the tympanum sculpture over the museum's main entrance. This piece, also executed by Gill, shows two heraldic kneeling figures, identified as Africa and Asia, flanking a tree (Figure 2.5). The Israel Museum website identifies the subject of the panel as "the meeting of Asia and Africa, with the palm tree symbolizing the land of Israel."[37] A more generic identification of the space would be less chauvinistic. Like Breasted, Gill referred to Jerusalem's location exclusively as either Palestine or the Holy Land. For Gill, in good Orientalist fashion, the resident Arabs were the land's true representatives. "In Palestine, among the Arabs, [humanity] is uppermost and unspoiled. I am not saying there is nothing wrong in Palestine. Wherever there are men there is sin and violence and selfishness and disease. Moreover there are poor in Palestine poorer than anything we can conceive in our up-to-date towns. In spite of all that it is the Holy Land and they live a holy life, whereas England is unholy and people can only live holy lives in secret." In contrast, Gill is unsympathetic to the innovations of Jewish immigrants. "The smart modern Jews are building smart modern towns and introducing

Figure 2.5. Jerusalem, Palestine Archaeological Museum, tympanum sculpture by Eric Gill.

smart modern ways, including smart modern prostitution, and smart modern factories, and smart modern clothes. Are these things good? They are not."[38] The meaning of the tympanum might better be understood in Breasted's terms: Africa and (Eur)Asia face each other across a land bridge bearing the Tree of Knowledge. Indeed, the sculptural program of the Palestine Archaeological Museum appears to be a version of that designed by Breasted for his own Oriental Institute at the University of Chicago. There the tympanum over the main entrance is also heraldic. It displays the East (as an Egyptian scribe accompanied by an African lion) presenting the West (a half-nude Caucasian, identified as an American by the bison recumbent at his feet) with the origins of the writing system (Figure 2.6). Figures personifying the interim civilizations of the East and West stand behind their respective representatives. No Israelite is included.[39]

The privileged position of the West in the ordering of the exhibition and in the programing of the decoration of the Palestine Archaeological Museum reverberates in its institutional structure. At the time of the establishment of the Palestine

Figure 2.6. Chicago, Oriental Institute, tympanum, designed by James Henry Breasted and executed by Ulric H. Ellerhusen.

Archaeological Museum, Rockefeller stipulated that "the responsibility . . . [for the museum's] future administration will likewise be carried on by the Palestine Government in such advisory relations with an international advisory committee as the Palestine Government may deem feasible."[40] The recognized government of Palestine, at the time the British Mandate Authority, established an archaeological advisory board to run the museum. The board consisted "of the heads of the principal archaeological schools in Palestine, with representatives of the religious communities . . . under the chairmanship of the Director of Antiquities."[41] This purely advisory body carried out its duties under the auspices of the Mandate Authority until April 1948.

On the eve of the British evacuation of Palestine in 1948, in one of the last acts of the Mandate government, the advisory board was precipitously reconstituted as the museum's owners.

> In view of the termination of the Mandate, it appears to the Government of Palestine to be desirable that the Museum should be placed in an independent position. With this end in view, the Government of Palestine is prepared, if the Rockefeller Foundation agrees, to introduce legislation providing for a Board of Trustees to hold the building, its contents, the land upon which it stands and the endowment fund, and to administer the Museum and the fund. It is proposed that this Board should be international in character and should include representatives of the principal archaeological institutions interested in the Near East, namely, the Oriental Institute of Chicago, American School of Oriental Research, Académie des inscriptions et belles lettres, institut français d'archéologie orientale, the British Museum, the British Academy, a Scandinavian Institution, together with two Palestinian and two Near Eastern representatives.[42]

Religious diversity, emphasized in the original descriptions of the advisory board, goes unmentioned in the constitution of its board of trustees. In a supplementary document, the fear of the museum falling into nonprofessional (i.e., non-Western) hands, is more apparent:

> It is considered desirable to make provision for ensuring that the Palestine Archaeological Museum and its contents shall be controlled and administered by archaeologists and persons of eminence for, and on behalf of, the people of Palestine as a whole and in the general interests of archaeology, And whereas it is considered desirable to associate with that control, representatives of those archaeological institutions, which are principally concerned with the archaeology of Palestine and the neighboring countries. . . . And whereas it has been decided for that purpose to

> transfer the ownership and control of the Museum to the Board hereinafter established . . . [the High Commissioner ordered the museum's privatization].[43]

This hysterical act of privatization turned out to be the first of two mistakes that had catastrophic consequences for the museum.

The Mandate ended disastrously in 1948 with the beginning of a war between the Arabs and the Jews that has had, since then, cessations but no real end. A letter from James L. Kelso, president of the board of trustees of the museum as well as the director of the American Schools of Oriental Research, to John D. Rockefeller Jr., written in December 1949, suggests how the museum fared.

> The new international Board of Trustees for the Palestine Archaeological Museum, as provided for by the order of the High Commissioner in 1948, has now met and is arranging for the re-opening of the Museum to the general public early in 1950. . . .
>
> It suffered no major structural damage during the fighting, but there was a variety of minor damages. Windows in particular were shattered, doors and gates damaged and the roof was struck in several places. Emergency repairs cost a little over 400 Palestine pounds. Permanent repairs will run approximately LP. 1,600.
>
> A part of the building was occupied by the Arab Legion during the fighting. Their "wear and tear" on the building was light and comes chiefly from the use of army boots on the floor coverings. Some walls will need repainting and some telephone and electric cables will need to be replaced. No thieving was discovered. Few armies in history ever treated a building so kindly. Since Mr. J. H. Iliffe, the Curator, left during the fighting, Mr. G. W. L. Harding was appointed Acting Curator at once. He is being continued in that post until a new Director can be secured. Mr. Harding is the Chief of the Antiquities Department of the Hashemite Kingdom of the Jordan with headquarters in Amman. . . . All Archaeological groups which appoint Trustees to the Museum have been requested to nominate candidates for the position of permanent Curator.
>
> The Endowment Funds which you gave are intact. They are still in the hands of the Crown Agents as they were during the Mandate. The future financial program of the Museum will be cramped for a time as the former Mandate Government blended the work of its Antiquities Department with that of the Museum in such a way that the Museum had financial resources beyond those produced by the Endowment which you presented to the Museum.[44]

Because of its location in East Jerusalem, the Palestine Archaeological Museum came under the control of the Hashemite Kingdom of Jordan. With the establishment of the barrier dividing Jordan and Israel, Jews, always unemphasized in the museum's displays, were newly excluded from its administration and its audience. Ironically, just at that time, artifacts of a peculiarly Jewish history became the museum's self-destructive obsession.

Dead Sea Scrolls

The Prix Femina is a literary prize awarded by a jury of distinguished women of letters to an author, male or female, for the best novel of the year. In 1904 its first recipient was Myriam Harry for her *La Conquête de Jérusalem* (1903).[45] In a later fiction, *La Petite Fille de Jérusalem* (1914), Harry describes the life of a young girl in Jerusalem from her birth through the suicide of her father, Mr. Benedictus. Benedictus, a Jew converted to Christianity and married to a narrow-minded Lutheran deaconess, owns an antiquities shop in the Old City from which he travels, buying and selling artifacts. He acquires what he believes to be the fragments of an ancient copy of Deuteronomy. He takes the texts to Europe for authentication and sale. The Berlin Museum offers to buy them, but the price they are willing to pay is inadequate.

> Professor Hartwig [a German academic and family friend] urged Mr. Benedictus to try his fortune in Paris, or better still, in London, where he was already so well known. Besides the English were remarkable for their predilection for all that was associated with the study of Hebrew. And surely enough, when Mr. Benedictus arrived in London with his treasured parchment, he created quite a sensation. Directly he set foot in one of the best hotels, he was besieged by interviewers, reporters and photographers. He was the hero of the hour.[46]

But Benedictus's longtime nemesis, a jealous French antiquarian, raises questions of the manuscript's authenticity.

> In the most uncompromising terms, he had pronounced the Deuteronomy parchment to be a forgery; [in consequence] the manuscript had been instantly withdrawn from the department in the British Museum where it had been closely guarded by detectives. . . . [Benedictus] had been most severely censured in the papers for bringing discredit on all the well-known Orientalists in Great Britain, whom he had succeeded in duping.[47]

Benedictus, distraught at the loss of his reputation, kills himself.

La Petite Fille de Jérusalem was translated into English as *The Little Daughter of Jerusalem* in 1919. The novel's remarkable popularity did not depend on the subtlety or verisimilitude of its writing. As a contemporary reviewer commented, Harry "often falls almost ridiculously short of realism—or soars above it, as one is pleased to look at the matter. . . . However, these ecstatic excursions into the Land of Nowhere may be forgiven, juvenile though they be, in view of the rich descriptions of oriental life."[48] The public was fascinated by the book's intimate depiction of both the trade in biblical artifacts and female life in the East. The author's ability to satisfy the voyeurism of her audience was grounded in her familiarity with the subject matter. Her novel is autobiographical. Myriam Harry was born Maria Rosette Shapira; her father, Moses Shapira, was a Jerusalem antiquities dealer. He claimed to have bought the leather text fragments that he took to Europe to sell from a Bedouin. The Bedouin, Shapira reported, had found the strips in a cave near the Dead Sea. In 1884, after the texts were pronounced forgeries by the French Orientalist Charles Simon Clermont-Ganneau, Shapira committed suicide in Rotterdam. Sixty-four years later, the first of the Dead Sea Scrolls were found in the same area as that Shapira had identified as the source of his fragments. The Shapira fragments themselves are now lost.[49]

The West's fascination with the East, as both exotic and biblical, has been exploited by modern fiction writers from Benjamin Disraeli and Émile Zola to Agatha Christie and Joel Rosenberg. That same fascination helps explain the public's sustained interest in the Dead Sea Scrolls. Between 1947 and 1956, caves near Qumran on the Dead Sea yielded the remnants of about eight hundred manuscripts, most of them of biblical or ritual content, written between the end of the third century BCE and the middle of the first century CE.[50] The acquisition of these fragments by various individuals and institutions from their Bedouin discoverers was notoriously competitive.[51] Hebrew University acquired some fragments, which are now housed in the Israel Museum. Others were purchased privately. The major player in the market was the Palestine Archaeological Museum.[52] In his introduction to the permanent public display of the scrolls in the museum, the museum's curator, Yusef Saad, describes the scrolls' affect on the institution.

> Unfortunately the Museum received no financial help towards the actual buying of the scrolls, and has during the ten years from 1949 to 1959 spent over JD [Jordanian Dinars] 65,000 ($183,000 [about $1.5 million now]) on this. In order to realize this large sum it became necessary at one stage to cash a part of its Endowment Fund, with a consequent loss of income of lbs. 2,000 a year, nearly a quarter of the total. Thus its activities have had to be somewhat curtailed recently. . . . Although there are still rumors of more scrolls in the hands of the Bedu, the Museum has exhausted itself financially and can do no more on its own, though the Trustees continue to try and find other sources of funds for the rescue of these unique and priceless documents.[53]

During the 1950s, the main site for the study of the Dead Sea Scrolls was the Palestine Archaeological Museum's "Scrollery" (Figure 2.7).[54] The building had been carefully planned with space for the scientific study of ancient artifacts, following the model of Breasted's projected Egyptian Museum, though on a smaller scale. With the discovery and acquisition of the Dead Sea Scrolls, research and its patronage shifted abruptly from excavated sites to parchment fragments.

Competition and controversy were not limited to the collection of the fragments. The museum became the locus of virulent academic intrigue.[55] Scholars battled not for the ownership of the scrolls, which were permanently installed in the Palestine Archaeological Museum, but for the control of their meaning. For patrons, scrolls were bought for intellectual, not physical, possession. A 1958 article from *Time* magazine suggests how this worked:

> A Manhattan church—All Souls Unitarian—announced last week that it had acquired a new and unique section of the Dead Sea Scrolls: the oldest complete Biblical copy of the Ten Commandments, probably dating from the end of the

Figure 2.7. Jerusalem, Palestine Archaeological Museum, "Scrollery." From Saad, *The Palestine Archaeological Museum and the Dead Sea Scrolls* (1965).

> 1st century B.C. The price of the scroll, slightly more than $5,000, was paid by a prominent mining tycoon with a hankering for archaeology and a strong dislike of publicity.... While dickering for fragments on behalf of Chicago's McCormick Theological Seminary with the Syrian cobbler Kando, who is unofficial middleman between the Bedouins and the scholars, [Dr. Frank] Cross and his fellow scholars had been offered an exceptionally large piece from Cave 4 for $12,000. An old hand at the Bedouin bargaining table, the scholars began making counteroffers. Finally, last summer, during the height of the Middle East crisis, Cross and Jordanian Curator Yusuf Saad of the Palestine Archaeological Museum sat down with Kando for a bit of high-class haggling over tea and Turkish cigarettes.... The bargaining went on for three sessions, and the price slowly descended to about $5,000. Then Cross and Saad hurried into the British Bank of the Middle East, just outside Jerusalem's ancient Damascus Gate, stepped nervously out again into the teeming, clanking tangle of Arabs and animals in Jericho Road with $5,000 in Jordanian pounds, and hurried back for the final transaction.... All Souls Unitarians will have to travel to Jerusalem to see their acquisition as Jordanian law prohibits any cave finds from being taken out of the country. But the church will have its share of scholarly glory; the new scroll will henceforth be known in bibliographies as the "All Souls Deuteronomy."[56]

Corporations were also involved in fund-raising. John Allegro, for example, received funding from Glaxo, Kodak, Kraft, Nestlé, Unilever, Cadbury, Eveready, Rover, and others in support of a scrolls-inspired treasure-hunt.[57]

If institutions and corporations invested in the scrolls for glory, scholars had scrolls bought for them for the exclusive right to their study and publication—again not for physical custody. Roland de Vaux, one of the principals of the Dead Sea Scrolls project, reveals the intimate relation between money and scholarship in a report presented in 1966 on the progress being made in the publication of the scrolls:

> Most of the material coming from the Cave 11 in Qumran was bought by the P.A.M. [Palestine Archaeological Museum]. Some fragments were found in subsequent excavation. In order to reimburse the Museum, it was decided that the Museum would sell to responsible institutions the exclusive rights of editing and publishing these manuscripts, against a payment of the sums disbursed by the Museum. At the same time, the ownership of the manuscripts was to be transferred to the Government of Jordan, in compliance with the decision of the Council of Ministers (17.vii.1960) which claimed government ownership for all the manuscripts found or to be found in the Dead Sea area.[58]

The Palestine Archaeological Museum might have survived the battle for custody of the Dead Sea Scrolls—its possession of artifacts that enthralled a popular as well as scholarly audience might, indeed, have enhanced its health. But the political conditions of Jerusalem made the museum directors' decision to bet all of its resources on the Dead Sea Scrolls another lethal one. Privatization and overinvestment in the Dead Sea Scrolls strangled the museum.

Controversy continues to cling to the Dead Sea Scrolls.[59] A *Time* magazine article from 1992 exemplifies the kind of titillating reportage that has excited public interest in the scrolls from the time of their discovery to the present.

> The Dead Sea Scrolls are an endless source of sensationalism. Supermarket tabloids would have us believe that these ancient Jewish texts reveal visitations from outer space, the cure for AIDS and the date the world will end. In a new book somehow inspired by the scrolls, Barbara Thiering of Australia's University of Sydney tells of a Jesus who was crucified but secretly revived at the Dead Sea and who wed a woman bishop at midnight on March 17, A.D. 50.
>
> Amid all the hokum, however, the latest discoveries on actual details in the scrolls are startling enough to generate legitimate headlines. Texts that are only now becoming widely available establish the first connection between the scrolls and Jesus' New Testament words about his role as the Messiah. . . .
>
> Scholars on the official committee worked on these remaining texts at a painfully slow pace while granting others severely limited access. By the late 1980s, scholarly temperatures reached the boiling point. One recent book claims Roman Catholic priests beholden to the Vatican conspired to cover up the texts lest they shake the doctrinal foundations of the mother church. The true reasons are more mundane: too few scholars monopolizing too much material, team members' personal problems, shortage of money, political and academic intrigue and plain incompetence.
>
> The breakthrough on access occurred in the fall of 1991 when *Biblical Archeology Review* of Washington capped a lengthy crusade by publishing a bootleg computerized reconstruction of the texts. Specialized research libraries then decided to ignore scholarly protocol and allowed outside experts to examine photos of the unpublished scrolls. Finally the *Review* published its own photo books.[60]

Some of the Dead Sea Scroll quarrels are narrowly philological contentions regarding the critical reconstruction of the texts. Most are broader and more acrimonious. Bitter complaints about the lack of access to the fragments because of the possessiveness of the scholars controlling them led not only to their unauthorized publication but also to adjudication of important cultural property claims in the Supreme Court of Israel.[61] Less litigious but just as rancorous have been the debates over the context and history of the scrolls.[62] Most scholars accept the hypothesis that in the first century CE the scrolls were in possession of an ascetic sect, the Essenes, though there is much dissension among researchers over the religious and social construction of this group. Other scholars argue that the Essenes are an academic fiction.[63] In any case, claims about the documents' relevance to the study of Judaism and Christianity tend to be apologetic, dogmatic, and contradictory. All of these arguments have their own politics, most of them personal and/or sectarian. More crucially, the tumultuous micropolitics of academic careerism and religious identity seem to have obscured the macropolitics of the state's theft of the artifacts.

Catalepsy

Catalepsy is a pathological condition characterized by a loss of consciousness accompanied by a rigidity of muscles that keeps limbs in any position in which they are placed; it may also be a seizure or trance characterized by a suspension of sensation and consciousness. In people, this state may last for hours or days; in buildings it may persist for years.[64] The Palestine Archaeological Museum in Jerusalem, aka the Rockefeller Museum, is now in a cataleptic coma. The museum offers no admission buttons or tickets, no suggested donations, no museum shop, no café, no docents. The museum is unheated in the winter.[65] The galleries are empty of visitors, haunted by the fragments of the past that occupy them. Between April 1954 and March 1955 there were 4,512 paying visitors and 3,558 free admissions to the museum.[66] Now visitors, if there are any, go unrecorded.[67]

The Palestine Archaeological Museum/Rockefeller Museum lingers in a state of suspended animation. Some of the labels have been changed, and at least one inscription apparently erased—that identifying the Islamic material in the last bay of the exhibition.[68] But the gallery order is the same. Displays have remained virtually unchanged since their installation. The museum thus presents its rare visitor with two distinct archaeological experiences: the first is that of the evolution of human culture before 1700, and the second is that of the state of museology of the 1930s. Displayed for the occasional postmodern observer are not only premodern artifacts but also modern techniques of exhibition. In its state of dormancy, the Palestine Archaeological Museum/Rockefeller Museum provides an architectural analogue to the urbanism of East Jerusalem. Construction—most of it ill advised and almost all of it aesthetically abominable—refigures Israeli West Jerusalem.[69] In Palestinian East Jerusalem, Israeli building is, under international law, all illegal and unrelentingly ugly. Permits for building, even restoration, are notoriously difficult for Palestinians to obtain.[70] The Palestinian urban setting of the museum, like the museum itself, is dying from paralysis.

East Jerusalem is being slowly suffocated. It is progressively isolated from the western parts of the city with checkpoints and from the Palestinian West Bank by the notorious "fence" and by illegal Jewish settlements. Israeli Jews are uncomfortable in East Jerusalem, avoiding it and, consequently, the museum.[71] The museum's entrance, policed by fully armed security guards, is yet another checkpoint.[72] To Palestinians it appears inaccessible. No parking is allowed. The parking lot is filled with the cars of the Israel Antiquities Authority housed there rather than those of visitors. The museum is absent from tourist itineraries. Its place on the tourist route, along with its Dead Sea Scrolls and many of its most precious artifacts, has been usurped by the Israel Museum. The Israel Museum's Shrine of the Book, designed by Frederic Kiesler and Armand Bartos, opened in 1965; it is either admired as great architecture or ridiculed as kitsch (Figure 2.8).[73] The deeply disappointing focus of its exhibition when I visited was a photocopy of the Isaiah Scroll, wrapped around the monumental Oldenburg-esque scroll handle that dominates the dimly lit, cave-like interior gallery space. The light-filled Scrollery of the Palestine Archaeological Museum is now a dark, compact shelf–filled archive (Figure 2.9).

Figure 2.8. Jerusalem, Israel Museum, Shrine of the Book, general view with the Hilton Hotel and the Knesset in the background.

The museum's morbidity is the result of a state politics infected by old colonial arrogance and current religious and ethnic antagonism. On the eve of its departure, the British Mandate Authority legislated the museum's advisory board into its owners. The British thus imposed on its successor state an institution run by foreigners (Westerners), not unlike that proposed by Breasted and Rockefeller to Egypt two decades earlier and rejected by that government as an insult to its sovereignty. Remarkably, the Hashemite Kingdom of Jordan tolerated these conditions until 1966. Then, with the backing of several members of the advisory board, the museum was finally renationalized. The institutions responsible for appointing members of the board of trustees were, nevertheless, invited to nominate members for a new board of advisors.[74]

With the 1967 war came the Israeli occupation of East Jerusalem and the Palestine Archaeological Museum. The Israel Antiquities Authority moved its headquarters from West to East Jerusalem and centered all its activities in the Palestine Archaeological Museum, which was officially renamed the Rockefeller Museum, presumably to sever the museum's connection with its Palestinian past. Using the

Figure 2.9. Jerusalem, Rockefeller Museum, archive.

museum's recent nationalization by the Jordanians as an excuse, the museum and its collections were confiscated. Jordan's nationalization of the museum was represented as a radical aberration. Its connection to international scholarly bodies is ubiquitously misrepresented. The entry for the museum in the *Encyclopedia of the Dead Sea Scrolls* (2000), for example, distorts the situation:

> Despite the international board of trustees appointed to oversee the museum, the Jordanian government chose to nationalize the museum on 1 November, 1966, and disband the board. . . . Following the events of the 1967 Arab-Israeli War and the reunification of Jerusalem, the Israel Antiquities Authority moved its headquarters from west to east Jerusalem and centered all its activities in the Palestine Archaeological Museum, which was renamed the Rockefeller Museum in recognition of the contributions of John D. Rockefeller, Jr.[75]

As far as I am aware, Israeli authorities never invited the international archaeological schools to nominate members for an advisory board that might protect the interests of the museum, as had the Jordanians.

Both Israel and Jordan are signatories of the Hague Convention on Cultural Property of 1954.[76] This convention includes in its definition of cultural property those movable or immovable works of importance to the heritage of every people, including buildings, such as museums and libraries, whose effective purpose is to preserve or exhibit such goods. It stipulates that contracting parties are pledged to prevent any form of theft, pillage, or misappropriation of cultural property. Further, in the occupation of the whole or part of the sovereign territory of another state, the signatory shall as far as possible support the competent national authorities of the occupied country in safeguarding and preserving its cultural property. Despite signing the Hague Convention, Israel has confiscated the precious possessions of a museum situated in territory recognized internationally as militarily occupied. The Palestine Archaeological Museum was robbed of its name, deprived of its board of advisors, and stripped of significant parts of its collection, including the Dead Sea Scrolls for which it had sold its inheritance. The museum has lost its lifeblood. And nobody seems to have noticed.[77]

The Palestine Archaeological Museum has been looted, but the booty is not *spolia.* It is not proudly exhibited as evidence of military prowess. The source of the plunder is not named in its display but hidden. Any bloodletting in its capture has been carefully concealed. Indeed, the body from which it was taken has not been slaughtered, but rather kept barely alive and in isolation in a pretense of civilization. But if the museum and its precious possessions are not *spolia,* they are certainly spoils.

PART II

DISEASE

3

AMNESIA

Bullet holes, a reminder to residents of their deadly surroundings and of their vulnerability, mark entrances to violent buildings.

—Camilo José Vergara, "Opening the Doors to the Ghettos"

The fact that domestic homicide cannot be predicted does not detract from our excellent ability to predict less lethal violence among chronic couples. Among couples with nine or more incidents, it can be predicted that they will have further incidents with 75 per cent accuracy. Chronically violent buildings can also be identified with 72 per cent accuracy, regardless of the specific couples living in them at any given time.

—Lawrence W. Sherman, "Preventing Homicide through Trial and Error"

Bullshit

"True," in common language, generally refers to that which corresponds to empirical experience with dependable consistency. A "lie" consciously contradicts the true. Princeton philosopher Harry Frankfurt usefully probes the word "bullshit" in relation to truth and falsehood through a consideration of the intentions of the speaker. Liars consciously contradict that which they know to be true. In order to hide the truth by their lies, they must recognize what truth is. For bullshitters, in contrast, truth is irrelevant. What bullshitters posit may be true or false—it doesn't really matter. Bullshit, Frankfurt writes, is a greater enemy of truth than the lie.[1] Bullshit is all too familiar now, but it is only the most ubiquitous of truth's spoilers. Another is amnesia.

Amnesia is the loss of memory. The cause may be physiological, a head injury, a medical condition, medication side effects, or substance abuse. Alternatively, amnesia may have a psychological basis, the result of a dissociative disorder. Dissociative amnesia is a significant loss of memory that cannot be medically explained. Among doctors and the lay public, this condition is broadly understood as a patient's unconscious suppression of an experienced trauma. It is widely assumed that the sufferer avoids reexperiencing a painful past event by forgetting it. The WebMD Internet site provides a popular description of the condition:[2]

> Dissociative amnesia occurs when a person blocks out certain information, usually associated with a stressful or traumatic event, leaving him or her unable to remember important personal information. With this disorder, the degree of memory loss goes beyond normal forgetfulness and includes gaps in memory for long periods of time or of memories involving the traumatic event. Dissociative amnesia is not the same as simple amnesia, which involves a loss of information from memory, usually as the result of disease or injury to the brain. With dissociative amnesia, the memories still exist but are deeply buried within the person's mind and cannot be recalled. However, the memories might resurface on their own or after being triggered by something in the person's surroundings.[3]

From the 1990s, however, research on memory loss linked to dissociation took a skeptical turn.[4] The contentious division, broadly between clinicians and researchers, has been titled the "memory wars."[5] Radically alternative explanations for dissociative amnesia are being explored. For example, Drs. Giesbrecht, Lillienfeld, Lynn, and Merckelbach comment in the *Psychological Bulletin*:

> Contrary to a widespread assumption in the clinical literature, dissociation does not appear to be related to avoidant information processing. Rather, it is associated with an enhanced propensity toward pseudo-memories, possibly mediated by heightened levels of interrogative suggestibility, fantasy proneness, and cognitive failures. Evidence for a link between dissociation and either memory fragmentation or early trauma based on objective measures is conspicuously lacking.[6]

Amnesia may result from a self-defensive reaction to a past trauma or a creative substitution of a fantasized memory for an actual one, and the sufferer may not be able to tell the difference.

There is another possibility: false amnesia. In a case of false amnesia the "sufferer" fakes memory loss in order to avoid self-incrimination.[7] Researchers from Wesleyan University describe the phenomenon:

> When called to testify about illegal actions, individuals may attempt to avoid perjury and evade responsibility for their previous actions by claiming that they cannot remember. These claims of "focal retrograde amnesia," whereby individuals report a relatively isolated, permanent memory loss for autobiographical events associated

> with a specific crime, can occur at rates of 25%–45% when defendants are charged with murder. Because genuine cases of focal retrograde amnesia in neurological patients are rare, researchers suspect that many defendants who present this memory problem when charged with a crime are actually feigning amnesia to avoid legal responsibility, especially when they face substantial incriminating evidence. In many of these instances, the individuals claim that the memory loss was due to their use of alcohol or drugs.[8]

False amnesia is a perpetrator's manipulation of the history of an act in order to avoid taking responsibility for its commission. The misrepresentation of events may even erode the culprit's ability to reconstruct the truth.[9] Both dissociative amnesia and false amnesia may signal not only an erasure of memory, but also the construction of a fictitious history. Recognizing the force of amnesia is relevant to the reconstruction of a building's biography.[10] In any attempt to understand bad acts of the past, the architectural historian, like the forensic investigator, discovers that the written and oral memory of a building offers truth, lies, and bullshit.

Figure 3.1. Santiago de Compostela, Hostal de los Reyes Católicos, south facade.

The Hospital de los Reyes Católicos, located in Santiago de Compostela in northwest Spain, was constructed to serve religious and therapeutic functions (Figure 3.1). As religion is popularly associated with benevolent spirituality and as caretaking is commonly identified with compassion, this structure seems an unlikely subject of fantasy substitution, prevarication, and bullshit. Nevertheless, the Hospital de los Reyes Católicos was the agent of tyrants and implicated in social trauma. Like the stories of a human criminal, the narratives of this building are not to be trusted.

Early Modern Trauma

In the Middle Ages, the three most powerful sites in Christendom focused on tombs: the empty one of the absent Jesus in Jerusalem and those filled with the remains of Jesus's disciples in Italy and Spain. Saints Peter and Paul, the Princes of the Apostles, had their basilicas in Rome. The body of St. James the Greater was miraculously translated to the Iberian Peninsula after his martyrdom in Palestine.[11] By the twelfth century, his remains were enshrined in a great Romanesque church in Compostela. All of these sepulchers were important pilgrimage destinations. Indeed, Rome and Santiago are the only two cities of Christendom awarded the papal privilege of celebrating a Holy Year. In Santiago the Holy Year is that in which James's saint's day, July 25, occurs on a Sunday. Pilgrims who visit the shrine of the apostle during a Holy Year receive a plenary indulgence. Indulgences are a remarkable Catholic invention by which the pious can repay the debts incurred by their sins before death with pious acts (including, in the past, donations to the church's civil and military projects), rather than after death with physical suffering. A plenary indulgence provides for a full remission of the recipient's sins so that no further expiation of her bad deeds is required in purgatory.

St. James was the beloved votary of Jesus. He witnessed Jesus's Transfiguration along with only Peter and John (Matthew 17:1–9). That James had a belligerent streak is suggested in the Gospels: he proposed calling down the fire of heaven on the Samaritan village that refused to receive Jesus and his apostles on their way to Jerusalem (Luke 9:51–56). James's latent hostility later became fully active. In Spain, violence was James's most prominent attribute. There he was known as Santiago Matamoros, St. James the Moor-Slayer, the patron saint of the Catholic conquest of the Iberian Peninsula. St. James was popularly represented as a mounted, sword-wielding knight trampling the bodies of Muslims (Figure 3.2).[12] The crusading trope of St. James and the Moors was revived in the form of a St. James's Cross badge, designed to be worn by Spanish troops sent to fight the American war in Iraq.[13]

The discussions of powerful premodern sanctuaries tend to concentrate on the immediate architectural frame of the saints' relics—the church. But relics' power also

Figure 3.2. London, British Library C. 18, e. i., No. 75, Indulgence of Pope Alexander VI, 1503, detail of Santiago Matamoros, St. James the Moor-Slayer. Rendition by the author.

permeated their neighborhoods. It is in the neighborhood of the great cathedral of St. James that some underobserved displays of architectural violence occur. The early modern Hospital de los Reyes Católicos is in the immediate vicinity of the great cathedral-tomb of St. James. The intimate association of a killer saint with a hospital turns out to be less ironic than one might hope. "Reyes Católicos" or "Catholic Kings" was the name conferred on Ferdinand and Isabella of Spain in 1496 by the Spanish Pope Alexander VI (Rodrigo Borgia) in honor of the joint rulers' fervent furtherance of the Catholic cause through good works and through violence. That violence was directed externally in wars of conquest and internally with the conscientious purging of misbelievers. In 1487, during the reign of the Catholic Kings, Pope Sixtus IV established the Spanish Inquisition; it was not finally abolished until 1834.[14] Interrogation under torture, spying, intimidation, and incitement of the fear of the Other certainly go on in the early twenty-first century. But the public burning of bodies and books made the consequences of challenging religious and political orthodoxies more immediate in early modernity than it is now.[15]

The Catholic monarchs announced their intentions to establish a hospital in Compostela in the portentous year of 1492, a year that marked the discovery of America, the expulsion of the Jews from Spain, and the fall of Granada, the last Muslim stronghold in the peninsula.[16] A late fifteenth-century traveler describes what happened in Granada: "[The king] ordered the demolition of the Juderia, which had been inhabited by more than twenty thousand Jews, in order to construct in their place, at his own expense, a great hospital and a magnificent church in honor of the Virgin, to serve as the cathedral."[17] Santiago was further away but benefited from Granada's conquest just as directly. Ferdinand had made a pilgrimage to the shrine of St. James before beginning his crusade against the Muslims; the new hospital in Santiago, like that of Granada, was a thank-offering, a gift to the apostle for his contribution to the destruction of the heretics. The structure served as a monumental ex-voto celebrating the expropriation of the religious Other.[18] The deadly work done by an ex-voto is revealed in the origins of the familiar term "devotions." As the scholar of Roman religion James Rives notes, "devotion" is derived from *vovere,* "to promise an offering to a god in return for the fulfillment of a request." *Devotio* and its cognates became "technical terms for a particular type of ritual in which a Roman general dedicated the enemy, and in some cases himself, to the gods of the underworld in exchange for a Roman victory. By the first century BCE, they had come to signify more generally any prayer or ritual that consigned some person or thing to the gods of the underworld for destruction."[19] Violence involved in the foundation of the hospital was not just etymological but historical.[20] The Hospital de los Reyes Católicos, announced in 1492 and funded in 1499, was designed and built by Enrique Egas between 1501 and 1511.[21]

The Hospital de los Reyes Católicos was the agent of monarchy. It ensured the Catholic Kings a monumental urban presence. It also secured the monarchs' persistent identity with St. James by means of the hospital's name, its privileged location in proximity to the cathedral, its vast size, and the high quality of its construction and decoration. The structure defines the north side of the great square, the Obradoiro, immediately to the west of the cathedral. The size of the structure is exaggerated by the austerity of its massive facade, which was built in the same material as the cathedral.[22] The royal signature is ubiquitously inscribed on the flesh of the building. Most publicly and legibly, the rulers are prominently figured in the building's great portal.[23] This portal controls the expansive front of the hospital by its centrality and by the contrast between the bleak plane of the structure's walls and the extreme elaboration of the entrance (Figure 3.3). The portal's high-relief ornament is realized in the busy, globular style of the plateresque ("in the manner of a silversmith"): the sculptural decoration appears to be modeled in toothpaste.[24] The portraits of the royal couple in the program of the portal establish their elevated position in the cosmic scheme of things. Flanking the entrance just above eye level are the figures of Adam and Eve, the initiators of human suffering. At the height of the scheme are Jesus and the Virgin. Between the originators of sin and its redeemers, in roundels ornamenting the spandrels of the arched entrance, are portrait busts of Ferdinand and Isabella.

The Catholic monarchs of Spain were the principal patrons of the building but not its exclusive promoters. The church was also committed to the institution. Indeed, the hospital, by its location, its mission, and its performance, expressed both religious and secular power: it was fully sacred *and* fully profane.[25] At the end of the fifteenth and beginning of the sixteenth centuries, Popes Innocent VIII and Alexander VI issued bulls promoting the hospital. Innocent VIII freed the hospital from local ecclesiastical intrusions.[26] Alexander VI established a confraternity for the continued support of the hospital. Membership was acquired by buying an indulgence. A copy of such an indulgence is held in the collection of the British Library. It is identified not only by its title, but also by the image in the lower left corner of the mounted St. James trampling on the decapitated heads of Moors (Figure 3.2).

> Having invoked the name of Christ and of Blessed James. Be it known to all Christ's faithful people that our Most Holy Lord Pope Alexander the Sixth has by his apostolic letters instituted in perpetual memory of the affair a certain confraternity in the great hospital which is being constructed in the city of Compostella, in which he has ordered that all persons of either sex who have spent a sixth part of a ducat for the building fund, for hospitality, for the sustenance of the poor and sick pilgrims of

Figure 3.3. Santiago de Compostela, Hostal de los Reyes Católicos, main portal, south facade.

> the said hospital be considered members of the confraternity and obtain the indulgences, favors and plenary remissions written below. . . .
>
> Item, he concedes to members of the confraternity that, on visiting at any season, including Lent, in which stations of the city [of Rome] are celebrated any church whatever of the place in which they may happen to reside, and devoutly saying five times on bended knee the Lord's prayer with the angelic salutation, they may obtain all and singular indulgences and plenary remissions which they would obtain if they passed through the holy places themselves. And just as if they had visited in person the aforesaid churches of the city within and without. . . .
>
> Item, he grants to women that four times in the year in the company of one or two honest women they may enter any convent of nuns whatsoever of any order, even of the recluses of St. Clare, with the consent of their superiors. And converse with them, and take refreshment, provided they do not pass the night there.[27]

A contribution to the hospital provided a female donor not only time off purgatory but tea with the nuns of her choice. The building was the agent of salvation.

The hospital's administration confirmed its Catholic genealogy. The staff was largely ecclesiastical, not secular—it had more priests than doctors. Though its financial and political well-being depended on the monarchy, the building's discipline was Catholic. Its administrator was a cleric; he did not, however, answer to the local hierarchy but directly to Rome. Patients were also expected to be Catholic devotees of St. James. Royal decrees up through the eighteenth century consistently reaffirm the hospital's prerogative to admit only those persons dedicated to the veneration of St. James.[28] The religious rigor of the institution conformed perfectly to its evolving Counter-Reformation context.

The hospital's architectural program, like its administration, might be identified as "inquisitional Catholic." Its design is marked by a heightened concern with the discipline of the body.[29] The building plan, like the facade with its central monumental entrance, is schematic (Figure 3.4). As all those who have spent time in churches know, bilateral symmetry imposes a hierarchy on a space—a dominant axis culminates at the locus of power, the altar. In a church or throne room, such order has a clear function. When bilateral symmetry occurs in other buildings, their function is distorted by a will to a similar spatial expression of authority. Observers should always be suspicious of the objectives of a bilaterally symmetrical building. The Hospital de los Reyes Católicos was bilaterally symmetrical. Religion controlled the spatial heart of the hospital, just as it regulated its central administration. At the core of the structure was the T-plan chapel. It was originally flanked by two identical courtyards around which were constructed wards and offices.

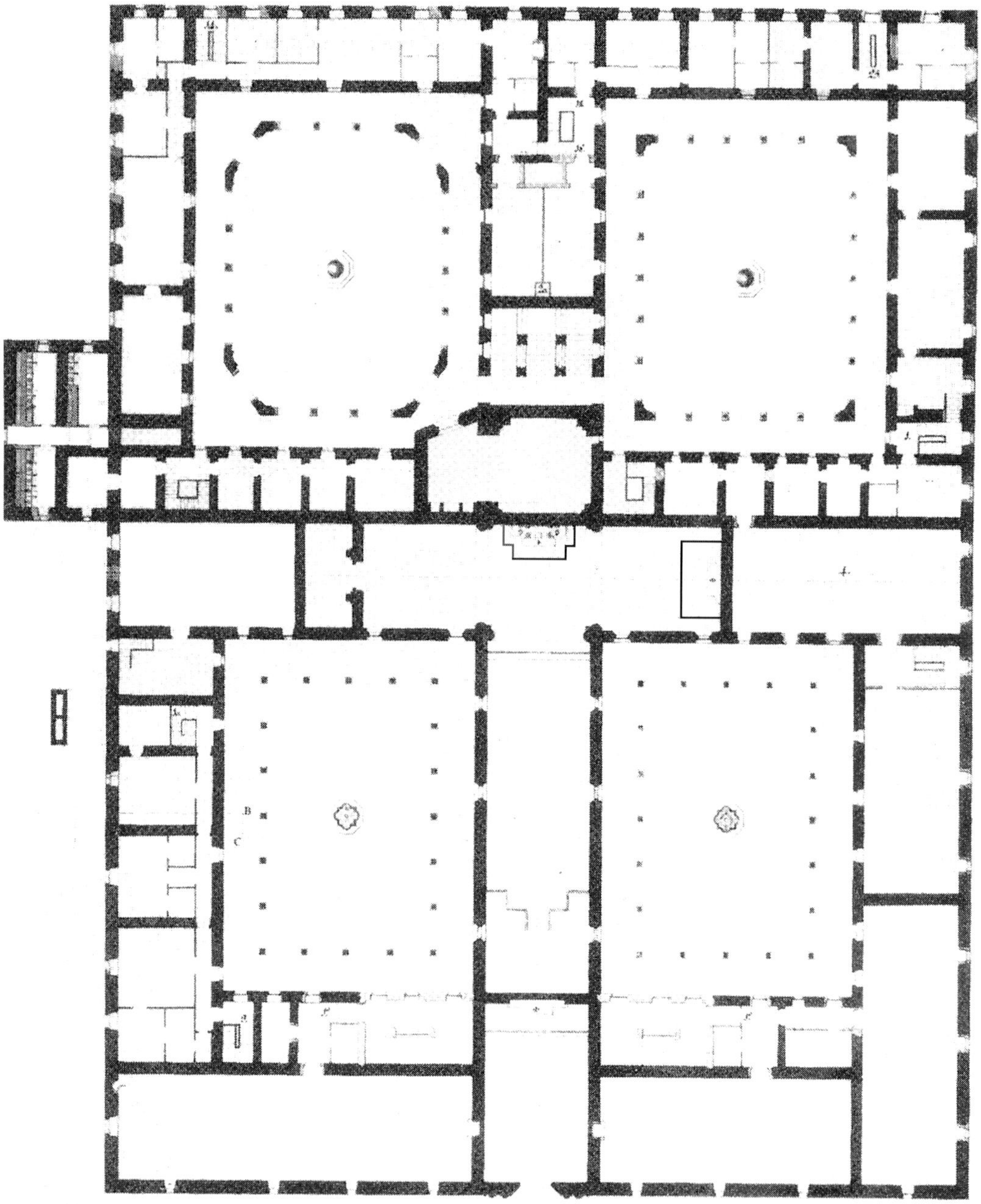

Figure 3.4. Santiago de Compostela, Hospital de los Reyes Católicos, ground floor plan from 1807. Modified by the author.

Certainly, the building gestured toward the care of patients. The sixteenth-century Jesuit theologian Luis de Molina lovingly described the hospital:

> I well believe that the standing of the royal hospital is so well known throughout the world that all I can say about it will be readily believed. It is enough to say that there are only a few days when, in the three principal wards, there are less than two hundred sick people; many more in jubilee year. But each patient is comforted with such care [that it is] as if the hospital was built only for his benefit. I wish I could expand here on the majesty of it so that everyone who has not heard will consider it as one of the great things of the world, because in addition to the sumptuousness and royalty of the building, it is a marvelous thing to sense the size of the house, the multitudes of its officials, their diligence, their regard for the patients, the cleanliness of the clothes, the care taken with meals, the order of the routine, the great care of the afflicted, the zeal for souls, the great dedication of the chaplains, the care of the doctors, the abundance of the pharmacy, and finally the full provisions for all things. One may hold it to be a crowning glory of Christendom as did its founders who were the Catholic Kings.[30]

The wards themselves were large, open spaces with high ceilings. The hospital had between eighty and one hundred beds, providing for two hundred patients. Each ward had a fireplace or oven and ventilation. Doors and windows were carefully constructed so that they could be opened easily. Dormitory floors were oak, not stone, so that patients' feet would not get cold. Benches were provided for ambulatory patients in the courtyard. But the building's attention to patients' bodies seems to have been limited to when they were completely covered. The latrine seems to have been separated from the structure, set over the steep incline at the back of the west side of the building, well away from the church.[31] In the Hospital de los Reyes Católicos there were apparently no bathing facilities provided for the patients.[32] Plumbing seems to have been limited to the fountains in the two courtyards. Medieval infirmaries had continued the practice of hygienic bathing adopted from Roman and late ancient hospitals.[33] Bathing disappeared from the habits of daily life in the sixteenth century.[34] Writing in 1523, Erasmus explains: "Twenty-five years ago nothing was more customary among us than public steam baths. Now these are out of fashion everywhere, for the new pox has taught us to avoid them."[35] Indeed, Spain seems to have been ahead of the early modern curve in eliminating the bath from the hygienic regime of healing.[36] Baths, like medical texts, seem to have been expurgated by the Inquisition.[37]

Indeed, the building was dangerous. Only a relatively healthy patient survived it. Even in the eighteenth century, after science had had some affect on the hospital's practices, of the approximately eight hundred neonates left annually at the hospital's doors, less than one hundred would survive their diet of soup and wine.[38] Apparently people recognized the hospital's threat. The sick of the city seem to have been only forcibly removed to it, as is evident from the constitutions for the institution provided by Charles V in 1524:

> Because many of the sick do not come to our Hospital, either because they can't, or because they don't know what is done here, they stay in the holy Church of Santiago, or in other places, where they die, we decree that the Administrator . . . shall provide for one or two people, who shall at least twice a day walk through the City and the Church to seek out sick pilgrims, and those that they find . . . they shall bring to our Hospital that they may be cured here.[39]

The brutal origins of the building and the harsh habits that it developed were aggravated by the changed cultural climate of the Reformation and Counter-Reformation. Pilgrimage contracted in the sixteenth century, though its decrease has been exaggerated in modern scholarship.[40] Pilgrimage was certainly an object of Protestant scorn and Counter-Reformation Catholic anxiety. Familiarly, Protestants disdained the materiality of Catholicism, denouncing relics, images, pilgrimage, and indulgences.[41] Less familiarly, the Catholic reforms of the Counter-Reformation discouraged long-distant pilgrimage in favor of local shrines as part of the church's effort to control and discipline the laity.[42] As the number of pilgrims lessened, the hospital's beds were filled with the community's indigent.

The decline in pilgrimage coincided with both the rise of capitalism and a European-wide shift in attitude toward poverty—from benevolence (poverty as part of the divine scheme) to condemnation (poverty as evidence of sin). In 1531, laws were passed making begging illegal, and pilgrimage was subjected to regulation that sought to control begging.[43] Support of the hospital as a pious act of charity to be rewarded by time off purgatory was displaced by civil obligation. Fear of poverty and contagion seem to have been linked. A city ordinance passed in Santiago in 1569 makes this association clear:

> Seeing as how in this city gather many beggars, some carrying contagious diseases and others feigning disabilities of various kinds, and a great many vagabonds, male and female, with neither jobs nor patrons, but wander around the city under the pretext of pilgrimage and devotion to the glorious apostle Saint James . . . [therefore] no poor person begging because of any disease or necessity, who may come to this city for pilgrimage or by any other route, shall be allowed to stay in the city more than three days, counting the day of entry and the day of departure and the

> day in between, and should they exceed these three days they will be put in the stocks and there restrained for four hours, and, if found again in the city without employment, shall be given two hundred public lashes.[44]

In 1589, St. James's relics were hidden in fear of a British invasion.[45] By the seventeenth and eighteenth centuries, the empty shrine of Santiago de Compostela was no longer a pan-European destination. The great church of St. James became the center of a regional devotion, with few pilgrims from abroad. One of those exceptional travelers was an Italian, Domenico Laffi, who in his remarkable 1681 account of his journey to Santiago de Compostela described the Hospital de los Reyes Católicos as well as the great church:

> Here there is a fine hospital that can hold a thousand sick people. The beds are arranged in the form of a cross so that everyone can hear Mass from a chapel which stands by itself in the center. There are three lovely courtyards all built of marble each one exhibiting a different classical order, one Corinthian, another Doric and the third Tuscan. Each has a spacious yard with a single fountain in the center. . . . The exterior of the hospital, just as much as the interior, is like a royal palace.[46]

Even as the pilgrimage to the shrine of St. James atrophied, the cathedral received an elaborate late-Baroque facade and a new palace complex for its episcopal administration. The hospital was also expanded: by the end of the eighteenth century two courtyards had been added symmetrically behind the hospital.[47] The new construction conceded nothing of its rigid ordering of space but rather reinforced the spatial constraints already in place. The extension provided more administrative office space but had little effect on the way the structure worked. No baths were added.[48] Through the first half of the eighteenth century, Spain's medical practices were, according to one of the state's more enlightened doctors, Andrés Piquer (1711–72), sunk in "decadence."[49] The hospital still looked like a palace, but it increasingly acted like a prison or an asylum, used by the city to remove sickness and poverty from its streets (Figure 3.5). Founded on blood money and raised in the discipline of the Inquisition, the great Hospital de los Reyes Católicos passed, in the mid-nineteenth century, into the possession of the county council of La Coruña.[50] It functioned then as a conventional hospital.

Modern Amnesia

In 1858 a fourteen-year-old child, Bernadette Soubirous, had a series of visions of the Virgin of the Immaculate Conception. These apparitions occurred in a grotto

Figure 3.5. Santiago de Compostela, Hostal de los Reyes Católicos, view of the exterior from the northeast.

near Lourdes, a French village close to the Spanish border. By the 1860s, Lourdes was one of the greatest pilgrimage shrines in the world, attracting many thousands of pilgrims annually.[51] The cult's popularity resulted in enormous benefit to the local economy and in political cachet for conservative Catholicism.[52] In 1878, the archbishop of Santiago, Cardinal Payá, began excavations in the crypt of the cathedral to look for the relics of St. James. Bones were found in 1879; by the time these were authenticated by Pope Leo XIII in 1884, the cult of St. James had already regained a good deal of its lost popularity.[53] The Camino, the great pan-European pilgrimage to Santiago, was reinvented. Camino stamps and certifications for pilgrims were, for example, institutionalized by legislation.[54] By the 1930s, the economic and ideological profits of the revived pilgrimage to Santiago were accruing to fascist Spain.[55]

The old hospital was put to work for the promotion of the fascist state. At the top of the dark stairwell in the remote northeast corner of the structure is a peculiar frieze of high-relief portrait busts identified with the names and occupations of those represented (Figure 3.6).[56] The frieze also bears an inscription: "This hostel was planned and constructed in nine months for the National Institute of Industry, 1953–1954." As this curious dedication frieze indicates, the state subjected the early modern building to modernization in the middle of the twentieth century: the old hospital was transformed into a new luxury hotel.[57] The Hostal de los Reyes Católicos was inaugurated by Generalissimo Francisco Franco himself on July 24, 1954, the eve of the apostle's day in Santiago's Holy Year.[58] The British Council representative to Spain during World War II, Walter Starkie, on his own pilgrimage to Santiago, records the excitement of the occasion as well as the centrality of Franco's role in the proceedings:

> "This year," said Enrique, "there will be even more people at Santiago than in past Holy Years, because Generalissimo Franco himself will be present and will make the offering to the Apostle."
>
> "We want to see the opening of the Hospital del Rey," said one of the French journalists. "They say it has been transformed into the finest hotel in Europe today."
>
> "Wonders will never cease," I said. "Why only a year ago I remember visiting the Hospital del Rey with friends who were doctors. Whoever did the transformation must have rubbed Aladdin's lamp!"
>
> "That was Franco," replied the Spaniard. "Obstacles do not exist for him. In less than a year patients have been moved to other hospitals and the ancient building founded by Queen Isabella has been transformed, as if by magic, into the last word in guest-houses for the crowds of North and South Americans who are arriving every day. You foreigners never thought that we Spaniards could hustle; you always thought of Spain as the country of mañana."[59]

Representing as it does the highest possible quality of accommodation, the hotel certainly acts to lend status to the state. At least in the minds of Starkie's traveling companions, the new hotel outperformed the Savoy in London and the Sacher in Vienna. Rich foreign travelers from liberal democratic states could be comfortable in a fascist one. Just as critically, the structure stages Franco as efficient and modern, masking his reactionary conservatism.

Figure 3.6. Santiago de Compostela, Hostal de los Reyes Católicos, northeast stairwell, frieze.

From the end of the Civil War until Franco's death in 1975, Spain remained a fascist state. Spanish fascism, in contrast to Nazism, was not genocidal.[60] Franco hated Freemasons more than Jews. Spanish fascism, like communism, assumed state control of the economy, but in contrast to communism, embraced the old industrial and agricultural elites. The poor remained poor under Franco. The fascist state was rabidly Catholic, glorifying the tradition of religious nondiversity. It branded nationalism with the militant crusading zeal of the fifteenth and sixteenth centuries and fueled it with a paranoid fear not only of communism but also of liberal democracy. Indeed, the ruling fascist Falangists even regarded the ultraconservative Roman Catholic order of Opus Dei as a dangerous liberal force.[61] Franco's fascism, like all fascisms, used the threat of hostile external forces to enforce consensus and crush critical discourse.[62] Disagreement with the state was treason. From the end of the Civil War to Franco's death, it is estimated that at least four thousand political prisoners were liquidated.[63] The number is uncannily similar to scholarly estimates on the number of those executed by the Inquisition.

Censorship in Spain was the intellectual glove on the fist of physical repression. In the 1940s and 1950s Spanish censorship was controlled by Gabriel Arias-Salgado, who acted as a new inquisitor.[64] The *New York Times* described censorship at the moment of Arias-Salgado's displacement in 1962:

> The new Minister of Information, Manuel de Fraga Iribarne, [is] a great improvement over his late predecessor, Gabriel Arias-Salgado, who was more suited to the sixteenth century. . . . Spain's censorship is one of the most thorough in the world. The Government has its political censorship; the Church its religious and moral censorship and the army its fierce, sensitive nationalistic censorship of anything that concerns military affairs. . . . In the law of April 22, 1938 (while the civil war was still on), the state was given complete control of newspapers, magazines, books, movies, manuscripts, radio and even musical scores. This is still the law. All political expression contrary to Government policy is illegal.[65]

Arias-Salgado's control of information shrewdly extended to the closely related spheres of propaganda and tourism. The state's understanding of the intimate link between propaganda and tourism is revealed in the preface of a decree of 1952 modifying the institutional structure of the Ministry of Information and Tourism:

> In order to attend to this service [of controlling public information] the law of January 30, 1938, reorganized the offices of Public Administration, the Subsecretary of the Press, Propaganda, and Tourism, including them in the Ministry of the Interior. A few years later they were constituted, by the law of May 20, 1941, under the Secretary General of Operations [Movimiento] and the Vice-Secretary of Popular Education, retaining the central administrator of Tourism in the Ministry of Governance [Gobernación], with the rank of director general. Then the organs of popular education passed to the Ministry of National Education by the decree/law of July 27, 1951. Finally, by the decree/law of July 15, 1951, those organizations dealing with various aspects of information have been reunited with those of tourism, in order to constitute one of the Departments of the Administration of the State, with the designation Ministry of Information and Tourism.[66]

If, by the early 1950s, the state had legislated the marriage of tourism with propaganda, the two had already been involved in a long-term relationship. A system of state-run hotels, the Paradores de Turismo de España, had been established during the dictatorship of Primo de Rivera in the 1920s.[67] A number of these paradors were distinguished medieval or early modern buildings remodeled to function as hostels. The fascists took tourism to a new propagandistic level during the Civil

War. The Rutas Nacionales de Guerra, or National Routes of War, were triweekly tours of the battlefields, including Guernica, organized for a foreign clientele (Figure 3.7). In his autobiography, Luis Bolín, former director of the Spanish State Tourist Department, reminisces:

> I was anxious to prove that war and travel were not incompatible, that foreign tourists were a possibility even before peace had been made. February [1938, the same month in which Franco appointed his first cabinet] was still with us when I announced that by 1 July we would have motor-coach tours from the French frontier to Oviedo, with intermediate stops at San Sebastian, Bilbao, Laredo and Santander and a chance to visit battlefields and places on the way as interesting as the remnants of the Iron Belt around Bilbao, the Fito Pass in the Sueve range, Covadonga in the Picos de Europa, and the ruined districts in the city of Oviedo, liberated four months before. The duration of the tour was nine days; the total price, £8 or its equivalent in other currencies, with transport in new buses, hotel accommodation, three daily meals, and the services of qualified guides all included. . . . When I announced my project nobody believed that it could be carried out. There were no buses and no guides, every bridge on the roads chosen had been blown up, hotels had to be refurbished and supplied. . . .
>
> The majority of our passengers were writers, lecturers and preachers, friends of ours and supporters of our cause, in quest of the truth and deeply impressed with what they saw. Led by the Abbé Jobit and M. Pichon, two hundred Friends of Spain came from France and, in seven crammed busses, departed on an extended tour. . . . We took them not only to Oviedo, but to Compostela. . . . The *Rutas Nacionales de Guerra* were the first conducted tours to operate in Spain.[68]

Tourism was a critical part of the state's political regime. By the mid-1950s it had become centrally important to Franco's economic strategy.[69]

Europe only slowly recovered from World War II. Spain, though a noncombatant in the war, had never recuperated from the economic devastations of the brutal Civil War (1933–36). Spain's economy continued to be stifled by fascism. Internal economic policies were autarchic. Moreover, as an unreformed fascist state that had materially abetted the Axis powers, Spain long remained a pariah. This alienation had economic as well as political consequences. Spain received no Marshall Plan aid. It was excluded from the United Nations until 1955. Franco's regime successfully breached Spain's isolation in the 1950s and 1960s by deploying one economic and cultural instrument—tourism—with the help of another, ideological one: anticommunism.[70] Franco used tourism both to demonstrate to European and American audiences the legitimacy of his regime and to bring hard currencies into the

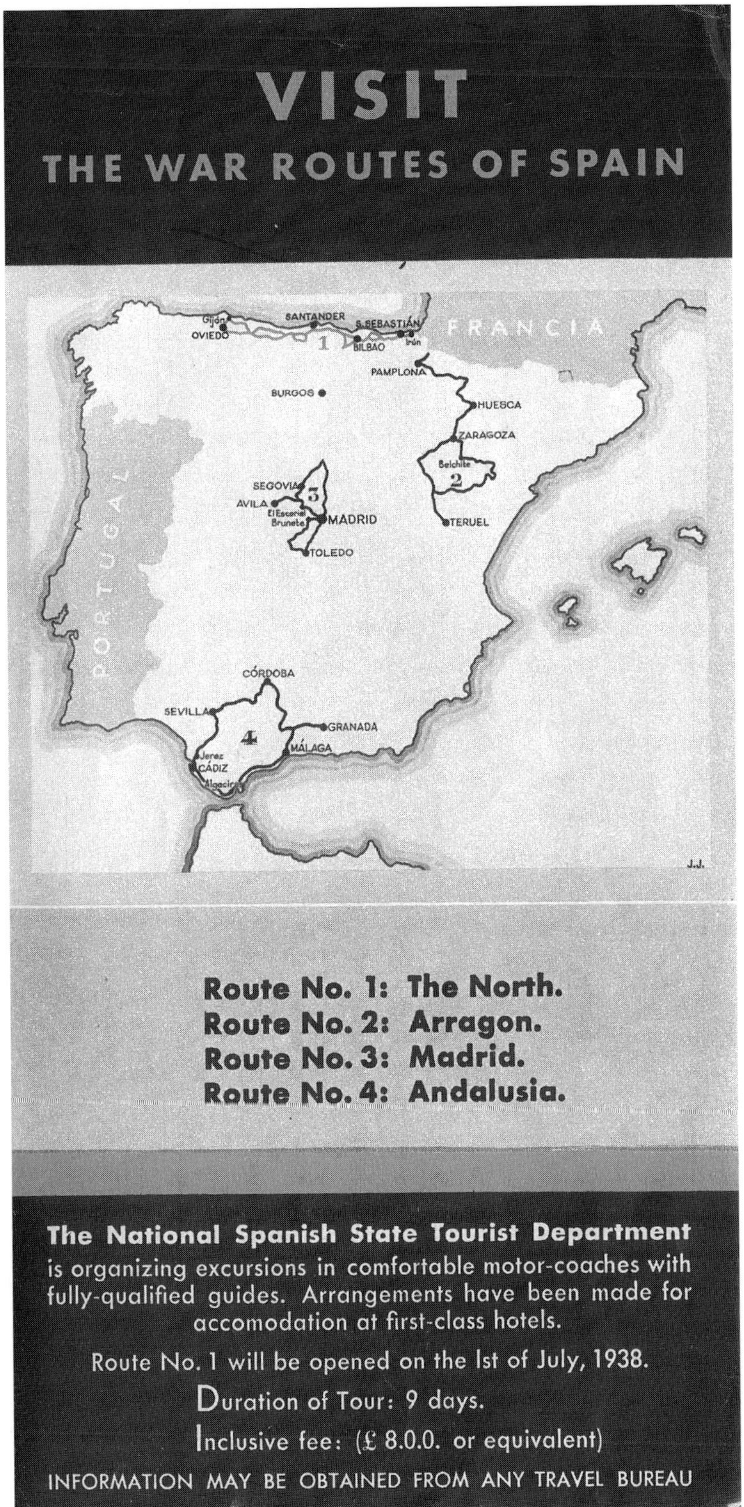

Figure 3.7. English-language brochure advertising the Rutas de Guerra (War Routes). Courtesy of the Mandeville Special Collections Library, University of California, San Diego.

country.[71] Its late invitation to join the European Union in 1968 indicates that Spain was able to overcome the West's critique of its fascist political system even before the country embraced democracy.

Convincing the West that Spain was an important anticommunist ally in the Cold War entailed an amnesia of convenience: the barbarities of Spanish fascism were displaced by fantasized memories of benevolent early modern monarchs. The facility with which this amnesia was embraced and promoted is displayed in one American's investment in Franco's Spain. In 1953, the same year that work began on converting the Hospital de los Reyes Católicos into a hotel, Conrad Hilton, a pious Catholic and a devout anticommunist, opened the first of his European Hilton International Hotels in Spain's capital city.[72] At the gala celebration in Madrid of the Castellana Hilton's completion, Conrad Hilton's remarks included an homage to Spain's modern political history framed by its illustrious early modern past:

> At the opening of the Castellana we tried to let the Spaniards who had never visited America know what ancient and strong ties exist between us through the imprint left by their explorers and missionaries of three hundred years ago in our country. . . . Now we had come to Spain to return the compliment. First to admit the great cultural debt the western peoples owe to the Spain of the past; second, to pause in admiration before a nation which had so thoroughly defeated Communism in our own twentieth century.[73]

Hotels were important agents of propaganda. There had been about ten paradors established by the Spanish government between 1928 and 1949; in the subsequent two decades over fifty more were opened. The American travel writers Sam and Jane Ballard forget that government is not supposed to function efficiently in the market:

> Today the traveler to Spain is assured of fine accommodations in paradores, where prices and standards are set by the government. You may be a seasoned traveler, but unless you have experienced a parador you have missed a rare treat. . . . In addition to 74 paradores within Spain, Paradores de Turismo operates two government-owned *hosterías* and two hotels. . . . The two hotels are the incomparable San Marcos in León and the Reyes Católicos in Santiago de Compostela.[74]

The chain of paradors, of which the Hostal de los Reyes Católicos became the flagship, had the same purpose as the Castellana Hilton—to celebrate Spain's ancient monarchic imperial history and its more recent anticommunist one.[75] Both effectively embodied imagined idealized pasts, forgetting Spain's histories of inhumanity.

For the Hostal de los Reyes Católicos to act its part in Franco's remodeling of Spain's image, its fabric as well as its history had to be altered. The building's old body was modified with excisions and implants. James Michener quotes a description by Alfredo de Ramón-Laca, the contractor who renovated the Hostal de San Marco in León, of the renovation process: "We're putting steel ribs right through the heart of the old building."[76] In the Hostal de los Reyes Católicos, the second-floor ward was converted into a ballroom; a first-floor ward became an elegant lounge. A chic restaurant replaces the hospital's morgue. Communal places of pain, suffering, and death are converted to private spaces of luxury and self-indulgence. The once waterless wards now have private marble bathrooms (Figure 3.8). Perhaps most revealingly, the chapel, cleared of its liturgical furnishings, is used as the setting for corporate lunches and wedding receptions (Figure 3.9). That core of the structure that instantiated its spiritual and ideological identity is now usually empty, silently occupied only by those institutional round tables perfectly sized to make communal conversation impossible. The building's heart has been removed. The poor stayed for nothing in the hospital; now the cost per night for a tourist is extravagant.

Obviously luxury is being sold. Less obviously memory is also for sale. The memory being marketed is, of course, a trivializing one of a lavish and benign monarchy. The building is an agent not of remembrance but of forgetfulness. It lost its memory along with its heart in the 1950s: its archives were removed and replaced by a daily guided tour of the premises.[77] The tour is certainly informative: the relevant dates of the structure and the achievements of its glorified early modern founders, the celebrity guests, the iconography of the gargoyles. No mention is made of dead neonates or fascist politics. The building was remade to sanction Francisco Franco as the heir of the Catholic Kings and champion of St. James and militant Catholic nationalism. The structure had always publicly and monumentally attested to the righteousness of an inquisitorial monarchy. It originally authorized the state's control of the bodies of the poor for the sake of religion and civil order. In the post–World War II era, the structure's pedigree legitimated Spain's version of fascism. It enabled the state's control of the bodies of the rich for the sake of profit and propaganda.

In early modernity, the acts of the Hospital de los Reyes Católicos were consistent with its form. The building performed according to its design as a disciplinary instrument of church and state. Now the structure shows serious signs of maladjustment.[78] Having earlier endured an inquisitorial trauma, the Hospital de los Reyes Católicos was later subjected to a fascist one. Its compulsory conversion from a dry body to a wet one, from a body with a relatively porous interior, breathing through its open courtyards, to an arrangement of hermetically sealed privatized

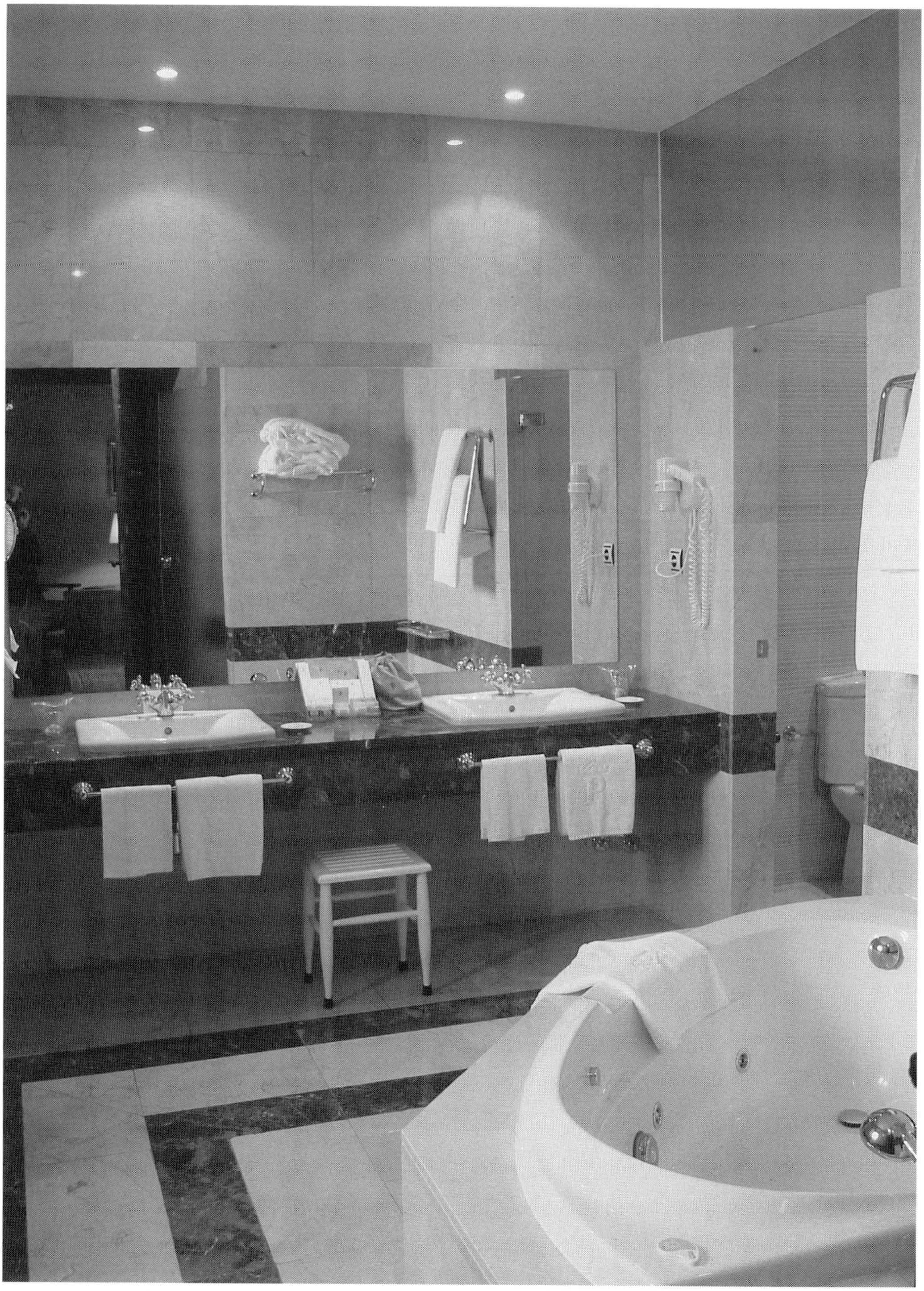

Figure 3.8. Santiago de Compostela, Hostal de los Reyes Católicos, guest bathroom.

Figure 3.9. Santiago de Compostela, Hostal de los Reyes Católicos, view south from the chapel.

compartments is part of that shock. Its forced impersonation of a palace is the other. The structure and its occupants suffer from amnesia. Coerced to act in ways inappropriate to its design and its history, the building's identity disintegrates; it becomes dysfunctional. At the time that I wrote this chapter in 2011, the travel website Tripadvisor ranked the hotel only as the thirteenth most popular hotel in the city.[79] The structure is a continuing nightmare for the architects and engineers who labor to graft modern devices—air conditioning, Internet connections, a luxury spa—onto an old body.[80] It also punishes its guests, who have to navigate the incoherence created by the imposition of a complex new program over an old plan. The building's revenge is not limited to harassing technicians and tourists. Its most effective reprisal is economic. Under Franco the building refused to make a profit.[81] Temple Fielding, one of the most popular travel-guide writers of the 1950s and 1960s put it perfectly:

> The multimillion-dollar Hostal de los Reyes Católicos, underwritten by the government, is a fantastic architectural and decorative monument—so opulent, so grandiose, and so extravagantly conceived that it's a wonder to the eyes. Commercially, however, this all-season retreat must always remain, through this very lavishness, a Taj Mahal–size white elephant.[82]

The Hostal de los Reyes Católicos provides the tourist who resides there with a memorable experience. It is ideally located for a visitor to Santiago de Compostela, adjacent as it is to the great Cathedral of St. James. The rooms are lavishly appointed. The service and the food are very good. But much of its appeal depends on its self-representation as a building with a glorious past—the "oldest hotel in the world."[83] The thirteen reviewers reporting on their stay to Tripadvisor gave the hotel a cumulative 4.5 (out of 5) rating. At the core of almost every response was the hotel's historical architecture. Quotations from four of the reviews are characteristic:

> It is a fantastic sensation staying in the oldest hotel in the world!

> Obviously, you are paying for the hotel as a whole, and it is a great experience. . . . I totally enjoyed my experience living in this palace.

> Sleeping in an important historic building on the main plaza of the city with a view of the main attraction [the Cathedral of St. James] is the reason why you should stay here.

> This is a place where you can breathe the history in the air. . . . We ate at the fancy restaurant in the lower level. . . . It was also a very medieval feeling space, with high arches and thick stonewalls. . . . (If you stay at this Parador and then eat at Botin in Madrid, you'll have stayed in the oldest hotel in the world and eaten at the oldest restaurant!)[84]

The guests' misunderstanding of history is the result of a not completely innocent gullibility.[85] The imposture of history produced by the building's manipulators is symptomatic of false amnesia. It is an invention to cover up their own part in killing disagreeable parts of the past.

Arguably, an authentic experience of a site depends not on witnessing it as spectacle but on being aware of how that spectacle is produced. The Hostal de los Reyes Católicos is certainly spectacle, but the state veils the historical sources of its performance. In the early twenty-first century historical illusion has become merely the tourist-generating habit of "heritage." History as a royal fantasy is assumed to be more profitable than history as imperial violence. But knowing that the hotel worked in its youth more like a prison than a palace might not diminish the tourist's desire to stay in the building. After all, the Sultanamhet prison in Istanbul has become a successful luxury Four Seasons Hotel.[86] Understanding the restaurant's origins as a morgue might not cause a tourist to be any less interested in eating there. In 2011, the Gourmand World Cookbook Awards were held in Le Cent Quatre—the renovated city morgue that has three restaurants.[87] Indeed, familiarity with the gritty experiences of the structure would ground the visitor's embrace of the building in awareness of its real tribulations rather than in false assumptions of its past contentment. If history replaced bullshit as its framing narrative, the Hostal de los Reyes Católicos might be a more effective agent of liberal democratic modern Spain, commercially and ideologically, than it was of its fascist predecessor.

4

URBAN TOXICITY

Jerusalem is a golden bowl filled with scorpions.

—An old Arab saying, recorded by C. R. Ashbee, 1918

It is a well known fact that not many people can endure living in Jerusalem any length of time. . . . The Holy City makes them morose or drives them insane; yes, and it even kills them outright. You cannot stop there a fortnight without hearing people say of this or that person, who has passed away: "Jerusalem has killed him."

—Selma Lagerlöf, *The Holy City,* 1918

Jerusalem Syndrome

Arguably Jerusalem has a longer history of trauma than any other continuously inhabited city in the world. It has been subjected to chronic destruction. In 586 BCE, after King Zedekiah rebelled against the Babylonians, Nebuchadnezzar laid siege to Jerusalem. The city was starved and then destroyed. Zedekiah's sons were slaughtered before his eyes, then he was blinded. The commander of the invaders "set fire to the temple of the Lord, the royal palace and all the houses of Jerusalem. Every important building he burned down" (2 Kings 25:9). Josephus describes the destruction of Jerusalem and its temple in 70 CE: "While the holy house was on fire, everything was plundered that came to hand, and ten thousand of those that were caught were slain; nor was there a consideration of any age, or any reverence of gravity; but children, and old men, and profane persons, and priests, were all slain in the same manner" (*Jewish Wars,* 4.5.1). In 1099 the crusaders pillaged Jerusalem and slaughtered its inhabitants. Fulcher of Chartres describes the scene on the Temple Mount: "Within this temple about ten thousand were beheaded. If you had been there, your feet would have been stained to the ankles in the blood of the slain. What more can I tell? Not one of them was allowed to live. They did not spare the women and children."[1] These spectacular historical assaults by external enemies are the best remembered of Jerusalem's bloody ordeals. Less familiar but more pervasive is the city's internal festering.

The savagery long suffered by the city has infected it. Buildings themselves are agents of conflict. Symptomatic is the Church of the Holy Sepulchre. First constructed by Constantine, the complex was repeatedly destroyed and repeatedly reconstructed, most notably by the Byzantines and the crusaders.[2] The resulting structure is a confusing spatial pastiche. Each compartment of its complexity is occupied by one of seven Christian denominations (see Plate 1). All claim rights to the whole of the space or to at least more of it than they are allotted. In 1909, the *New York Times* reported on the brawls provoked by proprietary conflicts over the possession of the building's parts:

> In these holiest places of Christian history Christian monks and priests quarrel and fight over hair-splitting questions of sectarian dignity and privilege, tear each other's hair, slap each other's faces, and shed each other's blood. Greeks, Latins, and Armenians, robed, mitered, hooded, and sandaled, with Syrians, Copts, Abyssinians, and what not of minor churches huddled on either side of the great Christian denomination, insult and conspire against each other, and condescend to vulgar fist brawls, while hosts of poor pilgrims, haggard, weary, and white with want, pour their pitiful savings into monastic treasuries in which are already piled gold and jewels enough to make the splendor of the Caesars look dim.[3]

A similar news report a century later suggests that the Church of the Holy Sepulchre remains contagious:

> On Sunday a clash between Armenian and Greek Orthodox monks broke out in the Church of the Holy Sepulcher, revered as the site of Jesus' crucifixion, burial and resurrection. The brawling began during a procession of Armenian clergymen commemorating the fourth-century discovery of the cross believed to have been used to crucify Jesus. The Greeks objected to the march without one of their monks present, fearing that otherwise, the procession would subvert their own claim to the edicule—the ancient structure built on what is believed to be the tomb of Jesus—and give the Armenians a claim to the site. The Armenians refused, and when they tried to march the Greek Orthodox monks blocked their way, sparking the brawl. . . . A bearded Armenian monk in a red-and-pink robe and a black-clad Greek Orthodox monk with a bloody gash on his forehead were both taken away in handcuffs after scuffling with dozens of riot police. Several Christian sects divide control of the ancient church. They regularly fight over turf and influence, and Israeli police are occasionally forced to intervene.[4]

Protestants are noticeably absent from the Holy Sepulchre's internecine battles. Until the middle of the nineteenth century Protestants tended to relegate the city of Jerusalem to the immaterial realms of the textual, ideal, and visionary. In their search for a direct, personal relationship with God, Protestants from the sixteenth century onward denounced those intermediaries between the human and the divine—priests, saints, relics, shrines—so central to non-Protestant Christian traditions.[5] As observed in the last chapter, pilgrimage, which combined all these things and added an association with those indulgences so despised by Luther, was particularly detested. The principal pilgrimage destination of the Holy Land, the Church of the Holy Sepulchre was, for many Protestant visitors, an object of ridicule. Remarks by the mid-nineteenth-century travel writer Fisher Howe are typical: "The impressions of sacredness, which would seem almost instinctively to attach to many localities, are measurably effaced by Mohammedan appropriation, or the gross superstitions engrafted by the ignorant and corrupt Christian sects. These remarks are specially applicable to the Church of the Holy Sepulchre."[6] Or again, the observations of Edwin Sherman Wallace, the viciously narrow-minded American Consul in Jerusalem between 1893 and 1898:

> It is a sickening fact that Moslem brute force must compel Christians to exercise, not charity toward each other, but common decency and decorum. But it is a fact, nevertheless, and will remain apparent to all, so long as priestcraft takes the place of New Testament Christianity and superstition supplants religion.[7]

Protestant travelogues and diaries are filled with pernicious and self-righteous denunciations of those with theologies, practices, and places distinct from their own. Protestant writings were at least as poisonous as those sites and acts they denounced. They are symptomatic of a peculiarly Protestant bigotry that festered in Jerusalem in the nineteenth and early twentieth centuries.

In 1901, Selma Lagerlöf, the first woman to win the Nobel Prize in literature, described Jerusalem's lethal present as well as its bloody past. The epigraph at the beginning of this chapter is part of a longer passage that describes the topography of the city in terms of its bloody past.[8]

> "How can a city kill? . . . I should like to know where that dreadful Jerusalem can be which is supposed to cause death!" So you decide perhaps to make a tour of the city. You go out through Jaffa gate, and turn to the left past the imposing four-corned Tower of David [and on to David's tomb and Zion]. . . . A strange feeling comes over you while walking there. You seem to hear the noise of battle, to see great armies advancing to attack the walls of the city, and kings driving through the streets in

> their chariots. This is the Jerusalem of War and Carnage, you think, horrified by the panorama of abomination and bloodshed. [But this is not the Jerusalem that kills.]
>
> [At] the East end of the city, you meet with something quite different. You now are come to the holy places, and here you think only of ancient High Priests and servants of the Temple. . . . And here you behold the pillar in the wall where 'tis said that Christ shall stand on the Day of Judgment holding one end of a long thread, fine as a hair, while Mohammad will stand upon the Mount of Olives holding the other end, and the dead, on awaking, must cross the Valley of Jehoshaphat on this thread. The righteous will reach the other side, but the wicked shall fall into the fires of Gehenna. . . . [But this is not the Jerusalem that kills.]
>
> [On the north] lies the naked hill which is probably the real Golgotha; yonder the grotto where Jeremiah wrote his Lamentations, just inside the wall is the Pool of Bethesda and beneath dismal arches winds the Via Dolorosa. Here is the Jerusalem of Disconsolation; of suffering; of Anguish; of Atonement. . . . [But not the Jerusalem that kills.]
>
> But going westward and northwest, what a contrast will appear to you! Here in the new part of the town which has sprung up outside the city wall are the palatial homes of the missionaries and the big hotels. . . . Here are the splendid mission schools, where the pupils are given free instruction, board, lodging and raiment for the sake of winning their souls. . . . Here lurks the demon of envy. . . . And it is here that you find what you have been seeking. This is the Jerusalem of soul hunting. . . . It is *this* Jerusalem that kills.[9]

For Lagerlöf, Jerusalem was at its most dangerous outside the walls of the Old City, in the new suburbs that developed only after the middle of the nineteenth century. There Europeans were particularly prominent.

Despite derisive skepticism about the reverenced sites of other Christians, Protestant desire to possess the Holy Land emerged in modernity. As described in greater detail below, Western imperial ambition and evangelical ferment worked to make the Holy Land newly attractive to Protestants in the nineteenth and early twentieth centuries. Euro-American tourism, millenarianism, missionary activities, and archaeology not only changed Jerusalem's landscape but also introduced a new affliction: Jerusalem Syndrome. The city infects sufferers of this syndrome with the delusion of a divine calling. Its victims commonly understand themselves as the embodiment of a biblical figure (Moses, John the Baptist, Ezekiel) or as a harbinger of the End of Days (the Messiah). The disease is described in the *British Journal of Psychiatry*:

> Since 1980, Jerusalem's psychiatrists have encountered an ever-increasing number of tourists who, upon arriving in Jerusalem, suffer psychotic decompensation [failure

> of defense mechanisms resulting in progressive personality disintegration[10]]. In view of the consistently high incidence of this phenomenon, it was decided to channel all such cases to one central facility—the Kfar Shaul Mental Health Centre—for psychological counseling, psychiatric intervention and, if deemed necessary, admission to hospital. Over the course of 13 years (1980–1993), 1200 tourists with severe, Jerusalem-generated mental problems have been referred to this facility. Of these, 470 were admitted to hospital. On average, 100 such tourists are seen annually, 40 of them requiring admission to hospital.[11]

Kfar Shaul Psychiatric Hospital, a state-run institution affiliated with Hadassa Hospital, was founded in 1951 in the repurposed Palestinian village of Deir Yassin, site of the infamous 1948 slaughter of more than a hundred men, women, and children by Irgun, the terrorist branch of the Zionist Haganah.[12]

Most of those who suffer from the syndrome "'are Protestant, and come from rural places in America. There are some Europeans, though, as well,' says Gregory Katz, the director of the emergency unit at Kfar Shaul. 'They tend to exhibit ecstatic behavior in holy places, and after some time it becomes a full-blown psychotic state. It's very short, but florid and acute with religious content and strange behavior.'"[13] One case study suggests that Jerusalem's pathology can even be contracted through the media.

> A 25-year-old US citizen was transferred to the Jerusalem Mental Health Center at Kfar Shaul Hospital from an emergency ward following a thwarted attempt to amputate his own testes. The patient's psychomotor development as a child was uneventful. He was described as a daydreamer in his teens but completed 12 years of education. . . . Two years before his arrival in Israel, he had experienced a religious revelation after watching an evangelical TV program. Soon after, he felt his inner self leave his body, believed he was reborn, changed his way of life and became a devoted believer. As an integral part of his wish to serve God and to free himself from lust, he became intent upon castrating himself, basing himself on literal interpretation of verses in the New Testament. He concluded that it was God's will that he perform the act in the Holy City of Jerusalem, the site of all revelations. His plan was to visit the Holy Places and to learn more about the roots of Christianity and then, to perform his act. . . . Once prepared for the mission, he initiated his attempt to castrate himself, using a razor.[14]

In this case, evangelical ecstasy envisions Jerusalem as the appropriate setting for self-mutilation. In other instances, Protestant anxieties raised by the materiality of holiness in the Holy Land led to similarly bizarre behaviors. Many of these acts took place outside the walls of the Old City.

European Periphery

Until the middle of the nineteenth century, Jerusalem had remained largely enclosed within its formidable sixteenth-century Ottoman fortifications. Palestinian villages and the houses of local landowners had established themselves in the landscape around Jerusalem since at least the eighteenth century.[15] But significant expansion outside the walls of Jerusalem occurred only after the political reforms implemented during the Egyptian rule of Muhammad Ali and continued later under the Ottomans during the Tanzimât or Reform Movement.[16] Global economic expansion, subsidized by the rapid improvement of travel and communication technologies, promoted Jerusalem's ethnic diversity, increases in its population, and the development of suburbs.[17] The forms of the buildings in the extramural neighborhoods of Jerusalem register the distinctive cultural habits of those who had them constructed.[18] It was in the new suburban periphery of Jerusalem that European and American presence was most apparent. With their new technologies and alien forms, the neighborhoods constructed by recent émigrés acted as agents of foreign social practices. A few examples must suffice to make this point.

The German Society of Templers, a Lutheran sect devoted to restoring the Jerusalem temple as a means of promoting Jesus's second coming, established themselves in Palestine at the end of the 1860s and began building a colony in Jerusalem in the 1870s (see D in Figure 2.1).[19] Count Bohémond d'Amenjen, the Roman Catholic aristocrat and longtime resident of Jerusalem in Myriam Harry's novel *La Conquête de Jérusalem,* describes the colony's construction:

> Not that I really bear any ill-will to these people for their heresies. Besides, I don't understand their disputes, and if they refuse to adore the Blessed Virgin, so much the worse for them. What I cannot forgive them for is the ugliness they spread all round them. And that on the pretext of progress! I ask myself how progress comes into their squeezing themselves into their absurd tight clothes or into the destruction of beautiful and sacred ruins, to be replaced by houses with tiled roofs and crockery ornamentations. . . . Do you see those heaps of tiles and of iron? And those bricks? To think of their bringing bricks from Europe, where here stone is to be had for nothing! They are going to build houses with green shutters and iron balconies. There are going to be chimney-flues. Perhaps factories will spring up later. There will be straight streets, gardens with gravel pathways, and glass balls, and long lines of cabbages.[20]

The houses of the German Colony were rather less exotic than the count makes out. A number of masonry techniques found in the Templer homes in the Holy

City were derived from local Palestinian practice: basement and ground floors were often vaulted; north walls were less thick than those receiving direct sun.[21] Their affect, nevertheless, was utterly alien. Houses were one- or two-story structures on small lots arranged neatly in a grid. Their plans were conventionally German, with a front door leading to an entrance hall and stairs with rooms on either side. The structures shared architectural details like neoclassical or Gothic-revival arches for door and window openings and green shutters. Their most distinctive feature was their red-tile gable roofs (Figure 4.1). Although terra cotta roof tile may have already been available in Jerusalem before the arrival of the Templers, they certainly popularized it.[22] Those roofs contrasted dramatically with the domed or flat roof-terraces of Jerusalem's traditional vernacular construction. A view of the contemporary Templer neighborhood in Haifa illustrates the foreignness of such a community (Figure 4.2).

When it was built the German Colony was understood by Jerusalemites as distinct—foreign not only because of the particular ethnicity and religious practices of its inhabitants, but also because of its imported construction materials and the

Figure 4.1. Jerusalem, German Colony, Imberger House, 16 Emek Refaim, 1877.

Figure 4.2. Haifa, Templer Colony, ca. 1900. Matson Collection, Library of Congress Prints and Photographs Division.

foreign conception of its domestic space. Into the twentieth century the Templer neighborhood remained peculiarly western in character even after it lost its separate religious identity. In 1924 it was still described by Eunice Holliday, wife of Clifford Holliday, the civic advisor of British Mandate Jerusalem, as un-Jerusalem-like:

> The German Colony, where most of the English people live, is not like real Jerusalem, it has little German red-roofed houses, and each house has a garden. There are heaps of trees and flowers, so that the roads are quite shady. It is a very nice place . . . though we both say we wouldn't like to live here permanently, because it isn't enough like Jerusalem.[23]

The German Templers were craftsmen and entrepreneurs. By the early twentieth century they were prominent in the building and tourist trades of Palestine, operating hotels in Genin, Nablus, Nazareth, Tiberius, Jerusalem, Haifa, and Jaffa.[24] The Templers retained their close association with Germany in the twentieth century. Members fought for the Axis in World War I; with the rise of Nazism in the 1930s, the Nazi flag was flown and *Mein Kampf* was read in Templer schools.[25] Britain had occupied Jerusalem since 1917, when it defeated Turkish forces there during World War I. After war between Britain and Germany was again declared in 1939, the Templers were deported. The German Colony is now one of the most prestigious, highly priced neighborhoods in Jerusalem.[26] Its value resides in its age and location, its trees and its shady sidewalks, not in its German-ness. Indeed, the most expensive properties in the German Colony on the market are identified as

"Arab style." By the late twentieth century the German Colony had been thoroughly acculturated. Nevertheless, "red roofs" retained their identification with alien appropriation, becoming a powerful political signifier of Israeli construction in the occupied territories.[27]

Just as the Templers constructed their Jerusalem as German, so Jews newly immigrated from Central and Eastern Europe sought to make the Holy City familiar.[28] Me'ah She'arim, begun in 1874, is symptomatic of a number of new Jewish neighborhoods outside the walls of the Old City (see C in Figure 2.1).[29] The patron of this particular neighborhood was a Jewish building society representing over one hundred recently arrived Ashkenazi Jewish families. Although the settlement was built in traditional stone by local Palestinian masons, its form was utterly alien. The complex was designed by Conrad Schick, a quirky German Protestant architect, archaeologist, and employee of the Episcopalian missionary group incorporated as the London Jews Society.[30] Row houses were initially arranged to define three sides of the property; later the compound was fully enclosed and gated. It is universally claimed now that enclosure was for protection. However, as it was originally open in its plan, like most of the other early neighborhoods in Jerusalem, the question is raised as to whose movements the enclosure was intended to restrain—those inside or those outside. Indeed, both the community and its architecture became ever more restrictive. Not only was the compound increasingly introverted, but also its inhabitants were progressively exclusionary.[31] The distinguished Israeli architect and architectural historian David Kroyanker describes the ideological closure of the neighborhood:

> Me'ah She'arim's character as a vibrant, innovative place changed with the arrival in Eretz Yisrael of the Brisker Rabbi, Moses Joshua Jodah Leib Diskin, known for his fanaticism, who settled first in the Old City in 1877. New neighborhood bylaws of his inspiration were enacted in 1883, to ensure spiritual purity. For example, no flat could be rented to a Safardi Jew without the approval of the "Defense Committee," lest he send his children to the Sephardi school of Alliance Israelite Universelle, considered a modern institution and boycotted by the fanatics. . . . Yosef Rivlin was no longer permitted to deliver sermons in Me'ah She'arim synagogues because he had taken part in founding the enlightened Even Yisrael quarter. . . . Extremism, introversion within the neighborhood confines, and detachment from the developing city of Jerusalem have continued to this day.[32]

The built landscape, constructed to enforce the increasing insularity of the community, became the agent of its inhabitants' isolation. The basic components of the compound were blocks of row houses made up of single-floor, two-room apartments of about 420 square feet (Figure 4.3). These blocks turned their backs on the city. Access to the individual house was not from the public street, but through a small private courtyard that opened from the shared space of the central compound. The walled enclosure of the unit contained a separate kitchen and, at its entrance, the toilet with its cesspool. Over time, second and third stories were added over the ground-floor buildings, and private courtyards were incorporated into interior living space. Similarly, the planned communal garden space of the complex was progressively eroded by construction of further apartments and institutional spaces—schools, synagogues, bakeries, and the like (Figure 4.4).

Jewish observers noted the unpleasant peculiarity of this form of Jewish housing. In 1907, a Jewish settler, Ze'ev Smilansky, critically compared the Jewish settlement in Jaffa with that of the Germans. Both, like their equivalents in Jerusalem, had been established toward the end of the nineteenth century.

> Passing through the neighborhood of the Germans near Jaffa, as well as the small German quarter [Valhalla] opposite Neve Zedek, it is a pleasure to see pretty, tastefully built houses embellished by courtyards full of trees and flower gardens which blossom almost all year long. . . . [In contrast, in the Jewish sector it] is saddening and shaming to find something akin to a new version of the ghetto. . . . Because the houses were so close together, the toilets were built one beside the other and, what is more, the houses are at the back of the courtyard and the toilets at the front, near the street entrance. Thus in walking the streets of Neve Zedek, one passes a long row of outhouses.[33]

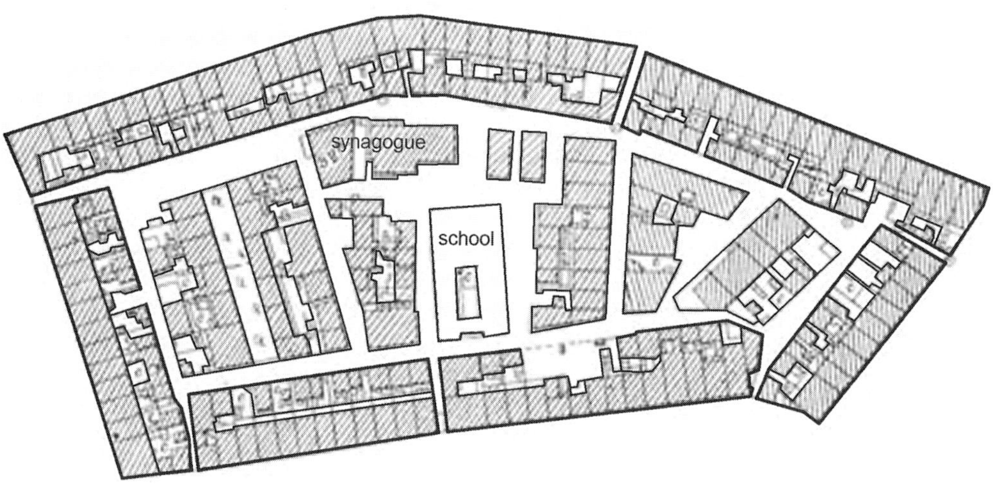

Figure 4.3. Jerusalem, Me'ah She'arim, plan of the complex.

Figure 4.4. Jerusalem, Me'ah She'arim, interior of the complex.

Others were also critical. The American consul to Jerusalem, Edwin Sherman Wallace, whose comments on the Church of the Holy Sepulchre were quoted above, despised Jews as well as non-Protestant Christians, though on theological grounds he was committed to the Jews' return to Palestine. He disparages the new Jewish suburbs of the city:

> Nearly every house has its garden or small vineyard about it where the air can have full play. Yet this is not true of all the Jewish colonies;[34] strange as it may appear, some of these people certainly prefer villainous surroundings. With every chance of having their precincts clean and comfortable and wholesome, they manage to keep them in the very opposite condition. They are satisfied to crowd together in small ill-lighted houses, all of which front on a court that too often is made the dumping place for the refuse of the colony.[35]

Criticism of Me'ah She'arim's architecture and inhabitants has certainly not been limited to the nineteenth and early twentieth centuries. The narrow, low-ceilinged rooms of Me'ah She'arim are, for instance, the claustrophobic expressions of repression and death in the disturbing production *Kadosh* by the well-known Israeli film director Amos Gitai.[36]

The negative assessments of the neighborhood resonate with its acts. Though the gates of Me'ah She'arim were removed by order of the civil government in 1915, the space continues to work hard to separate itself from the rest of Jerusalem. It colludes with its inhabitants, the closed, Haredi (ultra-Orthodox) community of Ashkenazi Jews, in despising outsiders—Zionists, Gentiles, women in slacks. They habitually spit on Christian clergy.[37] They regularly assault and beat those who do not conform to the extreme dress and behavioral prescriptions that they impose.[38] Warnings are posted at the entrances to the neighborhood outlining dress codes and forbidding access to groups (Figure 4.5). The architecture collaborates with its occupiers in the construction of an introverted religious extremism that contributes significantly to the present violence of Jerusalem.[39] The European ghetto had a poisonous afterlife in the Holy City.

Like the new European domestic buildings, European institutional structures reproduced allochthonous forms familiar to their patrons but alien to Jerusalem. Architect and early architectural conservationist George Jeffery describes the situation:

> Ever since the building of the great Russian hospice the different nations of Europe seem to have vied with each other in erecting immense blocks of buildings, very few of which can be considered satisfactory additions to the modern city springing up without the walls to the north. The French Hospice of Notre Dame de France is the

> most pretentious and most unsatisfactory. . . . But in poverty of design and total absence of all keeping with its surroundings perhaps the great German Hospice of St. Paul near the old Damascus Gate is even more successful. School buildings, Protestant chapels, hospitals, etc. all the constituent institutions of a large and remarkably mixed community are coming into existence. . . . In this northern district of the city the only group of buildings which can lay claim to any serious architectural character is the Anglican College of St. George, built by the present writer (1895–1910).[40]

Despite what he claims, Jeffery's own St. George is as alien to its settings as any of the foreign buildings that he lists. In addition to religious complexes, Westerners also established centers of archaeological study. The compound including the French École Biblique was built in a neo-Romanesque style in the 1890s. The church with which it was associated was constructed to the dimensions of the early Christian church that occupied the site in the fifth century. The American School of Oriental Research was founded in 1900, though its present structure north of Damascus Gate was built only in 1925. The British School of Archaeology was established in 1909 within a late Ottoman structure.

Figure 4.5. Jerusalem, Me'ah She'arim, view from outside the community toward the interior. Courtesy of Ben Dalfen.

These foreign institutional interventions in the expanding periphery of Jerusalem were symptomatic of the two means of engaging the materiality of the Holy Land that attracted Protestant professionals to the city in the later nineteenth and early twentieth centuries: archaeology and missionary work. The two professions—the first dealing with local artifacts and the second with resident bodies—had at least two things in common. It is well established that both participated fully, if not self-consciously, in the Western imperial project.[41] Less broadly recognized is that both were also bent on conversion. Protestant archaeologists effectively labored to redeem the land from its un-Protestant materiality by understanding it as a text. Sites were reread as documents providing *scientific* proof of biblical truth.[42] For most Christianities, sites touched by God continued to act miraculously with the residual power of the divine encounter. For Protestant biblical archaeologists, sites did not act miraculously at all. Rather, they behaved as empirical evidence of the literal correctness of the sacred text. Sites do not desire rituals, candles, incense, ex-votos, *proskynesis,* or priests; they do not heal the blind or cure the leper. Rather, sites demand devout interpreters and scholarly observers; they require graphic documentation and footnotes. The long list of publications in the field of biblical archaeology is an index of the biblical archaeologists' popular success.

In contrast to the biblical archaeologists' effective conversion of the land from connotative to denotative, missionaries' efforts to convert non-Protestants to Protestants were pathetically ineffective. Supported by one or another variant of the post-Reformation Christianities (Congregationalist, Lutheran, Baptist, Episcopalian, Methodist, etc.), missionaries came to Jerusalem in the nineteenth and early twentieth centuries to find new believers. Converts were sought particularly among the Jews, both because of a theological commitment to the conversion of the Jews in preparation for the world's final redemption and because of strict Ottoman sanctions against attempts to convert Muslims.[43] Replicating the non-Protestant Christianities' contestations over the space of the Holy Sepulchre, missionaries often fought among themselves, sometimes violently, over the few Jewish bodies that were converted.[44] Here resides the "demon of envy," the "Jerusalem that kills," observed by Lagerlöf.

The noxious combination of wealth and self-righteousness, archaeology and missionary zeal that contaminated some Westerners living in Jerusalem is witnessed in the career of Selah Merrill in Jerusalem. Merrill was a conservative Protestant, ordained as a Congregational minister in 1864, after his graduation from Yale Divinity School. He toured the Holy Land in 1869, dabbling in archaeology between 1874 and 1877 in expeditions sponsored by the American Palestine Exploration Society.[45] He returned to Jerusalem more permanently as U.S. consul during each of the Republican administrations from 1882 to 1907, altogether fourteen years.[46] His archaeological research and his civil administration were both expressions of the noxious sectarianism inflamed by the Holy City.

Merrill claimed scientific detachment. "In all my researches I aim to go upon the principle, that if I am conscientious and careful in collecting *facts,* the theories that are subsequently evolved from them will be more likely to correspond with the truth."[47] Despite his protestations of objectivity, even Merrill's archaeological publications were transparently vehicles of his religious and political partisanship. His denunciation of the Church of the Holy Sepulchre as the site of Jesus's burial was, empirically, deeply flawed.[48] William F. Albright, the "father of biblical archaeology," ascribes Merrill's misunderstandings to "his narrow Puritan attitude." More broadly, Albright comments that Merrill's book *Ancient Jerusalem* manifests "his prejudiced approach" to archaeology as well as his "lack of critical training."[49]

Merrill's contributions to the historical record document biblical archaeology's political, ideological, and acquisitive character more effectively than its scientific one. If his archaeological writings best display his religious biases, his cultural prejudices are explicitly articulated in his more popular publications. In several such works he notes that Arabs are good as servants, but Jews and non-Protestant Christians are good for nothing.[50]

> Poor Jews in Europe know that, if once they can get to Jerusalem, they will receive something, and although it be a mere pittance. . . . Hence they come here to live in wretchedness and poverty. As there is no work for them, they live in idleness. . . . The Jews throughout the world ought to be ashamed to foster such a spirit, or to perpetuate such a state of things. If we turn to the Christian population of Jerusalem, we find that matters are not much better than they are among the Jews, although there is not among them so much desperate poverty. The Protestants form only a very small community, and for a very significant reason—namely, a reason which expresses a radical difference between Protestantism and the various forms of nominal Christianity. Protestantism teaches independence and self-reliance; the Catholic and Greek churches teach exactly the opposite. Protestants are taught that they must earn their own living, and pay for what they receive. The Latin and Greek convents have vast properties in their possession, and every family belonging to either of these communities has its house rent free. . . . The worst of it is that priests and patriarchs foster this pernicious system. Consequently, how can Protestantism, which is directly opposed in its spirit and methods to such a system, gain any foothold on such ground? . . . It is no exaggeration to say that, taking the Jews and nominal Christians together, two-thirds of the inhabitants of the city are beggars, either actual beggars or polite beggars. . . . This state of things which I describe is becoming worse every year. Tens of thousands of pounds are sent here each year, and

> spent in these so-called charities, thus fostering qualities the very opposite of those in which industrious, enterprising, and prosperous people take pride.[51]

According to Merrill, Jews and non-Protestant Christians, as well as the Ottoman rulers, obstinately resist Protestant attempts to make the land more efficient and thereby closer to God.

> Palestine has suffered terribly under the oppression of the Turkish government, which has succeeded in reducing the country to a desert, and its inhabitants to the condition of beggars. But under a good [Protestant] government there is no reason why this interesting land should not be restored to its ancient state of fertility and beauty. When the favorable time comes, I believe . . . that the cities and towns will be restored and become again the centers of industry and the homes of people of intelligence and enterprise; and that the ruined churches and schools will be again rebuilt.[52]

Merrill represented Jerusalem as a victim suffering from incompetence, laziness, and ignorance. He assumed that Protestant missions, vehicles of capitalism and the Protestant work ethic, were the Holy City's only cure.

Merrill's bigotry extended from theology and ethnicity to architecture. Any attention paid to non-Protestant, postbiblical structures was, in Merrill's opinion, a waste of time. He warns the traveler not to squander "his mental energies on the question whether oriental Christianity and the oriental churches may not be wonderfully fine things," because "a few weeks or months of actual contact would suffice to restore him to his right mind on this plausible but delusive subject."[53] In contrast, most Western travelers in the Holy Land embraced the vernacular architecture of the region. The traditionally constructed villages were seen as rendering present the ancient landscape inhabited by biblical figures. The French travel writer Pierre Loti provides a typical description.

> Some of the houses seem as old as the patriarchs; others are new, only recently built; but all are alike: the same massive walls, of a solidity to defy the centuries, the same cubical proportions and the same little windows always in pairs. On the whole, there is nothing out of keeping, and Hebron is one of those rare towns that are not marred by a building of modern or foreign appearance.[54]

For Selah Merrill, in contrast, only Western intervention could make Palestine healthy, even when it came to architecture.

> Twenty or thirty years ago there was little to distinguish Nazareth from the common, unthrifty, neglected appearance of other Oriental towns, but within a recent period foreign influence, which has been almost wholly missionary in character, has worked a wonderful change in this respect, so that now a considerable number of attractive private residences and public buildings have been erected, all of white stone, which make it picturesque and beautiful.[55]

Merrill's disdain for all things Ottoman, Jewish, Catholic, and Orthodox is consistently expressed as practical, ethical, economic, and aesthetic, rather than political, cultural, or theological. But the narrow sectarianism and priggishness of his prejudices are unmasked in his treatment of a group of his own coreligionists—a Protestant commune known as the "American Colony." The architectural setting of the colony in another of the new neighborhoods on the periphery of Jerusalem helps explain Merrill's animosity toward those who lived there.

Local Affect

Late nineteenth-century Palestinian construction outside the walls of the Old City offers an autochthonous foil to the alien-ness of Jerusalem's European developments.[56] One of those communities, the Husseini neighborhood, also known as Sheikh Jarrah, preserves an enclave of architectural health in the midst of widespread urban pathology. Begun in the 1860s, north of Damascus Gate on Nablus Road, this neighborhood remained closely connected to the Old City (see B in Figure 2.1). The ten-minute walk from the neighborhood to Damascus Gate was no obstacle to continued use of the city's schools, markets, and places of business, though from the late 1870s, with the paving of Nablus Road, a market and shops developed around Damascus Gate.[57] In contrast, the suburbs built by foreigners tended to include within their compass the institutions necessary to their communal independence—schools, bakeries, and the like. The Husseini neighborhood was not only more local, but also in important ways more cosmopolitan than some of the other new communities.[58] With its substantial private houses, it was an indigenous version of the broad phenomenon of suburban emergence. In Istanbul and Cairo, as well as in Chicago and New York, the well-to-do built large family homes, often in proximity to those of other family members, on the urban periphery.

The new suburban residences of the Palestinian merchant and landowning classes were sited on generously scaled lots, in a setting of gardens and fruit trees. Often stone walls around the property assured its privacy.[59] The houses are built with traditional local materials and techniques: massive walls of limestone ashlar with more finely finished, often lighter colored limestone window surrounds, coins, and moldings (Figure 4.6). Thick walls support broad, high, groin or domical vaults; arched windows provide muted light; the interior space is cool and generous. Below the house are often vaulted substructures, and within the precinct there are always cisterns. The dwellings in the neighborhood grew as the family increased in numbers or in status. The organic character of these houses is evidenced in their production. Their walls and vaults perfectly express the craft and materials of their making. The irregularity of the stone floor, the imprecision of the angles, the subtle inconsistencies of the molding profiles all reveal the human labor engaged in the struggle to create a habitat with materials offered by the land. An awareness, conscious or unconscious, of the human touch in the modeling of the space and its details lends intimacy even to the large, communal rooms of these substantial structures.

Yehoshua Yellin, a Jewish immigrant, intellectual, and entrepreneur, describes the expansion of the Husseini neighborhood to the north:

Figure 4.6. Jerusalem, American Colony Hotel/Rabbah Effendi al-Husseini's house, view from the southwest before 1910. Courtesy of the Archive at the American Colony Hotel, Jerusalem.

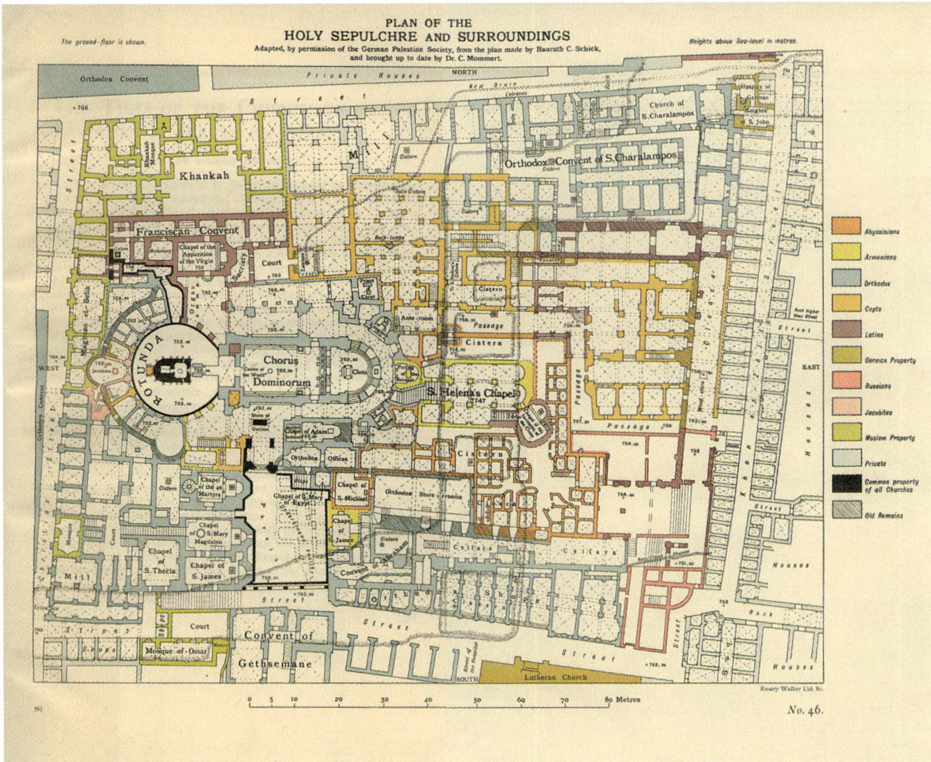

Plate 1. Jerusalem, Church of the Holy Sepulchre, plan of the church showing its sectarian divisions. Only those spaces defined by solid black are shared. From Ashbee, *Jerusalem*, volume 2.

Plate 2. Jerusalem, American Colony Hotel/Rabbah Effendi al-Husseini's house, sketch plan of the phases of the building. A. I, dark brown (between 1864 and 1876); IIA, ground floor, medium brown (between 1876 and 1886). B. IIB, upper floor, light brown (after IIA). C. III, ground floor, pink (1926). D. Final (after 1968).

Plate 3. Jerusalem, American Colony Hotel, view from the entrance hall into the central courtyard garden.

Plate 4. Las Vegas Strip, Wynn, casino interior.

Plate 5. Comparison of details: *(top)* David Roberts, *Jerusalem from the Mount of Olives*, detail; from Roberts and Croly, *The Holy Land, Syria, Idumea, Arabia, Egypt, and Nubia,* volume 1, plate 17. Courtesy of the Nasher Museum of Art, Duke University; *(center) Assassin's Creed,* Jerusalem, Altaïr outside Damascus; *(bottom)* David Roberts, *Sebaste, Ancient Samaria*; from Roberts and Croly, *The Holy Land, Syria, Idumea, Arabia, Egypt, and Nubia,* volume 1, plate 43. Courtesy of the Nasher Museum of Art, Duke University. Museum purchase with funds provided by Anita and John A. Schwarz III, Mr. and Mrs. Andrew Major, Bobbie and Michael Wilsey, and the Mary Duke Biddle Foundation (1996.1.44).

Plate 6. Comparison of details from *Assassin's Creed*: *(left to right)* Damascus, Jerusalem, Acre.

> In the past years a whole neighborhood of our Muslim fellow citizens was established northeast of our city, from the field of the Tomb of Simon the Just and eastward—a neighborhood of large, excellent-looking, wonderful, perfectly beautiful houses, without anyone in our city noticing it and without going there specially to see it.[60]

The Husseini family is one of the most distinguished of the Palestinian families of Jerusalem: between 1864 and 1914, six of the thirteen mayors of Jerusalem were Husseinis.[61] Members of the family continue to distinguish themselves in political, intellectual, and humanitarian arenas. Yellin describes the family as well as the neighborhood:

> In Jerusalem, the Husseinis held governmental offices in the "Idara" (the Pascha's Council), in the courts dealing with business and civil law, and in the municipality. . . . To be sure, the inhabitants of Jerusalem, in general, and ruling members of the municipality, in particular, until this day, remember favorably the abovementioned chief of the city [Salim Effendi] for all of the many improvements which he made during the long term of his service, both within and outside of the city, and for the many things he introduced into the city with his numerous activities: Because of him, all the streets within the city were paved with stone. And many paths were made outside the city in all four directions. On the eastern side, up to the "Tur" Gate; in the west, up to the neighborhood of "Beth Jacob"; in the south, up to the railway station; and in the north, up to the edges of the American neighborhood. Because of him, there were also constructed many shops above which were upper-story dwellings. During his tenure, there were built the large municipal hospital, the beautiful city park in the midst of which there was a large and beautiful coffee house and a place for the military orchestra. Because of him, lamps were set up in the city's streets and guards were appointed to protect the houses and shops, as were street cleaners to protect the city's cleanliness.[62]

Yellin's observations reflect not only on the Husseini family's status, but also on the Palestinian origins of the modernization of Jerusalem during the Ottoman era.

The first of the houses built in the Husseini neighbourhood was the home of a wealthy Palestinian merchant and landowner, Rabbah Effendi al-Husseini. The earliest construction on the site, dating between 1865 and 1876, was modest in both its scale and execution.[63] A second phase of construction, begun after 1876, made the home into one of the biggest and most lavish of its generation in Jerusalem. Indeed, it is often referred to as a "palace," although when compared with the mansions of Damascus, Beirut, and Aleppo, such a characterization is recognized as hyperbolic.[64]

The expanded structure was built around a courtyard (see Plates 2 and 3). Parts of the older house were incorporated into the new one as its east wing.[65] The masonry of the expanded ground level was conventionally Palestinian. The upper floors of the north, west, and east wings were more elaborately finished in a finely dressed, mottled-gray local limestone with sculptural details: pilasters, decorative keystones, and a handsome cornice. Some of the chambers of the upper floors were traditionally vaulted; others incorporate technologies associated with the contemporary expansion of the European community in Jerusalem—notably red roof tiling and iron roof beams.[66]

The west facade on Nablus Road was the public face of the home. It had a formal character: its central portal was emphasized by the balcony above it. The rooms behind this facade were also formal. On the second floor of the west wing was the gracious reception space of the house. It is well lit and beautifully decorated. Its elaborately painted, wood-panelled ceiling is further ornamented with a false dome set off-center toward the south, orienting the room in the same direction as al-Aksa mosque and suggesting that it also functioned as the prayer room of the house (Figure 4.7).[67] The west wing was not only the most formal part of the home, but following well-established regional conventions in domestic architecture, this wing was also a largely male domain in which business was done and male guests were received.[68]

The rest of the home constituted the domestic sphere. To the north were the private rooms of the owner's wives.[69] The south wing of the structure was a *liwan*: a vaulted space enclosed on three sides and fully open on the fourth, accessible from two flanking rooms.[70] *Liwan* houses are very common in the Levant. This triad of rooms was the shared space of the family. In the program of the new house, the east wing, adapted from the earliest structure on the site, retains something of its autonomous character, functioning as the kitchen with adjoining bathing and washing rooms, all of which typically shared a single hot water source. Areas associated with dirt and odor—spaces of impurity—were traditionally located at the margins of the domestic sphere when at all possible. Toilets were probably constructed outside of the house in a separate wooden structure. In the Levant generally, bathrooms became associated with sleeping areas only well into the twentieth century, after the use of modern sewage and plumbing systems had become familiar.[71] The courtyard was entered informally from the east, the side of the house that turned away from the public thoroughfare and toward the interior of the neighbourhood. The program of the new house is clear. The domain of the public and the male is separable from that of the private and the familial. Polluted spaces are isolated from clean ones. The space is ordered to provide good air circulation—most of the rooms open to fresh air on at least two sides. The kitchen is sited to the northeast, in the coolest part of the home, where it is most shielded from the direct sun. The house is generously functional, embodying and preserving tradition. It was the agent of local family values.

Houses like those found in the Husseini neighborhood are commonly evoked in nineteenth- and early twentieth-century Orientalist novels.[72] An affectionate description of a Palestinian house appears in Myriam Harry's *La Petite Fille de Jérusalem,* a novel mentioned in chapter 2. Though Harry was a nonbeliever, her novels reveal her familiarity with the Jewish, Christian, and Muslim neighborhoods of Jerusalem. Her autobiographical heroine, Siona, lives with her family briefly in a western-style apartment, which she despises. There she learns to knit. Later the family moves to a Palestinian house. There she learns to write poetry.

> They had had the wonderful good fortune to light on a villa belonging to the Agha Rachid which had been built considerably lower down on the road to Jaffa, partly in European and partly in Mussulman style. . . . The garden was a typical Persian

Figure 4.7. Jerusalem, American Colony Hotel/Rabbah Effendi al-Husseini's house, prayer room/salon, American Colony Album. American Colony Collection, Library of Congress Prints and Photographs Division.

> pleasure-ground, like that described in the Song of Solomon, where fruit-trees spread their heavily-laden branches over flower-beds.... "So picturesque and so romantic! You didn't see anything to equal it in the West, now did you, papa?"... The interior of the Villa Rachid was equally fascinating. The ground floor was completely Turkish in style and arrangement, and Siona ... delighted in the rooms with their domed ceilings, and the masked windows through which the daylight filtered so sparingly that Siona was reminded of the "dim religious light" of a peaceful chapel.... There Siona had developed a gift for making verses.[73]

More recent expressions of an appreciation of vernacular Palestinian suburban houses appear in travel accounts and novels.[74] A brilliant celebration of the life-affirming endurance of such a house and a graphic lament for its humiliations are presented in Amos Gitai's documentary films *House* and *House in Jerusalem.*[75] The real estate market, like novels and films, indicates that Palestinian stone houses are still, in the early twenty-first century, the best (most expensive) places in the city to live. They seem to offer some compensation for the hazards of occupying Jerusalem.

American Colony

Rabbah Effendi al-Husseini's home adapted local building traditions to a new suburban setting, supplementing the social and physical landscape of Jerusalem. It conditioned those who resided in it to the Holy City by its intimate attachment to the old urban landscape. One of its occupants was the American Colony.

In 1881 a group of Americans led by Horatio and Anna Spafford arrived in Palestine from Chicago to await the imminent arrival of the Messiah.[76] Horatio Spafford had been a successful lawyer in the United States before a series of family tragedies, including the loss of their four children in a shipwreck, awakened his and his wife's desire to witness the Second Coming. Following Horatio Spafford's death in 1888, his wife, Anna Spafford, became the indomitable leader of the group. Later leadership passed to their daughter, Bertha Vester. They lived initially as a commune of celibates:

> They had patterned their life at Jerusalem upon that of the early church there; lived together in brotherly love, more than a hundred and twenty of them; owned everything in common, and after twenty-five years of such an experiment still held fast to the belief of the early Christians at Jerusalem, that it was Christ's teachings that those calling themselves Christians should give all their accumulated earnings to the poor, and no one member of the great brotherhood be content if he could find anyone poorer than himself. They had carried absolute unselfishness to its extreme, and, truth to tell, seemed a most contented and industrious household.... I shall

> hereafter speak with reverence of any movement toward Christian socialism, the actual practical possibility of which, in one instance, has been demonstrated here at the birthplace of Christ by an undaunted body of American citizens.[77]

The architectural setting of the colony participated in shaping the character and quality of its work in Jerusalem. Initially the commune had settled in a traditional urban courtyard house just within the walls of the Old City, near Damascus Gate.[78] In 1896, the community rented, in addition, Rabbah Effendi al-Husseini's house in the Husseini neighborhood. When the owner died without a male heir, the property had passed, following Ottoman law, to male members of the extended family. In 1887, the multiple owners of the house apparently agreed to rent it to the London Society for Promoting Christianity amongst the Jews.[79] Less than a decade later they leased the structure to the American Colony. Some of the functions served by the home's various spaces stayed the same. The prayer and reception room of the Palestinian house, for example, became the parlor of the American Colony, remaining the place of social receptions and religious meetings; members of the American Colony did not attend services in any of the local Protestant churches (Figure 4.8). But the gendering of the space shifted dramatically. Both men and women came to the formal and informal events held in the communal spaces of the house: the parlor, the central courtyard, the rooftop patio of the south wing, and the gardens. The patriarchal Palestinian home, with its gendered domestic spheres, comfortably accommodated the matriarchal, porously gendered space of the American Colony.

Professionals as well as Presbyterians at home in the United States, the members of the sect passed the time awaiting Jesus's advent by becoming professionals in Palestine—nursing, organizing food kitchens, founding an orphanage, establishing a weaving workshop. They also provided teachers for local schools. As early as 1885, A. Loivy, the secretary of the Anglo-Jewish Association in London, offered his thanks to the Spaffords, having heard of their work from colleagues at the Lionel Rothchild School in Jerusalem.

> You have undertaken from the kindest and most disinterested motives the instruction of the pupils, who are making excellent progress in the English language, the subject of your tuition. The Committee, therefore, desires to tender you their cordial thanks for the admirable service you are rendering to the institution. . . . Your freedom from sectarian bias and your abhorrence of attempts at proselytizing places your sentiments and ours on the same level.[80]

By 1906, American Colonists were deeply engaged in an educational mission. Anna Spafford writes to a friend of the colony, "we were not only looking after the

Figure 4.8. Jerusalem, American Colony Hotel, reception.

Government Mohammadan Girls' School of about 450 scholars, but also several of our sisters were teaching in the Rothschild Jewish Girls' School, which, I think, outnumbered the other school, besides our teaching in three other Jerusalem boys' schools, Jewish and Armenian, and also there was always our home school attended by a good number of other native boys and girls."[81]

The colony attracted a few Britons and Germans as well as a large contingent of Swedes. Although the commune was not made up exclusively of Americans, it retained its American character by preserving English as the language of the colony's daily life and by nurturing American patriotism. In a letter home, C. R. Ashbee, civic advisor during the British Mandate, describes a party given at the colony celebrating the Fourth of July, 1918, to which the colony's Turkish, Palestinian, Jewish, and European friends were invited (Figure 4.9):

> The American gathering would have thrilled you. It was so absolutely, so naïvely American. We ate great swimming slabs of ice cream, and rose with our plates, and napkins folded in neat triangles, to the sound of "Hail Columbia." Then Columbia

> entered, such a dear, deadly earnest young woman, dressed in white, standing on a white box to make her taller, attended by two little pages got up as Red Indians, and she holding the Declaration of Independence . . . in one hand, and in the other a sort of trident crowned with cotton wool—to present foam, foam of the ocean. . . . Yes, she was "gotten" up like the Statue of Liberty in New York Harbor, and there were silver rays, spiky ones, coming out of her head. And there was a bevy of young ladies dressed up in Stars and Stripes, neatly flounced, who did figure dances . . . and we all saluted the flag. . . . No other people could do this sort of thing, and in Jerusalem in the twentieth century. . . . *Quand meme*—they're splendid people. . . . And the British Bishop of Jerusalem, he too, was there, taking himself very seriously, though, so good Anglicans whisper, this American "freak colony" has a religion all its own and follows some fanciful tradition of the Puritan fathers, enough to turn the color of any Anglican Bishop's gaiters. . . . But I'm not sure that the undenominational here isn't nearer to Christ's teaching.[82]

As Ashbee's final comment suggests, the American Colony sustained good works over a long period of time. When several hundred destitute Jews arrived in Jerusalem in 1882 having been moved by messianic enthusiasm to leave their native Yemen, the Sephardic and Ashkenazi Jewish communities in the city refused to acknowledge them as coreligionists. They survived only because of the aid they received from the American Colony.[83] The local Ottoman authority assigned to the American Colony the task of overseeing hospitals in the city on the eve of the British invasion of the city during World War I as well as maintaining the food distribution center. When the Palestinian village of Abu Dis was destroyed by an earthquake in 1927,

Figure 4.9. Jerusalem, American Colony, Fourth of July Celebration, ca. 1910. American Colony Collection, Library of Congress Prints and Photographs Division.

the American Colony established a temporary clinic there to tend the victims.[84] They helped everyone who needed it—Jews, Arabs, Christians—indiscriminately. The American Colonists were not missionaries. Their aid could be accepted because it came with no confessional strings attached.

The American Colonists also became increasingly entrepreneurial. Members of a prosperous Swedish farming community from the vicinity of Nås had joined the colony in 1896.[85] The Swedes contributed to the enterprising vigor of the colony as well as providing it with an economic security it had not previously enjoyed. The colony expanded its workshops and began to grow its own produce successfully. They established one of the first photographic workshops in Jerusalem and opened a tourist store in the Old City. A sense of how graciously the old house framed its new functions is conveyed in a letter written in October 1902 by Anna Spafford:

> We fill the new house [new to the American Colony] which contains twenty-two rooms. Besides this we occupy three houses which have respectively five and four rooms each. Then we occupy the lower part of a large house which contains five very large rooms and two small ones and three rooms for storing our stores. Some of the rooms in the smaller houses are used for Photography and silver plating and school rooms. Five rooms are thus used, leaving the rest for sleeping, parlour or salon as we call it here, and three dining rooms and one kitchen. Then we have added to one home two wooden rooms for cake baking and putting up jams, etc. which we sell. Then we have put up a good sized barn for our three horses and two donkeys and four cows and two calves, which we are raising. Then we have a carpentry shop, where all kinds of carpentry is done. Then we have a little blacksmith shop. So all together we work like a little village.[86]

In 1910, the commune purchased Rabbah Effendi al-Husseini's house from the family heirs.[87] Bertha Vester describes the problems encountered in the process:

> Since Rabbah Effendi's death his palace had been roughly used. It was large, and on this account difficult to lease, but it was exactly what we needed. We rented it at once. Nearly all the rooms were enormous and surrounded a beautiful open court. Rabbah Effendi had lived a patriarchal life there surrounded by his four wives and other relatives, retainers and servants. From Hadj Raghib and his son therefore, we rented the present American Colony building in Sheik Harah Quarter near the Kedron Valley, sometimes called the Valley of Jehoshaphat. Renting property in Palestine is not such an easy matter as it sounds. Innumerable heirs who have inherited bits and pieces all have to receive their share of the rent and sign the lease. Later, when we finally bought the property, we went through the same procedure. Every bit purchased increased the nuisance value of the unbought. The last two

> shares, from the Mufti of Jerusalem [Kamil al-Husseini] and his brother, whose mother had been Rabbah Effendi's fourth wife before she married the Mufti's father, were acquired at an exorbitant price.[88]

The recoding of the home's space by the social practices of its new inhabitants was instantiated by the building's remodeling after its purchase. An additional bay was added to the ground floor, filling in the southeast corner of the plan. More fundamentally, the house was reoriented. In 1926, the old formal (men's) entrance of the house to the west and the smaller, domestic (women's) entrance to the east were blocked up, replaced by a new entrance cut through the center of the south facade which was then monumentalized by a porte cochere.[89] A triple-arched separation was also introduced to the west side of the *liwan,* converting it to an entrance hall. The carefully ordered distinctions between the male and female, public and private domains of the house when it served a Palestinian family were erased.

Both before and after remodeling, the old Palestinian house was a central character in contemporary descriptions of the American Colony. These portrayals associate the group's good works with their special *place* in the city. Indeed, the place and its inhabitants became, literally, synonymous. In 1902, a pilgrim related the American Colony to the topography of Jerusalem:

> I had sought the Lord in many places in Jerusalem, but I found Him not. And I came to conclusion that if Christ came again to the city where He was crucified, died and was buried, He would go direct to this house of the American Family. There he would be known and loved. Not to the Church of the Holy Sepulchre would he go, where his professing followers, Catholics, Armenians, and Copts, often come to grief in sight of His reputed tomb so that Turkish soldiers must separate them and keep them from killing one another. Neither would He go to the fashionable German and English Protestant Churches where much would put Him in mind of His old tomb in Joseph of Arimathea's garden. But as in former days, at eventide, He turned His steps and crossed the Mount of Olives to the home of the sister at Bethany, He would hasten His steps to our friends outside the Damascus gate, and turn in there and hold Communion (sup) with them and they with Him.[90]

Another visitor to the colony described its atmosphere in a report in the *New York Times* in 1909:

> There is something indescribably peaceful in the home of these colonists, who are trying, in their own way, to live the unselfish life of the primitive Christians. . . . The beauty and tranquility of this life have made a deep impression upon Moslems, and many of the prominent officials of Jerusalem visit the American Colony. So

great is the influence exerted by its members that a daughter of its founder has been chosen by the city authorities as directress of a school of 300 Moslem girls, including the daughters of the mufti, or chief ecclesiastical officer of Jerusalem. In an old garden in the courtyard of the colony I met Faidy Effendi, the intelligent and much-respected Mayor of Jerusalem.[91]

The American Colony is rendered in texts as a place for Christians, Jews, and Muslims to meet as equals. It is also filmed that way. A farewell party for Sir Louis Bols, British chief administrator, at the American Colony was recorded in 1920 by the travel documentary producer Burton Holmes. The film was described by Bertha Vester:

> This film shows the Greek Orthodox Patriarch and other ecclesiastical dignitaries sitting with the guests enjoying the music by the American Colony band and drills performed by the children. Jamil Effendi al Husseini, the Grand Mufti, and Mrs. Norman Bentwich, wife of the Jewish Attorney General, are seen enjoying a good joke together, and Sir Ronald Storrs and Mrs. Ragib Bey Nashashebie, wife of Jerusalem's mayor, are having a confidential conversation. So we have a record of that unique gathering when British officials and civilians, with Jews and Arabs, mingled and had a good time.[92]

Remarkably similar is the party with the colony's friends from the diverse communities in Jerusalem that begins the 2010 film *Miral*, directed by Julian Schnabel.[93]

The American Colony's socialist enterprise and its unprejudiced engagement with non-Aryan non-Protestants made it the object of missionary spite.[94] In denying charges of discrimination against the colony, George E. Woodhouse, the Anglican bishop's commissary to the British consul, inadvertently reveals his prejudices:

> The statement that the Missionaries have joined in persecuting the sect is absolutely untrue as they are altogether ignored by all the missionaries here, as their rules and manner of life do not commend themselves to the English people. That they are "led in a path different from that trodden by the missionaries" is true. For I understand that the Moslems and Jews look on this sect as anti-missionary and non-Christian which is proved by the fact that one of the members is Directress of the Government (Mohammedan) School and others are engaged as teachers in the Alliance (Jewish) Schools.[95]

Despised in general by the Protestant missionaries, the colony had, as mentioned above, one particularly implacable persecutor: the American consul, Selah Merrill.

Merrill's animosity was certainly ideological. The communism of the colony embodied a threat to the Protestant ethic of *individual,* profit-driven, capitalist labor. Its matriarchal order threatened conventional Protestant patriarchy. Its embrace of those of other ethnicities and religious beliefs subverted the Protestant sense of racial and religious superiority expressed in missionary work. And its old Palestinian house revealed the unloveliness of the modern to which Merrill was committed.

Merrill's harassment of the colonists was often petty. In 1906, he forbid them to display the American flag at their shop in Jerusalem on July 4th and ordered that they not celebrate the holiday. But the violence of Merrill's hatred was most fully realized archaeologically. In 1891, he excavated ancient remains in the American Cemetery, exposing the coffins of the colonists. Later, with his colleague Rev. Edwin Sherman Wallace, Merrill colluded in the secret sale and subsequent destruction of the cemetery. Bodies were exhumed, removed from their coffins, hacked into pieces, and stored indiscriminately in packing cases in a temporary mass grave in the English Cemetery. A journalist, Alexander Hume Ford, described this "War of the Graveyard." At the funeral for a recently deceased member of the commune, the colonists discovered the desecration of their graveyard:

> [D]eep holes [were] visible, while fragments of bones, coffins, hair, and clothing were lying on the surface of the ground. In one place, the coffin of Mr. Spafford was still exposed, and was seen by his daughter . . . who was taken home in a fainting condition as a result. From that day to this has lingered "The War of the Graveyard," waged bitterly between two successive clergyman consuls [Merrill and Edwin Wallace] and a missionary on the one side, and on the other, the members of the American Colony, who have never asked more—and asked that in vain—than that the remains of their dead should be left to rest in peace.[96]

The American Colony never recovered all the bodies of their dead.

Merrill believed that the Ottomans, Jews, Catholics, Orthodox, and unorthodox Protestants made Jerusalem sick; ironically, it was his own predisposition to prejudice that made Jerusalem an effective pathological agent. He, and others like him, produced "the Jerusalem of soul hunting," the "Jerusalem that kills."

Hospitality

The American Colony, despite its abuse by Merrill and others, remained a site of benevolence in a brutal city. The last function of the American Colony, as a hostel, was taken on at the beginning of the twentieth century at the request of Baron Plato von Ustinov (grandfather of actor Sir Peter Ustinov). The baron owned a hotel for Western tourists in Jaffa and wanted an appropriate place for his guests to stay in Jerusalem. Theo Larsson, one of the Swedish members of the colony, describes the hostel:

> The growing numbers of overseas visitors to the Holy Land introduced the Colony to the business which is its sole function today. In the main, spring season, the Colonists had to move out temporarily to make room for all the guests who wanted to stay there, its charm and fine food being something of a novelty among local hostels at the time. The girls waited on them, and the young men acted as guides on tours around the country. Tourism was behind the development of other sidelines, like the Colony's photographic department, run by my father, which became famous throughout the Middle East and beyond for its views of the Holy Land and hand-coloured slides. Everything the Colonists touched seemed to prosper, but they never neglected their charitable works. Every day at noon a queue of needy people formed in the garden for soup or stew or whatever else the sisters had prepared for them. Colonists nursed the sick and the dying, and provided medical treatment for those who could not otherwise afford it.[97]

In 1996, the American Colony joined the Relais & Châteaux Association; now it is part of the Leading Small Hotels of the World chain founded by the Swiss Gauer Group.[98] Nevertheless, the hotel is still owned, tended, and administered by descendants of the members of the American Colony. East House and Palm House have been reoriented to face one another across a cul-de-sac, Louis Hugues Vincent Road.[99] Dar Al-Tifel, the girl's school so movingly described by Julian Schnabel in his film *Miral,* and a planned museum of Palestinian culture in a beautifully renovated old house occupy the end of the cul-de-sac. Opposite the hotel are three small shops, including an excellent bookstore. The gardens of Palm House are a summer restaurant. The complex acts like a neighborhood; arriving at the hotel feels like coming home. The long practice of unbigoted generosity associated with the American Colony is continued in the cosmopolitan hospitality of the hotel.

Violence in Jerusalem has escalated since the departure of the Ottomans. The American Colony is located at the literal seam of that violence, just on the Palestinian side of the savagely contested line drawn between the Jordanians and the Israelis during the 1948 war.[100] In the midst of the brutality of 1948 and the subsequent ferocity of the 1967 war and the intifadas, the American Colony never abandoned its neutrality. Its general manager is Swiss; its head accountant and its architect are Jewish Israelis; its chief engineer, its principal building contractors, and its staff are largely Palestinian. Some Israelis feel uncomfortable at the American Colony, but perhaps that is because it is the only public space in Jerusalem where Palestinians and Israelis meet together and act as equals. It may be the only place where peace in a violent city is possible. The Oslo peace accords were secretly drafted there in 1993.

The American Colony was once a peculiar Protestant sect, which, while awaiting the coming of the Messiah, abstained from bigotry and acted charitably and without discrimination toward Jerusalem's religiously and ethnically diverse poor. It formed a place from which no one was excluded on the basis of her station or convictions, a space of relative peace in a city of pervasive violence. Now the American Colony is a hotel in which the poor are no longer found, but where respect for difference is still habitual. A healthy building can be honest with itself. The American Colony has not misrepresented its history to attract consumers. The modifications made to the American Colony's old buildings to fit the contemporary requirements of a luxury hotel are transparent. They are not coded as archaeologically correct. While care has certainly been taken to preserve and accentuate what remains of the original buildings, no attempt has been made to re-create a particular, and therefore necessarily false, architectural past. Much more fundamentally, in contrast to the city in which it is found, the American Colony seems to have developed an immunity to sectarian and political hatred. In the early twentieth century, the American Colony was so wholesome that it was the only site in Jerusalem identified as entirely free of malarial parasites.[101] In the early twenty-first century, the American Colony retains its sanity by remembering its history in its embrace of social and political hybridity. Despite the toxicity of its urban setting, the old house of Rabbah Effendi al-Husseini, now a fancy hotel, remains healthy.[102]

PART III

ADDICTION

5

GAMBLING

Case 7. A 49-year-old married man with an 8-year history of Parkinson's Disease developed a compulsive gambling habit a month after increasing his ropinirole dosage. . . . Not until the dosage of ropinirole . . . was tapered and carbidopa/levodopa substituted did his pathological behaviors remit, with his wife reporting a "complete transformation." . . . "I have my husband back," she said. "It was like I was married to an alien."

—J. Michael Bostwick et al., "Frequency of New-Onset Pathologic Compulsive Gambling," *Mayo Clinic Proceedings,* 2009

Nearly half a million people gathered on the Las Vegas strip tonight to ring in the New Year and watch the Hacienda Hotel implode. The implosion, the centerpiece of a celebration that rivaled New York's, was preceded by 4 minutes of fireworks that used 3,000 aerial shells, a pyrotechnic waterfall and a fireball off the rooftop of the hotel moments before the building crumpled.

—"A Falling Hotel Vies with a Dropping Ball," *New York Times,* January 1, 1997

Cue

We all have our habits, most of them bad. But few obsessive behaviors, even bad ones, are addictions. Addicts are those who compulsively repeat acts that they and those who know them understand as self-destructive. Beyond their chronic failure to resist the deleterious object of their desire, individuals suffering from addiction have other diagnosable symptoms. They experience stress before their gratification, pleasure and abandon at its initiation, self-loathing at its end. They spend more time engaged in their indulgence than they intend, commonly neglect obligations or forgo beneficial activities for its sake, become irascible in its prolonged absence, and often try repeatedly to curtail it.[1] Addiction might have as its trigger any one of a variety of substances or behaviors. In addition to habit-forming drugs, the American Psychiatric Association has identified gambling as an addiction; other obsessions have been recognized as addictions by those who suffer from them, if not by the APA.[2] They include shopping, gaming, eating.[3] The diagnosis of these disorders may be contested, but all authorities acknowledge that "addiction" is not defined by its source. Rather it names the unquenchable craving for that which promises satisfaction but delivers despair. Overzealous advocates of rational choice claim that addiction is an expression of the liberty offered to the individual by the free market.[4] They are wrong. Addiction is slavery.

The term "addict" is derived from the Latin *addictus,* a slave not by birth or by military conquest but by unpaid debt.[5] "Addict" retains its sense of an oppressive and inescapable obligation that has economic as well as social and personal entailments. Modern addicts, like ancient ones, are usually exploited for someone else's gain. The ancient addict could lose control not only of his own body, but also of all his possessions, including his children. The children of modern addicts, while not bound to their parent's enslavers, are also often lost to their parents. Of course, ancient addicts were distinct from their modern counterparts. The *addictus,* in contrast to a conventional Roman slave, was legally protected from being put to death by his master. Modern addicts may die in the embrace of their enthrallers. Ancient addicts owed their debts to humans; modern addicts' creditors are chemical. The most powerful of these chemicals may well be dopamine, a neurotransmitter active in the brain's encoding of reward patterns.[6]

Humans are neurologically constituted to be particularly sensitive to evidence in their environment of prey (whether that "prey" is food or pleasurable activity) and other predators.[7] The search for contextual clues that predict reward or protection is constant, if not necessarily conscious.[8] A clue (from Middle English *clew,* a ball of yarn) is a thread that leads the subject out of danger (the Minotaur's labyrinth) to safety or even delight (Ariadne). When following a particular clue repeatedly results in gratification, that clue, with dopamine's help, becomes a cue. In common language, a cue is a hint that prompts an anticipated response. For the addict, a cue is a powerful signifier of imminent satisfaction. As Pavlov long ago demonstrated, the pleasure of possessing the object of desire begins precociously at the cue to its proximity.[9] This cue may be an event (like the ringing of the bell that induced Pavlov's dogs to salivate) that presages satisfaction or a place (like the cozy bar that induces an alcoholic to drink) in which satisfaction is habitually found. The cue is now recognized as being so powerful that, in the case of addicts, it displaces that which the cue once only signified. Cues "hijack" the neural systems related to the pursuit of rewards, perhaps permanently modifying the chemical structure of the brain (dopamine related neuroplasticity).[10] Even when the cued object is no longer desired, indeed even when it is despised, the cue may still result in an uncontrollable urge to pursue its associated object.[11] For pathological gamblers and video game players, visual cues may be particularly powerful.[12]

In the quotidian, buildings aren't addictive. Except for the aberrant architectural fetishist, a built structure, however attractive, does not lend itself to obsession. But a building may well function as a powerful cue for the self-destructive behavior of the addict. Some places may become cues by circumstances beyond their control. A public library with a bank of free-access computers may inadvertently become a cue for an Internet addict, but the structure cannot be held culpable for contributing to the self-abuse that goes on within it. However, most places that act as cues for addictive behaviors are not so innocent. Many buildings—because of their programmatic and decorative forms, their equipment, and their ambiance—offer spaces that might potentially provoke an addictive response. The local pub attracts adults with its dark wood finishes, faux Victorian details, and intimate alcoves designed to complement alcoholic consumption by conditioning its patron's sense of well-being. For a few dipsomaniacs, the place becomes a cue that incites an uncontrollable urge to drink. The local McDonalds targets children with its highly visible PlayPlace, marked by brightly colored, large-scale plastic climbing forms; it also rewards their consumption with Happy Meal toys. For not such a few of those tending to obesity, the place becomes a cue that incites an uncontrollable urge to eat.[13] Traps for the potential addict's discovery of their addiction can be cleverly set. No space is more carefully programmed for making addicts than the casino resort of Las Vegas, Nevada. An appreciation of the evolving sophistication of addictive design depends on a sense of Las Vegas's urban history.

Urban Cyborg

Buildings, like people, are in large part the products of their environment. How a building acts depends a great deal on its habitat. One explanation for the pathology of the casino resort in Vegas is the abnormality of its urban incubator. Las Vegas has the features of a cyborg—a sentient body with artificial additions.[14] The architectural progeny of cyberorganisms are bound to be less natural, perhaps even more dangerous, than normal offspring. In John Shirley's cyberpunk, neoliberal-nightmare novel *City Come a Walkin'*, San Francisco is a cyborg. The big banks, run by criminals, have displaced the government in the United States. Easily manipulated digital credit has been forcibly substituted for money. Mob bosses in each of the major cities of the nation plot the final usurpation of power and the consolidation of their new criminal cartel. Mafioso-bankers work in clandestine conjunction with far-right vigilantes, who brutally repress all forms of alternative popular expression from prostitution to pop concerts. Corporate gangsters ravage the city as well as its population. Architecture is a signifier of corruption. The venal destruction of the rich historic urban texture is contrasted to the enervating banality of the buildings of the new order. The ruin of a grand hotel represents the loss of civic self-esteem:

> The deserted wrecking site, the building three-quarters spooned out, showed the cutaway cells of one of the last nineteenth-century edifices remaining in the city. It had been a grand place once, the pride of the town, replete with carved angels upholding the cornices and ornamental roof-spouts. It had been a solid place, built for permanence of good wood and stone, and it would have served well for another century if not for the avarice of a certain land developer.[15]

Stu Cole, a hard-bitten, classic noir individualist and club owner, and his star performer, Catz Wailen, represent those who love urban life and who constitute its originality. Both use their particular geniuses to resist the irresistible cultural depredations of the villain, Rufe Roscoe, head of the mob. But the most powerful character of the novel is City, the reification of San Francisco's communal angst. City opposes the forces of evil with amoral violence. He explains himself to Cole through the protagonist's television:

> A TV is a media outlet for the city. A neuron in my brain. The means I use to transfer the image from video to electron-patterns, bring it through the wires and feed it into your TV—it's a form of telekinesis. Manipulating electronics with thought. At night I have the power in every cerebral battery in the city. A brain stores electricity. I can tap in, when they sleep. During the day I have only the power of those who sleep in the day—far fewer, so I am limited. Though I'm bolstered by people watching TV, since that's a form of sleeping. I'm the sum total of the unconscious cognition of every brain in the city. And I'm Rufe Roscoe, too—I'm his self-hatred.[16]

City is an urban cyborg with an electronic body and a human psyche created as an act of self-defense against the ravages of corporate greed. Las Vegas is posited in my text as a different kind of urban cyborg. City is opposed to a culture of predatory profit; Las Vegas is constructed to gain from human loss. City has consciousness; Las Vegas is conscienceless. City is an endogenous materialization of the local population; Las Vegas's organic social body has been reshaped by a series of prostheses appended by criminals, corporations, and the state. "Prosthesis" identifies an artificial augmentation that is attached to the periphery of the body to compensate for a real or perceived lack; whether the prosthesis benefits or discomfits its host, it changes its wearer's life.[17] Las Vegas has had several significant prosthetic interventions. Its robotic supplements help account for the odd shape of the city and for the remarkable agency of some of its buildings.

Las Vegas was begotten on a little water by a big railroad. The town was brought into being in 1905 by William Clark, the entrepreneur who built the railroad connecting Salt Lake City to Los Angeles and who speculated in the land along its path. Initially the community's conventional economy—transportation, mining, and real estate—produced a normative form. The railroad station, marker of the town's vital link to elsewhere, dominated the settlement's principal axis (Fremont Street) from its apex (Figure 5.1). Ordered around this axis was a street grid with the town's first businesses and residences, then churches and public buildings. The patchwork plan of the town was the result of off-axis grids laid out on the margins of Clark's settlement by subsequent real estate speculators. As late as 1930, with a population of less than five thousand in the whole of Clark County, Las Vegas was still a very small town watered by artesian wells in a large and hostile desert. The handsomely elaborated art deco Las Vegas High School (now the Las Vegas Academy), built in 1930 by George A. Ferris, documents the town's modest prosperity and conventional civic pride (Figure 5.2).[18]

Las Vegas's humble scale allowed it to survive in its harsh ecological niche. Not all its citizens were, however, satisfied with humble. Those interested in wealth recognized that money could not be grown locally; it needed to be imported.[19] Among the most effective conduits of wealth were tourists. And among the most effective lures for tourists was gambling. Gambling had been made illegal in Nevada in 1915; by the 1920s land speculators and businessmen were pressuring the Nevada legislature to relegalize it.[20] The interests of these lobbyists are clearly articulated in an open letter published simultaneously in several Nevadan newspapers on May 9, 1930, by Las Vegas property developer Thomas Carroll. Carroll writes at length promoting two complementary "subjects"—gambling and horse racing.

> The State adoption of these subjects will increase population, and constantly bring millions of dollars into Nevada. Real Estate values will very noticeably increase, and legitimate business of every kind will decidedly increase and prosper.
>
> These two subjects are the incidental and active parts of a brand new idea for Nevada, and this new idea is TO MAKE NEVADA THE PLAYGROUND OF THE UNITED STATES. Ours is the last frontier and border State. Thruout the Union it has the name and reputation of being an open and a liberal State. Our people can build on this name and reputation, to make Nevada the magnet and attraction for the wealthy of the nation to spend much of their time and money in Nevada, instead of in Havana, Mexico or Europe.[21]

If Nevada could offer "wealthy" Americans gambling and horse racing as well as fine winter weather and impressive landscapes, the state might become a viable

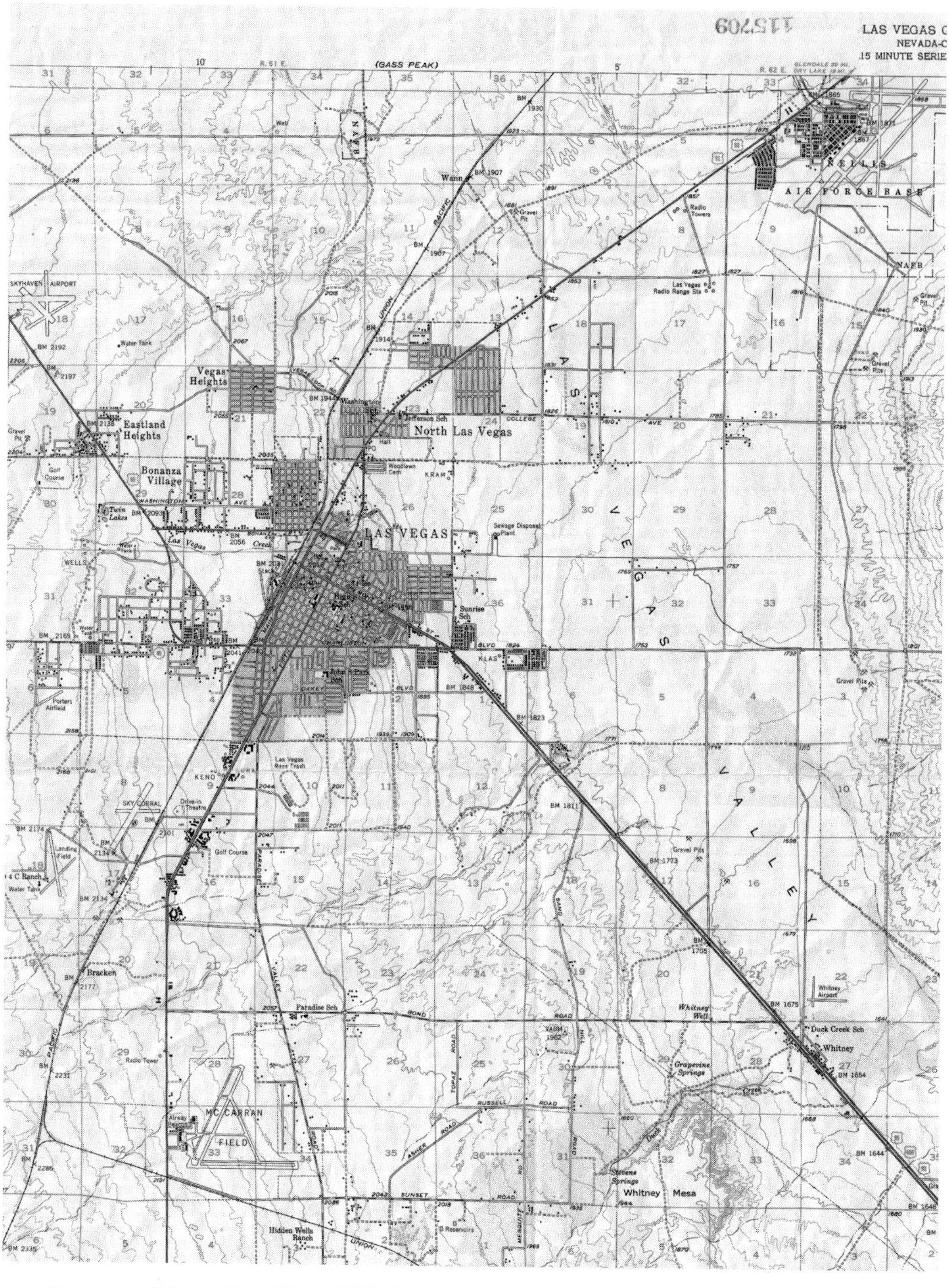

Figure 5.1. Map of Las Vegas, U.S. Geological Survey 1952, original scale 1:62,500. The Strip originates in the southwest quadrants 9 and 16 and extends between quadrants 20–21 and 28–29. Courtesy of the University of Texas Libraries, the University of Texas at Austin.

alternative to established holiday destinations abroad. The lobbyists were successful: gambling was legalized by the Nevada legislature in 1931.[22] Gambling was not the only lure fashioned in the Nevada Legislature. Sex was always a hot and available commodity in Nevada, the only state in the Union in which the legality of prostitution is decided by individual counties.[23] Other forms of sexual relations—namely marriage and divorce—also proved profitable. Nevada makes both extremely easy. Legislation also passed in 1931 allowed divorce after a mere six weeks of residency. It is less now. Weddings are even more immediately available. On its official website, the Nevada Commission comments on the efficiency of Nevadan nuptials: "And if time is an issue, it's no issue at all in Nevada. There are no waiting periods or pre-wedding blood tests required. And in certain round-the-clock cities, like Las Vegas and Reno, you can even find license bureaus open until midnight daily."[24] These legislative manipulations explain the ubiquity of two oddly complementary architectural types in Las Vegas: the casino and the wedding chapel.

In the same year, 1931, the federal government began work on the city's first, if remotely attached, prosthesis: Hoover Dam.[25] Hoover Dam is the city's colossal, permanently attached IV bag—continuously providing massive transfusions of water, electricity, and humans. Rendered in art deco like the Las Vegas High School, Hoover Dam engorged the city with resources and capital. It reshaped the city's economy and its form. Tubed and wired to Las Vegas, the dam not only provided the city with cheap water and electricity, it also attracted business. The dam, both during construction and after completion, was a draw for sightseers. Just as importantly,

Figure 5.2. Las Vegas, Las Vegas High School, now the Las Vegas Academy of Arts, George A. Ferris and Lehman A. Ferris, 1930.

Las Vegas was the supply center for equipment and materials as well as the primary diversion for its large and almost exclusively male workforce. Casinos began their incremental domination of Fremont Street. Their ascent was given a further boost by the ending of Prohibition in 1933.

The federal government added two further prosthetic appendages a decade later. The federally subsidized Basic Magnesium Plant was built about ten miles southeast of Las Vegas in Henderson. At the height of production during World War II the plant employed over thirteen thousand workers. About twelve miles northeast of the city the government constructed the airfield and base of the Army Air Corps Flexible Gunnery School, which, after World War II, was rescripted as Nellis Air Force Base. Both significantly increased the population of Las Vegas and the client base of the city's casinos.[26] These additions also contributed to the introduction of the most formidable of all of Las Vegas's prostheses: the Strip.

The Strip was a four-mile section of Los Angeles Boulevard (U.S. Highway 91), the principal highway connecting Las Vegas to southern California. It was a distinct appendage to the city, added just beyond its boundary and crucially outside its tax jurisdiction. Later the avenue, renamed Las Vegas Boulevard, took on a life of its own, independent of the artery to Southern California (U.S. Interstate 15). Indeed, in 1950 the Strip officially identified itself as Paradise, an unincorporated, census-designated place.[27] The Strip had three distinct generations, each of which iconically modeled contemporary America. From the 1940s into the 1970s, the Strip was modern, a postwar symptom of the experimental frivolity of the world's newly dominant industrial power. From the 1970s through the 1990s, the Strip was postmodern, the corporate poster-child of escapist excess en masse. In the early twenty-first century, the Strip might be described as posthuman, the embodiment of a globalization contingent on the insinuation of the digital into everything.

Modern Strip

"Modern" evokes figures of urbanism, industrialization, and capitalism. The individual is understood as responsible for his own destiny. Reason and its twin progeny, science and technology, assure human progress toward freedom. The Strip in its youth certainly celebrated one of the archetypical expressions of the modern—the automobile. The motorcar determined the Strip's plan and inspired its architecture. But the Strip embraced not only the celebratory forms of the modern, but also its deformities: anxiety, escape, excess, and atomic bombs.

By the 1930s cars had displaced the railroad as the privileged means of individual, middle-class travel. The highway became an increasingly generative source of California tourists for Las Vegas. In his 1932 autobiography, Frank Lloyd Wright wrote, with characteristic incoherence, of the highway as the liberator of the American spirit:

> The Motor Car More and More. Complete mobilization of our American people is one natural asset of the machine, fast approaching. Opportunity will soon come for the homeward-bound individual to pick up by the wayside anything in the way of supplies he may require, just as the stranger may find there entertainment and satisfactory lodging. In these United States great highways are becoming arteries of the integrated but otherwise decentralized great metropolis of the future. . . . As the importance of Freedom appears to the human mind the need of it increases in the human heart. So no doubt a new sense of quality in all these expressions will appear.[28]

Presumably on the basis of his recent Los Angeles experience, America's all-time favorite architect embraced urban sprawl as an affirmation of American freedom. The entrepreneurs of the modern Strip exploited it for profit. The casino-resort motels were designed to attract the attention of automobiles' drivers and their passengers. They were scaled to private vehicles and designed to accommodate a few hundred guests and their cars.

The first casino resort on Los Angeles Boulevard was the El Rancho, opened in 1941.[29] Another dozen casino-resort motels, including the Last Frontier, Flamingo, Desert Inn, Sahara, Sands, Riviera, Dunes, Hacienda, Tropicana, and Stardust, joined El Rancho on the Strip over the next two decades. Differences among these casino resorts were skin deep. Those skins came from different imaginaries: El Rancho and the Last Frontier, for example, referenced a nostalgically fantasized Wild West (Figure 5.3). The Last Frontier staged a frontier town as an attraction. It was reported in the *New York Times*: "The grounds of the hotel are a veritable museum of the Old West, with a jail built in 1870, an old school-house, stagecoaches, covered wagons, two trains of the year 1800 and a venerable Joss House built in 1860 in Elko, Nevada."[30] William Moore, the Last Frontier's architect, describes the construction of the resort's wedding chapel:

> We thought, because of the old churches that we had seen in western towns still existing in California and Nevada . . . that we could make a church a part of the wedding chapel business. Most of the wedding chapels [in Las Vegas] had the interior of a chapel or church, but the exteriors were usually an old home or part of another structure of some kind. . . . I went to California and took numerous pictures of an old church that existed and was in operation, and then brought the pictures back and induced Zick and Sharp to reduce them down in size using the whole

> scale of the church and the measurements that I took at the time I took the pictures, so they became a miniature of the actual church in operation in the state of California. They did make drawings, and we got our maintenance crew at the hotel to build it according to the drawings. . . . Then [we] hired a wedding chapel director.[31]

Because of its utility and mobility, this chapel, known as "The Little Church of the West," is the only surviving fragment of its generation of casino resorts. It has moved locations on three occasions. It now occupies its own minute, isolated oasis at the far end of the Strip. I spent an hour photographing the church on a Tuesday morning. During that hour, three weddings were performed (Figure 5.4). For those in more of a hurry for their nuptials, Las Vegas Boulevard provides drive-thru wedding venues.[32]

In contrast to the Wild West of the El Rancho and the Last Frontier, the Desert Inn, Flamingo, Sahara, Sands, Dunes, and Stardust evoked more exotic pleasures

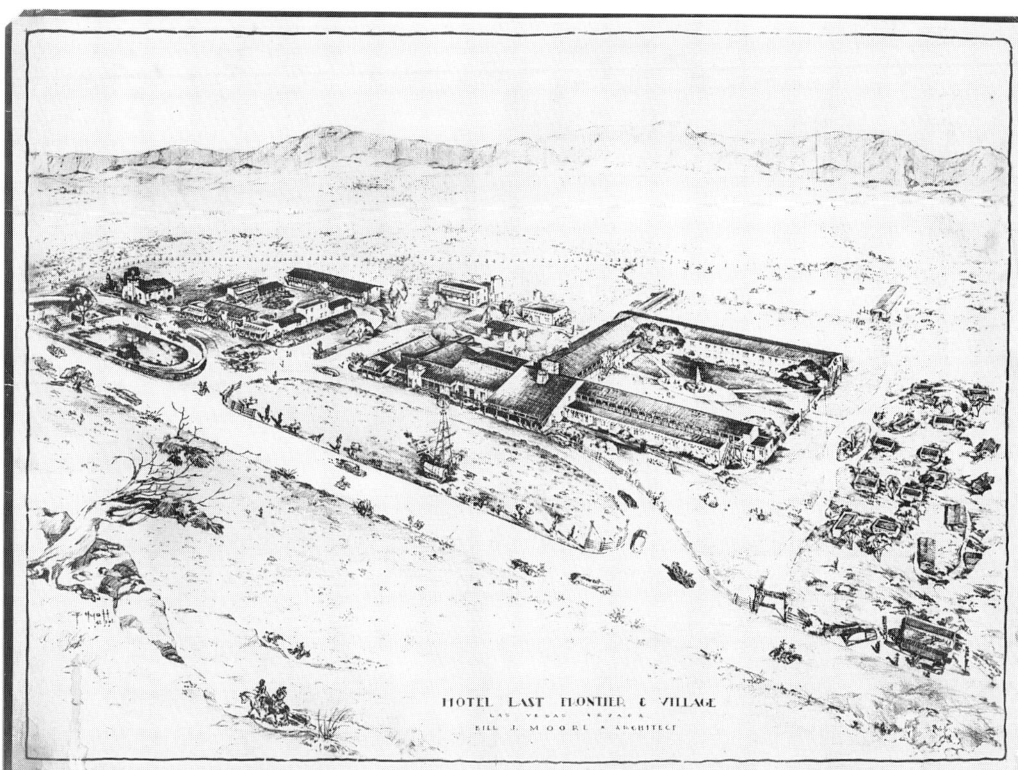

Figure 5.3. Las Vegas Strip, the Last Frontier, perspective drawing by William Moore, n.d. Courtesy of Special Collections, University Libraries, University of Nevada–Las Vegas.

mixed with LA cool. As different as they might look, all these casino-resort motels shared their spatial strategy. The formula was simple and persistent. Each casino was attached to the highway and separate from everything else. Each was identified by a large and distinctive sign on the boulevard and most had a signature "weinie" (as Walt Disney named the visually dominant castle-feature of his theme parks) marking the complex's focal structure. The property was protected from the desert and its neighbors by enfolding motel-room wings with their parking lots. William Moore, part owner of the Last Frontier as well as its architect, described the motel wings of this second casino resort on the Strip as taking "the form of an old fort—in other words, completely enclosed on four sides."[33] The bastion had two foci: a large structure—housing reception, the casino, dining rooms, and a theater—and an ample adjoining swimming pool. The swimming pool, like the casino, provided leisure activity for some guests and spectacle for others.

There was nothing new in the various architectural components of these casino complexes. In the United States, motels were already ubiquitous.[34] The informal, unintimidating familiarity of the motel form must have been one of the attractions

Figure 5.4. Las Vegas Strip, the Little Church of the West, originally built in 1942 as part of the theme town of the Last Frontier, now relocated.

of the Las Vegas resorts for middle-class Americans who had little experience with the established elite leisure spaces of either the city or the country. The traditional grand hotel of the metropolis and the traditional grand resort of the spa and the golf course both had their highly discriminatory rituals of admission and residence.[35] Less pretentious escape settings were, nevertheless, as familiar as the motel. From summer camps to dude ranches, destinations that provided all the necessary guest amenities at one site were commonplace. Indeed, middle-class resorts were a growth industry, particularly in the southern parts of the United States.[36] But if resorts and motels were established middle-class attractions, casinos were not. Casinos distinguished the modern Strip. In addition to advertising sports and nature as sources of leisure and rejuvenation, the casinos of the Strip promoted gambling and nightclub entertainment.

The first generation of Strip casino resorts shared more than their programmatic schemes. They also shared basic economic tactics: all depended on venture capital from elsewhere. Though each might have one or more legitimate owners licensed by the Nevada Gaming Control Board, most came to rely on funds from questionable sources. Benjamin "Bugsy" Siegel introduced organized crime to Las Vegas in the financing of the Flamingo. From 1946 to 1969, the external principals involved in the development of this remarkable prosthetic appendage of Las Vegas were mob related.[37]

Tom Wolfe, in breathless hyperbole, claims that the mob's involvement in the construction of casinos on the Strip affected their external form and internal ornament:

> Las Vegas happened to be created after the war, with war money, by gangsters. Gangsters happened to be the first uneducated . . . but more to the point, unaristocratic, *outside* of the aristocratic tradition . . . the first uneducated, prole-petty-burgher Americans to have enough money to build a monument to their style of life. They built it in an isolated spot, Las Vegas, out in the desert. . . . The important thing about the building of Las Vegas is not that the builders were gangsters but that they were proles. They celebrated, very early, the new style of life of America—using the money pumped in by the war to show a prole vision . . . *Glamor!* . . . of style.[38]

An architecture celebrating the popular was not, however, as Wolfe implies, a Las Vegas invention. It had begun much earlier, notably in Los Angeles. Sunset Strip came to Las Vegas in a variety of guises: in the adoption of its name, in the persons of its patrons and entertainers, and in the shape of its buildings. Guy McAfee, who owned a club on Sunset Strip before legalizing his operations by taking them to Nevada, reportedly imported the title "Strip" to the stretch of Los Angeles Boulevard outside Las Vegas.[39] The classic curvilinear abstraction of the ubiquitous deco forms of the twenties and thirties had been superseded in Los Angeles by the fragmented planarity of midcentury modern.[40] McAfee's club, Ciro's, opened in 1940, is an early version of the new cubistic sensibility. The 1946 Flamingo, designed by George Vernon Russell, was an expression of the same style. Russell is perhaps best known for his design of the "Circus Car," General Dwight D. Eisenhower's World War II mobile battle command post, and for his postwar, modernist, single-family homes for Angelenos.[41] But his work as a set designer in the film industry perhaps best explains the "forced perspectives, avoidance of rectangularity, color and effective lighting" in the Flamingo.[42]

Russell's basic program for the Flamingo followed that of the two earlier Strip casino resorts. But, in contrast to the faux Old West theming of the earlier establishments, the Flamingo embraced the modern. Its main facade was a collage of rectilinear planes, cleaved from the spatial core of the structure and only tentatively reattached (Figure 5.5). The interior of the casino was open and uncluttered, with lighting that dramatized strafing angles. The flamingo-pink of the faux-leather furniture ignited against the rain-forest green that controlled the interior palette (Figure 5.6). Later remodeling subdued its aggression inside but heightened the glitz of the exterior (Figure 5.7). The violent chic of the original Flamingo's design and its mob associations were expressions of the risky excitement of alternative entertainment after World War II. At its edges, the conservative society of postwar America experimented with its moral order. But for all its drama, the casino interior of the time was legible: the tables surrounded by neat rows of slots, with a bar as a backdrop and an occasional window. Like the arrangement of the casino resorts along the highway, form followed function—how things worked was clearly visible.

Spectacle complemented rather than obscured the operation of this first-generation prosthesis. Neon—the invention of Georges Claude, the French chemist who was also the designer of poison gases used by the French in World War I and later a Nazi collaborator—was famously used to emblazon the desert.[43] More idiosyncratic, and certainly more ethically problematic, was the modern Strip's appropriation of atomic bomb testing as entertainment. The military began testing atomic bombs in Yucca Flats, outside Las Vegas, in 1951. Daniel Lang described with brilliant brevity in a *New Yorker* article the local reception of the detonations, from the initial anxiety about their physical and economic impact, through the delirium of their display and publicity, to the annoyance with the government when the scale of the blasts was diminished.

> The Desert Inn's Sky Room, a glass-enclosed cocktail lounge with a sweeping panoramic view, was an especially popular spot for dawn parties. "It was a wonderful

Figure 5.5. Las Vegas Strip, Flamingo, exterior, George Russell, 1946.

Figure 5.6. Las Vegas Strip, Flamingo, interior, George Russell, after 1946.

Figure 5.7. Las Vegas Strip, Flamingo, postcard of exterior after remodeling by Pereira and Luckman, 1953. Author's collection.

> place for what the customers wanted," a waitress there told me. "They could sit around and listen to our piano player and look out the big windows and see the pretty hotel fountain and the guests swimming in the pool and the traffic speeding by on Highway 91, and then, just when they were starting to get tired, the A-bomb."[44]

The obscenities of the bomb—exposure of soldiers to the blasts, cremation of live animals, carcinogenic toxins floating eastwards—were forgotten in the thrill of witnessing the pyrotechnics of power. The caption to a newspaper image of an early Miss Atomic Blast is excruciatingly ironic:

> Radiating loveliness instead of deadly atomic particles, Candyee King, actress appearing at Last Frontier Hotel in Las Vegas, Nevada, dazzled U.S. Marines who participated in recent atomic maneuvers at Yucca Flats. They bestowed on her the title of "Miss Atomic Blast" finding her as awe-inspiring in another way, as was the "Big Bang."[45]

The last Miss Atomic Blast appeared in 1957.

In the same year, 1957, new legislation rescinded the Nevada requirement that all stockholders in a casino be licensed by the state.[46] The old law attempted to keep known gangsters from casino ownership but only succeeded in denying corporate investment in casinos, as all their stockholders could not be licensed. After 1957, expanded corporate resources along with the increasing toleration in the United States for behaviors previously understood as morally ambiguous provided the scaffold for a new class of proprietors on the Strip in the 1960s. The corporate entrepreneur and the corporation, with their elite operatives and middle-class investors, displaced the mob, with its proletariat roots and working-class pension-fund financing. There was, of course, considerable overlap, and, like the mob, the corporation was a nonlocal player.[47] The new corporate owners of the Strip modified its material forms as well as its financial practices.

The modern Strip was productively taught to us by Venturi, Izenour, and Scott Brown's *Learning from Las Vegas*.[48] This was the Strip of the "decorated shed"—a simple structure with elaborate signage and ornament, designed to be seen from a moving vehicle. The visual order of the modern Strip complemented the desert and the highway by which it was penetrated: episodic, horizontal, filmic. The casino-resort mise-en-scène, dazzling in the neon of Hollywood glamour, unscrolled like a diorama projected on the automobile's windscreen (Figure 5.8). All students of Las Vegas understand how much they learned about the modern Strip from Venturi et al.; they also recognize that this radically revisionist urban analysis was itself a quintessentially postmodern book. It retains modernism's exclusive concern with *form,* in the formidable tradition of New York's Museum of Modern Art. But that formalism is obscured by the book's celebration of popular forms, its fractured structure, its dependence on signs as well as its promotion of their signifying power. Further, *Learning from Las Vegas* ignores history. These features, as well as its unheroic subject, Las Vegas, make the text an important exemplar of postmodern architectural writing and practice. The powerful lessons about reading commercial architecture from the highway taught in *Learning from Las Vegas* may still be applied to a suburban strip mall, but they don't much help in understanding the corporate postmodern Strip.[49]

Postmodern Strip

In this text, "postmodern" defines a period not a style.[50] It labels the cultural, political, and economic features of its moment—an erosion of the modern distinctions between elite and popular forms, the shift in production from heavy industry to service, the commodification and homogenization of culture with globalization. The postmodern retained many of the features of modernity, though modifying them by a changed context. Its spaces were characterized by an oddly ahistorical

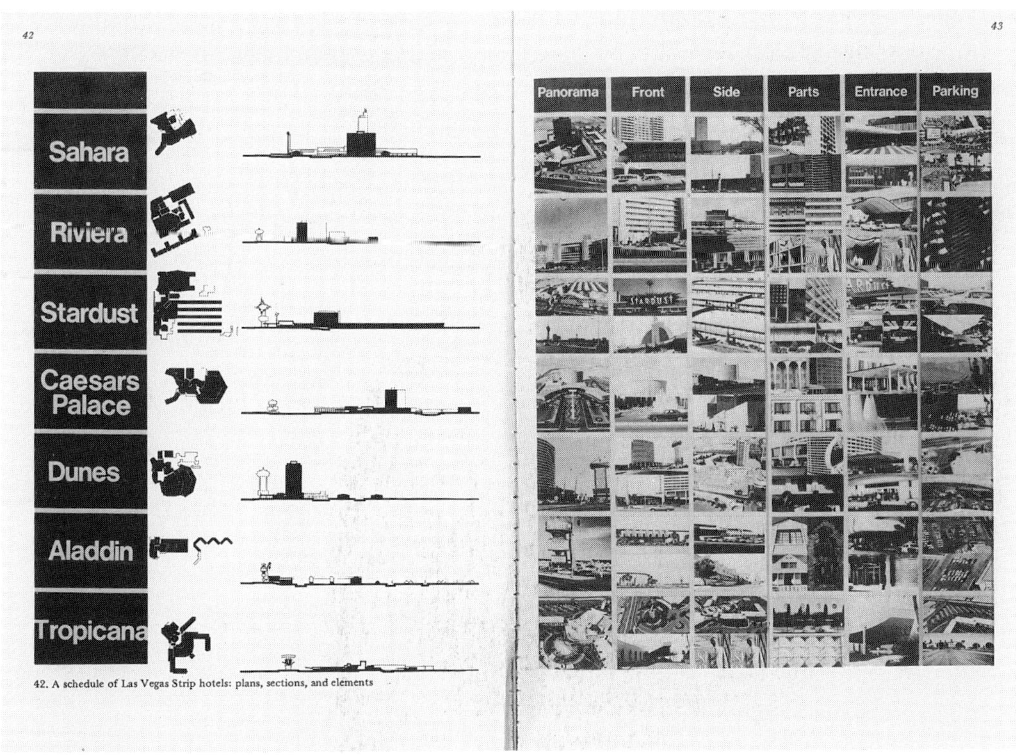

Figure 5.8. Venturi, Brown, and Izenour, *Learning from Las Vegas,* 42–43.

eclecticism, fracture, disorientation, and spectacularization. If the Las Vegas Strip offered a particular take on American modernism in the 1950s, by the 1990s the Strip had become a perfect index of postmodern America.

Howard Hughes, whose wealth was generated by respected capitalistic means including inheritance, came to Las Vegas in 1966. By the end of 1967 he owned six major casino resorts—20 percent of the rooms on the Strip—and was continuing to expand his holdings.[51] In 1968, he announced plans for the world's largest luxury hotel, complete with an indoor, electronically simulated golf course, but it was never constructed.[52] Hughes was a buyer of casinos, not a builder. He shifted the culture and economics of the Strip without reworking its appearance. In the late 1960s and early 1970s, Kirk Kerkorian, who earned his wealth in the airline and film industries as well as in land speculation, brought his money to Las Vegas. He also brought his architect, Martin Stern. Together they introduced, with great effect, the megaresort casino both to the Strip and to Wall Street.

High-rise hotel blocks were not new on the Strip. But before the late 1960s they were uneventfully small. The first of these, the Riviera (1955) was only nine stories with three hundred rooms. Initiating the new generation of behemoths on the Strip was Kerkorian and Stern's International Hotel (opened, 1969; later the Las Vegas Hilton). It marked not only a change in scale but also a reordered program. From the desert oasis encircled by guestrooms with a double focus on a swimming pool and a gambling hall, the casino resort was reconfigured as a great guestroom tower planted on top of an expansive gaming and entertainment platform. Like the basic arrangement of the earlier motel-casinos, this new program was not a local invention. Its spatial formula was well established already in the 1950s. Resort hotels such as the Caribe Hilton (San Juan, Puerto Rico, Toro/Warner, 1949) and the Beverly Hilton (Los Angeles, Welton Becket, 1956) had a ground-level platform housing the services and public functions of the hotel that served as an extended base for one or more guestroom towers.[53] As was the case with their predecessors on the Strip, casinos distinguished the new generation of casino megaresorts from their prototypes. They were also much bigger. Like one of Claes Oldenburg's giant sculptures, Kerkorian and Stern inflated their model. The number of hotel rooms multiplied: guestroom towers were supersized. The International's 1,500 rooms made it momentarily the largest hotel in the world outside the Soviet Union (Figure 5.9). Selling the International to Hilton allowed Kerkorian and Stern to build an even bigger version of the type. The two thousand plus rooms of the MGM Grand (1973, later Bally's) made it the largest hotel anywhere for a number of years. It was soon surpassed by its neighbors.

The Claes Oldenburg analogy might seem even more appropriately applied to the series of hyperthemed megaresort casinos of the 1990s. The Strip always had themed resorts—from the El Rancho and the Last Frontier with their Wild West motifs, through the gaudy classicism and toga-clad waitresses of Caesars Palace and the clowns and trapeze acts of Circus Circus, to the MGM Grand, a real hotel that thematized a fictional one.[54] But by the end of the 1980s, hotels had taken theming beyond surface ornament and signage to spectacle. Some hotels brought spectacle to the street: the Mirage (1989) has its volcano that erupts on the hour; Treasure Island (1993) its five-times-a-night live enactment of a pirate attack; the Bellagio (1998) its continuously choreographed fountains.[55] Other megaresorts assumed the form of their theme: Excalibur (1990) is a medieval castle; Luxor (1993) a pyramid; New York New York (1997) New York; the Venetian (1999) Venice.[56] These simulacra have, however, nothing to do with Oldenburg. They don't have an ironic, witty, critical bone in their bodies. Rather, they represent an appropriation of Disney, rendering the world placeless, historyless, and sanitary. Like the nations of Epcot (opened in Orlando in 1982), the theme parks of the postmodern Strip promise the personal experience of difference but deliver mass fantasy of the same.

Figure 5.9. Las Vegas Strip, the International Hotel, Kirk Kerkorian and Martin Stern Jr., 1969. Modified by the author from the Creative Commons website Classic Las Vegas, "Las Vegas Photos: 1960s."

The most symptomatic of all spectacles of the postmodern Strip were the theatrically staged, hyperviolent deaths of buildings: the casino implosions. A Las Vegas casino's life is short; few live longer than two or three decades. Steven Wynn (the current incarnation of the Hughes/Kerkorian Las Vegas financial colossus) initiated these extravagant pyrotechnics with the destruction of the North Tower of the Dunes in 1993. Well over a dozen implosions have been orchestrated since. In an uncanny semblance of the atomic blasts of the 1950s and 1960s, casino detonations have become an excuse for partying. Like the earlier demonstration of military state authority, these dramatic visualizations of corporate control also promote Las Vegas. The implosion of the Hacienda at 9 p.m. (not midnight) on December 31, 1996, was purposely scheduled for the celebration of the New Year at eastern standard time in order to vie for attention with the traditional Times Square ball-drop on national television.[57] Las Vegas implosions amplify Guy Debord's sinister understanding of spectacle as "capital accumulated to the point that it becomes image."[58] Destruction became entertainment.

Posthuman Strip

Though less familiar than modern or postmodern, "posthuman" also names a particular time—the present—through reference to its characteristic features.[59] Like the modern in postmodern, the human in posthuman is not erased but rather changed. Humans now are increasingly augmented and qualitatively changed by technology. At the core of the posthuman is the modified body; the human and the machine are increasingly equivalent. Through implantations, the body extends its longevity and strength; through accessorizing, the body enhances its information access. Simultaneously, the increasing fluidity of intelligence and treasure enables expanding state and corporate power. Like the human body, urban and architectural bodies are now increasingly penetrated and surveilled.[60] The Strip presents the paradigm of a posthuman habitat.

With the corporatization of Las Vegas beginning in the late 1960s, the inhumanly scaled casino-resort hotels began resetting the visual order of the Strip. By the second decade of the twenty-first century, the shift is complete. In the remodeling of older establishments like the Flamingo and construction of new ones like the International, casino resorts absorbed front parking lots into their gaming spaces. Automobiles were no longer part of the casino's ornamental facade. The casino megaresort, in contrast to the modern casino motel, extends its visual hyperbole and swollen scale to the sidewalk. Now the Strip is witnessed with vertical anamorphic tilt—as in the canyons of New York City, buildings are experienced obliquely. Casino resorts are no longer legible sheds framed by asphalt parking lots, decorated with elaborate marquees, and labeled by massive roadside signs. Rather, their facades bully the pavement; whole structures are only visible on the web or from a great elevation. The displacement of an objective perspective outside the casino disorients the observer in preparation for the placelessness of its interior. Visitors to the Strip in its youth knew where they were; visitors now may not. The most coherent view of the posthuman Strip is through the portal of a jetliner, not from a car window. That view is offered to over 40 percent of Las Vegas's nearly forty million annual visitors: McCarran International Airport, nestled next to the Strip and expanded in the early 1980s in response to the Strip's development, now competes with Interstate 15 as the primary means of access to Las Vegas.[61] From a height, the monumental, isolated hotels of the Strip still appear to be ordered with linear regularity along the shallow stage space of Las Vegas Boulevard. This distant impression of the Strip's rationality is false; it disappears with proximity.

The cause of the Strip's irrationality lies not just in the physical relation between the boulevard and its buildings, but also in its dysfunctional treatment of human density. In 2011, if a website can be believed, fourteen of the world's twenty largest hotels were on the Strip.[62] Las Vegas's Venetian has more hotel rooms on offer than does the city of Venice.[63] The Strip's massive hotels, the entertainments they offer, and the staffing they require all generate hideous congestion. By the 1990s, pedestrians began to challenge the automobile's hegemony, though not with great success. Street traffic became a nightmare; being a pedestrian proved life-threatening (Figure 5.10). The Las Vegas poet-policeman Harry Fagel describes the situation:

> Cars are like cave bats blind and
> Hungry and seeking sustenance from the
> Teeming insects that swirl and whoop in the
> Darkness.[64]

Between 1995 and 1997, 142 pedestrians died in Clark County; 190 people were injured on crosswalks even when obeying the light. Traversing the Strip was locally known as "the six-lane dash to death."[65] The thirteen pedestrian bridges built since 1998 are the most obvious response to pedestrian overload. These interventions along the Strip, though claimed to be for the safety of pedestrians, are actually designed to protect the autonomy of automobiles and to improve the revenues of the megaresorts. They work to minimize the human impediment to vehicular traffic. Clark County Public Works spokesman Bobby Shelton is quoted as saying "that the bridges [at Sands Avenue/Spring Mountain Road/Las Vegas Boulevard], by removing the 80,000 to 100,000 pedestrians who cross that intersection using crosswalks each day, will allow twice as many vehicles to get through each traffic light. Fewer cars will be stopped at intersections, which would also help air quality."[66] Pedestrian bridges, subsidized by the resort owners, also serve to funnel bodies directly into casinos. Despite protests to county officials from the owners of small businesses on the Strip, several bridges, like that connecting the Cosmopolitan and Crystals, part of CityCenter, and that between the Venetian and the Mirage, empty their human contents directly into corporate complexes.

The segregation of human and vehicular traffic is also apparent at the main entrances of some of the larger casinos. In grand urban hotels of the nineteenth and twentieth centuries, the great porte cochere on the avenue led both guests and the pedestrian public to their lavishly ornamented and poshly furnished lobbies. The lobbies of the grand casino resorts are, as in the past, sumptuously decorated, but apart from the marble registration counter and concierge desk, furnishings have disappeared. The lobby is not for loitering (or even for the comfort of guests waiting to be registered). More relevant to the discussion of circulation on the Strip: the lobbies of some resorts are readily accessible only to vehicular traffic. Most blatantly, at the Venetian barricades and security personnel protect the principal

Figure 5.10. Las Vegas Strip, traffic.

entrance of the hotel from pedestrians (Figure 5.11). To access the registration area without wheels requires a circuitous negotiation of retail and gaming spaces. The obstacles for pedestrians on the Strip—bridges, traffic, signage—export the disorientation notoriously associated with the inside of the casino to its outside. The elaborate cocktails ubiquitously carried on the street signify the casino's seepage into urban space. The consciously created confusion of the gaming venue has now spread to the public parts of the Strip. Cars know where they are going; humans often do not.

The scale of buildings now, as in the past, has been an expression of power and status.[67] But in Paradise, size is more about profit than about reputation. Indeed, the megaresort casino hotels are monuments to economies of scale and the corporations who profit from them.[68] Among the largest hotels on the Strip are its most recent additions: the Wynn, Encore, and Aria. The Wynn and Encore are owned by Wynn Resorts, a company deeply invested in China. The Aria, with over four thousand rooms, is part of the multibuilding CityCenter complex, a joint venture

Figure 5.11. Las Vegas Strip, the Venetian, hotel entrance blocked to pedestrians; enlarged sign inset.

of MGM Resorts International and Infinity World Development Corporation, a wholly owned subsidiary of Dubai World. In addition to the Aria by Pelli Clarke Pelli Architects (known best for their Petronas Towers in Kuala Lumpur), CityCenter has structures by a roster of starchitects including Rafael Viñoly, Helmut Jahn, Norman Foster, Daniel Libeskind, and Kohn Pederson (Figure 5.12).[69] Architainment is the most recent spectacle introduced to Las Vegas. This latest megaresort complex attached to the Strip is, however, more than spectacle. CityCenter reveals its purpose in its name. It marks the usurpation of the bodily core of the old Las Vegas by its prosthetic supplement (Figure 5.13). The artificial appendage is now in control of the body. Las Vegas is an urban cyborg, and casinos are its life's blood.

The modern Strip sought to attract the detached male. The postmodern Strip experimentally directed its interest to families. The posthuman Strip consumes everyone over eighteen indiscriminately, but contemporary casino design demonstrates that it finds women particularly tempting.[70]

Figure 5.12. Las Vegas Strip, CityCenter, Crystals, Daniel Libeskind, 2009.

Casino

Of course, product design is everywhere driven by the desire for profit. But some products, particularly packaging and advertising, are carefully devised to function as effective cues for behavioral addictions. The same case holds in architecture. Arenas feed the lunacy of the sports fanatic, malls abet the frenzy of the compulsive shopper, tanning salons enable the dependency of the tanning habitué.[71] Nowhere is programming more predatory than in the Las Vegas casino. The casino is the offspring of a maze and a labyrinth.[72] A maze—like amazement—is not a material site but an emotional state of astonished bewilderment; the confusion of its complexity is more conceptual than somatic. Indeed, it is seductive. "If a visitor has a propensity to gamble, the maze layout will evoke it," writes Bill Friedman, retired guru of casino design.[73] In contrast, the labyrinth is a built place of bodily entanglement; its partitions physically frustrate the escape of those imprisoned within it, staging their death.[74] Its prototype was constructed by Daedalus to entrap Greek youths and maidens extorted by King Minos to feed the Cretan Minotaur. Its contemporary manifestations in Las Vegas act in an uncannily similar manner. The

Figure 5.13. Las Vegas and the Las Vegas Strip, Google Earth view, with the diminutive city in the foreground and the engorged Strip in the background.

casino tyrannizes the great plinth of the megaresort, devouring the humans who are channeled through it from the hotel's guestroom towers and pedestrian walkways. In contrast to the terrifying labyrinth of Crete, the brilliant ornament and animation of the Las Vegas casino anesthetizes its victims (Figure 5.14).

The viscera of the casino are its gaming spaces, which have been scientifically programmed to siphon away the substance of those who experience it.[75] Most of that science has been undertaken, directly or indirectly, with funding from the gaming industry. Studies in the field, published from the late 1970s through the early 1990s, appeared in academic journals addressed to the marketing and service industries. Articles tended to be broad investigations of the affective qualities of commercial interiors.[76] Subsequent research has applied earlier findings to specific environments, notably casinos.[77] The tenor of these studies is suggested by a concept central to them: "servicescape." Servicescape is defined as all those affective features—program, decor, lighting, cleanliness, attitudes and appearance of attendants, smell, sound—that contribute, first, to the initial impression that a commercial setting makes on its patrons and, second, to those patrons' decision to "repatronize" the site. The servicescape is most important, it is argued, to those businesses in which the lingering of consumers is desirable. The bottom-line success of a casino depends upon its servicescape. This genre of social scientific research is quantitative, nonnarrative, and ethics free.

Bill Friedman's *Designing Casinos to Dominate the Competition* provides templates of both casino research and casino planning in the 1990s. Friedman makes the claim—important for architectural historians—that the greatest determinants of a casino's success are spatial:

> Six factors have an important influence on player counts: interior design, location, number of hotel rooms, marketing, management, and operations. . . . Location is the single most important factor, because it determines the size and demographic composition of the available marketplace. Interior design, the second most significant impact, can even improve or reduce the expected potential of a given location. The research findings in this book lead to a heretical business concept: *interior design is far more important in determining potential player counts than management, marketing, and operations combined.*[78]

Friedman's book provides corporations the formula for financially rewarding casino spaces: in addition to the six factors of influence, Friedman's volume offers thirteen principles of persuasive interior order to maximize a casino's revenue. Those principles can be condensed. Successful casinos, however large, should provide prospective gamblers with a maze of intimate play spaces defined by low ceilings, soft barriers,

Figure 5.14. Las Vegas Strip, Caesars Palace, casino interior.

and distinct decors. Empty space and clear sightlines should be avoided. Themes as spectacle may work on the outside of a casino as an attraction, but inside present only distractions to gamblers. Gambling machines and tables should provide the interior's principal decoration.[79] The success of a building is judged entirely on the basis of its profitability. Aesthetics in the Kantian sense of the good and the beautiful erode income.

In the posthuman generation of Las Vegas resorts, the familiar spatial formulas of the postmodern have been modified. Not only must the gaming spaces in Las Vegas increasingly compete for tourists with casinos around the country as well as elsewhere in the world, but they must also vie with high-end retail for local attention. A CityCenter representative explained to me that 60–70 percent of Las Vegas resorts' profits used to come from gambling and 30–40 percent from accommodation, dining, entertainment, and retail. Now those figures are reversed.[80] The luxury shopping mall of CityCenter, Crystals, designed by Daniel Libeskind, has speculatively displaced the casino from Strip frontage. It is presented as architectural spectacle (Figure 5.12). In the Wynn/Encore complex, Caesars Palace, and the Venetian, a public resort entrance may well lead to a shopping mall rather than a casino. The retail space of those casinos is voluptuously framed. Broad, luxuriously carpeted galleries, lit by sculpturally grand chandeliers, offer access to high-end retail shops. But the sumptuous halls still lead to the core of the resort—the casino.

The casino remains the viscous matrix for an aggregate of bars, nightclubs, theaters, and restaurants. Some elements of Friedman's formula are still in place. Decoration continues to contribute to the visual entertainment of the space and to reinforce the theme of the hotel. At Caesars Palace the ceiling is ornately coffered, and the carpet is faux-mosaic; at the Encore brilliantly hued giant butterflies float on the carpet, and small white ones in the ceilings help disguise video cameras and sprinklers. Decoration masks the casino's evident vastness, while not distracting gamblers from their games. Other casino conventions also remain very much in place.[81] Time—that most elemental of modern regulatory systems—is still unmarked. There are no clocks. Rhythms are measured in game sequences, not hours; time is not social, but personal. Space as well as time is still arranged for forgetfulness. That which is basic for bodies' minimal maintenance is readily available: food and toilets. Drinks, still free to players, add to the gambler's dissociation. The superego doesn't stand a chance. Everything is ordered to make those playing games unaware of themselves.

Nevertheless, in the high-end resort, the casino's old Friedmanian formulas have been modified to better serve its enduring task of maximizing profits. Directions for navigating the resort are more prominently posted than in the past. Plans of the hotel are stationed at its junctions, though these brilliantly colored maps are hardly more legible than the space itself. Oxygen is still pumped into the casino, but it is now fresher and branded by carefully selected scents. Each of the high-end casinos has its particular perfume.[82] The outside, excluded from the postmodern casino, has been reintroduced inside. Elaborately crafted gardens are glimpsed from gaming spaces; gaming spaces are glimpsed from gardens (see Plate 4). In the Wynn, the high-rollers baccarat table is located in a grove of three-hundred-year-old *Aloe bainesii* trees, kentia palms, orchids, and peacocks.[83] Early every morning gardeners replace the plants that are no longer perky. Indeed, these gardens are wonderfully unnatural: people touch the leaves and smell the flowers in an attempt to determine whether or not they are artificial. Daylight too can occasionally be seen in the distance, though it still seems always to be early evening in the casino.[84]

Newly added nature does not rationalize the casino interior but increases its incoherence. The spatial disorder of the gaming arena supplements the maniacal human and mechanical activities that it stages. Clusters of slot machines contribute to the casino's complexity as well as to its bottom line. Scopic and audio digital technologies make these engines of accumulation visually and phonically despotic. Lights and sounds are pulsating, but spasmodic. Offered is a disorienting cacophony of digitally recorded coin-cascades overlaying multitracked robotic percussion keyboard play, xylophone, and bells, with accompanying pinball machines.[85] Sound is coordinated with wins; it is also deployed to convince gamblers that they have won when they have lost.[86] The slots' sound system significantly contributes to the casino's distinctively dissociative ambiance. It discourages both making conversations and overhearing them. The slot machine, as the casino's biggest and most consistent profit-generator, usurps more of its space.[87] It makes money for the casino by attracting high-volume, if low-stakes, largely female gamblers. The sales and marketing director of a Vegas-based slot machine maker comments: "The idea is to create a sense of winning by pulsing all the human senses with sounds and animated symbols and paylines flashing, non-aversive visual and auditory cues."[88] Slot machines are also one of the most addictive forms of gambling.[89]

> In Connecticut, a couple leaves a nine-year-old boy in a car overnight in freezing weather while they gamble at Foxwoods Casino. In Mississippi, parents also leave their twelve-year-old son in a vehicle, but with a revolver for protection. In Niagara Falls, casino operators complain that slot machine players are urinating into the plastic coin cups supplied by the casino or onto the floor beside the machines. Some wear adult diapers.[90]

Anthropologist Natasha Dow Schüll, on the basis of interviews with inveterate gamblers, summarizes their sense of immersion: "In the zone of machine play that compulsive gamblers describe, the conventional means of self-enterprise—money, time, sociality, and bodily existence—are disengaged from the agenda of maximizing self, and put in the service of self-liquidation."[91] Extreme players regard even winning as an unwonted diversion. The posthuman slot machine has been refined to augment its addictiveness. The machines are now somatically modeled. Recently introduced, for example, are slot-machine chairs with speakers built into the headrests. How machines are fed has also changed; they no longer eat coins, only credit slips, credit cards, and bills. How they are played has been similarly modified: a button has replaced the lever of the old one-armed bandit. Computerization has facilitated the use of club cards that allow the player to accrue reward points for complimentary meals and hotel expenses. All these features make the machines increasingly efficient both in extracting money from their players and in keeping players playing in the same casino for a longer period of time. Perhaps the most important of these posthuman innovations, however, is the slot's video digitalization, a development that heightens the immersive abjection of the gamer's experience.[92]

Playing the player is becoming increasingly technologically sophisticated. Among the technologies of immersion being developed to make slot machines ever more enticing are those with three-dimensionality.

> REELdepth™ games use Multi-Layer Display technology, an ingenious layering of two or more Liquid Crystal Displays (LCDs) that creates the visual effect of true depth without the use of 3-D glasses. The MLD technology allows players to view and play dozens of their favorite games by switching from a 3-reel to 4-reel to 5-reel to video reel to poker within seconds—all on the same AVP machine.[93]

Players no longer have to change locations in order to play a variety of games—REELdepth™ enables them to transform the machine in which they are ergonomically comfortable from an old-fashioned three-reel slot, with compellingly real reels rotating behind a glass screen, to a video slot that rewards wins with persuasive encounters with their favorite film characters—Indiana Jones, Batman, Godzilla, Aladdin. Players may even participate in their favorite television shows, like American Idol (Figure 5.15). These machines give a new dimension to the gambler's engagement in play: virtual space.[94] Virtual space presents a compelling illusion of depth where there is only flatness. Added to the visual and auditory excitement of the casino interior is the thrill of heroic narrative and celebrity. The latent addict doesn't stand a chance. The machine attaches to the body and then absorbs it. The addict, like the city in which she finds herself, is a cyborg.

All cities are unique, but Las Vegas is particularly peculiar. Here that peculiarity has been figured in the trope of a cyborg in order to emphasize its artificial, if not

Figure 5.15. Las Vegas, Golden Nugget Casino, American Idol slot machine.

unnatural, form. Whether Las Vegas, with its almost exclusive emphasis on service industries, will stay peculiar remains an open question. It seems likely that other metropolises will morph into the model that it presents. Las Vegas already functions as a prototype for such posthuman cities as Dubai and Macau. Las Vegas's tight corporate ties with those cities and the powers that control them suggest that urban cyborgs, like the dinosaurs in *Jurassic Park,* have learned to reproduce. More broadly, Las Vegas provides an example for more conventional cities of how to cope with increasingly hostile environmental and economic conditions by exploiting consumers. Better than just about any other city, Las Vegas has learned to profit from the contemporary individual's embrace of self-absorption. Cities are, of course, not the only instruments to take advantage of the current caress of the pleasures of expensive oblivion. This same escape is also sought within that space from which Las Vegas derives its latest slot-machine technology: the video game.

6

DIGITAL PLAY

Inspired by historical events and characters. This work of fiction was designed, developed and produced by a multicultural team of various religious faiths and beliefs.

—Opening disclaimer, *Assassin's Creed,* Ubisoft, 2007

Second Life couples can now make their relationships official. Whether you're married or just connected, you can designate your partner on your profile in-world and make your relationship visible to the rest of the community. Send your proposal to the avatar of your dreams using the form below. Partnering, like real life marriage, costs money. To create a partnership will cost each partner L$10. If you decide to divorce later, the person requesting the divorce will be charged L$25.

—Linden Labs, August 2011

Video Game

The Las Vegas casino suggests how a building, as a cue, may act as an agent in an addict's compulsion. Architectural agency is more intense, however, when a space is not the cue that triggers an addictive impulse but is itself the substance of abuse. For those dependent on video games or immersive worlds, play is the addiction and virtual space is its medium. Johan Huizinga, in a brilliant analysis of the ludic as a critique of fascism, argues that a defined space is a necessity for play:[1]

> More striking even than the limitation as to time is the limitation as to space. All play moves and has its being within a playground marked off beforehand either materially or ideally, deliberately or as a matter of course. Just as there is no formal difference between play and ritual, so the "consecrated spot" cannot be formally distinguished from the play-ground. The arena, the card-table, the magic circle, the temple, the stage, the screen, the tennis court, the court of justice, etc., are all in form

> and function play-grounds, i.e. forbidden spots, isolated, hedged round, hallowed, within which special rules obtain. All are temporary worlds within the ordinary world, dedicated to the performance of an act apart.[2]

Arena, temple, stage, court of justice are all buildings. Even the card table, magic circle, and screen are spatially defined. The buildings and landscapes of digital contexts are here referred to as the field-of-play's architectonics. "Architectonics" recognizes the virtuality of structures coincidentally with their visual persuasiveness.[3]

The centrality of architectonics to the video game is evident even in the title of its earliest manifestation: *Spacewar!* (Figure 6.1).[4] Invented at MIT in 1962–63 and subsequently played in computer research labs throughout the country, *Spacewar!* can still be experienced on the Internet.[5] The field of play is black. White specks are unevenly distributed across its plane. At the center is a gyrating X, a death star, that exerts a magnetic or gravitational force. Outlined in white are two distinctively shaped spaceships. One takes the form of a bomb, the other a pencil. Simple keyboard controls allow crude maneuvers: the vessels rotate left or right, thrust forward, and fire dash-like missiles. The vessels enter the field from opposite corners and are drawn toward the death star at an accelerating pace. The object of the game is to destroy the enemy spaceship while avoiding being blown up by either the alien vessel or the death star. When a spaceship moves outside the frame, it reappears following the same trajectory on the screen's opposite side. When a vessel is destroyed, it reappears where it began the game, in its respective corner of the display. Although

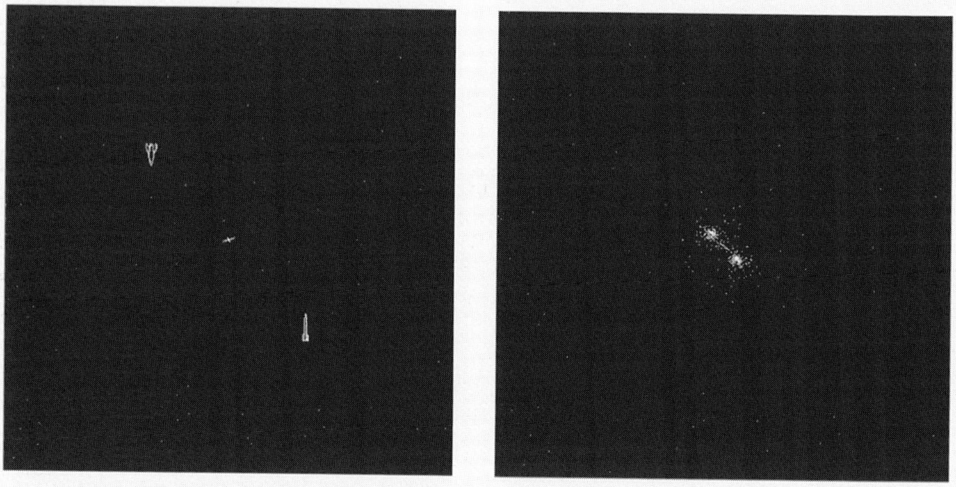

Figure 6.1. *Spacewar!*

the world within the screen can go on continuously, game play cannot. The vessels run out of ammunition.

The black-and-white graphics and the motion controls of *Spacewar!* now seem primitive, but they remain remarkably evocative. The static black ground with its points of light (arranged as the constellations in the heavens of the real world) efficiently renders the vast three-dimensionality of the universe. The distinctly different shape of each of the vessels promotes player identification with his proxy.[6] The inexorable pull of the death star and the ponderous response of the vehicle to the controls effectively excite anxiety. The destruction of the Other presents exhilarating proof of your skill. Your own destruction coerces the continuation of the game in a search for the redemption of your self-esteem. The spatial basics of video games were in place already in its first embodiment: an arena that may be perceived as boundless, but that is strictly bounded; a mobility that may be perceived as unrestricted, but that is rigidly restricted; an agency that allows the player to kill, but that may end in his own virtual death.

If the "space" in *Spacewar!* is indicative of the critical category of architectonics in video games, the "war" in its title is symptomatic of their violence. Not all video games are violent, only the most popular. First- and third-person shooter games—those in which the player or his avatar attacks figures or objects within the frame—are to video games what slot machines are to the casino: the most addictive and the best source of corporate profit.[7] DFC Intelligence, a market research organization, predicts that by 2015 the video game industry will be doing over $70 billion of business.[8] Much of that profit will come from teenagers. In 2009, the California Assembly, like many other groups and individuals, understood these games as dangerous to their children. They took action to criminalize the sale of violent video games to consumers under the age of 18.[9]

> Exposing minors to depictions of violence in video games, including sexual and heinous violence, makes those minors more likely to experience feelings of aggression, to experience a reduction of activity in the frontal lobes of the brain, and to exhibit violent antisocial or aggressive behavior. Even minors who do not commit acts of violence suffer psychological harm from prolonged exposure to violent video games.[10]

The legislative body defined a violent video game as one "in which the range of options available to a player includes killing, maiming, dismembering, or sexually assaulting an image of a human being" in a manner that "appeals to a deviant or morbid interest of minors, . . . is patently offensive to prevailing standards in the community as to what is suitable for minors . . . [and] causes the game, as a whole, to lack serious literary, artistic, political, or scientific value for minors." Further, a violent video game "enables the player to virtually inflict serious injury upon images of human beings or characters with substantially human characteristics in a manner which is especially heinous, cruel, or depraved in that it involves torture or serious physical abuse to the victim. . . . Pertinent factors in determining whether a killing depicted in a video game is especially heinous, cruel, or depraved include infliction of gratuitous violence upon the victim beyond that necessary to commit the killing, needless mutilation of the victim's body, and helplessness of the victim."[11]

Violence, in contrast to pornography and obscenity, is, however, protected as free speech. The Supreme Court struck down California's attempt to limit the sales of violent video games to children.

> Video games qualify for First Amendment protection. Like protected books, plays, and movies, they communicate ideas through familiar literary devices and features distinctive to the medium. And "the basic principles of freedom of speech . . . do not vary" with a new and different communication medium. . . . This country has no tradition of specially restricting children's access to depictions of violence. And California's claim that the player participates in the violent action on screen and determines its outcome, is unpersuasive.[12]

It appears that the Supreme Court justices do not, themselves, play these games. Their ruling demonstrates, in any case, how violence is valued in the United States. A game in which lovemaking takes place is problematic; a game in which women are raped then beaten to death is just fine.[13]

Intensive, often brutal encounters are a principal attraction of many of the best-selling digital games, both those usually played solo on a console—like *Grand Theft Auto* and *Call of Duty*—and those played with others on the web, like *World of Warcraft*. With very few exceptions, perhaps most notably Lara Croft in the *Tomb Raider* series, the protagonists of video games are male. In judging the dozens of sophisticated games published each year, the novelty of the weapons and the agility of the player's avatar are focal considerations. The plot is less central to a review than the quality and originality of the game's action. But emphasized both in the advertising of the latest games and in the reactions that follow their distribution is also the persuasiveness of the space of play offered by the game. Video game producers compete in the development of technologies that present the gamer with increasingly illusionistic settings.[14] Indeed, academic complaints are made that too much attention is given to illusionism: "Contemporary video game designers badly need to concentrate on the game idea itself in order to shift the emphasis away from realistic visualization and back to the core topic of the game."[15] But violence and veracity are closely connected: both escalate in the most popular games. An analysis of a single game, *Assassin's Creed,* probes the relationship between violence and verisimilitude. It also suggests that the art and politics of video games, if not their economics, distinguish them from slot machines.

Assassin's Creed

In another decade, Ubisoft's *Assassin's Creed,* once one of the best-known video games in the world, may well be a largely forgotten episode of popular culture. The game, which was technologically cutting edge when it debuted in 2007, may not even be playable, given the rapidity with which hardware and software are developing. Nevertheless, because of its particular use of the past and the virtuosity of its settings, *Assassin's Creed* allows observations about digital architectures, the politics of history, and addiction that should continue to be relevant so long as illusion is part of the immersive persuasion of video games.

Assassin's Creed is pulp fiction played as a third-person-shooter video game.[16] The framing narrative is set in 2012 in the lab of Abstergo Industries, a corporation using its profits to gain control of the world. An evil scientist attempts to extract the memory of supernaturally powerful Solomonic vessels ("Pieces of Eden") from the DNA of his kidnapped victim, Desmond Miles (played by the gamer), the descendant of the man who possessed them at the end of the twelfth century. To discover the mystical objects' location, Desmond is forced relive the role of his ancestor, Altaïr, in the Third Crusade during the crucial year of 1191. Herein lies the core story. Most of the action occurs in the cities of Damascus, Acre, and Jerusalem, and in the hostile, ancient-ruin-filled territory encompassing them (Figure 6.2). In the background, two great historical heroes, the Christian king Richard the Lionheart and the Muslim sultan Salah ad-Din Yusuf ibn Ayyub (Saladin), contend with one another for control of the Holy Land. The foreground is occupied by Altaïr Ibn-La'Ahad/Desmond Miles, the plot's protagonist, and Robert de Sablé, the villain of the story, who contend with one another for control of the minds of the people. Altaïr's character development from petulant, arrogant, and two-dimensional to wise, humble, and two-dimensional is written into the program. The gamer does not control Altaïr's intellect or temper, only his physical movement, his acquisition of weapons, and the progressive refinement of his combat skills. The order of action and its outcome are predetermined; only how efficiently Altaïr progresses through the narrative depends on the gamer.

Altaïr, an Assassin, and Robert de Sablé, Grand Master of the Templars, are representatives of two thoroughly romanticized historical communities. The English word "assassin" is derived from imaginative medieval accounts of the Hashshashin,

Figure 6.2. *Assassin's Creed,* Jerusalem, Altaïr at the Dome of the Rock.

a heretical Shi'a Muslim sect.[17] From the Middle Ages to the present, its members have been represented as expert killers-for-hire. The infamous daring of the Hashshashin was ascribed to the manipulative use of hashish by their leader, the Old Man of the Mountain. The Knights of the Temple, Christianity's first military monastic order, was established in Jerusalem after the city's bloody fall to the crusaders in 1099. Both Muslims and Christians recognized the Templars, along with the Hospitallers, as the Latin Kingdom's most disciplined and ferocious warriors. The order was destroyed by a rapacious king, Philip the Fair, in collusion with a weak and greedy pope, Clement V, on Friday the thirteenth of October in 1307.[18] Mythologized already in the Middle Ages, the Templars have been thoroughly reimagined in modern novels from Sir Walter Scott's *Ivanhoe* to Dan Brown's *Da Vinci Code* and Raymond Khoury's *Last Templar. Assassin's Creed* supplements that tradition of fictionalization. A characteristic attribute of the subgenre of Templar narratives is violence, to which *Assassin's Creed* makes a significant contribution.

The skills that Altaïr acquires are those that allow him more effectively to stalk and kill his victims and escape capture after accomplishing the deed. The dexterities he develops—running, fighting, hiding, leaping, climbing, riding—are in keeping with the skills deployed in the twelfth century, though they are performed with unnatural prowess. Altaïr has an astonishing ability to free-run. He scales structures, including minarets and church towers, with alarming aptitude; he leaps and swings between buildings with awesome agility; he dives from high places into piles of straw with astounding accuracy. The weapons that he procures are also conventional for the twelfth century: fists, swords, daggers, throwing knives. The digitally driven human figures that react to Altaïr—beggars accosting him, guards wearily watching him, bystanders exclaiming on his odd behavior when he climbs buildings, the Templars attacking him—are mechanical in their movement. Their gestures are robotic, not spontaneous; their drapery is brittle, not pliant; their speech is repetitive, not improvised. There are no children. Only in brutal combat does the game image shift to filmic hyperrealism. Blood spurts from the wounds of Altaïr's victims; they writhe in pain before they die.

The excitement of control and conquest is graphically charged. Although killing is the principal action of the game, it is by no means the gamer's only thrill.[19] Tourism is another. The gamer in *Assassin's Creed,* like a Western tourist in the Holy Land, has the apparent freedom to explore the landscape, thereby creating her own, unique, experience.

Patrice Désilets, creative director of *Assassin's Creed,* describes the space of the game as the principal vehicle of the gamer's "freedom":

> Right from the beginning of the conception, thinking about how we would do the next generation of games, it was really important that the player could go anywhere and interact with everything. In *Assassin's Creed* you can experience your freedom in three big cities—Jerusalem, Acre, and Damascus. . . . The way we did our cities was basically to have a lot of blocks already with their own game play. So we have buildings where everything is interactive . . . but we also have other ingredients that the character can interact with that are all architectural elements. So there are beams, poles, merchant stands. . . . They are all ingredients that are historically accurate that are put together. . . . You have freedom of choice. . . . Create your own experience.[20]

"Freedom" here is the false sense of spatial access that gamers, like tourists, savor when their investigation of an alien territory feels authentic. Devices in the game that support travel are not unlike those the tourist depends on—navigational tools (compass, maps, guidebooks, and cheats [Internet hints for navigating difficult tasks]) as well as observation points and major attractions. Exploration is rewarded with little adventures and small treasures. Such freedom is, of course, illusory. Tourists in *Assassin's Creed,* like those in the nondigital Holy Land, are highly restricted in their movements. Despite Désilets's claims for Altaïr's mobility, the game is full of arbitrary restraints. Altaïr cannot climb rocks or trees, though he easily scales the highest tower. Altaïr drowns in a harbor; his sophisticated skill-set does not include swimming. Altaïr has trouble turning in small spaces because of the bulky camera (providing the gamer's viewpoint) that he carries, like a large, invisible backpack, usually behind his left shoulder. Further, Altaïr is initially banned from great swatches of the cities to which he is sent. Those urban areas become accessible to Altaïr only with his promotion. I had to accomplish a number of assassinations before I, as Altaïr, was at liberty to become a virtual tourist. Even then, finding a position from which to make a good screen capture (photograph) almost always involved killing guards. Games, like life, limit a player's autonomy; rules (conventions, laws) restrict freedom. Mastering those constraints may well be a source of satisfaction for both gamer and tourist, but "freedom" is too ideologically burdened to bc that movement's appropriate descriptor.

In addition to movement, visual lures are central to both video game play and tourism. *Assassin's Creed* creates spaces that invite investigation. Indeed, what made it and its several sequels top-selling games between 2007 and 2014 are their effective evocations of space. The two-dimensional screen opens to a three-dimensional interactive arena through which the player moves her avatar. The illusion of space that is essential to the player's immersion in the game depends both on the compelling rendering of volumes and their persuasive staging.

The settings in *Assassin's Creed* are utterly engaging. The human scale and compact complexity of the buildings allow both congested and secluded spaces. There are gardens and fountains. In contrast to the robotic human figures in the game, the buildings are more convincing the more closely they are considered. The photographic skins or "textures" used by the game's creators are beautifully compelling: masonry, sculpture, ceramic tiles, Oriental carpets, stone, wood, and metalwork (Figure 6.3). The topography of *Assassin's Creed* is punctuated with historical monuments, some of them shared with the Holy Land. The Dome of the Rock in Jerusalem is the most successful of these reproductions, perhaps because of the geometric simplicity of its perfection (see Figure 6.2). The Church of the Holy Sepulchre is less convincing, and the Great Mosque of Damascus is less accurate. Famous structures occasionally even appear where they don't belong—the Treasury of Petra as the site of the Ark of the Covenant buried below al-Haram al-Sherif/ Temple Mount in Jerusalem, the sculptures from the ambulatory of St. Sernin in Toulouse on the facade of the Cathedral of Acre, and parts of the Templar's great castle in Tomar, Portugal, compounded with the Assassin's fortress of Masyaf. Historical accuracy is claimed for the setting, just as it is for the context of the plot and its characters.[21] But unlike many of the faux historical buildings in the tourist's world, the bits of archaeological *realia* in *Assassin's Creed* conjure the remote past without pretense to reconstructing it.

The appeal of the setting in *Assassin's Creed* certainly does not depend on its archaeological correctness. Nor is it the result of cinema vérité. The game avoids

Figure 6.3. *Assassin's Creed,* Damascus, Altaïr shopping for a carpet.

both the appearance and the didactic valence of capturing the grittiness of the world. There are remarkably realistic passages, like the birds feeding on human carrion that flap away at Altaïr's approach while the flies on the bodies remain buzzing around their meal. But the game has neither the ethos nor the formal devices of documentary. Similarly, despite the photographic sources of the skins of the game's architecture and objects, its settings avoid the unsettling preoccupation with surface that characterizes the work of the photo-realists of the 1960s, 1970s, and later. The glitz and shimmer of the shop window, the diner, and the pop-culture still-life of photo-realist painting conjure an uncanny nostalgia that remakes America's commodities into human products. *Assassin's Creed* and the paraphernalia necessary to play it certainly participate in a globalized commodity-fetishism, but the game doesn't depict it.

Picturesque

The persuasiveness of the landscape in *Assassin's Creed* inheres not in its realism but in its particular picturesqueness.[22] The modern guidebook for finding and describing historical monuments—a genre invented by John Murray III and Karl Baedeker in the 1830s—was preceded by the modern guidebook for finding and describing the picturesque view.[23] "The picturesque" as a mode of sightseeing in nature was popularized in England by William Gilpin at the end of the eighteenth century.[24] Gilpin provided a paradigm for engaging the aesthetically pleasurable landscape: the surprise and delight of discovery, the identification of the proper view, the recognition and recording of its picturesque parts, the judgment of nature against art, and the final rendering of a memory through the artful translation of the sketch into a painting. Gilpin defined the picturesque in terms of contrasts (rough and smooth), compositional framing, and recession. Engaging objects—ruins, rustics, travelers—rendered with clarity in the foreground, monumental vestiges (preferably of a medieval church or castle) depicted as mass in the middle ground, and, in the background, hazy clouds, hillsides, or mountains bounding the composition (Figure 6.4). Picturesqueness lies in aerial perspective: the distillation of hue close at hand and its dilution far away; the luxuriance of its light and the richness of its shadow in the foreground, the tenderness of both in the distance; the visual fullness of the immediate and emptiness of the remote.[25]

In the nineteenth century, the devices of the picturesque were particularly effective in rendering a foreign view for an audience back home. The picturesque tamed the alien without domesticating it. The familiarity of the mode of presentation allowed the naive viewer to feel comfortable with the image. The picturesque enhanced the pleasure of such witnessing. The exotic vista depicted with lyrical virtuosity in the picturesque manner was very profitably realized by panorama painters and travel artists.[26] The work of the Scottish artist David Roberts exemplifies this once popular means of appropriating "elsewhere." His *Jerusalem from the Mount of Olives* demonstrates his mastery of the picturesque (Figure 6.5). The intricate violence of the foreground with its dramatic diagonals fixing a lonely group of witnesses in the middle ground contrasts with the stable horizontality of the walled city in the background, mixing the sublime with the beautiful. The warm palette of the work is more saturated in the foreground, paling in recession. The contrast between light and shadow decreases with distance.

David Roberts worked as a detail painter in private homes and as a landscapist on public panoramas before establishing himself as a travel artist with a productive trip to Spain.[27] He made his reputation and garnered membership to the Royal Academy by authoring one of the most lavish lithographic art-print collections ever produced: *The Holy Land, Syria, Idumea, Arabia, Egypt, and Nubia.*[28] Roberts's plates were first published between 1840 and 1845 in the form of separate fascicules for subscribers. The collected fascicules comprise a magisterial, three-volume set of 257 folio polychrome prints.

Roberts's lithographs were represented by the artist and his publisher as literal renderings of the Holy Land. Critics corroborated the accuracy of the representations. John Ruskin, the preeminent nineteenth-century authority on art, commented:

Figure 6.4. William Gilpin, *Three Essays,* a contrast of a nonpicturesque (smooth) mountain view with a picturesque (rough or broken) mountain view, facing page 19.

Figure 6.5. David Roberts, *Jerusalem from the Mount of Olives.* From Roberts and Croly, *The Holy Land, Syria, Idumea, Arabia, Egypt, and Nubia,* vol. 1, plate 17. Courtesy of the Nasher Museum of Art, Duke University. Museum purchase with funds provided by Anita and John A. Schwarz III, Mr. and Mrs. Andrew Major, Bobbie and Michael Wilsey, and the Mary Duke Biddle Foundation (1996.1.18).

> It had chanced . . . that David Roberts had brought home and exhibited his sketches in Egypt and the Holy Land. They were the first studies ever made conscientiously by an English painter, not to exhibit his own skill, or make capital out of his subjects, but to give true portraiture of scenes of historical and religious interest. They were faithful and laborious beyond any outlines from nature I had ever seen.[29]

Earlier Western representations of the Holy Land tended to the overly imaginary or the hopelessly familiar. William Finden's *Landscape Illustrations of the Bible: Consisting of Views of the Most Remarkable Places Mentioned in the Old and New Testaments, From Original Sketches Taken on the Spot* of 1836 exaggerated the landscape; Luigi Mayer's *Views in Egypt, Palestine, and Other Parts of the Ottoman Empire from Original Drawings in the Collection of Sir Robert Ainslee* of 1801 imposed Bavaria on Palestine.[30] Of course Roberts also modified the actualities of the scenes that he rendered, aggrandizing the scale of some structures in relation to others and eliminating elements deemed ugly from the environment. But Roberts's distortions were neither theatrically excessive nor culturally condescending; they were, rather, picturesque.

Roberts's picturesqueness depended not just on formal, compositional elements, but on the technology of the relatively new medium in which it was rendered—lithography. Lithography, invented at the very end of the eighteenth century and perfected in the second quarter of the nineteenth century, displaced etching as the most popular means of art reproduction. Etchings are made by scratching or otherwise abrading with tools or with acid the surface of a metal plate. The ridges catch the ink and transfer those un-brush-like marks to the paper into which the plate is pressed. In contrast, the lithographer, working with a brush, applies a gluey substance to a polished stone, much as a painter applies paint to a canvas. The stone is moistened, pigmented, then wiped. The ink, adhering only to the applied adhesive, is then pressed onto paper.[31] The master lithographer's gestures take the same form as those of a painter; his prints look like paintings or drawings. A print's audience tends to elide the intervention of the printmaker and see only the immediacy of the artist's vision. Viewers looking at Roberts's lithographs were reassured of the landscape's accessibility by indexical evidence of the presence of the Western artist within it.

By the end of the nineteenth century, photography superseded lithography as the conventional technology of representing both art and the world. Photography seemed to do away with the artist-interpreter mediating the viewer's experience of the visual object. The photograph's claim to reproduce reality was promptly accepted by its popular audience; the photographer's claim to be an artist was, in contrast, long contested. Postcards and stereographs took over the mass market for images of the Holy Land. But photographs erode agency. They conceal their maker by eliminating his literal touch. They also congeal their subjects: the long exposure times of late nineteenth- and early twentieth-century photographs precluded movement. The early views of Jerusalem are starkly inanimate, a lack for a Western audience who understands it as sublimely vital.[32] The lifelessness of the scene and the apparent absence of the artist render the Holy Land less rather than more accessible.

David Roberts's renderings were broadly distributed in the nineteenth century. The ostensible objectivity of *The Holy Land*'s lithographic prints, their compelling artistry, and their relative affordability contributed to the remarkable popularity of the collection. Multiple editions of these prints of the Holy Land, both legitimate and pirated, circulated to an unprecedentedly large European and American audience.[33] They became *the* models for the representation of the Holy Land in illustrated bibles and travel books. After a hiatus of interest in Roberts's prints, they are again highly marketable. They now adorn tourist agencies' promotional pamphlets and decorate the walls of hotels in the Middle East. Indeed, Roberts's lithographic series, as I have argued elsewhere, has proved to be the most pervasive and enduring set of images of the Middle East circulated in the West.[34] *Assassin's Creed* participates fully in Robertson's visual legacy. The juxtaposition of a screen shot of Altaïr outside Damascus with details from Roberts's *Sebaste, Ancient Samaria* and his *Jerusalem from the Mount of Olives* suggests that these images shared the inheritance of the picturesque (see Plate 5). The sweet ochres of the distant city with its romantic skyline, its delicately wrought volumes given substance by the shadows cast by imaginary clouds—in the worlds of Roberts's prints and Altaïr's game it seems always to be late afternoon. The picturesque is alive and well in *Assassin's Creed.*

Not only did Roberts's prints inform the Western imaginary of the Middle East, but that imaginary left a lasting impression on the Holy Land. During the British Mandate in Palestine, for example, Jerusalem was remodeled to conform to the Western tourist's picturesque expectations of the Holy City: its walls were restored, a framing green space imposed, and building codes imposed to limit the use of modern building materials.[35] The picturesque is implicated in imperialism. The question remains, does the picturesque do the same kind of conservative political work in a video game that it did for the empire? I would argue that although *Assassin's Creed* embraces the devices of the picturesque, the mode does very different work for the gamer than it did for the nineteenth-century Western viewer. In *Assassin's Creed,* Altaïr, not the painter's brushstroke, is the index of the gamer's presence in the world. These landscapes are experienced not through identification with the Western painter but with the body of a heretical Muslim avatar. The Middle Ages is familiar gaming territory. From *Dungeons and Dragons* to *Medieval II: Total War* and *World of Warcraft,* neomedievalism occupies a remarkably large territory in the digital realm. More narrowly, the crusades have attracted game developers—Paradox Interactive's *Crusader Kings* and Starbreeze AB's *Knights of the Temple: Infernal Crusade,* for example. But the explicit and sympathetic treatment of ethnicity in *Assassin's Creed* is unusual. Among the most popular medieval-revival video games, it seems to be alone in having an explicitly Muslim, albeit heretical, protagonist.

The Western gamer's new Eastern ethnicity, imposed by the narrative, is reinforced by its settings. The devices of the picturesque are deployed not to mask cultural difference, but to code and characterize it. The game's palette and musical score track ethnic difference (see Plate 6). The mood of play changes from city to city. Damascus, the richest and most Muslim of the urban centers, is golden—its hues are warm and its settings lavish. Its souk is well stocked; its structures are elaborate and beautifully ornamented. Its architectural centerpiece is the Great Mosque, rendered with an imaginary verisimilitude complete with opulent early eighth-century Byzantine mosaics. Minarets and domes create the city's filigree skyline. Acre, the poorest and most Christian of the venues, is rendered in desaturated blues. Smoking ruins and dead bodies, reminders of its recent capture by the crusaders, pollute the city. The dominant motif of the distant view is the steeple: the great cathedral, with its unfinished facade, commands the jagged skyline. There are more beggars in Acre than elsewhere. Jerusalem, with its mixed Christian/Muslim population, is rendered in between the golds of Damascus and blues of Acre—in green tones. In the game, as in history, Jerusalem has competing centers of the sacred: al-Haram al-Sherif, with the magnificent Dome of the Rock, and the Church of the Holy Sepulchre (see Figure 6.2 and Plate 6).

Differences in class as well as culture are articulated in building materials and sculptural details. From the decaying slums of Acre to the mosaicked palaces of Damascus, neighborhoods in each city are identified by their relative wealth. Even more clearly, class and culture are recorded in the visages, dress, and voice of the cities' populations—the French, Italian, German and (largely) English speaking Christians of Acre look and sound very different from the Arabic and (largely) English speakers of Jerusalem and Damascus. A similar concern for ethnic diversity is also recorded in Jesper Kyd's soundtrack for the game, which won the ELAN (Electronic Arts and Animation) award for the "Best Video Game Soundtrack" in 2008. In an interview, Kyd describes his efforts to render acoustically the communities of the different cities of the game:

> The team wanted the sci-fi element . . . mixed into a historical score. . . . I also mixed in primal, meditative and deeply spiritual elements. . . . We recorded the choir at the Bastyr [University] Chapel in Seattle. All the male and female vocals, chants, Middle Eastern prayers, percussion and ethnic instruments were recorded live with Hollywood players . . . with a lot of performers from the Middle East.
>
> [Each city in the game has its own musical character.] Acre is a Christian city with a western style instrumentation palette . . . so I added extra elements such as piano, harp, acoustic guitar and violins to keep the score fresh, multi-layered. . . . Here the musical tone is the most tragic because Acre endured a massive battle and is in ruins.
>
> Damascus is the proudest of the cities and a Muslim stronghold that had never been overtaken. So the music here uses more traditional Middle Eastern arrangements from this time period and a slightly heroic tone. I recorded Muslim male vocals, whispering noises, chanting and prayers; ethnic instruments such as the

> Ud (a middle-eastern guitar), Ney flute, mizmar (snake charmer / reed-based instrument), Mijwiz, Buzuq (duduk), other live hand percussion and traditional Egyptian instruments.
>
> For Jerusalem, I mixed melodic elements from both Damascus and Acre to represent the clash of the two religions. The overall tone is deeply moving, emotional and spiritual by employing a lot of large choir music and solo Gregorian priest chanting and whispering references from the Bible recorded in Latin. To represent the strong Western influences of the Holy City I also mixed acoustic guitar, orchestra strings as well as solo female performances including Arabic, Bulgarian and other western style male and female vocals.[36]

The audio and visual refinements of *Assassin's Creed* provide its multicultural subtext.[37] This multicultural setting is not a politically correct, unbiased one. Jews have no presence in the narrative or, with the exception of an ahistorically monumental synagogue in Jerusalem, in the urban setting. The West, by the territories it occupies as well as in the actions of its population, is represented as more brutal and avaricious than its Islamic enemies. In *Assassin's Creed,* both Robert de Sablé and Altaïr work for "peace" in the Holy Land. The Westerner seeks to impose a kind of ur-fascism on the region by finding and controlling magical "Pieces of Eden" that would give the Templars mind-numbing power over the population. Altaïr works for peace through the elimination of evil men who feed upon the war—the slavers, arms-dealers, treacherous governors, and book-burners of whatever religious creed. All of Altaïr's victims are also part of the Templar conspiracy. He is penalized by the game if he kills an innocent civilian.

Assassin's Creed was developed for a French company by the largely Canadian staff of their Montreal office; recording was done with native Arabic speakers in Los Angeles. The game's message is not that of Christian and Western triumphalism but rather rational skepticism. The disclaimer that appears at the opening of the game is the epigraph of this chapter. It alerts the player to the game's politics. The notice, "Inspired by historical events and characters," obviously refers to the chronicle of the Third Crusade and particularly to the assassination targets, all historical figures who died at the time that the story takes place.[38] But "inspired by historical events and characters" might also be taken to refer to the Iraq War and George Bush. The narrative concentration on the elimination of warmongers as well as the unprecedented cultural partiality with which the game presents its Muslim sites and actors reveals something of the international community's horror at Bush's invasion of Iraq and its deadly aftermath. Video games, like novels or films, and in contrast to slot machines, may bear powerful political messages.[39] At least in the case of *Assassin's Creed,* the spaces of the game are agents of ideology.

Warcrack and SLunkie

Obsessive video gaming was not included as a separate addiction disorder in the fifth edition of the American Psychiatric Association's canonical code book, the *Diagnostic and Statistical Manual for Mental Disorders* (*DSM-V*); efforts to introduce it into the latest edition proved unsuccessful.[40] Nevertheless, there is evidence that those fixated on computer play ruin their real lives in their passionate embrace of their virtual ones. Extended frenetic play has led to child neglect, cardiac arrest, and death.[41] In gaming, as in gambling, the visual may be a particularly powerful source of an addict's cues.[42] The emergence and spread of this addiction coincides with the development of interactive Internet play. Certainly two extremely popular Internet sites—the massively multiplayer online role-playing game (MMORPG) *World of Warcraft* and the virtual world of *Second Life*—have both generated web-based groups of self-identified addicts, most notably wowdetox.com and sl-addiction.com. In a poll on sl-addiction, 36 percent of those responding indicated that they spent between four and six hours a day in *Second Life*; 32 percent admitted to more than eight hours a day.[43] *Second Life* is the subject of a documentary film about four individuals whose obsessive engagement with the game ruined their real lives; addicts of both games have published autobiographical accounts of their affliction.[44] *World of Warcraft* and *Second Life* both, therefore, offer documentation for a critical investigation of the distinct contributions made by architectonics to the addictive potential of Internet play.

World of Warcraft is the most populated and probably the most profitable MMORPG presently in operation.[45] It reportedly has twelve million active players. On January 10, 2011, *World of Warcraft*'s producer, Blizzard Entertainment, Inc., announced that the third expansion of the game sold a record-breaking 4.7 million copies in the first month of its release. The game is described without literary pretense on its website:

> Azeroth is a world of swords and sorcery. Its lands are home to a vast number of races and cultures, led by kings, chieftains, lords, ladies, archdruids, and everything in between. . . . Among all these different kingdoms, cultures, tribes, and territories, two major power blocs are locked in a struggle for dominance. . . . On one side is the noble Alliance, which comprises the valiant humans, the stalwart dwarves, the ingenious gnomes, the spiritual night elves, the mystical draenei, and the bestial worgen; on the other side is the mighty Horde, made up of the battle-hardened orcs, the cunning trolls, the hulking tauren, the cursed Forsaken, the extravagant blood elves, and the devious goblins. . . . In World of Warcraft, you play the role of a fantasy hero. Over the course of his or her life, your character will brave thousands of quests,

> learn new and powerful abilities, amass (and likely spend) vast fortunes of gold, and find hundreds of powerful weapons, enchanted rings, artifacts, suits of armor, and more. . . . The core gameplay of World of Warcraft revolves around fighting monsters and completing quests. . . . You will be able to deal with most monsters you encounter by yourself, but the true challenges and the big payoffs await in the world's many dungeons and raids, which can only be conquered by groups of heroes working together as a team.[46]

World of Warcraft is about acquiring wealth through team/gang violence.

Wealth and violence are not limited to in-game play. The game provides an annual revenue of over $4 billion to its corporate producer, Activision Blizzard. The game is more brutally mined by less regulated companies.

> Last year, nearly $2 billion in virtual currency was traded in China, according to the China Internet Network Information Center. Some experts say they believe there is a much larger underground economy in the virtual world. Some smaller gaming companies have even set up what are called virtual sweatshops, cramped quarters where young people play online games to earn credits that the companies then sell at a profit to overseas customers in Taiwan, South Korea and even the United States. This practice is popularly known in the online gaming community as gold farming.[47]

Players with real world money buy digital enhancements and possessions. The selling of virtual weapons, armor, and avatars has been banned from eBay, but they are still available to anyone with a credit card through less carefully monitored sites.

Wealth and violence certainly have their attractions. *World of Warcraft* offers them in a particularly seductive guise—a magical medievalized world familiar from C. S. Lewis's *Chronicles of Narnia*, J. R. R. Tolkien's *Lord of the Rings*, and J. K. Rowling's *Harry Potter* series. It is gorgeous, with Disney-quality rendering, color, and imagination, if not Disney-quality animation. The settings of play, from idyllic Edens through underwater lost cities to postapocalyptic wastelands, and architectures of adventure, including castles, dungeons, and sanctuaries, are lavishly rendered. The monsters and humanoids, fairies and dwarfs that occupy those spaces, are fabulously detailed and arrayed. Even brute ugliness is beautiful. Eye-cocaine. A description by a player provides a sense of the various delights offered by the game's landscape:

> Alterac Valley is a big battleground with various buildings and constructions that you can choose to conquer or skip, depending on your strategy. The Alliance put up a good fight in one of their advanced bunkers and it took us numerous attempts to finally capture it. The fights were fierce and all classes of combatants were involved. I

> died several times myself along the way, but since the graveyard was nearby, I was able to come back and continue the fight. Finally, we were done, and when the flag eventually converted to our color, I emerged from the bunker, still pumped with adrenaline and ready to move on to the next target, but the landscape outside just stopped me in my track. The moon was rising behind the hills and a pond way down below the valley was reflecting its silvery rays. The entire scenery looked so peaceful and it contrasted so starkly with the intense scrimmage I was just submitted to that I paused and took this picture [Figure 6.6]. The two blue banners in the distance are set on the Alliance fortress, which is our next goal. . . . Say what you want about *World of Warcraft*, but I have yet to come across a game that, one year and a half after I started playing it, is still making me live such intense and gratifying moments.[48]

In the player's description, Alterac Valley is an arena for battle that readily converts into a picture postcard. The beautiful, here rendered in a gift-and-barter medievalizing habitat, exonerates violence. Historical fantasy and aesthetics collude to

Figure 6.6. *World of Warcraft*, Alterac Valley. From Beust. "Order and Chaos in Alterac Valley."

distance the brutality of war while making its pleasures available. The satisfaction that *World of Warcraft* and games like it provide may be dangerous, as Nick Dyer-Witheford and Greig de Peuter speculate.

> [Among the genres of video games] the neomedieval role-playing fantasy remains dominant: if one wants to get away from things, where better than an imaginary of precapitalist folklore? How ironic, then, that these worlds become sites where primitive and futuristic accumulation now meet on a new frontier of profit. . . . [The conventional concern is that gamers will] abandon quotidian actuality to addictively sojourn in virtual fantasy. Perhaps so; but is this more disturbing than the converse possibility: that virtualities such as World of Warcraft will increasingly *coincide* with the actuality of Empire's biopolitical regime—a game of chimeras, populated by cyborgs, governed by capital?[49]

Like cyberpunk novels such as *City Come a Walkin'* and *Snowcrash,* the game may offer a preview of the dystopic future as well as an escape from a problematic present.

Judging from the accounts of *World of Warcraft* addicts, dependence is driven by the camaraderie of battle and by the progressive acquisition of wealth and status. Contributing to the game's power over the player is also its endlessness. *World of Warcraft,* like a slot machine and unlike *Assassin's Creed,* has no conclusion. Though the lavish settings of the game world are carefully analyzed in assessments of the game and its expansions, *World of Warcraft*'s visual properties are rarely ascribed an important role in addiction. This lack of reference by addicts to the pictorial conditions of the game is perhaps explained by the passivity of its habitats. Gamers can't modify their environments. Game play in *World of Warcraft* is creatively social; the setting is not. The illusionistic, three-dimensional world of *World of Warcraft* and the robots and avatars that populate it are crafted by the corporation, not by their users. Unconsciously the lush landscapes of the game may well act initially as lures and later as cues for the addict, but their agency in immersion is difficult to track. In *Second Life,* in contrast to *World of Warcraft,* addicts are more aware of the fatal attractions of the game's architectonics.

Second Life

Corporations control the world; police and postal services are privatized; the U.S. federal government is reduced to a fascistic bureaucracy, having ceded its governmental obligations and resources to private firms. The Mafia, with their emphasis on family values, are the good guys; the CIA, now the CIC (the Central Intelligence

Corporation of Langley, Virginia), are the bad guys. Computer code is power. The elite of this dystopian real world meet in a more entertaining virtual one, the Metaverse. Its main artery is eerily similar to the Las Vegas Strip.

> Hiro is approaching the Street. It is the Broadway, the Champs Élysées of the Metaverse. It is the brilliantly lit boulevard that can be seen, miniaturized and backward reflected in the lenses of his goggles. It does not really exist. But right now, millions of people are walking up and down it. . . .
>
> Like any place in Reality, the Street is subject to development. Developers can build their own small streets feeding off of the main one. They can build buildings, parks, signs, as well as things that do not exist in Reality, such as vast hovering overhead light shows, special neighborhoods where the rules of three-dimensional spacetime are ignored, and free-combat zones where people can go to hunt and kill each other. . . . In order to place these things on the Street, they have had to get approval from the Global Multimedia Protocol Group, have had to buy frontage on the Street, get zoning approval, obtain permits, bribe inspectors, the whole bit. . . . Put a sign or a building on the Street and the hundred million richest, hippest, best-connected people on earth will see it every day of their lives. It is a hundred meters wide, with a narrow monorail track running down the middle. The monorail is a free piece of public utility software that enables users to change their location on the Street rapidly and smoothly. A lot of people just ride back and forth on it, looking at the sights. . . .
>
> Your avatar can look any way you want it to, up to the limitations of your equipment. If you're ugly, you can make your avatar beautiful. . . . You can look like a gorilla or a dragon or a giant talking penis in the Metaverse. Spend five minutes walking down the Street and you will see all of these. . . . [Available at Walmart are cheap, ready-made avatars including two, Brandy and Clint, reminiscent of the Barbie and Ken dolls of the twentieth century. Brandy's purchaser can choose one of] three breast sizes: improbable, impossible, and ludicrous. Brandy has a limited repertoire of facial expressions: cute and pouty; cute and sultry; perky and interested; smiling and receptive; cute and spacy. Her eyelashes are half an inch long, and the software is so cheap that they are rendered as solid ebony chips. When a Brandy flutters her eyelashes, you can almost feel the breeze.[50]

The vicious, postcorporatist United States described by Neal Stephenson in his cyberpunk novel *Snow Crash* has not yet been fully realized. In contrast, the digital entertainment world imagined by Stephenson is operational. Phillip Rosedale, inspired by *Snow Crash,* developed a Web version of the Metaverse.[51] *Second Life,* a virtual space that went online in June 2003, is sustained by Linden Labs, a company based in San Francisco. In 2011, *Second Life* had a digital land mass similar in size to that of the Judean Desert, about 775 square miles, produced and stored in several thousand servers. But *Second Life* has a much larger population than its arid equivalent: over twenty million registered residents, made manifest in "uniquely named" avatars, occupy this territory. Each avatar enjoys limited citizens' rights including ownership, movement, and access to the Linden-dollar economy.

Second Life is an adult playground: not a game, but a space of creative play, an alternative social world.[52] In some ways that social world parallels real life. *Second Life* citizens are no better or worse than those in real life. Of course, avatars may act differently than their handlers do in real life. After all, players come to the digital world with different forms and degrees of commitment.[53] Some avatars do in *Second Life* that which their handlers would like to do in real life but don't dare. Like humans, avatars are generous, caring, thoughtful, smart, selfish, nasty, petty, and stupid. Prevarication and misrepresentation are commonplace in *Second Life,* just as they are in the real world. Most players are in-world for entertainment (e.g., live music performances, soft porn, shopping, art exhibitions) or other forms of personal gratification (e.g., creating objects, practicing religion, exploring, attending discussion groups, book clubs, and poetry gatherings). Some enroll for educational purposes (teachers, students, and researchers, particularly anthropologists and psychologists, but also art historians and doctors).[54] Others (griefers) seem to have joined just to make the lives of other users miserable. A very few are in-world to make a real-world living (e.g., as builders, land speculators, skin-makers [skins = avatars' bodies], fashion designers, police). As in both the real world and video games there is violence in *Second Life.* I've witnessed evangelicals burning books and been told of buildings destroyed by griefers.[55] My avatar, Benevolent String, has been killed three times: shot twice while photographing in the Favela and once eaten by a shark while swimming in waters signposted as dangerous. In *Second Life* as in both the real world and games like *World of Warcraft,* there is money as well as violence. Lindens can be converted into real world currencies.[56]

Despite the possibility of wealth and tumult in *Second Life,* play is not, for the majority of its citizens, *about* either accruing riches or pursuing power. The social world of *Second Life* is quite different than that of real life in other ways as well. Most fundamentally, the social hierarchy in *Second Life* is much flatter than in real life. That is not to claim that all players in *Second Life* are equal, either economically or socially. *Second Life* has a land-based economy.[57] Property leasing sustains Linden Labs. As in real life, without access to land, inhabitants have no place to display their buildings and goods. There are rich land barons and property speculators in *Second Life,* but wealth is much more evenly distributed there than in the United States and status is less directly tied to it.[58] A player's prestige depends more on her cultural capital (her communication and building skills) than on her economic capital (how many Linden dollars are in her account). For those with access to computers, admission to *Second Life* is free. Experience, not class, determines a player's social location and mobility. A limited selection of basic avatars, like Stephenson's Brandy and Clint, are provided gratis to new users, along with the tools to modify them. "Newbies," or unskilled neophytes, are obvious to older inhabitants from their cloned appearance and lack of grace. Newbies may well understand themselves as disadvantaged. But the condition of newbie-ness is too ephemeral to be a meaningful signifier of "class." With the exception of those regions coded for nudity and sexual activity, which can be accessed only by citizens verified as adults by on-file credit card information, venues are not closed to them. Older residents, with very few exceptions, are sympathetic and helpful, not aloof and exclusionary. Most fundamentally, after ten to twenty hours of experience newbies metamorphose into individuated and coordinated avatars. Avatars can acquire the devices to move and dress with relative sophistication simply by looking carefully through the many freebies that are offered in-world. It is possible to have a good time in *Second Life* independent of money and power.

In addition to being relatively more egalitarian (if less democratic) than the real world, *Second Life* cultivates greater creativity among its inhabitants. Users first exercise their imaginations on their avatars. Though head covering is required in some regions and nudity in others, self-representation in most places in *Second Life* is unrestricted. Almost all but very short-term visitors to *Second Life* remodel the standard avatars they chose at the time of their admission. There are avatar animals, robots, and mythical creatures, as well as an elaborate assortment of humanoids (Figure 6.7).[59] As in the Metaverse, avatars in *Second Life* tend to look more beautiful, more handsome, more outrageous than folks you meet in the real world. All these embodiments are projections of their makers' sense of themselves. I attempted to mirror myself in Benevolent: she wears jeans and a leather jacket; she is skinny and has short gray hair; she needs glasses. But significant breast reduction was beyond my skill level, and wrinkles are nowhere to be found. It is harder to judge by appearances in *Second Life* than in real life.

If creative work begins with avatars, it certainly doesn't end there. In contrast to *World of Warcraft* or *Assassin's Creed,* the contents of *Second Life*—its hills, lakes, trees, animals, birds, houses, shops, cities, slums, garbage dumps—are produced by its inhabitants. Linden Labs creates the land parcels (sims) and the water that surrounds them; it also designed Welcome Island, the landing site for new avatars. The world's citizens have created most of the rest of this extraordinarily rich environment. Admission into the world comes with prims (basic three-dimensional, modifiable blocks) and textures (photographic skins that surface the prims) from

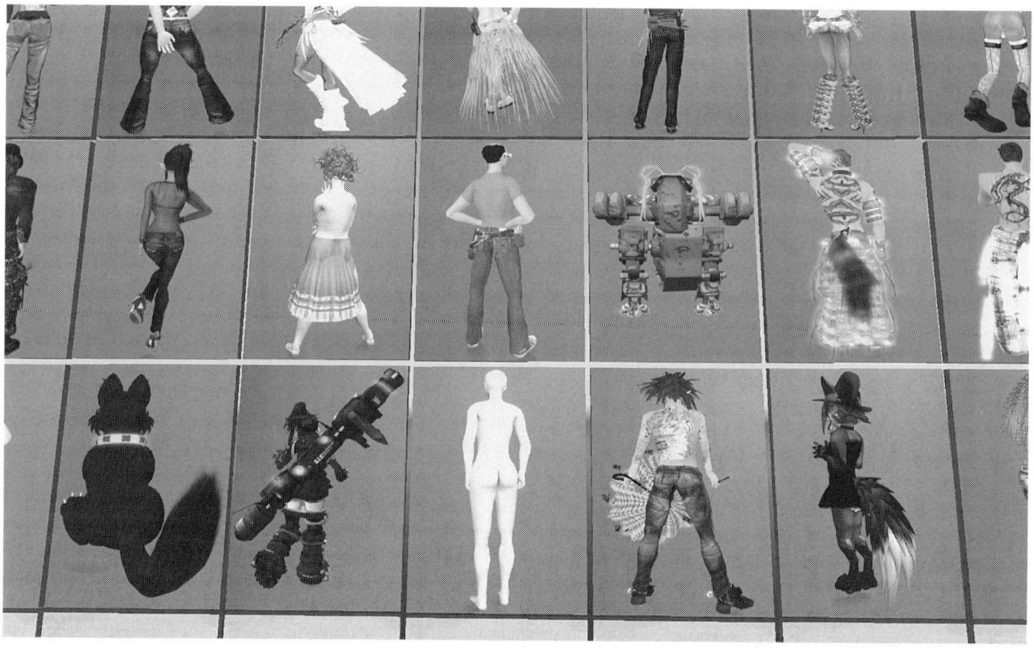

Figure 6.7. *Second Life,* Gracie Kendal's Gallery, detail of the exhibition of the artist's project "1000 Avatars" (Coyote, 118.172.1430).

which the world is built. It also provides the tools by which these construction materials can be creatively manipulated. Free classes for basic and advanced design and construction of objects and buildings are offered at numerous sites. The persistent display of things in-world, unless they are small enough to be attached to an avatar, depends on access to land—whether rented, owned, or gifted. But avatars can make anything from jewelry to palaces in free sandboxes found throughout the world and store them in their inventories for use or exchange at any later time. If commodities are fungible, as defined in the Introduction, they are necessarily anonymous. The real world is filled with commodities. From the hamburgers that we eat to the beds that we sleep on, we know the histories of very few of the many things in our lives. In contrast, there are no commodities in this technical sense in *Second Life,* only works. Although they are utterly reproducible, objects in-world are never anonymous. In contrast to most things in the real world, products in the virtual world have an easily traceable history. Players can click on any entity they encounter to discover who crafted it and who now owns it. Although economic interactions in *Second Life* appear to be similar to those of the contemporary globalized economy—from shopping malls and real estate offices to wedding chapels and divorce lawyers—they also reinvent premodern economic modalities. In *Second*

Life, as in the Middle Ages, most inhabitants know who made the chair they sit on and the shirt that they wear. Similarly, the gift economy is much greater in *Second Life* than in real life. Residents can make objects for sale or for gifting without paying taxes. Avatars are in general more generous than their handlers.

Freed not only from economic and material restraints, but also from the practical responsibilities of building codes, many *Second Life* buildings, like many of its avatars, are delightfully unusual. Gifted architects exhibit their imagination in fanciful constructions that exploit *Second Life*'s brilliant palette and lack of gravity (Figure 6.8).[60] All construction in *Second Life* is purely aesthetic, in the sense in which Ruskin uses the word: "The term 'æsthesis' properly signifies mere sensual perception of the outward qualities and necessary effects of bodies."[61] Buildings in digital environments are not restrained by weight-bearing technologies. Their roofs do not leak and their foundations do not subside. They do not decay. They are destroyed without creating waste. Old forms may be readily exchanged for new ones. In their fugitive insubstantiality, *Second Life* buildings behave more like fashionable real-life clothing rather than real-life structures. *Second Life* buildings present no primordial presence in the landscape; the nooks and crannies of residue memory are evanescent. The sadness at the loss of a comforting space may not be as great in *Second Life* as it is in real life, but it is more often encountered.

Figure 6.8. *Second Life,* opening of the Guggenheim Museum in the Frank Lloyd Wright Virtual Museum (Usonia, 109.80.21).

Although *Second Life* architecture is certainly distinct from real-life architecture, the buildings of both worlds share important properties. As in real life, in-world buildings have authority. Large compounds and big buildings imply wealth in the immersive world, just as they do in the physical one. Built space in both worlds also defines function—casinos, art galleries, churches—and shapes communities. Further, architectures in immersive worlds, like those in real life, reveal a great deal about their makers. The form that a patron gives to her building is as much an expression of her interests, peculiarities, and understanding of the world as the figuration that she gives to her avatar. Finally, virtual structures, like material ones, may well act as agents in their environments. Buildings manipulate the movement of their users and condition not only their actions but also their thinking, often without their subjects' conscious realization. Indeed, the ways in which architecture models behavior may be even more obvious and demonstrable in *Second Life* than in real life. It may be claimed that structures modeled in *Second Life* model the lives of their users not only in *Second Life* but also in the real world.

Some modeling in *Second Life* is conventional. Many users provide themselves with the semblance of residences that they wish that they possessed in real life—a castle in the mountains, a bungalow in a rural village, a small domed cubicle of Jerusalem stone with a Turkish carpet, an espresso machine, and a sea view. Others exercise *Second Life*'s modeling capacity for the reproduction of the buildings that they love in real life. For two years, I took students to the Frank Lloyd Wright Virtual Museum, where talented *Second Life* architects had reconstructed several of Wright's most famous houses, as well as a virtual Guggenheim Museum (see Figure 6.8). The spatial relations of buildings like the Robbie House and Falling Water are difficult to understand from plans and images. Students more readily grasped the interlocking volumes of these complex homes from virtual explorations of their interiors. The Frank Lloyd Wright Virtual Museum was a nonprofit group in *Second Life* that raised funds for land rent and other expenses by having parties on the premises for group members, not unlike museums in real life. Unfortunately, the site was shut down for copyright infringement by the real life Frank Lloyd Wright Foundation.

Hated as well as loved buildings are found in-world. Two versions of the Dome of the Rock exist in *Second Life* at the time of writing. One, at Ummah of Noor, is prominently positioned and carefully crafted. Its *Second Life* architect, Ahmeed Loire, built it from a love of the building and for its symbolic significance to Islam. The other, at SL Israel (Israel, 119.69.26), is crudely rendered and hidden by an enclosing wall (Figure 6.9). It was constructed by the Israel Department of Tourism as one of a number of iconic destinations in Israel, including the Dead Sea (where a visiting avatar can float above the water and have a mud bath), the Church of the Holy Sepulchre, and Tel Aviv. My avatar had the following conversation with the taxi driver I met at the landing point:

BENEVOLENT: Are you a regular taxi driver?
YONATAN: Just today. lol [lots of laughs]
BENEVOLENT: Thanks for the ride.
YONATAN: You are welcome.
BENEVOLENT: What is there to see here? I'm just a tourist.
YONATAN: Well, it is like a puzzle of the big sites in Israel.
BENEVOLENT: Which is your favorite?
YONATAN: I think the underwater observatory. And nuking the temple mount [Dome of the Rock]. But that is another subject. lol
BENEVOLENT STRING: ? But the Temple Mount is so beautiful.
YONATAN: It is political like everything in life.
BENEVOLENT: But since everything is political, why destroy that which is most beautiful?
YONATAN: To build something even more beautiful of course . . . a new temple. . . . I tell you its in planning for a long time now.

Figure 6.9. *Second Life,* Comparison of the Dome of the Rock constructed by Ahmeed Loire, exterior and interior (Oases, 94.109.40) with the Dome of the Rock constructed by the Israel Ministry of Tourism, exterior and interior (Israel, 119.69.26).

BENEVOLENT: I don't think that I have ever been somewhere more beautiful than the Temple Mount.
YONATAN: That's why I say I am all for redecorating lol.[62]

As in real life, buildings in *Second Life* are political agents. As in real life, most buildings in-world work subtly to condition the beliefs of their makers and behaviors of their users.[63] Evidence of such spatial persuasion is provided by a comparison of two complexes—one Republican and the other Democratic—constructed to serve as campaign settings for the 2008 U.S. presidential election. The "Unofficial Obama Headquarters" was typical of the sites devoted to Barak Obama's campaign (Figure 6.10). The structure was located on an island between a wind farm and research offices. The size of a supermarket, this two-storied hypermodernist building was all virtual steel, glass, and plastic. Emphasis was on the periphery of the interior of the structure: high-tech devices in the form of wall plaques and computer consoles framed the space. These information instruments offered direct Internet access to voter registration, volunteer opportunities, and the candidate's position papers. The cool, gray space was barely furnished. The few aluminum benches in the building presented no attractive alternative to studying the data provided. Indeed nothing in the venue suggested social interaction—there was no coffee bar, no overstuffed sofas. The space was empty of things; it was also empty of avatars. The one visitor that I encountered was self-identified as a non–U.S. citizen.

In contrast to the emptiness of Democratic venues, Republican sites in *Second Life* were full. Characteristic was "The Straight Talk Café: John McCain and Sarah Palin for America" (see Figure 6.10). The point of entry for avatars teleporting to the site was a gazebo at the center of a town square. The square was elaborated with patriotic monuments including an equestrian statue of Theodore Roosevelt, a series of relief portraits of the American astronauts framing an American flag, and a model of the Wright brothers' first airplane. On a hill above the square was the Washington Monument adorned with bronze plaques with American battle scenes from World Wars I and II, the Korean War, the Vietnam War, the Gulf War, and the "Iraqi" War. The architecture framing the central square was classicizing. Establishing the axis were monumental buildings with colonnaded, pedimented porches. One of these buildings was the Straight Talk Café, a Georgian structure, its interior wood-paneled and furnished as a meeting place with a bar and comfortable couches as well as informational materials on McCain and negative posters of Obama. The Straight Talk Café site acted like a town square from a nostalgically remembered United States of the 1950s or from Main Street in Disney World.[64] The site was by far the most popular 2008 campaign venue in *Second Life* that I experienced. It seemed to attract as many Democrats as Republicans. Debate was

Figure 6.10. *Second Life*, "Unofficial Obama Headquarters" (Silicon Island, 70.182.26) and "The Straight Talk Café: John McCain and Sarah Palin for America" (Sagamore, 166.152.31).

lively and arguments were heated, but for the most part remarkably civil. Volunteer security avatars were always present, but I never witnessed an eviction. Though continuously modified, the site remained in place through 2011.[65]

The digital environments of the Republicans and Democrats in *Second Life* uncannily resembled their political campaigns in real life. The Democrats urged change, exploiting new media as a means of conveying their message. Correspondingly, the major Democratic sites in *Second Life* tended to be digitally articulated either as modern or as vernacular spaces without historical reference. Venues were typically open, nonhierarchical, and directionless. Technology had a dominant presence. Communication was primarily textual—political positions had to be read by the visitor, not intuited. The sites presumed a coolly rational clientele. Mechanically accessed messages were largely positive, devoted principally to describing the presidential candidate's positions. The buildings appeared even during the campaign period to be temporary or only temporarily political. All of the locations were didactic and programmatically a little dull. They were also all minimally inhabited. The Democratic sites in *Second Life* were empty and unpoliced. They were provisional, abstract spaces designed for the purpose of disseminating ideas and information. The only social engagement that they promoted occurred elsewhere—in real-life political activism. All the Democratic sites disappeared after the election. They were nomadic spaces.

In contrast to the Democrats' focus on change, the Republican campaign emphasized the renewal of traditional values. The architecture of their campaign venues corporealized those values through familiar and reassuring forms. Republican complexes tended to be established in stable *Second Life* communities. The human scale and conventional appearance of buildings were given much greater emphasis. The style of choice in the two major Republican sites was classical. Classicizing architectural forms were, from the nineteenth century through the early twentieth century, associated with the gravitas of conservative institutions that represented political, cultural, or economic authority: legislatures, courthouses, museums, banks. Classicizing principles establish an authoritative order: bilateral symmetry contributes to a clear articulation of hierarchy; reference to the Greek and Roman past lend that symmetry the weighty sanction of revered tradition. These spatial practices were put to use in the Republican sites.

Though textual materials were certainly available at Republican sites, communication was image oriented. Ideas were visually conveyed by monuments and pictures: great events and great men. The sites appealed to the patriotic through reference to the illustrious national past. Attacks on the opposition were much more prominent; polemical violence was greater. Surveillance was more extensive. The Republican locations tended toward the iconic and dogmatic. The labor involved in the planning and construction of these sites was apparent. The producer's dedication to architecture was complemented by a devotion to programming. The Republican sites were coded by their makers to act effectively not in real life but in *Second Life.* Discussions and lectures were organized and advertised. There were, in addition, beach parties, dances, and conversations that attracted avatars of different political persuasions. This commitment to the immediacy of avatar interaction was instantiated in the sites' settings. They were less boring than the Democratic venues. The end of the campaign affected the discourse in the Republican sites, which generally shifted from civil contention to uncivil, occasionally racist, invective, but it did not immediately affect their settings. The real-life griefers on talk shows and in Washington, D.C., infected the political discourse in *Second Life.* Many of the Republican sites remained in place after the election.

The Republican and Democratic 2008 campaign sites in *Second Life* suggest how virtual architecture might both embody and affect its users' understanding of the world and how they act within it. They also describe the possibilities and limitations of considering *Second Life* as a site for productive political interchange. Immersive worlds, in their virtual place-making, present spatial possibilities for the production of a public sphere unavailable to other web-based forums—political blogs, Facebook, Twitter. Immersive worlds provide architecturally articulated spaces that attract individuals and sustain their communal interaction.[66] These venues, by their spatial order and programming, also affect the discourses that they accommodate. The recognition of the force of space-shaping in the production of politics might make a contribution to the transparency of a democracy. The spatial lessons offered by *Second Life* in 2008 were not repeated in 2012. There was an Obama Unofficial Headquarters, empty of machines as well as avatars. The site of the Republican "Straight Talk Café" is now a vacant lot labeled "Land Foreclosed: GOPs didn't pay their bill." *Second Life,* which ended its policy of educational subsidies in 2010, is not the place it used to be. Nevertheless, the potential that it presented for an immersive public sphere might usefully be remembered.

Agents of Immersion

Four vehicles of obsessive behavior have been considered in Part III: slot machines (Las Vegas), video games *(Assassin's Creed),* MMORPGs *(World of Warcraft),* and virtual worlds *(Second Life).* They have much in common.[67] All may be broadly understood as entertainment, that is, pleasure as distraction from the mundane. All were developed within a capitalist economy with the object of increasing the profits of their producers. All depend on players who have sufficient sources of both leisure time and money to invest heavily in their own diversion. All are potentially addictive.

Although these modes of play have many commonalities, their differences are significant. Each mode has its characteristic means, its own end, and its particular demographic. A slot machine requires no skill; its players are adults, marginally more females than males. For its user, though not for its corporate owner, the slot machine offers an exercise in pure chance. Its player's frustrated objective is the acquisition of real wealth. Video games and MMORPGs, played primarily by male teenagers and young adults, require eye-hand coordination and problem solving abilities. They promise virtual power, sometimes expressed as riches. The digital world of *Second Life* is not a game, but a field of play requiring considerable sophistication; its users include adults of both genders as well as of all nationalities. Its rewards are social, cultural, and only very occasionally financial.

Each of these modes works best within a distinct venue. Slot machines are conventionally sited in casinos; the location of play is a physical space of spectacle. They are named "machine" with good reason: players relate directly to a device that looks and acts like a machine. Its bulk signals a heavy apparatus. A glass panel persuasively displays the revolving reels that imply the same cumbersome contraption that operated slots in the mechanical age. Only when the slot machine is opened for maintenance is the deception fully revealed: the hefty casing is empty. It encloses not a ponderous mechanism with levers and cogs but a small computer board. Slot interactivity has changed: it no longer feeds on physical coins or acts when its arm is pulled; now it consumes digital slips and invites its buttons to be pushed. Despite new forms of screen-touching and narrativity, the device itself does most of the work of play. Slots gorge on the passivity of their users. In the other modes described in this section, the computer, either in a conventional form or as a game console, is manifest, not hidden. The user manipulates the action on the screen from a physical position in front of it. The two-dimensional diagrams depicting movement, inventories, and maps that float on the surface of the screen confirm its flatness, disrupting the impression of recession behind it and betraying that depth as illusion.

Each mode makes different demands on the attention of the player, though all have the capacity to capture that attention with such intensity that it has been identified as "immersion"—absorption into the immediacy of play. At its extreme, immersion might be understood as the loss of identity. For the sake of clarity, if at the cost of oversimplification, the heavily laden terms "identity" and "identification" are used narrowly here. "Identity" (derived from Latin, *idem* [same] and *entitas* [thingness]) names a dynamic perception not a stable property. Although unstable, "identity" is a sameness in a thing recognizable because of its temporal persistence. Our bodies fully participate in our identities. In addition to the peculiarities of our physical being, those qualities in our acts and ways of thinking, moral and practical, that, additively, seem particular to us constitute our identities. In slot-play, the machine is the agent of the addict's loss of identity. Natasha Schüll describes an instance in which a slot-player loses herself:

> Carla, a nurse in her late thirties whom I met at Trimeridian, felt sudden cramps one day while driving down Boulder Highway and pulled into a gas station to gamble. As she began to gamble, she was overcome with a numbness that lasted until her last quarter ran out, whereupon she felt severe pain, looked down, and saw that she was hemorrhaging. "It interferes with the pain receptors or something," she said.[68]

In more interactive digital settings, the compulsive player enters a world of action in a form not her own, binding herself to her avatar.[69] In her identification with the fictive personality through whom she manipulates conditions within the screen world, she changes, however temporarily. Here "identification with" signals the human act, conscious or unconscious, of recognizing, in a separate entity, something of one's own self. "Identification with" is never independent of emotion, but it does not imply any particular emotional response. "Identification with" is distinct, for example, from "empathy for," which implies sympathy with the object, as well as distance from it.[70] "Identification with" is diametrically opposed to "identification of," which suggests objective understanding and authoritative control. "Identification with" is subjective; it greases the slide into immersion.

"Identification with" is very differently articulated in video games, MMORPGs, and virtual worlds. The degree of the player's investment in her avatar may well affect her level of identification with it. In video games like *Assassin's Creed,* the avatar might be elaborated with acquired paraphernalia, but its appearance and character are nonmodifiable parts of the program. The player's share in defining her avatar is somewhat greater in MMORPGs like *World of Warcraft,* in which the player may chose from a wide variety of avatar types. Once selected, however, change is again limited to extrinsic additions. In immersive worlds such as *Second Life* in which the avid player's avatar may be her alter ego, her identification with her avatar is potentially more complete. In some cases, the distinction between the player and her avatar collapses. A few examples must suffice to make this point. In James Cameron's *Avatar*—a video game in the form of a film—Jake Sully gives up his human identity for the Na'vi identity of his avatar.[71] Bluntly and Amie, the characters in the film *Life 2.0* who fall in love in *Second Life* and leave their respective families to be together in real life, provide a second instance. Celia Pearce, who includes her avatar, Artemesia, as the coauthor of her book *Communities of Play,* offers a third.[72]

Place provides the context for the player's abdication, however brief, of her real-life identity. For slots, the architectural spectacle of the casino is a cue for the addict. In video games and MMORPGs the virtual space created by landscape and architecture is far more important than the words to the game's plots and actions. Structures define the playground and promote the player's active engagement with the fictive world of the game. In *Second Life* the user's power to manipulate space, like her power to manipulate her avatar, facilitates her association with the virtual world and her dissociation from the real one. In all three modes of play, digital space is essential to the illusion of freedom that conditions immersion. Spatial models function effectively as an addictive cue in all of these media. What would the Na'vi be without the luscious nature of Pandora? Would Bluntly and Amie have fallen in love without the faux-somatic pleasures of a virtual luxury yoga spa? Why would the expatriates of Uru, described by Artemesia, work so hard to reconstruct their original setting in *Second Life* if the environment did not embody their understanding of themselves as a community? The hook of the built landscape is distinct in each medium: characteristic settings contribute in identifiably different ways to their immersive seductiveness. In each of these modes of play, buildings and sites appeal to their targeted audiences as agents of addiction.

Conclusion

Buildings/Things, Bodies/ Texts, History/Theory

PIE, n. An advance agent of the reaper whose name is Indigestion.
—Ambrose Bierce, *Devil's Dictionary*

They that trust in the Lord shall be as Mount Zion, which cannot be removed, but abideth forever.
—Psalm 125:1

Although the agency of built forms has been neglected, the agency of things has attracted a good bit of critical attention—from Mauss and Heidegger to Gell and Brown. It might be assumed that the theorizations of things' acts would provide useful paradigms for theorizing the operations of buildings. Certainly some of the sophisticated assessments of things that have been written are useful in the investigation of buildings. Others, however, function as obstacles to the appreciation of architecture's distinctive effects on its social and physical landscape. Indeed, I argue here that the theorization of buildings as agents has much to contribute to a consideration of how things in general perform in the world.

Relics

Ambrose Bierce's definition of "pie" is amusing because it so unexpectedly makes a benignly passive object into an apocalyptic agent. It is witty because it puts life back into a thing after modernity has so thoroughly stamped it out. Industrialization and capitalism have made most objects into fungible commodities, eliminating their particularities, their histories, and their ability to act.[1] The daily experience of commodities as lifeless—chairs, aspirin, cross-trainers, washing machines—confirms the Cartesian relegation of all *things* to the weak, material side of the great mind/

body divide. Nevertheless, certain classes of things, like relics, totems, fetishes, and idols, continue to be recognized at least by some audiences as agents. Relics are portable fragments of the sacred that are so filled with the aura of their divine source that they perform in its place: healing the sick, punishing the evil, even raising the dead. Relics are most often associated with holy bodies—martyrs, ascetics, and other pious persons who in their different ways gave up their bodies for the sake of God. But some relics, identified as contact relics, may also be a part of things that were suffused with the divine through a close physical connection, like the cross of the Crucifixion, the rocks with which the protomartyr Stephen was stoned to death, or even bits of a terrain trod upon by a holy subject. In 1903, for example, an early medieval box of such stones, labeled with their places of origin ("from Bethlehem," "from the Mount of Olives," "from Zion," and "from the Life-Giving Anastasis"), was discovered in the most sacred of Western treasuries, the altar of the Sancta Sanctorum—the Holy of Holies—in Rome.[2]

One of the great theorists of the Middle Ages, Thomas Aquinas, citing an equally formidable theorist of late antiquity, Augustine, writes about the source of relics' power:

> As Augustine says (*De civitate Dei*: i, 13): "If a father's coat or ring, or anything else of that kind, is so much more cherished by his children, as love for one's parents is greater, in no way are the bodies themselves to be despised, which are much more intimately and closely united to us than any garment; for they belong to man's very nature." It is clear from this that he who has a certain affection for anyone, venerates whatever of his is left after his death, not only his body and the parts thereof, but even external things, such as his clothes, and such like. Now it is manifest that we should show honor to the saints of God, as being members of Christ, the children and friends of God, and our intercessors. Wherefore in memory of them we ought to honor any relics of theirs in a fitting manner: principally their bodies, which were temples, and organs of the Holy Ghost dwelling and operating in them, and are destined to be likened to the body of Christ by the glory of the Resurrection. Hence God Himself fittingly honors such relics by working miracles at their presence.[3]

Aquinas recognizes that things associated with our beloved, especially his body, retain something of his aura even after his death. In the case of a saint, that aura is acknowledged also by God, who "works miracles at their presence" ("in eorum praesentia miracula faciendo"). For Aquinas the relic acts not on its own but as God's agent.

In 2011, hundreds of thousands of pious believers waited in line for hours in order to touch the Virgin's girdle, brought to Moscow from its haven on Mount

Athos. The relic is believed to aid women in conception, pregnancy, and birth.[4] Not only do old relics still have life, but also new relics occasionally appear:

> The Vatican said doctors had taken a quantity of blood from the pontiff [John Paul II] while he lay dying, which had been sent in four containers to the blood transfusion center at the Bambino Gesu hospital in Rome. Two "remained at the disposal" of his private secretary, Stanislaw Dziwisz, who was later made a cardinal and the archbishop of Krakow. The remaining two phials stayed in the hospital where they were "devoutly safeguarded by the nuns" who work there as nurses. Both had been put into reliquaries: ornate relic containers that are usually made with precious metals and stones. One of the reliquaries was to be returned to the hospital. The other would be exhibited on Sunday and then be kept with other relics in the Vatican.[5]

If relics are still active in some places, they are all but extinct in others. In the Protestantized cultures of North America and northern Europe relics rarely retain their agency. Offered here is a description of the unsuccessful struggle of one relic-like thing to claim more than the humble, passive place of a curiosity. This example demonstrates at least two aspects of the lives of things. First, it suggests that even objects that are not commodities are now manipulated in ways that disempower them. And second, the odd manner in which this relic-like thing is handled establishes that it still retains the power to make its post-Reformation Protestant possessor anxious.

Tribune Tower

The Chicago Tribune Tower is best known for the international competition held in 1922 for its design.[6] Less familiar is the story of the nearly 150 bits of famous places embedded in its fabric.[7] In some ways, this Gothic skyscraper is a monumental, twentieth-century equivalent of the Sancta Sanctorum reliquary in Rome. At street level, the north, south, and west faces of the Tribune Tower are studded with bricks, stones, marble fragments, and metal slices from significant sites representing all fifty states and dozens of foreign countries (Figure C.1 and Figure C.2). The easily transportable portions are physically nondescript. Like the relics in Rome, they have no intrinsic value and make no aesthetic claims. They would not be welcomed at the Cloisters. Only their accompanying inscriptions save them from utter anonymity. The site of origin of each fragment is engraved in ceremonial uncials on the wall beside it. Some of these fragments have been in place from the time of the building's opening in 1925. More were introduced into the structure's

Figure C.1. Chicago, Tribune Tower, general view.

Figure C.2. Chicago, Tribune Tower, west facade, detail, including fragments from Rome, Colosseum; Pompeii, Stabian Baths; South Dakota, Badlands; Kiev, Monastery of St. Michael; and Rome, St. Peter's Basilica.

fabric through the early 1950s. The few additions since the 1950s include a piece of the Berlin Wall and a shard from the World Trade Towers.

Robert R. McCormick, part owner and editor of the *Chicago Tribune,* was personally responsible for the Tribune Tower's display. McCormick, who died in 1955, was a member of Chicago's ruling elite. He was a politically right-wing Presbyterian—a committed patriot of the northern variety and a fervent isolationist. Symptomatically, when Charles Lindbergh came to Chicago in 1940 to speak to an antiwar rally that included among its organizers pro-Nazi groups, he stayed with McCormick.[8] McCormick acquired his fragments in different ways. Some were given. Stones from Petra were presented by a business associate and Tribune stockholder, Dr. Henry D. Lloyd:

> My dear Bert: Having the Tribune fairly constantly in mind for its exceeding goodness to all its stockholders, when I was in Petra last March it occurred to me that it was conceivable you might like a stone from Petra to set in the front wall of the Tribune Tower. In as much as I had my own boat in Beirut, and was traveling by automobile, the problem of transportation was simplified. These stones are now in Boston awaiting your pleasure in the matter.[9]

Most of the fragments embedded in the building were collected by the Tribune's foreign correspondents on McCormick's direct orders. As a letter written in 1934 by one such correspondent, John S. Steele, indicates, the required pieces were not always legitimately obtained:

> I am shipping one of these stone cannon balls to you. I don't know whether it would be wise to label it as coming from Pevensey Castle. The Office of Works refused to let us have one on the grounds that they were part of an ancient monument. But we acquired it by the process which, I believe, was known in the war as "winning." Anyhow it should arrive in Chicago within the next couple of weeks.[10]

The cannon ball in the wall of the Tribune Tower is, despite Steele's warning, fully labeled. Other pieces were solicited from local repositories.[11]

McCormick did not document his intentions for these fragments. The choice of sites representing each of the fifty states may broadly reveal McCormick's opinion of the state from which it comes: California, a piece of the Petrified Forest; Connecticut, a fragment from the Old Chapel of Yale University (where McCormick matriculated); Kansas, a bit of John Brown's cabin; Georgia, a stone from the notorious Andersonville Prison. Bits from foreign places may register McCormick's sense of the political reach of the United States. Stones from famous battlegrounds, like

Omaha Beach and Corregidor, and from famous buildings, like St. Peters in Rome, the Houses of Parliament, and the Pyramid at Gaza *[sic]*, suggest an assumption of America's military and cultural authority.[12] But the agenda of the program was left unspecified. Indeed, an investigation of the most privileged of the Tribune Tower fragments reveals an ambivalence about the power latent in all of the bits embedded in the building.

Marked by its prominent location—isolated, at eye level on the front, *interior* wall of the WGN (World's Greatest Newspaper) Radio Lobby of the Tribune Tower—the most carefully framed object in McCormick's odd collection is also the most relic-like (Figure C.3). It is relic-like in its substance—a sampling of bits of stone and mosaic tesserae from the Grotto of the Nativity in Bethlehem. It is also relic-like in its presentation—the fragments are encapsulated in sapphire-colored glass, embedded in the wall, and framed in a gold star imitating that which marks the traditional site of Jesus's birth. Finally and most oddly, this thing is relic-like in its narrative. From early Christian times, relics kept company with texts. An explanation for a thing so obviously without intrinsic material worth was consistently required, whether in the form of stories ("Martydom of Polycarp"), testaments ("Testament of the Forty Martyrs") or letters like the one of Paulinus of Nola (354–431) sent in 403 to his colleague Sulpicius Severus.[13]

> I have found . . . a fragment of a sliver of the wood of the holy Cross to send you as a worthy gift. . . . This goodly gift was brought to me from Jerusalem by the blessed Melania, a gift of the holy bishop John there. . . . In this almost indivisible particle of a small sliver take up the protection of your immediate safety, and the guarantee of your eternal salvation. . . . It is said that this request is granted only by the kindness of the bishop and it is likewise by his gift alone that these tiny fragments of sacred wood from the same cross are made available to win great graces of faith and blessing. . . . [Be impressed by the cross, not by] the arrangement by which I have enclosed this relic . . . in a golden casing. Rather in this adornment I have imitated your faith. I sent you your own exemplar clothed with gold, for I know that you have within you, like gold tried in the fire, the kingdom of God—in other words, faith in the cross, by which we enter the kingdom of heaven.[14]

This letter attests to the genuineness of a relic by identifying its source (the True Cross), by referencing its sacred provenance (Jerusalem), and by naming its distinguished patrons (Melania and Archbishop John). The rich materiality of the gold reliquary seems a bit of an embarrassment to the author, but the exquisite container, like the text, plays an important role in the corroboration of the relic's importance. At least since the Council of Trent in the sixteenth century, relics have been regularly attended by a certified statement of "facts" similar to those found in Paulinus's letter. These formal statements, named Authentics, conventionally display, at the top, the name of the high-ranking ecclesiastic who vouched for the relic's authenticity, with the date, signature, and seal at the bottom. The formula for the body of the text includes a public pronouncement of the source of the relic and a guarantee of its legitimacy as well as the description of the vessel in which it has been sealed.

A letter concerning the Grotto fragments filed in the Tribune Tower archive has the attributes of both Paulinus's missal and Authentics. It was written in 1950 by the Associated Press's bureau chief in the Middle East, L. S. Chakales, to McCormick's executive assistant, Keith B. Capron.

> The fragments I gave to Colonel McCormick are from the actual Cave of the Nativity. They were scraped from the ceiling of the cave by the Archbishop of the Orthodox church, which is situated directly above the cave and through which every denomination must pass to reach the shrine. Under no circumstances can the

Figure C.3. Chicago, Tribune Tower, interior wall of the WGN Lobby; Bethlehem, Fragments of the Grotto of the Nativity.

> archbishop be identified publicly as the source. However, it could be stated they came from a person who had access to the cave. Their authenticity can be guaranteed and proven by the archbishop and the mayor of Bethlehem, but the archbishop naturally would be reluctant to make it public. However the mayor, Issa Bandak, I am sure would confirm them. We were his guests in his home which is situated in a convent which is a part of the church of the Nativity for Christmas, 1949, when the fragments were given to us. In fact, it was his influence that brought about the archbishop's unusual action. We went down the morning after and saw the white spot in the roof of the cave. In addition, we also got four tiny pieces of mosaic that were scraped away. We attached great importance to the fragments. It must be recalled the cave has been there for 2,000 years and it remains virtually intact. In that time souvenir hunters should have leveled the area for miles around, but miraculously it remained intact. I would like to emphasize these fragments came from the cave in which Christ was actually born and not from the immediate vicinity.[15]

Like Paulinus's missal, this letter was written to explain the gift to its recipient. Like Authentics, the letter specifies the sacred body from which the fragment was taken (the Grotto of the Nativity), who produced the fragments (the Greek Orthodox archbishop), and who will authenticate them (the mayor of Bethlehem). The message also makes it clear that the fragments from the cave were removed clandestinely ("under no circumstances can the archbishop be identified publicly as the source"). The text thus presents a narrative worthy of the great medieval tradition of *sacra furta,* the theft of relics.[16] Relics could not legally be bought, but they could be gifted or stolen. Robbery was a popular part of legitimating the acquisition of relics in the Middle Ages. While the letter makes no claim about the fragment's ability to preserve the recipient, it does suggest that the source of the fragments is "miraculous" ("It must be recalled the cave has been there for 2,000 years. . . . In that time souvenir hunters should have leveled the area for miles around, but miraculously it remained intact.")

These bits of a holy site, which in many ways resemble relics, do not, however, act like relics. They have no effect. No one, so far as I can tell, reveres them. When I asked the archivist if they had ever performed a miracle, she assumed my question was a joke. The tissue of a structure, removed from a powerfully living body, offers no sign of vitality as a relic. It is reduced to the docile pathos of a curiosity. A curiosity is a thing that is selected and contemplated because of its oddity. It is a diversion. By their bizarre misplacement, the relic-like fragments from the Grotto of the Nativity become a corporate ornament. McCormick's eccentric installation of these fragments from the Grotto of the Nativity in the lobby of his office building betrays his ambivalence about the agency of things. Like the ancient *spolia* discussed in chapter 2, these fragments are powerful enough to prove their current possessor is more so. At the same time, in contrast to ancient *spolia,* they are displayed as mere ornament in a space that cannot be sacralized by their presence: their aura expires.

The pieces of the Grotto cannot work religiously. Like the other Tribune Tower fragments, they also fail to function museologically or ideologically. In fact all these pieces of other places hardly act at all. They might even be dead. I questioned thirty or so Chicagoans about the Tribune Tower. Only one had ever looked at it and its odd facade ornament carefully, four knew about the fragments but had never attended to them, and the rest were familiar with the building but ignorant of its incrustations. The scraps of old buildings and distant sites embedded in the Tribune Tower are largely ignored. On the rare occasions when they are noticed, they are typically regarded as a source of amusement rather than amazement.[17] The Tribune Tower facade attracts attention by the remarkable array of things that it presents. But, in its impressive pastiche of places, the fragments are reduced to mere curiosities. Certainly the pieces manifest McCormick's confiscatory power. But they more eloquently attest to his neurotic idiosyncracy in gathering and displaying such a collection. The fragments of the Tribune Tower retain the power to index madness.[18]

McCormick's aberrant attempt to control potentially powerful things may perhaps be understood as a material manifestation of a long-running Protestant anxiety about auratic objects.[19] That anxiety is embedded in the shift in the relationship between texts and things during the Reformation. Even in premodern, largely illiterate Christian communities, texts were, of course, essential to religious practice. However, as suggested in our discussion of relics, texts then shared their authority with more popularly accessible, material vehicles of divine will—priests, rituals, images, as well as relics and sacred places. Roman catholicism and Eastern orthodoxies still honor those ancient habits. In early modernity, however, Protestants gave texts a much more exclusive role in understanding God's convictions. Texts, like John Calvin's *Treatise on Relics,* no longer authenticated the agency of sacred things, but rather argued objects' impotence.[20] Now even secular texts are commonly deployed to discipline the agency of things.

Thing Theory

One such disciplinary text is Heidegger's "The Thing." An earthen jug provides his example of "thingness." "The vessel's thingness does not lie at all in the material of which it consists, but in the void that it holds."[21] The jug's gift is "giving out"—to the human or the divine. "The gift of the outpouring is a gift because it stays earth and sky, divinities and mortals [the 'fourfold']. Yet staying is now no longer the mere persisting of something that is here. . . . It brings the four into the light of their mutual belonging."[22] "The jug's essential nature, its presencing, so experienced and thought of in these terms, is what we call *thing*."[23] The jug's "presencing" consists in its act of bringing the human into relation with the world. For Heidegger, the thing is only a thing for man. "Men alone, as mortals, by dwelling attain to the world as world. Only what conjoins itself out of world becomes a thing."[24] Like the artwork or the dwelling, the thing allows the mortal to locate himself in the world.

Of course, Heidegger's argument leaves most things unthingly. Further, Heidegger's definition of the thing only seems to make the thing as well as the beholder who appreciates its thingness heroic. But, on the contrary, Heidegger leaves even those things that act as things stripped of their own singularity. His jug has no particular shape, no irregularity, no maker. It has no history. Heidegger's treatment of the thing that makes the world present to him is poetic but inattentive. That same lyric vagueness is just as marked in his piece "The Origin of the Work of Art."[25] There Heidegger doesn't care that the shoes in a Van Gogh painting that the author epically ascribes to a peasant woman are the artist's own.[26] How can generic things be heroic? They cannot. In the end, the only hero in Heidegger's text is Heidegger.

Heidegger's "The Thing" has had a wide readership. It is cited early in Bill Brown's engaging and influential article "Thing Theory," which appeared in the 2001 special issue of *Critical Inquiry* devoted to Things.[27] Indeed, much of the current scholarly interest in deploying a Heideggerian phenomenology to question old assumptions about human interactions with the world has congealed around thing theory. Thing theory has been broadly and productively understood as a demand that new attention be accorded to the nonhuman object.[28] Oddly, however, the object is remarkably absent from Brown's own text. Following Heidegger, Brown's initial definition dismisses objects generally, retaining only those objects—"things"—that have specially caught our attention by frustrating our attempt to take them for granted.[29] Moreover, Brown's things are attended to not because of their goodness but because of their badness. Objects only become things by not functioning as they should: the window is a thing when it is too dirty to see through; the toy is a thing when it trips us. But even those objects privileged by Brown as things because of their excessive and negative effect on us are oddly aestheticized. His examples come almost exclusively from literary sources or from the art world. The "things" by which Brown exemplifies thing theory are not objects at all but representations. Indeed, ideas about ideas make up the bulk of Brown's text. An arrangement of quotes from philosophers and critical theorists from Ponge and Simmel to Derrida and Appadurai constitute much of his generative argument. The human subject is not superseded in our attention by the material object but rather by the thing's interpreter. The author, like the reader, is protected from objects by layers of literary reference.

Brown displaces things with theory. Here, using Martin Heidegger and Claus Oldenberg, Brown puts typewriter erasers in their nonplace:

> You could say that today's children were born too late to understand this memorial to another mode of writing, or you could say that Oldenburg (cleverly) re-created the object too late for it to be generally understood. It is an object that helps to dramatize a basic disjunction, a human condition in which things inevitably seem too late–belated, in fact, because we want things to come before ideas, before theory, before the word, whereas they seem to persist in coming after: as the alternative to ideas, the limit to theory, victims of the word. If thinking the thing, to borrow Heidegger's phrase, feels like an exercise in belatedness, the feeling is provoked by our very capacity to imagine that thinking and thingness are distinct.[30]

For Heidegger, the earthen jug, like Van Gogh's shoes, may be sites where the fourfold is revealed, but their specific histories are beside the point. A typewriter eraser for Brown is a site of the uncanny, only controllable through art and language.

Brown's need to make things subservient to language suggests that objects make him anxious. A forty-five-minute interview of Brown by Austin Allen recorded in 2010 for BigThing.com confirms this sense. Brown answers with enthusiasm and at length a query as to his favorite works of literature. Indeed, he answers with coherence, authority, and brilliant objectivity all of the interviewer's questions but the last: "What are a few of your favorite things?" Most of us would probably answer something like "cream colored ponies and crisp apple strudels." But Brown responds personally and incoherently:

> Right, what are a few of my favorite things? This is an ongoing question that I have, it's an ongoing question that I pose to my therapist and my therapist poses to me, which really does have to do with whether or not I write about things because I, myself, care deeply about them, or whether I write about things because I see other people caring about them and I'm trying to figure it out. So is it, is my writing about things therapeutic or does it serve some other function? A few of my favorite things, you know, I would say that there certainly [are] objects in which I take great pleasure, but mostly, I'm a failed collector, by which I mean, I really tried, so, stereoscopes, for instance, right, and stereoviews. Early 20th century, I've got three of those, somebody gave me one, I thought, "That's cool," bought another one, bought another one, bought some stereoviews, that's as far as I got, and, you know, if anybody wants to make it happen, because it just, and I thought, those would be great,

> you put them on a shelf and to me it just seemed like, they seemed like dust collectors, and I never find myself spending more time with them. And that's not the only instance, I mean, I have tried to be some sort of a collector and I'm just not. It's like one of those people who, you know, always gets a chess set because people think you love chess sets, but it turns out you never wanted chess sets, but you now have a big bunch of them. So it could be that my writing about things is my effort to figure out my absence of cathexis on objects, that could be, too. But it's not as though I don't, I mean, I do like, love the material world. I like beautiful furniture, I like beautiful houses, clothes, and things like that. But that's different from being possessed by possessions the way I think most people are who are in some sense normal, that is, I think that it's a normal relation to have to the object world.[31]

Disquietingly, Brown's therapist displaces the interviewer. Brown condemns himself as a failed collector; at the same time the objects that he unsuccessfully attempts to engage act themselves as collectors (of dust). They are dead to him. He confesses that he is unable to engage with things in the world in a normal way; he is self-diagnosed as abnormal, perhaps even unhealthy. Objects apparently drive Brown a little crazy.

McCormick's odd appropriation and display of building parts suggests an anxiety about things similar to Brown's. After all, the act of collecting is one familiar means of attempting to control both things and the angst that things generate. Jean Baudrillard observed that a collector's pleasure arises "from the fact that possession relies, on the one hand, upon the absolute singularity of each item—which means that it is equivalent to a human being, and eventually the subject himself—and on the other, upon the possibility of envisaging a set or series of like items, in which is implied a prospect of limitless substitution and play. . . . Actually, there is a strong whiff of the harem about all this, in the sense that the whole charm of the harem lies in its being at once a series bounded by intimacy and an intimacy bounded by seriality. Surrounded by the objects he possesses, the collector is pre-eminently the sultan of a secret seraglio."[32] The harem, in Western discourse, is the archetypal expression of male control of his greatest threat, the unruly female.[33] Thing theory is a theoretical equivalent of the harem. Rather than liberating the fragments of the Tribune Tower, thing theory only offers them another form of bondage.

Animating Theory

If thing theory saps the life of a thing, theory of a less phenomenological, more sociomaterial ilk provides it some sustenance. Anthropology has been particularly active in enlivening things. In an attempt to free itself from the racist assumptions of Western cultural superiority of nineteenth- and early twentieth-century ethnography, anthropology began taking the animated things of the Other more seriously.[34] Working toward a rational explanation of how things fully participate with humans in structuring the communities that they studied, anthropologists have provided a number of productive models for thinking of things as agents.[35]

Marcel Mauss's brilliant study *The Gift* first appeared in 1924. In it, Mauss persuasively posits that the power of things, like that of people, depends on their function within social relations. He focuses on gifts, which he demonstrates are never free. Gifts always require reciprocation. He effectively presents gift-exchange as a more socially constitutive equivalent of the market economy. The thing is at the center of Mauss's implied critique of a contemporary liberalism obsessed with individualism; he asks the question: "What power resides in the object given that causes its recipient to pay it back?"[36] Based on studies of the Maori, Mauss suggests that the thing given has an identity derived from its originating location and owner.

> What imposes obligation in the present received and exchanged, is the fact that the thing received is not inactive. Even when it has been abandoned by the giver, it possesses something of him. Through it the giver has a hold over the beneficiary just as, being its owner, through it he has hold over the thief. This is because the *taonga* [gift] is animated by the *hau* [spiritual power] of its forest, its native heath and soil. . . . The *hau* follows after anyone possessing the thing. . . . The thing itself possesses a soul. . . . To retain that thing would be dangerous and mortal, not only because it would be against law and morality, but also because that thing coming from the person not only morally, but physically and spiritually . . . exert[s] a magical or religious hold over you. Finally, the thing given is not inactive. Invested with life, often possessing individuality, it seeks to return to what Hertze called its "place of origin" or to produce, on behalf of the clan and the native soil from which it sprang, an equivalent to replace it.[37]

Mauss's gifts attest to a tenacious acculturation. They have much in common with the "witness objects" identified by Baudrillard in *For a Critique of the Political Economy of the Sign,* which, independently of their possessors' intentions, reveal their origins.[38] Mauss's gifts cradle nostalgia; the meaningfulness of great-grandmother's ring or a lost lover's handkerchief is enfolded in its possessor's identification with the thing's longing to return to its owner. Conversely, the meaninglessness of many gifts given in a commodity culture issues from their utter independence from both their givers and their sites of conception. The fragments of the Tribune Tower, whether extorted, stolen, or freely given, lost their power in part through their alienation from a system of gifting that would assure reciprocity and return. Henry

Lloyd's stones from Petra function not as a gift but as a receipt for generous dividends and a lien on future profits.

Mauss's understanding of powerful things functioning within an exchange economy makes the life of a thing dependent on its place within the human community. Arjun Appadurai's introduction to the formidable collection of essays that he edited, *The Social Life of Things: Commodities in a Cultural Perspective,* popularized as well as systematized Mauss's insight. Appadurai's catchy phrase "commodities, like persons, have social lives" is frequently quoted.[39] But Mauss's suggestive comparison between gifting and monetary economies becomes more categorical and less suggestive in this text. First Appadurai explicitly denies objects' agency: "Even if our own approach to things is conditioned necessarily by the view that things have no meanings apart from those that human transactions, attributions and motivations endow them with, the anthropological problem is that this formal truth does not illuminate the concrete, historical circulation of things." He observes that anthropologists know ("from a *theoretical* point of view") that things depend entirely on humans, but that they may act ("from a *methodological* point of view"), when it is useful to do so, as though objects themselves generate meaning.[40] Second, Appadurai subverts nonmodern objects and forms of exchange by defining just about everything as a "commodity." "Let us start with the idea that a commodity is *any thing intended for exchange.*"[41] This move eliminates the distinction between the commodity, as an utterly fungible object from which all marks of place and history have been erased, and the product, which retains signs of its crafting and consequently something of its origins. In an otherwise Marxian analysis, Marx's understanding of the labor-erasing force of the modern industrial commodity is obscured and history disappears.

Though Appadurai's contribution to the life of things should not be overestimated, the piece offers a fuller appreciation of the role of exchange in making things what they are. He also usefully adopts and develops Mary Douglas's observations on "enclaved" objects, certain valuables in nonmodern economies that "resemble coupons and licenses in modern industrial economies."[42] Enclaved things are valuables taken out of circulation to establish or maintain their possessor's status. Such a notion suggests a possible understanding of McCormick's bizarre collection: perhaps he sought to establish his authority and that of the Tribune Tower by wresting pieces of high-status structures from their origins, then taking them out of circulation by enclaving them in his building. But if that was McCormick's strategy, it failed, revealing the limitations of analogizing nonmodern economic terms to modern ones.

For Appadurai as for Mauss, things work not as discrete actors but as participants in a social or economic matrix. Another anthropologist, Alfred Gell, goes further, theorizing the agency of the singular object outside systems of exchange. The subject of Gell's *Art and Agency,* published posthumously in 1998, is the ethnographic artwork, which he names "index." Art is a particular type of thing that I have avoided in this text because of the peculiar complexity of aesthetics. However, if "powerful thing" is substituted for Gell's "index," his defense of powerful things as agents offers a way of understanding how objects affect their users. Like Mauss and Appadurai, Gell recognizes that "culture has no existence independently of its manifestations in social interactions."[43] But he goes further in investigating the animation of objects. He posits that particularly powerful things connect with the world in a way much like persons through an "abduction of agency."[44] "Abduction" was defined by Charles Sanders Peirce as a logical form distinct from induction and deduction by which conclusions are drawn on the basis of "inference" from familiar experience.[45] For example, the smell of fresh bread suggests the presence of fresh bread, while not proving it.[46] Or the slot machine's sound of the clinking of coins suggests getting rich, while not actually making it so. Particular objects affect their audiences through abductively acquired vitality: things act because their effects are apparent.[47] Gell's theory does not make the relic-like thing embedded in the wall of the Tribune Tower any more active, but it helps explain its inertia. It refuses to act because nobody believes it will.[48] In Gell's, Mauss's, and Appadurai's conceptual models, objects have lives, but those lives all depend on their human hosts.

In his introduction to actor-network-theory (ANT) of 2005, the sociologist Bruno Latour allows objects a greater independence.[49] Latour's cogent understanding of the social as a collectivity or a network depends on the recognition of the animate character of the object. His network is a processual system in which humans and nonhumans are equally enmeshed as actors. Indeed, Latour insists that nonhumans "have to be actors and not simply the hapless bearers of symbolic projection."[50] He offers a useful definition of things as actors:

> Any thing that does modify a state of affairs by making a difference is an actor—or, if it has no figuration yet, an actant. Thus, the questions to ask about any agent are simply the following: Does it make a difference in the course of some other agent's action or not? Is there some trial that allows someone to detect this difference? . . . [A hammer that hits nails or a kettle that boils water] are actors, or more precisely, participants in the course of action waiting to be given a figuration. This, of course, does not mean that these participants "determine" the action, that . . . hammers "impose" the hitting of the nail. . . . Rather it means that there might exist many metaphysical shades between full causality and sheer inexistence. . . . Things might authorize, allow, afford, encourage, permit, suggest, influence, block, render possible, forbid, and so on.[51]

Tools for Latour are actors participating in an agent's work, if not themselves agents. His persuasive and often-cited debunking of the National Rifle Association's "Guns don't kill people, people kill people" exemplifies his attribution of the transformative effect of tools on their users:

> What does a gun add to the shooting? In a materialist account, *everything*: an innocent citizen becomes a criminal by virtue of the gun in her hand. The gun enables, of course, but also instructs, directs, even pulls the trigger. . . . Every artifact has its script, its potential to take hold of passersby and force them to play roles in its story.[52]

That same example also suggests something of the ethical core of Latour's project. He ascribes the viscosity of his network of human and nonhuman actors to the inevitable struggle over the perpetual inequalities in the world. ANT works to identify the ingredients in that uneven social topography.[53] Latour's work provides a crack through which might slip the consideration of the ethics of objects' behaviors.

The few socioanthropological theorizations considered here afford us the understanding that things, like people, require a social matrix to act, and, further, that within that matrix, things, like people, may well operate as agents. But when objects fall out of circulation within the social, do they inevitably disappear, as seems to be the case with the debris embedded in the walls of the Tribune Tower? However unnoticed, don't those fragments remain in place, continuing to accrue history and its marks? Certainly these theorizations of things provide useful models for thinking through the lives of buildings and sites. But places are different than things, notably in their greater resistance to commodity status as well as in their relative scale and stability. Consequently, understandings of the ways places act in the world cannot depend solely on thing theory, even in its broadest definition. Indeed, the theorization of spatial objects like buildings and places may, in the end, teach thing theory a thing or two.

Phenomenological Flatness

We find ourselves now negotiating a "spatial turn"—the shift from a historicizing industrial nineteenth century to a spatializing postindustrial late twentieth/early twenty-first century. Philosophers, sociologists, and materialist literary scholars (e.g., Lefebvre, Foucault, Deleuze, Jameson) have made the globalized world more available to our understanding by theorizing the new prominence of space in its construction. Much preturn thinking about space was characterized by a functional

Cartesianism, as was the case in geography and urbanism at midcentury. Only the residue of this old-fashioned positivism survives. Another powerful preturn understanding of space, particularly embedded in religion, art, and literature, was phenomenological. Two examples suggest the continued currency of that way of thinking about space.

First example: Edward Soja contributed significantly to converting the field of geography from dowdy to trendy. His book *Thirdspace* is a riff on Lefebvre's *Production of Space,* whose message is diluted by adding metaphysics: "All excursions into Thirdspace begin with this ontological restructuring, with the presupposition that being-in-the-world, Heidegger's *Dasein,* Sartre's *être-là,* is existentially definable as being simultaneously historical, social, and spatial."[54] But phenomenology gets in the way of understanding space for many of the same reasons that it is inimical to an appreciation of the agency of things. Heidegger's consideration of spatial objects is clearly articulated in his discussion of dwelling. Dwelling is the site of the coming together of the fourfold (earth, sky, gods, mortals) in the form of a structure. "*Dwelling,* insofar as it keeps or secures the fourfold in things, is as this keeping, *a building.*"[55] A farmhouse in the Black Forest takes the same role in Heidegger's "Building Dwelling Thinking" that Van Gogh's shoes play in his "Origin of the Work of Art" and the earthen jug holds in "The Thing." It is a transparent vessel filled with Heidegger's seductive description. The object disappears; only the author's language remains. The vivid rendering of a building's effect on the writer may well move the reader to identify with him, but it diverts her empathy from the house itself. Heidegger assumes the primacy of language to architecture: "Who gives us a standard at all by which we can take the measure of the nature of dwelling and building? It is language that tells us about the nature of a thing. . . . Man acts as though *he* were the shaper and master of language, while in fact *language* remains the master of man."[56] In phenomenology, language and its consummate human manipulator displace the spatial object and flatten space narcissistically into a mirror.

Second example: John Corrigan's contribution, "Spatiality and Religion," in *The Spatial Turn: Interdisciplinary Perspectives* also embraces phenomenology, though in the guise of Mircea Eliade. "Space exists in time. One of the most influential theorists of religion, Mircea Eliade (1961), took time and space together in his influential formulations of 'sacred time' and 'sacred space.' . . . The cutting edge of the study of religion and space should incorporate to an increasing extent analysis of time alongside space."[57] Eliade's phenomenology here is cited not as a footnote to the historiographical past of religious studies, but rather as a template for the future understanding of religious space. But Eliade is not an adequate model: his phenomenological space, like that of Heidegger, deflates to flatness when it is probed.

Within the field of religious studies, Eliade's work has apparently somehow survived its persuasive demystification by Jonathan Z. Smith.[58] Outside his own discipline Eliade's mystical phenomenology remains even more commonly cited.

Eliade's reference to Zion in his still popular book *The Sacred and the Profane* reveals how Eliade schematizes topography, erasing those historical peculiarities in which its agency resides.[59] He describes Zion as a primordial appearance at the moment of creation.

> A universe comes to birth from its center; it spreads out from a central point that is, as it were, its navel. It is in this way that, according to the *Rig Veda* (X, 149), the universe was born and developed—from a core, a central point. Hebrew tradition is still more explicit: "The Most Holy One created the world like an embryo. As the embryo grows from the navel, so God began to create the world by the navel and from there it spread out in all directions." And since the "navel of the earth," the Center of the World, is the Holy Land, the *Yoma* affirms that "the world was created beginning with Zion."[60]

Zion begins the world. For Eliade, it is the archetype of sacred space.

> When the sacred manifests itself in any hierophany, there is not only a break in the homogeneity of space; there is also revelation of an absolute reality, opposed to the nonreality of the vast surrounding expanse. The manifestation of the sacred ontologically founds the world. In the homogeneous and infinite expanse, in which no point of reference is possible and hence no *orientation* can be established, the hierophany reveals an absolute fixed point, a center.
>
> So it is clear to what a degree the discovery—that is, the revelation—of a sacred space possesses existential value for religious man; for nothing can begin, nothing can be *done,* without a previous orientation—and any orientation implies acquiring a fixed point.[61]

Sacred space, produced by hierophany (Eliade's neologism for that which is divinely manifested) alone provides the spatial stability necessary for "religious" man's meaningful action.[62] The timelessness of divine emanation offers the unchanging nexus that "founds the world." Zion is not only the archetype of sacred places but also the antitype of all other spaces. The power that Eliade ascribes to Zion is not an indication of its agency but of God's. Zion is a cipher, a disembodied placeholder, a fixed, unchanging revelation of God's presence in the world put there for the orientation of religious man. Other phenomenologists make similar claims about less famous places. Heidegger's farmhouse in the Black Forest, for example, seems, like Zion, to precede man's proper understanding of the world. Rather than being epiphanically revealed, however, the farmhouse is epiphanically recognized.

Heidegger displaces a farmhouse with a text of his own making; Eliade reduces Zion to religious texts. The work of another canonical phenomenologist, Gaston Bachelard, clarifies the reason for textualizing sites. Poetic reverie on a once inhabited space is a device for acquiring self-knowledge: "There is ground for taking the house as a *tool for analysis* of the human soul. With the help of this tool, can we not find within ourselves, while dreaming in our own modest homes, the consolations of the cave? . . . And by remembering 'houses' and 'rooms,' we learn to 'abide' within ourselves."[63] Bachelard explores not a space, but a memory. His examination takes the author, not the building, as the object of investigation. For Bachelard, as for Heidegger and Eliade, a space is powerful only insofar as it reveals man to himself. As is the case with Heidegger's Black Forest farmhouse, textuality provides the means of eliminating those specificities from a site that might challenge the author's control of it. Textualizing a place or an object involves its detexturing. The author becomes the object's sole observer. The reader is not invited to look at the site's peculiarities; she cannot *see* anything beyond that which the author puts before her eyes. The site is robbed of the singularities of its idiosyncratic body and thereby stripped of its agency. However persuasively poetic, Eliade and Heidegger, like Brown and others who adopt their practices, flatten things and places by projecting on them only their own consciousness. Some phenomenologists, like Maurice Merleau-Ponty, take account of the body, history, and the world's given-ness.[64] But those of a Heideggerian or Eliadean persuasion—like Christian Norbert-Schulz and Yi-Fu Tuan—may argue for the power of places, but empty sites of their agency by locating the sources of their force outside of history either in the self or in the transcendental.[65]

I suggest that phenomenologizing a site tends to eliminate its substance along with its history. Lodged in the author's memory, a site cannot be eroded or reconstructed. As Bachelard proclaims, "phenomenology liquidates the past."[66] The phenomenologist's control of a space is lost if he concedes that it has a history independent of his own. The timelessness characteristic of Bachelard's and Heidegger's places is also essential to Eliade's understanding of religion. He ascribes to the Jews the imposition of history on a pure, ahistorical Christianity:

> The "Judaization" of primitive Christianity is equivalent to its "historicization," that is, the decision of the first theologians to connect the history of Jesus' preaching and of the earliest Church to the Sacred History of the people of Israel. But Judaism had "historicized" a certain number of seasonal festivals and cosmic symbols by connecting them with important events in the history of Israel.[67]

Eliade's sense of the corruption of religion by history was sustained by his virulent anti-Semitism, if it were not rather its consequence.[68]

I find that Eliade's discomfort with historical time is made manifest in his fiction. Eliade's best-known novella, *Youth without Youth,* opens in late 1930s Bucharest.[69] Its protagonist, Dominic Matei, is an aging Romanian academic approaching seventy, whose enduring desire to find and describe the originating meaning of life remained frustrated. Dominic's preoccupation with this search for Truth even led him to reject love when it was offered to him. Nevertheless, his investigations were thwarted by his inability to fully control ancient languages. Finding himself in an early stage of dementia, Dominic travels to a distant town to commit suicide. There he is hit by lightning, causing a miraculous revitalization of both his body and mind. To avoid being apprehended by the Romanian security for his purported links with the Romanian fascists or abducted by the Gestapo for scientific examination in Germany, he disguises his identity with the help of his doctor and the Rockefeller Foundation. His heightened intelligence collapses time. Beautiful women sacrifice their youth to provide him with access to both the past and the future, allowing him to approach the Truth that he has long been seeking. Dominic returns from his fantasy only to die as an old man in the snow outside his old café. *Youth Without Youth* is creepily autobiographical. Written by a sixty-nine-year-old Romanian historian of religions, a former Nazi sympathizer associated with the fascist Iron Guard, the novella is full of only partially masked personal fixations and experiences. In his academic writing Eliade substitutes myth for history; in his fiction, history is displaced by a dream. In both, the past is the projection of the author's self. The work bears no resemblance to that of Borges, as suggested on the book jacket of the most recent English-language edition. Wit and irony are utterly absent from the text. This novella about a misogynist's self-obsession has more in common with the plots, if not the literary distinction, of Goethe's *Faust* and Oscar Wilde's *Picture of Dorian Gray.* It is a story that provides insight only into its author's preoccupation with his own mortality.

History, I would argue, restores Zion's agency. Zion (from Hebrew; Sion from Greek), perhaps the Jebusite name of the fortress that fell to King David (fl. 1000 BCE) and the Israelites, appears often in the Hebrew Bible.[70] Zion's prominence in Psalms—that book of the Bible, Old Testament or New, most used by Christians—assured the name's familiarity to Christians of all varieties as well as to Jews. Of course, "Zion" is commonly deployed synecdochically, as a part of Jerusalem standing in for the whole of the city. "Zion" also named a specific hill of the Holy City. At the time of David, Zion was the toponym for Jerusalem's southeast outcrop, adjacent to the Temple Mount (see F in Figure 2.1). There, according to 1 Kings 2:10, King David was buried in the tenth century BCE.[71] Despite the claim made in

Psalm 125 and echoed in Eliade that Mount Zion "cannot be removed, but abideth forever," it later migrated to the west. Apparently when Herod built his grand new royal palace to the west of the Temple Mount, Zion, as a place associated with kingship, moved too, settling itself on the city's highest promontory, the southwest hill.[72] At least by the first century CE the toponym Zion had fled, along with the city's elites, from Jerusalem's long-occupied, slummy southeast hill to its recently invested southwest hill (Figure E in 2.1 and Figure C.4). The new identity of the southwest hill is clearly articulated in Josephus's description of Jerusalem with which he prefaces Titus's conquest of the city (*Jewish Wars,* 5.4.1).

From late antiquity the southwest hill has retained its assumed identity.[73] "Mount Zion" remains the name on the map of the city for the height just outside Zion Gate/Bab el-Daoud (David's Gate). This height, having attracted a famous name, subsequently generated a good bit of aura. From late antiquity to early modernity,

Figure C.4. Jerusalem, Mount Zion, from the southwest. Dominant is the Church of the Dormition of the Virgin; the "Tomb of David" is marked by the small minaret beside it. American Colony Collection, Library of Congress Prints and Photographs Division (LC-DIG-matpc-06556).

through occupations by the Byzantine Empire, Islamic caliphates, the Crusader Kingdom, and the Mamluks, Mount Zion was a generative Christian holy site. There, the building associated with the first Christian congregation of Jerusalem was incorporated into a great basilica, the Mother of All Churches. The place bred a clutch of sacred spaces, among which were the sites of the Last Supper (the Cenacle), the foot washing, the Pentecost, and the death of the Virgin Mary.[74] Also attracted to the church's vicinity were the house of Caiaphas, the place of Peter's repentance, and the first tomb of the protomartyr Stephen. In early modernity the Mother of All Churches even delivered a historical impossibility: King David's Tomb. A monolithic crusader cenotaph placed in the room below the Cenacle provoked its identification by the Jews as the burial place of the king, precipitating the site's appropriation by the Ottomans and its conversion into a mosque. Between the sixteenth and mid-twentieth centuries the site remained under Muslim control.

Zion's fecundity made it messy. It accumulated the material debris of its multiple auratic enclaves. Interaction among the spatial objects of the site, its human occupants, and their narratives contributed to its spatial complexity. Often destroyed and always rebuilt, expanded and contracted, the site survives as a maze. Unstable, messy, fertile Zion suggests that Eliade's order of epiphanic appearances should be reversed: topographically prominent sites attract names and narratives that participate in the production of the aura, allowing it to be identified *post factum* with a divine eruption. Now the church/mosque is occupied by the right-wing, settler-identified Diaspora Yeshiva. Despite all archaeological evidence to the contrary, the Diaspora Yeshiva still shamelessly identifies their property as "David's Tomb" (Figure C.5). They do so to legitimize Zionist claims to a site that had been in Christian and Muslim possession for the last eighteen centuries. Eliade's Zion, the epitome of religious authoritarianism, has been adopted to the political requirements of the site's current occupant. Like Eliade's Zion, that of the Diaspora Yeshiva masks the site's history, disguises its social and political affects, and promotes its function as ideology. It seems to me that such an understanding of Zion accords it a seemingly privileged status while literally stripping it of the remarkable history that makes its actual agency legible. The elimination of history in Eliade's phenomenology, as in Heidegger's, flattens its objects but makes room for barbarism.

Materialist Spatial Theory

The atemporal, ideal space of phenomenology is politically dangerous. It slips noiselessly into ideology. Physical sites with complex pasts and disordered dispositions, like those described in this book, are not so easily managed; they offer history as resistance to dogma. Immersive worlds, websites, and video games, by their very

Figure C.5. Jerusalem, Mount Zion, so-called David's Tomb occupied by the Diaspora Yeshiva.

disembodied-ness, also potentially disrupt the neat ordering of power. Physical and cyber sites both provide proverbial grist for the mill of nonphenomenological, materialist spatial theorizing. Indeed, I mean to show how historical, embodied places and digital spaces may even nuance the most powerful contemporary conceptualizations of spatiality. A survey of some of the canonical theorizations of space suggests how. In this exercise, "Zion" acts as a placeholder for the other buildings whose biographies are presented in this text. "Place of immersion" serves as a proxy for those digital spaces that provide an escape for their human occupants.

French philosopher Michel Foucault made foundational contributions to current considerations of space.[75] Among his insights, his identification of heterotopia (other places) is particularly relevant to understanding the force of material sites. Utopias, he observes, "are sites with no real place"; in contrast, heterotopias are those real places in every society "that have the curious property of being in relation with all the other sites, but in such a way as to suspect, neutralize, or invert the set of relations that they happen to designate, mirror, or reflect."[76] Heterotopia—museums, hospitals, arenas, cemeteries, theaters, casinos—are physical, bounded, time bending, and transformative. Foucault marginalizes religious space and its hierarchical ordering of the world by positing it as part of a remote past, the medieval "space of emplacement."[77] Zion is certainly a heterotopia. Its current exploitation as a religious site reveals how auratic places continue to exist, maintained to manipulate the sacred for profane profit. Zion suggests how Foucault's analysis might usefully be extended to the holy—providing religious space with a social mobility and economic dimensionality that was previously underacknowledged. Sacred space is often treated as though it were unquestionably moral; rethinking it as a Foucauldian heterotopia requires that it take more responsibility for its ethical conduct. Foucault's model allows a modern desacralizing of space, without its disempowerment.

Gilles Deleuze and Félix Guattari's masterly discussions of space in their *A Thousand Plateaus* and *The Fold* have also had a widespread effect on contemporary spatial thinking.[78] The rendering of social contestation in terms of "striated" and "smooth" space is indicative of the resonance of their work.[79] Striated space is saturated, sedentary, and urban; smooth space is vacant, nomadic, and rural. The striated is instituted by the state apparatus, controlled and characterized by hierarchy; the smooth is empty of established authority, invites control, and breeds new sovereignties. Striated space is occupied by means of strategy; smooth space negotiated by tactics.[80] Most critically, striated and smooth spaces are never static, but always changing. Zion certainly presents a persuasive historical illustration of Deleuze and Guattari's model of the striated as agonistic. I'd like to suggest that, in addition, Zion adds to that model both texture and depth. Zion's generative disorder thickens the weft of striation's warp. Zion also suggests how attractive high places are for striation, providing a greater three-dimensionality to Deleuze and Guattari's topography. At the same time that historical sites invest striation with greater density, immersive places provide luminosity to the nomadism of the smooth.

De Certeau educates our perspective on high places. A high point offers control, real or imaged. "It transforms the bewitching world by which one was 'possessed' into a text that lies before one's eyes. It allows one to read it, to be a solar Eye, looking down like a god. The exaltation of a scopic and gnostic drive: the fiction of knowledge is related to this lust to be a viewpoint and nothing more."[81] De Certeau captures the sense of control offered by the view from above and identifies that elation as an illusion. But I might add that height transforms the coercive physical complexity of the urban into a tractable representation not only for the individual, but also for the state. Further, height allows being seen as well as seeing; it provides both the panoptic control of the surrounding space and the articulate expression of authority within the panorama.[82] Zion, as a locus of history, demonstrates how height is a lure for state power. Zion is (mis)remembered as the place of state power, the fortified palace of David. Later the state was represented there by its institutions. Like the temple on the Acropolis in Athens or the Twin Towers in New York, from late antiquity to early modernity, Zion's height was controlled by an alternative face of the state.[83] The church that became a mosque on Mount Zion was, in late modernity, displaced by another religious expression of the state apparatus, the Diaspora Yeshiva. The site acts as the agent of authority, conferring on transient power the semblance of permanence by monumentalizing it within the landscape. Zion shows that permanence to be impostrous. Digital worlds also offer their manipulators a fictitious sense of control from an elevated distance. Those concerned with maintaining some semblance of an individual's right to privacy are investigating how computers look back, observing their observers.

Digital sites also offer the means of refining current understandings of the civic arena. Jürgen Habermas brought the "public sphere" into focus as the space of civil, intellectual engagement of the population with the politics of the state.[84] In his historical introduction to the public sphere, Habermas positioned the exchange of ideas within specific material conditions, referencing physical sites from the *oikos* to the coffee house, as well as developments in technology and the economy. Subsequent discussions of the public sphere among historians, sociologists, and philosophers have concentrated almost exclusively on its centrally important discursive content and technological media. Indeed, now that those concerned with the degeneration of the public sphere have turned their attention to its survival on the web, physical space has all but disappeared from any assessment of its vital signs. The brief description of the figuration of the 2008 campaign venues of *Second Life* provided in chapter 6 suggests, I would argue, the effect as well as the affect of architecturally articulated space, real or virtual, in the formation of the polity. Buildings, even digital ones, apparently modify the acts of those who use them. In virtual life, as in real life, muggings are more likely to occur in back allies than in the lobbies of five-star hotels. If buildings inform behaviors, certainly they must also contribute to the shape of politics.

Among the most influential of contemporary theorizations of space is Henri Lefebvre's *Social Production of Space.*[85] Lefebvre compellingly renders space as actively produced rather than passively ubiquitous. His triadic understanding of spaces as conceived (representations of space—symbolic forms like maps and Lefebvre's own theorization), perceived (spatial practices—the fixed and framed space of authority), and lived (representational spaces—the subjective and unmappable space of the daily) offers a compelling critique of familiar Cartesian dualities (time/space, full/empty, sacred/profane). It seems to me that Lefebvre's writing also facilitates the modern reseeing of space in terms of labor. In premodernity, space was experienced as work, except perhaps by theologians. The body's toil in making space was always present, as expressed by its naming (foot; hand, for horses; mile, as 1,000 Roman double paces; acre and dunam for the day's plowing). After the Revolution, the French legislated a rationalized space: it was labeled by its abstract division (meter comes from the Greek for measure). Western space began losing its connection to physical exertion. In modernity, intellectuals are in particular need of Lefebvre to remind them of the work involved in producing space. Fertile as it is, the Lefebvrian model, like those of Foucault, de Certeau, Habermas, and Deleuze and Guattari, might be modestly augmented by a fuller embrace of spatial objects and immersive places as coagents in the labor of making space.

Crux: Agents, Nonagents, Quasi Agents

In this book I argue, through example and analysis, that architectural agents, like the more mobile bodies with which they collaborate, make social space and contribute to its ethical valence. A casino on the Las Vegas Strip is a tease that morphs into an addiction. The Cloisters Museum in New York imposes quiescence on objects excised from active spaces, inviting their audiences to collude in their passivity. The Hostal de los Reyes Católicos in Santiago de Compostela cannot disguise the bloody acts of its inquisitional origins under the guise of a five-star hotel. In Jerusalem, the Rockefeller Museum presents its dismemberment as bodily evidence of the depredations of occupation, and the American Colony Hotel documents the potential of buildings to resist systematic discrimination. As their histories show, all of the buildings in this text perform spatially in a way similar to the objects in

Bruno Latour's ANT. To further substantiate this claim I offer three final analogies: first, an analogy between the graphic and plastic marks of pictorial space and material objects in physical territory; second, an analogy between material and virtual places; and finally, an analogy between humans and animals.

The recognizable representation of a three-dimensional space on a two-dimensional plane depends on legible marks. A blank sheet of paper may be transformed into a landscape by a single line. Marks are also essential to seeing the physical landscape. Space is perceptible only when it is marked. As Leibniz observed, "The parts of space are fixed and differentiated only by the things that are in it."[86] Of course, neither the marks on the paper nor the marks in the landscape must be made by human hands. A snail might leave a line on a sheet of paper. In the physical world, marks may be natural features of a landscape—mountains, springs, caves. Or they might be made by animals—spore, tunnels, nests. Animals as well as humans certainly understand and react to spatial marks, both often for the purpose of defining territories. Indeed, noticing the utility of certain marks in the landscape and augmenting them with others is a particularly common human/animal activity. Even the etymology of "mark" reveals its territoriality and records the human compulsion to make it. The *Oxford English Dictionary* traces "mark" to the Old English *mearc* and the Old Frisian *merke* meaning mark, character, border, and relates it to Middle Dutch *marke,* signifying limit, boundary, borderland. With surprising consistency, spatial marks define inclusion, exclusion, and the movement in between.

Spatial marks act as signifiers: symbols, icons, indices.[87] They appear in a variety of forms. Here I distinguish a few of those forms: mass, point, volume, verge, track.

Mass. Mass is topography—the thickness or crumple of paper; the mountains, seas, deserts of territory; the pyramids of architecture.

Point. A white point on a black screen implies a universe (see Figure 6.1). A point that takes on fullness functions as a monument. It identifies the center or circumference of possession. By its scale, material, and figuration it often also establishes its own status and consequently that of its producer or claimant. It may promote the aura of the space and act as its protection. The herm—a human bust on a squared pedestal displaying male genitalia—embodies the land's fertility, works as a political signifier, and acts apotropaically for those who respect it.[88]

Volume. The volume is a discrete geometry, regular or irregular: an exterior that promises an interior or an interior that predicts an exterior. By its scale and elaboration, the volume signifies its function and status. Buildings are, for the most part, volumes. The facade of the bungalow invites the visitor inside. The fire in the hearth registers the cold of the outside.

Verge. The verge is an edge, an extended separation. It delimits territory. The verge that acquires bulk excludes those who are outside its circumference or contains those within it. That exclusion and containment may take the form of physical restraint, or, as in the case of the Great Wall of China, its power might lie in its manipulation of identity.[89]

Track. The track is often perpendicular to the verge. The track is a mark that identifies passage. Worn by repetition, it implies deletion or erosion rather than fullness. The track reveals transience in a way that other marks work to mask it. Tracks can, of course, be tarmacked into I-95 or ironed into the Great Western Railroad, but that their existence depends on consistent movement is always apparent.

I define these terms to emphasize that, in the physical world, all embodied marks—points, masses, volumes, verges, tracks—create space by their various actions. They function both as visual referents to extension and as haptic encounters. These spatial marks work for blind as well as sighted navigators. They also work for animals.[90] They are agents that facilitate and limit any physical negotiation of terrain. Despite the ubiquity and power of these marks, humans, if not animals, are often unconscious of their effects. Humans don't attend to particular humans in a crowd unless provoked by their appearance (he's wearing all purple) or their actions (she's trying to get in front of me). Nonprovocative humans obviously remain agents even when they go unnoticed. Similarly, humans don't attend to particular objects in their environment unless provoked by them. Nevertheless, both provocative and nonprovocative spatial objects also remain agents.

My analogy between the pictorial space of a drawing and the physical space of the material world services a further analogy between the material world and inhabited digital universes. Although marks seem to be even more obviously necessary for the legibility of space in virtual environments than in material ones, they work in similar ways in both. Digital structures on a screen, like structures in the world, can control the landscape of which they are a part by their scale, their symmetry, their closure, their gaps, their ornament, and their scripts. Virtual architectures act in virtual space very much like buildings act in the physical landscape, manipulatively staging the observer's engagement with her environment. By its dominance of the visual field, a massive wall or a bilaterally symmetrical interior exerts physical and ideological control over those within its frame. Alleys and sewers provide the avatars who find concealment within them the tactical means of subversion. The power of virtual places, like that of physical sites, is evident in the abstract means devised by humans in an effort to control them: measurements, maps, plans, symbols, and codes. Again, virtual spaces, like physical spaces, also perform as forceful social and political agents even when they are overlooked. The screens we encounter and the channels through which we move are haptic moderators of our practical action in immersive worlds. Physical and virtual structures are equally "real" in the way that they affect their users' conscious or unconscious behaviors.[91] Virtual spaces, like actual ones, can, for example, act as effective cues for addiction.

Despite similarities in their roles, physical buildings and virtual spaces are, of course, very different phenomena. Those differences inflect the ways that they work as well as the ways that they imply that space should be theorized. Most obviously and fundamentally their substances distinguish them. A building is corporeal and made of matter; it is tethered to the earth; the builder's imagination is constrained by the laws of physics. A virtual space is immaterial and constituted of electronic data; the laws of physics impose no limits on its maker's creativity. One is in the world and the other on a screen. This manifest and fundamental physical difference involves others. Most obviously, the physical body (human or animal) of the observer is in the world but outside the screen. The world and the screen both, of course, provide intellectual and somatic exercises, although buildings engage their users in a bodily experience that does not necessarily require a lot of thinking and virtual spaces provide mental ventures that do not necessarily demand much physical action. But with rare exceptions in real if not in fictional conditions, the body is not in danger in virtual spaces. Pain and death are always a possibility in built structures—tripping on a step or being pushed out a window—as Bernard Tschumi has so brilliantly illustrated (Figure C.6).[92] In contrast, even those virtual spaces designed to be dangerous kill only avatars, who are usually revived by rebooting.

Less apparent, but, it seems to me, equally important, are the distinct differences in the economic and historical effects of physical and virtual spaces. A material building is not fungible and, consequently, as I argued in the Introduction, not a commodity. Digital structures, in contrast, are utterly fungible—simulacra that circulate comfortably as commodities. The model of a Q Castle that you buy in *Second Life* and that is stored in your inventory is identical to every other example of the infinite number reproducible by its maker (Figure C.7). The disembodied fungibility of virtual spaces effects their relation to time. Both physical and virtual structures have a time of beginning and a time of ending, even if those times are unknown. A beginning and an end constitute a chronicle, not a diary. Idiosyncratic growth and decay are essential not only to living, as humans understand it, but also to history. Although a video game has a history, that history has more in common with the history of a text than with the history of a human or of a building. The context of a video game changes, its reception shifts, its hardware varies, but its components neither develop nor deteriorate independent of their software. Time alters

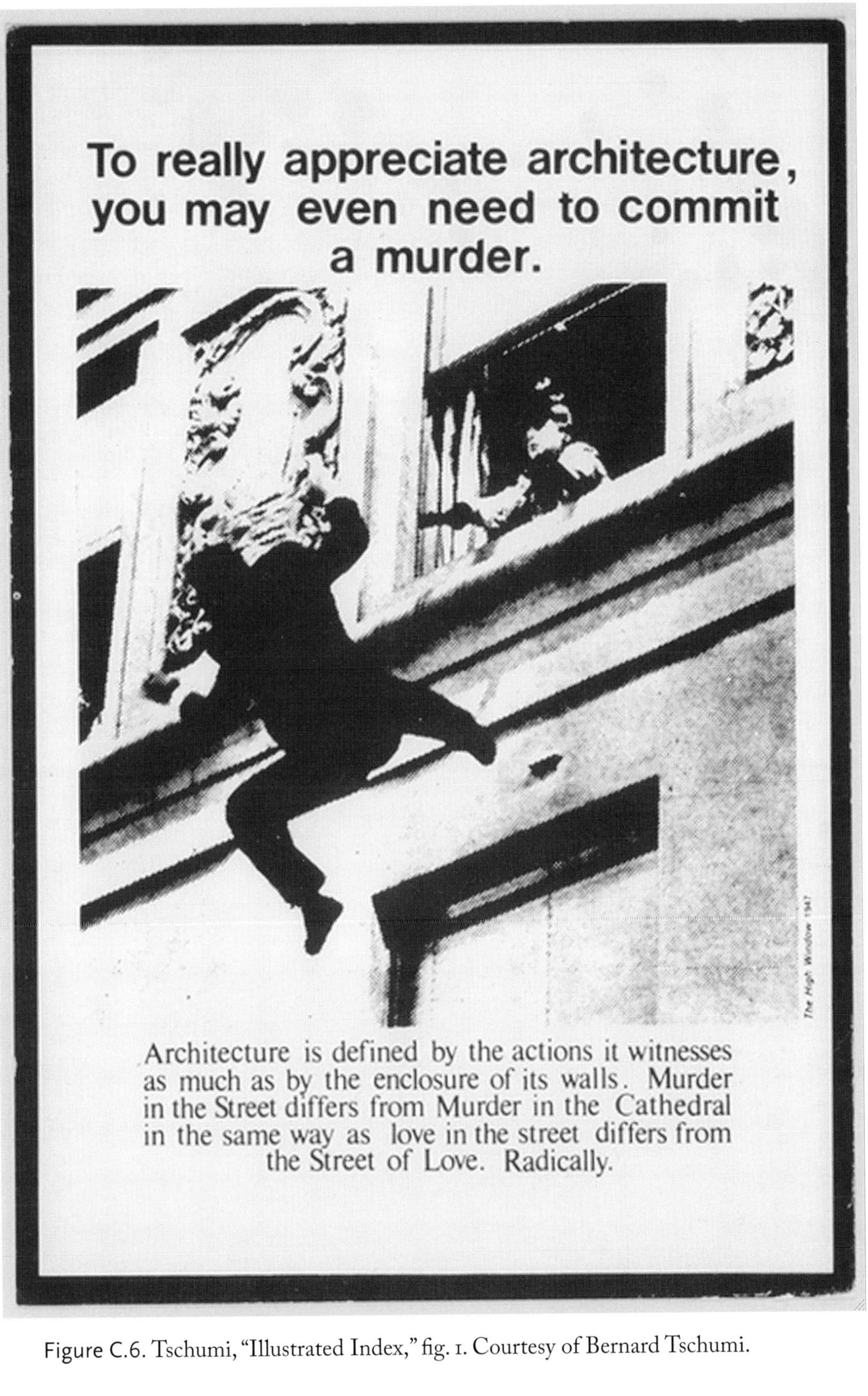

Figure C.6. Tschumi, "Illustrated Index," fig. 1. Courtesy of Bernard Tschumi.

the built environment but leaves the digital setting unaffected. Corroded environments certainly exist in video games and immersive playgrounds, but they were created that way. Experience makes no mark on the digital space. Built structures leave signs of their use and their erasure; digital spaces disappear without a trace (Figure C.8; compare Figure 6.10). Buildings witness history differently than do virtual structures, and that difference affects their agency. Buildings in the world are more subtle agents of nostalgia than buildings in video games. Physical structures not only stage the original experience of those whom they affect, but also, in their own degeneration, register the passage of time from the initial engagement. Like those who use them, physical buildings participate in time's corruption. Virtual spaces stay the same or disappear. Digital buildings might be better identified as quasi agents rather than agents. It is no wonder that phenomenologists don't embrace video games as vehicles of introspective self-knowledge. Phenomenology, which tends to the solipsistic, avoids encounters with forms to which memory does not readily adhere.

Phenomenologists of the Heideggerian variety have not found much purchase in immersive worlds. Nothing about digital environments that I have presented here will change that. Computer-generated places have not attracted much attention from materialist spatial theorists either. In contrast to phenomenology, theory of a more material and social disposition avoids turning the world into the self and,

Figure C.7. *Second Life*, Q[uality] Castles (Castles, 128.118.27).

instead, turns the subject out into the world. Consequently, I am hopeful that the consideration of the space of video games and digital playgrounds here and in chapter 6 demonstrates that the world into which we are turned may be virtual as well as physical.

One final analogy—between humans and animals—extends the reach of materialist spaces and further limits those of phenomenological ones. Material spatial theory, in contrast to phenomenology of the Heideggerian variety, does not necessarily subordinate things to humans. Nevertheless, animals, like virtual worlds, have also been relatively neglected in materialist theories of space, though certainly not in theory more broadly.[93] Here I introduce physical buildings' capacity to relate to animals as a small piece of evidence of their distinctive agency. Animals are, after all, fully interactive with buildings. In contrast, animals don't react in a distinct way to phenomenological spaces like Eliade's Zion. Animals also rarely make anything of digital screens except in exceptional experimental conditions.[94] The collaboration of animals in the argument for buildings' particular agency contributes to making it a more effective critique of Cartesian mind/body dualism. As Derrida and others have observed, that dualism bleeds from the man/thing and man/animal

Figure C.8. *Second Life,* section of the digital world formerly occupied by "The Straight Talk Café: John McCain and Sarah Palin for America." Caption: "Land Foreclosed: GOPs didn't pay their bill" (Baku, 117.142.31).

bias to the self/other of genocide. Derrida, in a typically idiosyncratic text that looks like a script, makes this point:

> [Pause for a moment: to dream of the face the Heideggerian corpus would look like the day when, with all the application and consistency required, the operations prescribed by him at one moment or another would indeed have been carried out: "avoid" the word "spirit," at the very least place it in quotation marks, then cross through all the names referring to the world whenever one is speaking of something which, like the animal, has no Dasein, and therefore no or only a little world, then place the word "Being" everywhere under a cross, and finally cross through without a cross all the question marks when it's a question of language, i.e., indirectly, of every thing, etc. One can imagine the surface of a text given over to the gnawing, ruminant, and silent voracity of such an animal-machine and its implacable "logic." This would not only be simply "without spirit," but a figure of evil. The perverse reading of Heidegger. End of pause.][95]

Heidegger's *Dasein*—Being of the heroic mortal—suggests that, in the twentieth century, the line between the privileged human and the rest of the world was inscribed with the added enthusiasm of racial superiority.[96] In any case, with the help of postcolonial thinking, the human Other is no longer so easily obscured and dismissed. Animals may now work more effectively as a vehicle for grasping the neglected, dismissed, and forgotten. They certainly contribute a further dimension to an argument for buildings' agency. The behavior of animals also confirms the sense that sites of immersion, in contrast to material places, would be best coded not as agents, but as quasi agents.

This book begins with an understanding of "agency" that allows buildings to act in the landscape. It ends by contrasting a building's agency to the nonagency of phenomenological sites and the quasi agency of computer-generated simulacra. Phenomenological sites are timeless, nonspatial loci produced by thinkers with remarkably little reference to the external world. They are persuasive only to their authors and some of their readers, not animals. Such sites certainly function ideologically or psychologically, but not physically. They are not agents. Immersive sites effectively act upon humans, but because their immateriality resists the somatic body, memory slips away from them. They may manipulate humans but not animals. They are quasi agents.

What is the reward for the work of recognizing sites as agents? By ascribing agency to buildings, their ethical dimensions are more fully disclosed; a structure's potential for violence as well as for benignity is more evident. Understanding a building as an idiosyncratic historical agent allows its witness to explore her empathy with buildings' mistreatment and destruction. If I can make that case compelling, the acts of buildings—whether good or bad—will be more readily recognized and, consequently, promoted or disciplined. Perhaps most importantly, by taking seriously the effects of history on a building and a building's contribution to the construction of the past, we will better understand our own roles in conditioning the present and our own responsibilities to fashioning the future.

Notes

Introduction

1. For an engaging introduction to these complexities, see Macintyre, "Social Structures and Their Threats to Moral Agency."

2. W. Anderson, *Dictionary of Law,* 42. For a more modern, more detailed, but less cogent legal definition of "agent," see Law and Martin, *Dictionary of Law.*

3. Bourdieu, *Outline of a Theory of Practice,* 79. Bourdieu was, of course, describing human agents, not architectural ones.

4. Mishima, "The Priest of Shiga Temple and His Love," 61.

5. Consciousness is the elemental attribute of agency in Asad's critique of understanding agency as essentially resistance to power. Asad, "Agency and Pain."

6. Sher, "Out of Control."

7. Sutton, "Nature of the Early Law of Deodand"; Pervukhin, "Deodands."

8. Gross, *Select Cases from the Coroners' Rolls,* 77.

9. Pietz, "Death of the Deodand."

10. H. Black, *Black's Law Dictionary,* 62–63.

11. Citizens United v. Federal Election Commission, 558 U.S. 08-205 (2010).

12. For the case and for counterarguments, see French, "The Corporation as a Moral Person"; Velazquez, "Debunking Corporate Moral Responsibility"; Welch, "Corporate Agency and Reduction"; Arnold, "Corporate Moral Agency."

13. Stone, *Should Trees Have Standing?*

14. Stephenson, *Snow Crash,* 281–83.

15. J. Black, *Oxford Dictionary of Economics,* 67. For a review of the use of the term in the social sciences, see D. Miller, "Consumption and Commodities." In his thought-provoking article on things, Kopytoff insists: "Although the singular and the commodity are opposites, no thing ever quite reaches the ultimate commodity end of the continuum between them. There are no perfect commodities." Kopytoff, "Cultural Biography of Things," 87. Such a claim cannot be sustained if Black's definition of "commodity" is accepted.

16. Even nonplaces have a life. Augé, *Non-Places.*

17. Ernest Richmond, advisor architect to the Wakf, Report, March 1919, quoted in Ashbee, *Jerusalem,* 1:9.

18. Zola, *Pot Luck,* 8.

19. Tschumi, *Questions of Space,* 58.

20. Hooper, *Poltergeist.* For a productive discussion of discomforting buildings, see Vidler, *Architectural Uncanny.*

21. Merleau-Ponty, *Phenomenology of Perception,* x–xi.

22. D. Smith, "Phenomenology."

23. Gauchet, *Disenchantment of the World.*

24. On the critical term *habitus,* see Bourdieu, *Outline of a Theory of Practice,* especially chap. 2.

25. Bentham, "Panopticon." For the classic analysis of the power of the Panopticon, see Foucault, *Discipline and Punish,* particularly 195–228.

26. Ruskin, *Modern Painters,* vol. 3, part 4.

27. Ruskin, *"A Joy For Ever" and Its Price in the Market,* 57.

28. Jacobs, *The Death and Life of Great American Cities,* 369, 16.

29. Bevan, *Destruction of Memory;* T. Smith, *Architecture of Aftermath.*

30. Sudjic, *The Edifice Complex.*

31. Harris, *Building Lives,* 3.

32. Godish, *Sick Buildings,* 5. Also see Murphy, *Sick Building Syndrome and the Problem of Uncertainty.*

33. Gruber, *Biomimetics in Architecture,* 7.

34. McNeill and McNamara, "Life and Death of Great Hotels."

35. Arnold and Sofaer, *Biographies and Space.*

36. In my own university's Department of History, of the nearly forty full-time regular faculty, at the time of writing only two are premodern specialists.

37. Written on December 16, 2012, after the shootings at Sandy Hook Elementary School in Connecticut.

38. Scarry, *Body in Pain,* 14.

39. For a review of various theoreticians' definition of "place," see Cresswell, *Place.* Cresswell's own distilled definition is a useful one: "Place, at a basic level, is space invested with meaning in the context of power" (12).

1. Murder

1. Dennis, Foote, and Perkins, *Laws of Early Iceland,* 1:146.

2. Miglio, "Old Norse and Old English Language Contact," §4.4.

3. Mike, "Is Denver's Animal Murder Act Constitutional?"

4. Camas Davis, who raises rabbits for eating and gives classes that include their slaughter, is regularly subjected to such abuse. Davis and Glass, "Animal Sacrifice, Act Two."

5. McSpadden, *Famous Sculptors of America,* 180.

6. Apparently as an art student in Paris he supported himself at least in part with taxidermy. Kimbrough, *Drawn from Life,* 23–24.

7. Benedict, *Holy Rule,* chap. 4.

8. Ibid., chap. 6.

9. In classical Latin, *claustrum* is a means of closing or shutting in; when referring to physical objects, a bolt, bar; when describing space, an enclosure, prison, den; a barricade, dam, fortress. Simpson, *Cassell's New Latin Dictionary.*

10. For an excellent introduction to the history and function of the cloister, see Meyvaert, "The Medieval Monastic Claustrum."

11. For Hugh of Folieto's *De claustro animae,* see Whitehead, *Castles of the Mind,* 61–86.

12. For speculation on the origins of cloisters, see Horn, "On the Origins of the Medieval Cloister."

13. Benedict, *Holy Rule,* chap. 52.

14. For secular judgments carried out in monastic cloisters, see Albrecht, "Der Kreuzgang als Gerichtsstätte." For examples of the other functions, see Meyvaert, "The Medieval Monastic Claustrum."

15. As Robert Browning's *Soliloquy of the Spanish Cloister* powerfully suggests, this interaction was not inevitably positive. Browning, *Poems in English.*

16. See, for example, Dale, "Monsters, Corporeal Deformities, and Phantasms"; Seidel, "Installation as Inspiration"; Pressouyre, "St. Bernard to St. Francis"; P. Klein, "Zur Einführung"; Davril, "Fonctions des cloîtres dans les monastères au Moyen Âge"; P. Klein, "Topographie, fonctions et programmes iconographiques des cloîtres." For some contemporary authors, the materiality of the cloister can be safely displaced by its reading as a text. Carruthers, "The Poet as Master Builder"; Whitehead, *Castles of the Mind,* 61–86. In contrast, still compelling is Meyer Schapiro's understanding of the aesthetic power of medieval sculpture. Schapiro, "On the Aesthetic Attitude in Romanesque Art." For a useful discussion of Schapiro's continued relevance, see Camille, "'How New York Stole the Idea of Romanesque Art.'"

17. For the Cloisters, in addition to texts included elsewhere in the notes, see T. Miller, "The Cloisters"; "The Cloisters: Another Technique in Museum Design"; Forsyth, "Five Crucial People in the Building of the Cloisters"; B. Young, *A Walk through the Cloisters*; Blumenthal, "The New Cloisters."

18. The seclusion of the Cloisters is not just apparent. For the negotiated commitment of New York City to maintaining a bus line to Fort Tryon Park, see Correspondence: Bus Route to the Cloisters, June–December 1937, Cloisters Papers and Correspondence Files.

19. For the mythical dimension of this retreat, see Goehring, "The Dark Side of Landscape."

20. My italics. "Introduction to The Cloisters," corrected in Barnet and Wu, *The Cloisters,* 11–12.

21. *New York Times,* "Big Tract Donated by Rockefeller Jr. to Save Palisades." The monograph devoted to the park-development of the Palisades details John D. Rockefeller's long commitment to the Palisades project but never mentions the Cloisters. Binnewies, *Palisades.* I could also find no mention of the Cloisters in the Rockefeller Archive folders with correspondence concerning Rockefeller's land acquisition and the Palisade Park development. See Cultural Interests: Palisades Park, 1902–44, Rockefeller Foundation Archives Collections.

22. Cuxa Cloister, as constructed at the Cloisters, measures 90 ft. by 78 ft. (27.43 × 23.77 m). An NBA/NCAA regulation basketball court is 94 ft. long by 50 ft. wide.

23. Where supplementary stone was required to construct the resized cloister, it was taken from the same quarries as the original. "The Cloisters: Another Technique in Museum Design," 50.

24. For a critical reading of the medievalizing plan, see Report by Wilhelm Reinhold Valentiner on the Plan for the Cloisters Museum, August 20, 1931, Cloisters Papers and Correspondence Files. For an authoritative discussion of the early stages of the design process, though with a different take than my own, see Leuchak, "'The Old World for the New.'"

25. Breck is actually commenting here on Barnard's Cloisters in his introduction to the museum after John D. Rockefeller Jr. gifted it to the Metropolitan Museum, but it also

matches his vision of how the new building should act. Breck, "The Opening of the Cloisters," 114.

26. Letter from Joseph Breck to Charles Collens, March 23, 1931, Cloisters Papers and Correspondence Files.

27. Report by Joseph Breck on Tentative Plans for the New Cloisters, 1931, Cloisters Papers and Correspondence Files.

28. Ibid.

29. Fergusson, "Medieval Architectural Scholarship in America, 1900–1940."

30. Report by Charles Collens on a Trip in Connection with the Mediaeval Museum at New York, 1931, 10, Cloisters Papers and Correspondence Files.

31. Rorimer's dedication to the project is amply documented in his papers. The James J. Rorimer Papers, 1927–66, Cloisters Papers and Correspondence Files.

32. The exterior ashlar is granite quarried near New London, Connecticut. Doria limestone from Genoa is used on the interior.

33. Rorimer, *The Cloisters,* 94.

34. Explanation of Preliminary Sketches probably provided by Charles Collens, 1931?, Cloisters Papers and Correspondence Files

35. For example: "I had no idea that such a setting could exist here—the building which is not a copy but a creation, the spaces in which treasures can be themselves." Letter from Harrison Griswold Dwight, Assistant Director of the Frick, to John D. Rockefeller Jr., September 20, 1938, Cloisters Papers and Correspondence Files.

36. My italics. Address by John D. Rockefeller Jr. on the Occasion of the Opening of the Cloisters in Fort Tryon Park, May 10, 1938, Cloisters Papers and Correspondence Files.

37. *New York Times,* "Southern Leaders Decide to Abandon Fight on Wage and Hour Bill."

38. Fair Labor Standards Act of 1938, Pub. L. No. 75-718, 52 Stat. 1060 (1938).

39. Letter from John D. Rockefeller Jr. to John D. Rockefeller Sr., February 1, 1917. Quoted in Fosdick, *John D. Rockefeller, Jr.,* 335–36.

40. For a discussion of Rockefeller's interest in porcelain and a critique of his taste, see Abe, "Rockefeller Home Decorating and Objects from China."

41. The Cloisters's spectacle works differently than that usefully characterized by Jonathan Crary: "Spectacle is not primarily concerned with a looking at images but rather with the construction of conditions that individuate, immobilize, and separate subjects, even within a world in which mobility and circulation are ubiquitous. In this way attention becomes key to the operation of non-coercive forms of power." Crary, *Suspensions of Perception,* 74.

42. For an engaging discussion of the relation between museums and iconoclasm, see Tamen, *Friends of Interpretable Objects,* chap. 3.

43. The *Mona Lisa* measures 30.35 in. by 21 in. or 637.35 square inches; the Annunciation panel measures 26.25 in. by 24 in. or 630 square inches.

44. Compare this frank Romanesque rendering of the Annunciation with the dense version of the same subject by Robert Campin of Tournai of about 1425, found in the Spanish Room of the Cloisters. In the latter, not even the Virgin attends to the subject's central message.

45. Hoving, "A Long-Lost Romanesque Annunciation." The most recent publication of the panel adds little more than bibliography to Hoving's account. Melcher, *Die mittelalterlichen Kanzeln der Toskana,* 270–73.

46. Richa, *Notizie istoriche delle chiese fiorentine, divise ne'suoi quartieri,* 4, 18.

47. Included in the San Leonardo pulpit are the Tree of Jesse, Nativity, Adoration of the Magi, Circumcision, Baptism, and Deposition.

48. Hoving, *King of the Confessors,* 76–88.

49. E. Smith, "George Grey Barnard"; Schrader, "George Grey Barnard"; M. Young, "George Grey Barnard and the Cloisters"; "The Cloisters"; Dickson, *George Grey Barnard, Centenary Exhibition*; McSpadden, *Famous Sculptors of America*; Dahler, "George Grey Barnard's Cloister."

50. Barnard's ambitious program for the capitol was described in the *New York Times*: "Barnard's idea is to crown the great entablature above the main portal with a series of bronze groups, gigantic in size, men, chariots, and horses, groups which may be termed the 'Apotheosis of Labor.' Against the entablature comes a series of eight granite caryatids in four groups of two each; the rest of the sculpture, so far as practicable, will be on lower planes, closer to the eye and easier to be seen, and carved in marble or granite. Among the themes that have already suggested themselves to the sculptor are typical groups of Indians, the Scotch-Irish, the English, the Pennsylvania Germans, and the Quakers. The caryatids on the main facade may indicate the laboring men, on whose shoulders the State rests, such as farmers, ironworkers, miners, foresters or lumbermen. Allegorical groups of men, women, and children will be placed near the chief portal to represent the primitive forces underlying human society, groups as a specimen of which 'The Hewer' may be taken, and these will be executed bravely in huge nudes like those of Barrias and Rodin." *New York Times,* "Pennsylvania's New Capitol." Barnard describes his financial difficulties in great detail in a cablegram sent to the *New York Times.* Barnard, "Sculptor Tells of Great Loss."

51. *New York Times,* "American Sculptor Is Lauded in Paris."

52. *New York Times,* "Rare Relics Kept from America by French Protest." Barnard's desire to acquire further monuments was by no means extinguished. A *New York Times* article suggests that Barnard's lust for monuments turned elsewhere: "Gainsboroughs, Fragonard screens, pillars from Tuscan villas, armor worn by Jeanne d'Arc, tapestries from queens' bedrooms, whole ceilings torn from Moorish palaces, effigies of dead kings, and crown jewels of living ones, are coming over to grace this new imperial country. Stone by stone, six temples will be transported to New York in the near future, according to the plans of George Grey Barnard." *New York Times,* "New Sack of Europe—by Americans."

53. His admission charges, Barnard claimed, were to raise money for French war orphans and widows. The new Cloisters never had guards in period costume, though some visitors desired it. "Dear Sir: In my recent visit to the Cloisters, I was very much impressed by the surroundings, the simplicity of its style and the treasures exhibited within the walls of the museum. However, for the sake of its ascetic looking atmosphere, I think it would add greatly to the prestige of the institution, if periodical sounds of an organ with music of the masters, and the public be ushered by monks rather than ordinary guides." Letter from Christopher Tallis to James Rorimer, Director of the Cloisters, August 4, 1938, Cloisters Papers and Correspondence Files.

54. His description dates from after Rockefeller's purchase of the site but before its replacement by the new museum. His comment appeared in an essay critical of Rockefeller Center titled, "Frozen Music or Solidified Static? Reflections on Radio City," which was first published in the *New Yorker* on June 20, 1931, and has since been republished in Mumford, *Sidewalk Critic,* 56. Perhaps his love of Barnard's Cloisters in part explains his dislike of Rockefeller's Cloisters. See Mumford, "Pax in Urbe."

55. Barnard Papers, Philadelphia Museum of Art Archives.

56. Barnard's italics. Letter from G. G. Barnard to Joseph Breck, May 11, 1925, Rockefeller Foundation Archives Collections.

57. Relations between Barnard and Rockefeller were already strained. Barnard completed an Adam and Eve Fountain in 1923 for the Rockefeller estate in Pocantico Hills, New York. Rockefeller demanded under contract that Adam's penis be covered by a cloud, while Barnard, through various means, including unauthorized work on the statue, resisted his patron's stipulations. Moffatt, "Re-Membering Adam."

58. Barnard continued to collect medieval objects after he sold his first collection to Rockefeller. A catalog of his second collection was published posthumously. The collector's lack of interest in documentation is generously ascribed to his exclusively aesthetic interest in the material, though it might just as well have been ascribed to his focus on the market. "Mr. Barnard regarded his treasures with the eyes of an artist, not of an art historian, and in the course of his life so many works of art had been brought to his attention that it was possible only in rare instances to identify objects in the collection by means of his notes and correspondence." Robinson and Weinberger, *George Grey Barnard Collection,* xi. I want to thank Professor Stan Abe for bringing this catalog to my attention.

59. Letter from G. G. Barnard to John D. Rockefeller Jr., November 21, 1927, Rockefeller Foundation Archives Collections. See this and other documents concerning the sale of Barnard's property and objects to John D. Rockefeller Jr. between 1925 and 1927, in Rockefeller and Barnard, "Cultural Interests."

60. *New York Times,* "G. G. Barnard Plans Art School Here."

61. Schrader, "George Grey Barnard," 3.

62. Barnet and Wu, *The Cloisters,* 9.

63. According to Stephanie Cassidy, the archivist of the Art Students' League of New York, Barnard only taught there for three seasons between 1900 and 1903. I am very grateful to Ms. Cassidy for supplying this information to me in a communication dated June 19, 2007.

64. Rorimer, *Medieval Monuments at the Cloisters.*

65. Rorimer, *Medieval Monuments at the Cloisters,* rev. ed.

66. Rorimer, *Medieval Monuments at the Cloisters,* 9.

67. Durliat, "La fin du cloître de Saint-Michel de Cuxa"; Mallet, "Dispersion et restauration du cloître de Saint-Michel de Cuxa."

68. For the restoration, see Mallet, *Les cloîtres démontés de Perpignan et du Roussillon,* 56.

69. These are documented by Duméril and Lespinasse, *Une abbaye cistercienne du Comminges.*

70. Barnet and Wu, *The Cloisters.*

71. "The Cloisters," 617. No doubt the source for this quote was Barnard himself.

72. For Saint-Guilhem's dismemberment and reconstruction, see Saint-Jean, *Saint-Guilhem-le-Désert,* 25–30. At least some of the capitals of the Bonnefont cloister have been attributed to a Franciscan monastery at Tarbes. Barnet and Wu, *The Cloisters,* 14–15.

73. The art dealer René Gimpel recognized Barnard's venality, writing "January 15 / Joseph [*sic*] Barnard. An excellent American sculptor, very much engrossed in carving himself a fortune out of the trade in works of art." Gimpel, *Diary of an Art Dealer,* 211. The passage reads more sarcastically in French. Gimpel, *Journal d'un collectionneur.*

74. For a further discussion of the term "commodity" as it is used in this text, see the Introduction.

75. For a range of assessments on the negative effect of the market in archaeological finds on historical understanding, see Brodie et al., *Archaeology, Cultural Heritage, and the Antiquities Trade.*

76. For an extended meditation on (textual) fragments, see Frey, *Interruptions.*
77. Mussot, "Monastères et tourisme."

2. Spoils

1. For the conception of benign and destructive expenditures of excess that informed this chapter, see Bataille, *The Accursed Share.*

2. The still magisterial work on *Wunderkammer* or cabinets of curiosities is Schlosser, *Die Kunst- und Wunderkammern der Spätrenaissance.* Also see Bredekamp, *The Lure of Antiquity and the Cult of the Machine.*

3. Bennett, *Pasts Beyond Memory.* Also see two very useful exemplifications of museological self-awareness: Karp, *Museum Frictions*; Karp and Lavine, *Exhibiting Cultures.*

4. For a critical consideration of *spolia,* see Brilliant and Kinney, *Reuse Value.*

5. For museum taxonomies as a control of cultural objects' excesses, see Clifford, "Objects and Selves—an Afterword."

6. For a description of the exhibited collection from 1948, see Perrot, *Le Musée archéologique de Palestine a Jérusalem.*

7. For archaeological institutions during the British Mandate, see Gibson, "British Archeological Institutions in Mandatory Palestine."

8. C. Breasted, *Pioneer to the Past,* 22. Also see Abt, *American Egyptologist.*

9. Breasted was in Egypt between 1891 and 1894.

10. J. Breasted, *The Oriental Institute.*

11. A souvenir pamphlet with interior and exterior renderings by William Walcot from designs by Welles Bosworth was produced for the occasion of the presentation of Rockefeller's gift to the Egyptian people. Cairo Museum: The New Egyptian Museum and Research Institute at Cairo, Rockefeller Foundation Archives Collections.

12. The Egyptian Museum is a classical beaux-art structure designed by Marcel Dourgnon; it was opened to the public in 1902. For a modern history of Cairo, see Abu-Lughod, *Cairo,* 102.

13. On the development of this site in relation to old Cairo, see Wharton, *Building the Cold War,* chapter 2.

14. For a description of these strings and a more detailed consideration of the Orientalism of Breasted's project, see Abt, "Toward a Historian's Laboratory."

15. Abt, "Breasted-Rockefeller Egyptian Museum Project."

16. Davis, *Shifting Sands.*

17. For insight into the devotional character of archaeology in Jerusalem in the mid-nineteenth century, there is no better source than Robinson, *Biblical Researches in Palestine and the Adjacent Regions.*

18. Much has been written on the subject. For further discussion of the politics of archaeology and a brief bibliography, see below, chapter 4.

19. Letter from John D. Rockefeller Jr. to Raymond B. Fosdick, December 16, 1926, Rockefeller Foundation Archives Collections.

20. Fosdick was the son of a schoolteacher, born in rural upper state New York and educated at Colgate, Princeton, and Columbia. He was, for many years, a public servant, working on police reform before being appointed by Woodrow Wilson to be under–secretary general of the League of Nations. He ended his public-spirited career as the president of the Rockefeller Foundation. His autobiography is a poignant reminder of what we have lost with the end of political civility. Fosdick, *Chronicle of a Generation.*

21. Letter from Raymond B. Fosdick to Thomas M. Debevoise, August 3, 1927, Rockefeller Foundation Archives Collections. Or again, "If Dr. Breasted should send a draft of such a letter to Lord Plumer and with it a confidential note suggesting that because of the Egyptian situation it seemed wiser for Mr. Rockefeller not to state conditions for his gift but rather to have the project described as suggested in the draft, Lord Plumer would, of course, understand fully the reasons for following such a course; in fact, it is quite possible that the British Government would also be pleased to avoid arousing in Egypt the feeling which might result from a comparison of the terms of offers made by Mr. Rockefeller for two such similar projects." Letter from Thomas M. Debevoise to Raymond B. Fosdick, August 4, 1927, Rockefeller Foundation Archives Collections.

22. A copy of the deed dated 1711 is found in the Rockefeller Museum Archive, Jerusalem. I am very grateful to Professor Rafaat Abou-el-Haj for translating this document for me. For an introduction to the Khalidi library in Jerusalem, see Little and Turgay, "Documents from the Ottoman Period in the Khālidī Library in Jerusalem."

23. Letter from Lord Plumer to Charles Breasted, January 15, 1927, Rockefeller Foundation Archives Collections.

24. Letter from John D. Rockefeller Jr. to Lord Plumer, October 11, 1927, Rockefeller Foundation Archives Collections.

25. "The Palestine Archaeological Museum"; Iliffe, "Palestine Archaeological Museum, Jerusalem"; Saad, *The Palestine Archaeological Museum and the Dead Sea Scrolls*; Sussman and Reich, "History of the Rockefeller Museum"; Herbert and Heinze-Greenberg, "Anatomy of a Profession"; Fuchs and Herbert, "A Colonial Portrait of Jerusalem"; Fuchs and Herbert, "Representing Mandatory Palestine"; Ibrahim, *West Meets East.*

26. Breasted and Harrison apparently both wanted to construct an asymmetrical structure. In a letter to Fosdick, Breasted comments on the plans that he received of the projected museum. "From the beginning the architect has expressed the conviction that the building site would require an asymmetrical building, and Mr. Ryerson and I went into this question very thoroughly, with the result that we both agree with the architect. The plans at present submitted are for a *symmetrical* building, and I have now written Harrison that the donor and his advisers are in favor of an *asymmetrical* building. I take it that the architect will now proceed to design such a building, which will require considerable modification of the present plans." Letter from James Henry Breasted to Raymond B. Fosdick, July 27, 1927, Rockefeller Foundation Archives Collections.

27. The Supreme Court Building in Jerusalem, opened in 1992, was designed by Israeli architects Ram Carmi and Ada Carmi-Melamed. Like the Palestine Archaeological Museum, the design suggests engagement with the historical traditions of the land. The inner court recalls Islamic palace architecture and was inspired by Harrison's interpretation of the Islamic tradition. Goldberger, "A Public Work That Ennobles as It Serves"; A. Schultz, *Ada Karmi-Melamede and Ram Karmi, Supreme Court of Israel, Jerusalem.* In the pamphlet given out as part of the tour of the Supreme Court Building, however, all reference to Islamic antecedents is erased: "The Courtyard, made of stone, suggests the arid conditions of the desert which borders Jerusalem. A narrow water channel bisects the Courtyard. The arches resemble the gates of Jerusalem during the Roman period. The stone quarried from the earth and the water reflecting the sky represent the biblical symbols of truth and justice. The courtyard is inspired by a verse from Psalms, 'Truth will spring up from the earth and justice will be reflected from the heavens,' (Psalms 85:12)." The observer is left to wonder whether the willful misidentification of the architectural precedents of the building as Roman rather than Islamic reveals a bias in Israeli law as well as in its architectural appreciation.

28. Geddes, "Jerusalem Actual and Possible," 29–30.

29. Observations made on a visit in 2005.

30. Iliffe, "Palestine Archaeological Museum, Jerusalem," 7–8.

31. The message was written in response to a grateful telegram at the time of the opening of the museum in 1938 from Sir Arthur Wauchope, high commissioner for Palestine. Communication sent by Sir Arthur Wauchope, High Commissioner for Palestine, to John D. Rockefeller Jr., January 20, 1938, Rockefeller Foundation Archives Collections.

32. Letter from James G. McDonald to John D. Rockefeller Jr., July 9, 1946, Rockefeller Foundation Archives Collections. For McDonald, see Breitman, Stewart, and Hochberg, *Refugees and Rescue.*

33. Comment on the Palestine Archaeological Museum from the *Boston Transcript,* November 18, 1927, Rockefeller Foundation Archives Collections.

34. The italics are Breasted's. J. Breasted, *The Oriental Institute,* 1–2.

35. Ibid., 6.

36. Collins, *Eric Gill,* 187–90.

37. Israel Museum, "West Meets East."

38. Gill, *Autobiography,* 251–52.

39. The sculptor was Ulric H. Ellerhusen. For the iconography of the tympanum, see *Oriental Institute: Symbolism.*

40. Letter from John D. Rockefeller Jr. to Lord Plumer, Rockefeller Foundation Archives Collections.

41. Iliffe, "Palestine Archaeological Museum, Jerusalem," 19.

42. High Commissioner and Council of Ministers, "Order of Transfer of Ownership of the Museum."

43. The Palestine Archaeological Museum Order, 1948 (Palestine Order in Council, 1948. Order Made by the High Commissioner under Section 3. Supplement no. 2 to *The Palestine Gazette* no. 1663 of 22nd April, 1948), Palestine Archaeological Museum Files.

44. Letter from James L. Kelso to John D. Rockefeller Jr., December 29, 1949, Rockefeller Foundation Archives Collections.

45. For Harry, see Haag, "Myriam Harry"; Bourin, "Prix Fémina—Myriam Harry."

46. Harry, *Little Daughter of Jerusalem,* 264.

47. Ibid., 272.

48. *Washington Post,* "Peace of the Harem."

49. For the possibility that the Shapira fragments were authentic, see the account—dismissed by archaeologists—by Allegro, *The Shapira Affair.* For the context of Allegro's argument, see J. Brown, *John Marco Allegro.*

50. For an overview of the Dead Sea Scrolls and a sense of the complexity of their publication, see Reed, *The Dead Sea Scrolls Catalogue*; Schiffman and VanderKam, *Encyclopedia of the Dead Sea Scrolls*; Magness, *The Archaeology of Qumran and the Dead Sea Scrolls.*

51. Much has been written on Dead Sea Scroll conspiracies, ranging in form from biographies to novels: e.g. J. Brown, *John Marco Allegro*; J. Rosenberg, *The Copper Scroll.*

52. Minutes of the trustees' meetings in the 1950s were preoccupied with finding money to buy scroll fragments.

53. Saad, *The Palestine Archaeological Museum and the Dead Sea Scrolls,* 12–15. The decision to use endowment funds to repay Dead Sea Scroll debts was made in a meeting of the museum's trustees in 1957. Minutes of the 13th Ordinary Meeting of the Board of Trustees, June 1, 1957, Palestine Archaeological Museum Files.

54. For descriptions of the working conditions at the beginning of the project and later, see J. Brown, *John Marco Allegro,* 26–40; Reed, "Jerusalem Report."

55. For example, see J. Brown, *John Marco Allegro*; Galor, Humbert, and Zangenberg, *Qumran, the Site of the Dead Sea Scrolls.*

56. *Time,* "The Oldest Decalogue."

57. Allegro, *Search in the Desert,* xi–xii.

58. Report on the Editing and Publishing of the Dead Sea Scrolls Preserved in the Palestine Archaeological Museum, June 3, 1966, Palestine Archaeological Museum Files.

59. Publications on the Dead Sea Scrolls are innumerable. For a summary of their history from 1947 to 1960, see the impossibly titled Fields, *Dead Sea Scrolls: A Full History.* The volume both describes and embodies the controversies associated with the scrolls. For exemplary essays on the historical context and interpretation of the scrolls, see Lim and Collins, *Oxford Handbook of the Dead Sea Scrolls.*

60. Ostling, "Is Jesus in the Dead Sea Scrolls?"

61. For a discussion of this case and its international copyright implications, see Lim, Carmichael, and MacQueen, *On Scrolls, Artefacts and Intellectual Property.* The judgment of the court is included as an appendix.

62. For an example of academic quarrels and state exhibitions, see Golb, "The Current Controversy over the Dead Sea Scrolls."

63. Magen and Peleg, "Back to Qumran."

64. Modified from the definition offered by the U.S. National Library of Medicine and the National Institutes of Health, "Medline Plus."

65. The official website warns: "Visitors are advised to wear warm clothing in the winter because the Museum is not heated!" Israel Museum, "Rockefeller Archaeological Museum."

66. Secretary's Report: April 1954 through March 1955, May 7, 1955, Palestine Archaeological Museum Files.

67. There was no attendant at the entrance to the museum when I visited it May 19, 2005; indeed, I was the only presence in the building until I began removing the brown paper that covered the Holy Sepulchre lintel sculptures. Only then did a guard armed with an uzi appear to forbid me taking such liberties. On two subsequent encounters with the museum, in November 2006, I noted a total of three other visitors. Uzi Dahari, deputy director, Israel Antiquities Authority, in a conversation in his office at the Rockefeller Museum, indicated that attendance records are kept at the Israel Museum. In response to my inquiry, James S. Snyder, the Anne and Jerome Fisher Director of the Israel Museum, found that formal admissions numbers are not kept (December 15, 2006). I also visited the museum in 2009, at which time it was receiving artificial resuscitation while the Israel Museum was being extensively renovated. Visitors unhappy with finding the Israel Museum closed were bused to the Rockefeller. In 2012, I found the museum returned to its comatose state.

68. In 2009 I was unsuccessful in my attempt to locate the "gallery books" in the archive of the Rockefeller Museum. I am grateful to the library of the University of Colorado at Boulder for sending me one of the "gallery books" in their collection. These books took the form of a mimeographed typescript bound in cardboard. They offered a detailed description of the objects and concluded with a description of the photographs in the gallery. *Gallery Book: Iron Age.* By 2012, artifact lists had been placed in a few of the rooms.

69. Furstenberg and Susser, "Future Shock." For a devasting critique of Israeli architectural practice, see Segal and Weizman, *A Civilian Occupation.*

70. Ferrero-Waldner, "The EU and the Middle East Peace Process." In contrast, illegal construction by Jewish settlers in East Jerusalem and the West Bank is sanctioned. J. Anderson, "Israelis Act to Encircle East Jerusalem." For an overview of the failure of the Oslo Accords to curtail state terrorism, see Elman, "Jerusalem and the Demise of the Oslo Peace Process."

71. At the "Jerusalem Across the Disciplines" conference at Arizona State University, Tempe, in February 2007, a nonacademic member of the audience made the absurd claim that she, as a Jewish woman, could only go into East Jerusalem with an armed guard.

72. When I visited the museum in 2012, trash was conspicuously left on both sides of the entrance booth. I sent photographs of the scene to the director of the Israel Museum.

73. For example, Spencer, "The Israel National Museum."

74. Although his majesty's government has "absolute discretion as to the constitution of the Advisory Board to the Museum, the Government wishes to cooperate with past members of the said board in the management of the Museum. I shall therefore be glad if you will kindly convey to me through the Governor of Jerusalem . . . your wishes as to the learned delegate whom you wish to represent you on the Museum's Advisory Board." Letter to the Institutions with Members of the Board of Directors of the Rockefeller Museum, August 21, 1966, Palestine Archaeological Museum Files.

75. Zias, "Palestine Archaeological Museum," 635. For a Palestinian perspective, see Taha, "History and Role of Museums in Palestine."

76. International Committee of the Red Cross, "Convention for the Protection of Cultural Property in the Event of Armed Conflict."

77. With very few exceptions. Oyediran, *Plunder, Destruction and Despoliation.*

3. Amnesia

1. Frankfurt, *On Bullshit.*

2. The American Psychiatric Association provides the professional view: "Dissociative Amnesia most commonly presents as a retrospectively reported gap or series of gaps in recall for aspects of the individual's life history. These gaps are usually related to traumatic or extremely stressful events. Some individuals may have amnesia for episodes of self-mutilation, violent outbursts, or suicide attempts. Less commonly, Dissociative Amnesia presents as a florid episode with sudden onset. This acute form is more likely to occur during wartime or in response to a natural disaster or other forms of severe trauma." American Psychiatric Association, *Diagnostic and Statistical Manual of Mental Disorders,* 4th ed., 300.12. (This definition, like a number of others, is clearer in the 4th edition than in the 2013 5th edition.)

3. Johnson, "Dissociative Identity Disorder (Multiple Personality Disorder)."

4. Holmes, "The Evidence for Repression."

5. Crews, *Memory Wars.*

6. Giesbrecht et al., "Cognitive Processes in Dissociation," 617.

7. Porter et al., "Memory for Murder." For an authoritative set of essays on criminal memory, see Rogers, *Clinical Assessment of Malingering and Deception. DSM-V* remains neutral: "There is no test, battery of tests, or set of procedures that invariably distinguishes dissociative amnesia from feigned amnesia. Individuals with factitious disorder or malingering have been noted to continue their deception even during hypnotic or barbiturate-facilitated interviews. Feigned amnesia is more common in individuals with 1) acute, florid dissociative amnesia; 2) financial, sexual, or legal problems; or 3) a wish to escape stressful circumstances." American Psychiatric Association, *Diagnostic and Statistical Manual of Mental Disorders,* 5th ed.

8. Sun et al., "Does Feigning Amnesia Impair Subsequent Recall?," 81.

9. Bylin and Christianson, "Characteristics of Malingered Amnesia." For research that suggests that feigned amnesia does not lead to a degraded memory of a crime, see Sun et al., "Does Feigning Amnesia Impair Subsequent Recall?"

10. Koolhaas, "A Foundation of Amnesia."

11. For three distinct *translatio* traditions, see Márquez Villanueva, *Santiago.*

12. In addition to the crude block-print offered as an illustration here, see, for example, the more robust image of the Matamoros by Carreño de Miranda, *St James the Great in the Battle of Clavijo.*

13. Short, "Spanish Troops in Iraq to Wear Christian Badge."

14. Rawlings, *Spanish Inquisition.*

15. For a powerful description and analysis of the spectacle of torture, see the account of the execution of Robert-François Damiens in Foucault, *Discipline and Punish,* chap. 1.

16. Jetter, *Santiago, Toledo, Granada,* 19. Innocent VIII initially promoted a hospital at Santiago de Compostela in a papal bull of 1487. Also see Jetter, *Das europäische Hospital von der Spätantike bis 1800,* 92–104. For a programmatic and formal discussion in English of the series of large hospitals built in sixteenth-century Spain, see Wilkinson-Zerner, "Hospital of Cardinal Tavera in Toledo."

17. Münzer, "Viaje por España y Portugal en los años 1494 y 1495," 95–96.

18. For the donations to the cathedral from Granada, see López Ferreiro, *Historia de la Santa A. M. Iglesia de Santiago de Compostela,* app. 43, pp. 152–60.

19. Rives, "Magic, Religion and Law," 56–57.

20. Local violence was also required: land was bought and water rights were seized over the objections of the Benedictines of St. Martins. Jetter, *Santiago, Toledo, Granada,* 25.

21. Egas was also the architect of the Catholic Kings' two other grand hospitals in Toledo (1494, 1504–14) and Granada (1504, 1511–22). Ibid.

22. Foundation documents specified that the facade should be built in ashlar masonry ("catería") similar to that of the cathedral. The building material of the rest of the exterior went unmentioned. At least originally the public "face" was apparently the only one that mattered. Ibid., 30.

23. On the inside, all warming ovens were backed with heavy masonry bearing the monarchs' coat of arms.

24. Bury, "Stylistic Term 'Plateresque.'"

25. The building reveals the treachery of that invidious modern dyadic construction of space so popularly and misleadingly articulated in Eliade, *The Sacred and the Profane.* For an extended critique of Eliade, see the Conclusion.

26. The foundation and institutional documents in the hospital's archive include pontifical bulls in favor of the Hospital de los Reyes Católicos received between 1499 and 1641; charters, provisions, and royal orders, the earliest of which is 1497 (1) and the latest 1821 (837); sixty-three manuscripts of the Cabildo, the governing body of the hospital with reports and accounts; documents of the Guild of the Apostle Saint James, deeds, testaments, lawsuits, admission lists, etc. For a catalog of the hospital's documents, see Fernández Catón, *El archivo del Hospital de los Reyes Católicos de Santiago de Compostela.* Also see López Ferreiro, "Colección Diplomática," 501–627. For a discussion of the foundation documents, see Jetter, *Santiago, Toledo, Granada,* 29–49.

27. Dodgson, "Rare Woodcuts in the Ashmolean Museum—VII," 14. Also see Lyell, *Early Book Illustration in Spain,* 283–84; Rhodes, "Further Notes on an Indulgence of Alexander VI."

28. García Guerra, *El Hospital Real de Santiago,* 39.

29. Some sense of the violence done by the Inquisition to the mind as well as the body is provided by Francisca de los Apóstoles, *Inquisition of Francisca.*

30. Molina, *Descripción del reyno de Galizia,* fol. 12r. I want to thank Camila Maroja for correcting and improving my translation of this passage.

31. The privy included in the plan may not date earlier than the eighteenth century. I have presumed that it took the place of an earlier facility. On premodern anxieties about bodily wastes, see Kuriyama, "Forgotten Fear of Excrement."

32. For a useful survey of water in medieval monastic establishments, see Bond, "Monastic Water Management in Great Britain."

33. Crislip, *From Monastery to Hospital.*

34. A more positive presentation of the Renaissance hospital is made by Henderson, *Renaissance Hospital.* The author, however, makes no mention of bathing.

35. Erasmus, "Colloquies: Inns," 372.

36. For a contrast between the medieval and the early modern use of water, see Guillerme, *Age of Water,* especially chaps. 3 and 5. For an assessment of attitudes toward health in premodernity, see Zimmerman, "Diseased Body in Premodern Europe."

37. For the particular severity with which medical texts were expurgated in inquisitional Spain, see Front, "Expurgation of Medical Books in Sixteenth-Century Spain."

38. García Guerra, *El Hospital Real de Santiago,* 315–79.

39. Constitutions of Charles V of 1524, cited by ibid., 39.

40. Julia, "Pour une géographie européenne du pèlerinage à l'époque moderne et contemporaine."

41. For example, Erasmus, "Colloquies: A Pilgrimage for Religion's Sake." For a later, sustained parody of the pilgrimage to Compostela, see Southey, *Poetical Works,* 245–68.

42. Pilgrimage to Santiago continued, if on a reduced scale, into the nineteenth century. For example, see Laffi, *Viaggio in ponente a San Giacomo di Galitia e Finisterrae.* For a discussion of attempts to control mendicancy, see Julia, "Pour une géographie européenne du pèlerinage à l'époque moderne et contemporaine," 6–22.

43. Julia, "Pour une géographie européenne du pèlerinage à l'époque moderne et contemporaine," 26–37.

44. Ordinance of the city of Santiago, 1569, quoted by Vázquez de Parga, Lacarra, and Uría Ríu, *Las peregrinaciones a Santiago de Compostela,* 116.

45. Pack, "Revival of Pilgrimage to Santiago de Compostela," 346.

46. Laffi, *A Journey to the West,* 166–67.

47. Jetter posits that the back courtyards were added between 1768 and 1798 by Manuel de los Mártires and Ramón Pérez Monroy. Whether or not these two additional courtyards were part of the original plan is unclear. Jetter, *Santiago, Toledo, Granada,* 53–54. Also see Carro Otero, "1785: Proyecto para ampliar el 'Gran Hospital' fundado por los Reyes Católicos."

48. Perhaps these additions were connected to the unproductive profit made by the Bourbon monarchy from the exploitation of Mexican mines and labor during the silver boom of the first half of the eighteenth century. On this silver boom, see Flynn and Giráldez, "Cycles of Silver."

49. Quoted by Israel, "Counter-Reformation, Economic Decline, and the Delayed Impact of the Medical Revolution in Catholic Europe," 41.

50. Fernández Catón, *El archivo del Hospital de los Reyes Católicos de Santiago de Compostela,* 11.

51. By far the best description that I have read of Lourdes and its devotions in the nineteenth century is that of Zola, *Lourdes.*

52. Perry and Echeverría, *Under the Heel of Mary.*

53. For suspicions about the authenticity of these relics, see Duchesne, "Saint-Jacques à Galice."

54. Fernández Fuster, *Teoría y técnica del turismo,* 2:65–70. Santiago de Compostela was designated as a World Heritage Site in 1985. González and Medina, "Cultural Tourism and Urban Management in Northwestern Spain," 448–49.

55. The Camino continues to be essential to the regional economy. "The Way of St. James is the *star product* of Galicia's tourism policy, and is also considered as one of the interregional *brands* in Spain's national Plan of Objectives for the Promotion of Tourism Overseas. Precisely, on the occasion of the Xacobeo 2010, the Ministry of Industry, Tourism and Commerce signed an agreement with the communities of Aragon, Basque Country, Asturias, Cantabria, Castile and León, Galicia, La Rioja, and Navarre to increase the international visibility of this touristic-cultural circuit." My italics. Fernández-Poyatos, Aguirregoitia-Martínez, and Boix-Martínez, "The Way of Saint James and the Xacobeo 2010 in the Tourism Websites of the Spanish Autonomous Communities," 25.

56. Arq Joanis Gomez Gonzalez; Arq Jefezus Ferdinandus Morenus; Arq Julius Canus; Arc di Rafrael Dela Joya; Constructor Rodolfus Lama; Alphsus Biperecius; Aparejatoris Ferdinadus Ortiz Echague.

57. For the funding of the paradors under Arias-Salgado, see Rosendorf, "Be El Caudillo's Guest." At the time of writing, the future of all of the Spanish paradors is in question. Daley, "A Fond Past with an Uncertain Future." For the building's corporate history, see note 75 below.

58. "El domingo se inaugura la hostería real de Compostela"; Vila Jato, *Parador de Santiago "Os Reis Católicos,"* 256–57.

59. Starkie, *Road to Santiago,* 262.

60. Eco, "Ur-Fascism." For an introduction to Spanish fascism and its leader, see Lewis, *Latin Fascist Elites,* chap. 5.

61. Opus Dei was founded in Spain in 1928. Allowing me to use Opus Dei here as a foil is its familiarity from the popular novel by Dan Brown, *The Da Vinci Code.* For an academic affirmation of the prelature's practices, see Fortunato, "Opus Dei's Box-Office Triumph." For an introduction to the movement, also see the founder's foundational text: Escrivá de Balaguer, *The Way.*

62. For academics, the repressive censorship of post–World War II fascism might be most powerfully signified by the realization that until 1962 the Falange controlled all academic appointments and the granting of degrees in Spain. The fascists lost their hegemony only with the official recognition of the degrees of the university of the Opus Dei, the Estudio General de Navarra, at Pamplona in that year. Welles, *Spain,* 160–61.

63. For a useful discussion of the historiography of repression in post–Civil War Spain, see Cabrera, "Developments in Contemporary Spanish Historiography." For concentration camps and slave labor during the Franco regime, see the collection of essays by Molinero, Tintó Sala, and Sobrequés i Callicó, *Una inmensa prisión.*

64. Correyero Ruiz, "La propaganda turística española en los años del aisleamiento internacional."

65. *New York Times,* "Censorship in Spain."

66. Franco and Arias-Salgado y de Cubas, "Ministerio de informacion y turismo."

67. Read and Manjon, *Paradores of Spain,* 6–10. A serious corporate history of the paradors has yet to appear.

68. Bolín, *Spain,* 303–5.

69. For another construction of a propagandistic tourist site, see Basilio, "A Pilgrimage to the Alcázar of Toledo."

70. Sánchez Sánchez, "Turismo, desarrollo e integración internacional de la España franquista"; Holguin, "'National Spain Invites You.'"

71. For example: "Captain Bolin [undersecretary in the Ministry of the Interior] frankly stated the Nationalist authorities believed it was good propaganda for them to demonstrate that behind the front life was orderly and normal in their territory. . . . It is admitted in official circles here that the foreign exchange brought into the Nationalist treasury by tourists, will, of course, be much appreciated." Carney, "Battlefield Tours Started in Spain." For Spanish legislation controlling tourism, see Roca Roca, *La regulación jurídica del turismo en España.* Also see Rosendorf, "Be El Caudillo's Guest"; Correyero Ruiz, "La propaganda turística española en los años de aislamiento internacional."

72. For Conrad Hilton's religious and ideological commitments, see Wharton, *Building the Cold War,* 8–9, 146–47.

73. Hilton, *Be My Guest,* 263. Also see Hamblin, "In Nineteen Lands, Instant America."

74. Ballard and Ballard, *Paradores of Spain,* 2–3.

75. From 1954 to 1986, the Hostal was not officially part of the system of paradors but controlled by another state corporation, ENTURSA, Empresa Nacional de Turismo, SA, which owned a chain of eight luxury urban hotels. Martínez, *El Instituto Nacional de Industria en el sector turístico*; Martínez, "La empresa pública en el sector turístico español." Because of its deficits, ENTURSA was privatized and sold to the prestigious Italian CIGA chain in 1986. In the 1990s, it was again acquired by the state and integrated with the paradors. Miguel García, "An Examination of International Promotion in a Spanish Hotel Network," 40–42. For background, see Vergés, "Why Governments Sell Public Firms."

76. Michener, *Iberia,* 740–41.

77. The archives were removed during the conversion of the hospital to a hotel; they were permanently incorporated into the collection of the Universidad de Santiago de Compostela in 1969. Fernández Catón, *El archivo del Hospital de los Reyes Católicos de Santiago de Compostela,* 11.

78. For a useful discussion of another maladjusted reuse, see Weiner, "From Victorian Asylum to 'Princess Park Manor.'"

79. TripAdvisor, "Parador Hostal Dos Reis Catolicos."

80. Esperanza Senande, interview with author at the Hostal de los Reyes Católicos, Santiago de Compostela, May 16, 2006.

81. I have been unable to get more recent account information.

82. Fielding, *Fielding's Travel Guide to Europe,* 1284–85.

83. García Sanchéz, "Santiago de Compostela and Its Parador." *The Guinness Book of World Records* awards the distinction of oldest hotel in the world to the Nisiyama Onsen Keiunkan in Yamanashi, Japan.

84. TripAdvisor, "Parador Hostal Dos Reis Catolicos." I checked this site first in March 2007. In October 2011, the comments were remarkably similar in tone and content.

85. Carr, "Travel Advisory"; Vila Jato, *Parador de Santiago "Os Reis Católicos."*

86. Old prisons have, after all, become popular subjects for reconstruction as boutique hotels. Gregor, "A Room for the Night (Not 40 to Life)."

87. Pfeiffer, "Many Genres, One Giant Space."

4. Urban Toxicity

1. Fulcher of Chartres, *The First Crusade,* 91.

2. For a recognition of the Holy Sepulchre's disorder, see Venturi, *Complexity and Contradiction in Architecture,* 58–59. For a description of how the building became complex, see Ousterhout, "Architecture as Relic and the Construction of Sanctity."

3. Creelman, "Profanation of the Holy Sepulchre."

4. M. Friedman, "Monks Brawl at Christian Holy Site in Jerusalem."

5. For good introductions to the Protestant relation to visual culture, see Eire, *War against the Idols*; Koerner, *Reformation of the Image.* Nevertheless, many Protestants were obsessed with things from holy places. See, for example, Wharton, "Relics, Protestants, Things."

6. Howe, *Oriental and Sacred Scenes,* 352–53.

7. Wallace, *Jerusalem the Holy,* 184.

8. Selma Lagerlöf received the Nobel Prize for her novel *Jerusalem.* For the English translation, see Lagerlöf, *Jerusalem: A Novel.*

9. Lagerlöf, *The Holy City,* 65–80.

10. Dorland, *Dorland's Illustrated Medical Dictionary.*

11. Bar-El et al., "Jerusalem Syndrome," 86.

12. The hospital has been judged to be "not fit for animals." Siegel, "Psychiatric Hospitals 'Not Fit for Animals,' Knesset Panel Hears."

13. Del Castillo, "Mad for Jerusalem."

14. Zislin et al., "Male Genital Self-Mutilation in the Context of Religious Belief," 258.

15. This point is worth making because the area around the city is sometimes represented as empty before foreign construction was begun outside the walls. Early travelers mention Silwan and Lifta. The deed of the Khalidi house, which formerly stood on the site of the Palestine Archaeological Museum, is dated to 1711. (See the discussion of this site in chapter 2.) For a description of the extramural Arab estates, see Kark and Landman, "Establishment of Muslim Neighbourhoods in Jerusalem," 117.

16. Kark and Oren-Nordheim, *Jerusalem and Its Environs.*

17. Development is documented by a series of topographical maps of the city: Sir Charles William Wilson (London, 1864–65), Sir Charles William Wilson (Southampton, 1876), Henri Nicole (Paris, 1886), and Conrad Schick (Leipzig, 1894–95). For excellent, high-resolution reproductions of these maps, see Jewish National and University Library, "Ancient Maps of Jerusalem."

18. Still the most convenient description of development outside the walls of Jerusalem, including those structures mentioned in this paragraph, is Ben-Arieh, *Jerusalem in the Nineteenth Century.*

19. Carmel, *Die Siedlungen der württembergischen Templer in Palästina 1868–1918,* 44–46; Ben-Arieh, *Jerusalem in the Nineteenth Century,* 2:127–32.

20. Harry, *Conquest of Jerusalem,* 189–91.

21. D. Goldman, "Architecture of the Templers," 278.

22. Ibid., 133–34. Red roof tiles were apparently being produced in Jerusalem at the Schneller German-Arab vocational school as early as the 1870s. Kroyanker and Wahrman, *Jerusalem Architecture,* 22–24. For further discussions of red tile in Jerusalem, see Carmel, *Die Siedlungen der württembergischen Templer in Palästina 1868–1918,* particularly 44–46; Kroyanker, *Jerusalem.*

23. Holliday, *Letters from Jerusalem during the Palestine Mandate,* 43.

24. Sauer, *The Holy Land Called,* 111.

25. Hope, *Hotel Tiberias,* 237–41.

26. For example, Internet real estate advertisements for prestigious properties in Jerusalem always list the German Colony among the city's most desirable neighborhoods. E.g., Ben Ishai, "Jerusalem Real Estate Guide."

27. Monk, "Review of *Bauhaus on the Carmel and the Crossroads of Empire,* by Gilbert Herbert and Silvina Sosnovsky."

28. Parfitt, *Jews in Palestine, 1800–1882.*

29. For the Jewish neighborhoods of Jerusalem, see Ben-Arieh, *Jerusalem in the Nineteenth Century,* 2:108–12; Kroyanker and Wahrman, *Jerusalem Architecture,* 33–133; Halper, *Between Redemption and Revival,* 139–50.

30. Wilson, "Obituary of Dr. Conrad Schick"; Masterman, "Important Work of Dr. Conrad Schick"; Goren, *For the Sake of Jerusalem.*

31. Rivlin, *Me'ah she'arim.*

32. Kroyanker and Wahrman, *Jerusalem Architecture,* 133.

33. Quoted by Kark, *Jaffa,* 115.

34. Wallace makes an exception for the Jewish community Mishkenot Sha'ananim, established through the philanthropic efforts of Sir Moses Montefiore.

35. Wallace, *Jerusalem the Holy,* 95.

36. Though the film represents Me'ah She'arim, it was not shot on site. Gitai, *Kadosh.*

37. O. Rosenberg, "Ultra-Orthodox Spitting Attacks on Old City Clergymen Becoming Daily."

38. Kershner, "Religious-Secular Divide, Tugging at Israel's Heart."

39. The descriptors are those of the Israeli urban historian David Kroyanker. Kroyanker and Wahrman, *Jerusalem Architecture,* 133.

40. Jeffery, *A Brief Description of the Holy Sepulchre, Jerusalem,* 191–92.

41. For the politics of archaeology, see Silberman, "'If I forget thee, O Jerusalem'"; Abu El-Haj, *Facts on the Ground*; Monk, *An Aesthetic Occupation*; Hicks, "From 'Questions that Count' to Stories that 'Matter' in Historical Archaeology"; Greenberg, "Contested Sites."

42. Biblical archaeology in its most apologetic form was American. As discussed in chapter 2, a German-trained archaeologist, like James Breasted, tended to be more critical in the application of archaeology to the Bible and vice versa. For a useful analysis of the varieties of biblical archaeology, see Davis, *Shifting Sands.*

43. For a balanced view of missionary work in the Holy Land, see Marten, "Imperialism and Evangelisation."

44. A sense of the bitterness and pettiness of Protestant squabbling is provided by Finn, *A View from Jerusalem, 1849–1858.* For a convert's perspective on the ordeal of being fought over by Anglicans and American evangelicals, see Diness et al., *Capturing the Holy Land.*

45. *Macon Weekly Telegraph,* "Explorations in Palestine"; Merrill, *East of the Jordan,* ix; Ben-Arieh, *Jerusalem in the Nineteenth Century,* 2:280–81. Also see Bates, "Archaeological News."

46. Kark, *American Consuls in the Holy Land,* 323–26.

47. Merrill, "Modern Researches in Palestine," 118.

48. Merrill, *The Site of Calvary.*

49. Albright, "Selah Merrill 1837–1909."

50. Merrill, as American consul, was responsible for the well-being not only of the few American Jews who lived in Palestine at the time, but also for the equitable distribution of the *halukah*—those monies that were collected by Jews in the Diaspora for support of their coreligionists in Palestine about which he so bitterly complained. Further, a few hundred Jews

who had emigrated from Russia had gained U.S. consular protection before Merrill took office. S. Goldman, "The Holy Land Appropriated," 157.

51. Merrill, "Jerusalem," 102–3.

52. Merrill, "Modern Researches in Palestine," 125.

53. Merrill, "Jerusalem," 99–100.

54. Loti, *Jerusalem*, 12.

55. Merrill, "Nazareth the Home of Jesus," 9.

56. The development of the Palestinian neighborhoods has not been thoroughly documented. Old scholarship dealing with Palestinian domestic architecture focused on the village dwelling. Much of this research was based on the ahistorical premise that, as unchanged traditional forms, these houses reproduced the setting in which Jesus lived. For an early twentieth-century account of this persuasion, which includes references to earlier literature of the same sort, see Dalman, *Arbeit und Sitte in Palästina.* The volume was published posthumously—Dalman died in 1941. Such assessments persist, e.g., Richardson, "Towards a Typology of Levantine/Palestinian Houses." Most new scholarship tends toward the social-scientific, making arguments about the cultural construction of Palestinian suburbs rather than about their architecture. There are, of course, important exceptions. See, for example, references herein to Ron Fuchs's work. More detailed investigations have been devoted to the German and Jewish neighborhoods developing contemporaneously in Jerusalem.

57. Kark and Oren-Nordheim, *Jerusalem and Its Environs*, 120–21.

58. I make this point because the Palestinian house tends to be treated by Israeli researchers as a subject of alien ethnography. In this literature Palestinian building tends to be marginalized; e.g., "the Arab Muslim population of Jerusalem showed little initiative in the realm of construction" (ibid., 115). Or even eliminated; e.g., "The map of Jerusalem drawn by Sir Charles William Wilson in 1864 (who directed the 1864–66 survey of Jerusalem) shows only barren hills and a few dirt trails leading to the city within the walls. The only buildings outside the walls are Mishkenot Sha'ananim, the Montefiore Windmill, the Russian Compound and the Monastery of the Cross" (Eylon, "Focus on Israel: Jerusalem"). As documented in note 15 above, this is not the case.

59. In the Old City, Palestinian houses tended to share walls with their neighbors; small interior courtyards provided privacy. For the Palestinian house, see Fuchs, "The Palestinian Arab House and the Islamic Primitive Hut"; Fuchs and Meyer-Brodnitz, "Emergence of the Central Hall House Type"; Fuchs, "Palestinian Vernacular Architecture." For high-quality photographs of historic Palestinian houses, see Khasawneh, *Memoirs Engraved in Stone.*

60. Quoted by Kark and Oren-Nordheim, *Jerusalem and Its Environs*, 120.

61. Nashif, "Palestinian Arab and Jewish Leadership in the Mandate Period," 115–16.

62. Yellin, *Memoirs of a Son of Jerusalem*, 180. I am grateful to Professor Kalman Bland for his translation of this passage.

63. For a properly illustrated and more complete discussion of the building phases of Rabbah Effendi al-Husseini's house, see Amiri and Wharton, "Home in Jerusalem." For the date of construction, see Kroyanker, *Jerusalem Architecture*, 117–18.

64. See, for example, the stunning publication of Bayt al-'Aqqad in Damascus, Mortensen, *Bayt al-'Aqqad.*

65. The courtyard house is a popular, autochthonous form in the Middle East. It has attracted considerable attention from architects as well as historians. See, for example, the typological studies of Petruccioli, "The Courtyard House"; Petruccioli, *After Amnesia.* More useful as historical assessments are several of the articles in Edwards et al., *Courtyard Housing.*

66. See above, notes 22 and 27.

67. For domestic prayer spaces, see Campo, *Other Sides of Paradise,* 32–34.

68. For example, see Zako, "Power of the Veil."

69. They are identified as such by Vester, *American Colony Family Album,* 25.

70. Bloom and Blair, *Grove Encyclopedia of Islamic Art and Architecture,* 2:336–39.

71. Ragette, *Architecture in Lebanon,* 190.

72. Disraeli, *Tancred or the New Crusade* (1871 edition), vol. 2, book 3, 12–13; Herzl, *Old New Land,* 71–73.

73. Harry, *Little Daughter of Jerusalem,* 175–77.

74. For example, Hoffman, *House of Windows.*

75. Gitai, *House / A House in Jerusalem.*

76. For primary sources on the American Colony, see Vester, *Our Jerusalem*; Larsson, *Seven Passports for Palestine*; Matsson, *American Colony of Jerusalem*; Levy, "An American Colony." For secondary sources, see Dudman and Kark, *The American Colony*; Gröndahl, *Dream of Jerusalem*; Hummel and Hintlian, "American Colony in Jerusalem"; Ariel and Kark, "Messianism, Holiness, Charisma, and Community"; Shamir, "'Our Jerusalem'"; Gavish, "The American Colony and Its Photographers."

77. Ford, "Our American Colony at Jerusalem," 644.

78. This structure now houses the Spafford Children's Center. In the last years it has been carefully renovated. I am grateful to Dr. Jantien Dajani, the center's director, for introducing me to the building.

79. Sapir, "Conrad Schick and His Works for the English Mission of Jerusalem," 76.

80. Letter from A. Loivy to H. G. Spafford, November 20, 1885, American Colony Collection.

81. Letter from Anna Spafford to Alexander Hume Ford, December 18, 1906, American Colony Collection.

82. Ashbee, *A Palestine Notebook, 1918–1923,* 9–10.

83. Ariel and Kark, "Messianism, Holiness, Charisma, and Community," 645.

84. Vester, *Our Jerusalem,* 298–99. For the earthquake, see *New York Times,* "Many Killed and Hurt in Palestine Quake."

85. It was her novel describing this millennial move that won Lagerlöf the Nobel Prize: Lagerlöf, *Jerusalem: A Novel.* The novel is still brilliant, as is its filmic version produced nearly a century later: August, *Jerusalem.* In the film, the powerful rendering of the extreme settings compensates for the flattening of the characters: the austere and beautiful cold of Sweden contrasts to the austere and beautiful heat of Jerusalem; the stoicism demanded by the weather in the north is tested by the violence of disease, aridity, and social ostracism in the south. The villain in both renderings is Hellgum, the born-again evangelical preacher who returns to his Swedish homeland from America as a dark shadow preying upon rifts in the religious fabric of the community. The novel *Jerusalem,* published in Sweden in 1901, depicted recent events with resonant sympathy. Bille August succeeded in recovering that same compassion in his rendering of a now remote historical moment. Indeed, Hellgum's evangelical megalomania and the Holy City's violence so compellingly described in the film seem all too contemporary. Unfortunately, the simple human goodness also so powerfully represented in *Jerusalem* now seems quaintly out-of-date.

86. Letter from Anna Spafford to George and Sarah, October 5, 1902, American Colony Collection.

87. A photograph of what seems to be a copy of a deed of March 10, 1910, is found in the American Colony Collection.

88. Vester, *Our Jerusalem,* 175–76. A slightly different version is given by Theo Larsson, who names the price of the building as US $40,000 in gold. Larsson, *Seven Passports for Palestine,* 11.

89. Vester, *American Colony Family Album,* 25.

90. Levy, "An American Colony."

91. Creelman, "Profanation of the Holy Sepulchre."

92. Vester, *Our Jerusalem,* 283.

93. Schnabel, *Miral.* I experienced a comparable gathering at the memorial service held for Val Vester in June 2008. For an obituary, see *London Times,* "Val Vester: Hotelier."

94. The most detailed account of the events described here was that written by Bertha Vester, the daughter of the founders of the American Colony, Horatio and Anna Spafford. Vester, *Our Jerusalem,* 158–59, 197–207. A brief version is provided by S. Goldman, "The Holy Land Appropriated," 164–65. The documents recording the questionable role of the British government and Episcopal church in the affair are published in Lipman, *Americans and the Holy Land through British Eyes,* 150–63, 81–83. For the most politically effective account of Merrill's treatment of the American Colony, see Ford, "Our American Colony at Jerusalem." For the American Colonists' accounts of their persecutions, see Notes and Letters Concerning American Consuls Merrill and Wallace, 1884–98, American Colony Collection.

95. Lipman, *Americans and the Holy Land through British Eyes,* 155. The Public Record Office documents concerning the American Colony (PRO FO78 78/4837, 4924, 4925, 4939) are usefully published in that volume.

96. Ford, "Our American Colony at Jerusalem," 649.

97. Larsson, *Seven Passports for Palestine,* 15.

98. The choice of management company was carefully made; the decision to appoint a Swiss firm rather than a local one was a critical political one for maintaining the American Colony's famous neutrality. Paul Vester, interview with author in Topanga, Calif., February 22, 2007. On that neutrality, see Feron, "Correspondent's Choice."

99. Vincent was one of the monumental figures of Jerusalem archaeology. Albright, "In Memory of Louis Hugues Vincent." This street name and a few others in the area indicate that it was the favored location of the foreign archaeological institutes. The Albright Institute of Archaeological Research (formerly the American School of Oriental Research) is located just down the road.

100. The line marking "the seam" between East and West Jerusalem has now been permanently inscribed by Israeli town planners with the six-lane Highway 1 and the Jerusalem Light Rail. Barghouti, *Boycott, Divestment, Sanctions,* 151–65. On the Israeli side of the line there is a relatively new institution that balances the American Colony opposite it—the Museum on the Seam. This museum, unlike the deeply intolerant Museum of Toleration, is truly about the ethical treatment of the Other.

101. By the distinguished epidemiologist Peter Mühlens. Weyer, "In memoriam Peter Mühlens." Bertha Vester ascribes the American Colony's health in this case to the screens they put over their doors and windows to keep out the flies, but which also excluded infected mosquitoes. Vester, *Our Jerusalem,* 186.

102. Two further unpublished descriptions of the house are worth quoting. The first is from a manuscript by Victor Hugo Wickström, Swedish writer and member of Parliament, in "The Best Recollections of My Journey: With the Swedes in Jerusalem," 1901, American Colony

Collection. "They [members of the American Colony] took me through all their apartments. How light! How nice! How scrupulously clean! The open garden was planted with flowers and green. Balconies offered comfortable places for sitting. The dining room floor was covered with genuine Swedish rag carpet and different dwelling rooms shone dazzlingly white with curtains and spreads. They had separate weaving, baking and washing rooms, and special departments for shoemaking, tailoring, goldsmiths, gold and silver plating, photography, etc. These make what the Colony needs, what is surplus is sold. Besides this the Colony has bought up a business of photography and olive wood works, where the public can buy extremely tasteful articles, also bunches of pressed flowers, picked and put together by the members of the Colony." The second was written by a Reform rabbi: Levy, "An American Colony." "Entering the house the visitor steps into the central salon or meeting room. If he be so fortunate as to come on Sunday, he will be invited to take part in the services. . . . The salon is paved with marble and with its broad windows curtained with dazzling white hangings, lamps covered with tasteful shades, and bunches of fresh roses and ferns in all the corners of the room, it presents a novel kind of sitting room. The center of the ceiling [is opened by a dome] and on a background of gold stars shine out, all surrounded with a garland of flowers. Nearby the organ may be seen five women and the men who act as the elders of the congregation. . . . The poor, and especially the despised lepers of Jerusalem, count the Americans as their best friends and constant helpers. Amid the motley throng of ne'er-do-wells with which Jerusalem is overfilled, the American colony stands out in relief, by its thrift and general helpfulness. The Mohammedans esteem the colony most highly, but the missionaries, strange to relate, are their most violent opponents. This is especially true of American missionaries . . . who not long ago committed the sacrilege of digging up the bodies of their dead and selling the cemetery to the Catholics so as to add to the missionary funds." For further, more available published descriptions of the American Colony, see Larsson, *Seven Passports for Palestine,* 12; Sontag, "An Undiplomatic Skirmish in a Pasha's Palace in Jerusalem"; Kark and Oren-Nordheim, *Jerusalem and Its Environs,* 123; Reichs, *Cross Bones,* 197–99; Shahid, *Jerusalem Memories,* 21.

5. Gambling

1. For a fuller account, see Goodman, "Addiction: Definition and Implications," 1404.

2. "In addition to the substance-related disorders, this chapter (292.9) also includes gambling disorder, reflecting evidence that gambling behaviors activate reward systems similar to those activated by drugs of abuse and produce some behavioral symptoms that appear comparable to those produced by the substance use disorders. Other excessive behavioral patterns, such as Internet gaming, have also been described, but the research on these and other behavioral syndromes is less clear. Thus, groups of repetitive behaviors, which some term *behavioral addictions,* with such subcategories as 'sex addiction,' 'exercise addiction,' or 'shopping addiction,' are not included because at this time there is insufficient peer-reviewed evidence to establish the diagnostic criteria and course descriptions needed to identify these behaviors as mental disorders." American Psychiatric Association, *Diagnostic and Statistical Manual of Mental Disorders,* 5th edition.

3. Lemon, "Can We Call Behaviours Addictive?"

4. For a remarkably influential example of such ideologically motivated arguments, see Becker and Murphy, "A Theory of Rational Addiction." For a compelling critique, see

Rogeberg, "Taking Absurd Theories Seriously." The application of free-market values to biology nevertheless continues. Hardy-Vallée, "Decision-Making in the Economy of Nature."

5. Woess, "Personalexekution und cessio bonorum im römischen Reichsrecht."

6. Iversen, *Dopamine Handbook*; Previc, *Dopaminergic Mind in Human Evolution and History.* Also see Goodman, "Neurobiology of Addiction."

7. For a classic statement on this subject, see Bruner, "On Perceptual Readiness."

8. Kavanagh, Andrade, and May, "Imaginary Relish and Exquisite Torture." I am grateful to Dr. Carey Morewedge, Department of Social and Decision Sciences, Carnegie Mellon University, for this reference.

9. Pavlov, *Conditioned Reflexes.* Now brain-imaging technologies appear to trace it. Suri and Schultz, "Temporal Difference Model Reproduces Anticipatory Neural Activity."

10. Hyman, "Addiction: A Disease of Learning and Memory"; O'Brian, "Neuroplasticity in Addictive Disorders."

11. W. Schultz, "Responses of Monkey Dopamine Neurons to Reward and Conditioned Stimuli"; Berridge and Aldridge, "Decision Utility, Incentive Salience, and Cue-Triggered 'Wanting.'"

12. Crockford et al., "Cue-Induced Brain Activity in Pathological Gamblers"; Han et al., "Brain Activity and Desire for Internet Video Game Play." A raft of books has been published on gaming addiction, for example, Clark and Scott, *Game Addiction.*

13. Mello, Rimm, and Studdert, "The McLawsuit"; Brownell and Gold, "Food and Addiction," 439–40.

14. "Cyborg" as used here has the politics but not the optimism of the foundational work on the subject: Haraway, "A Cyborg Manifesto." For a consideration of the contemporary city as cyborgian, see Swyngedouw, "Metabolic Urbanization."

15. Shirley, *City Come a Walkin',* 201–2.

16. Ibid., 58.

17. For a poignant example of a host's ambiguity about her prosthetic attachment, see Verlager, "The Prosthetic Eye."

18. Nicoletta and Morgan, *Buildings of Nevada,* 214.

19. Rothman, "Colony, Capital, and Casino."

20. Moody, "Nevada's Legislation of Casino Gambling in 1931."

21. Carroll, "To the People of Nevada."

22. *Los Angeles Times,* "Gambling Bill Wins Approval."

23. Prostitution is not legal in Clark County. Stingley, "Keeping Their House in Order."

24. Nevada Commission on Tourism, "Nevada Weddings."

25. For an engaging history of the dam, see Hiltzik, *Colossus.*

26. For the role of the Democratic politicians in securing Works Progress Administration funds from the Roosevelt administration, see Gottdiener, Collins, and Dickens, *Las Vegas,* 14–15.

27. Paradise, Nevada, includes the Strip, McCarran International Airport, and the University of Nevada–Las Vegas. Its police force and fire department are independent of those in Las Vegas.

28. Wright, *An Autobiography,* 329.

29. Hess, *Viva Las Vegas,* 26–36.

30. *New York Times,* "News Notes from the Field of Travel."

31. Patrick, *An Interview with William J. Moore,* 41–43.

32. At the Little White Chapel, for example, patrons push a button from their car window to call the minister to the drive-thru window.

33. Patrick, *An Interview with William J. Moore,* 5.

34. For a good photographic survey of early motels, see Liebs, *Main Street to Miracle Mile,* 168–91.

35. Wharton, *Building the Cold War,* 173–75.

36. Roehl and Van Doren, "Locational Characteristics of American Resort Hotels."

37. The role of the mob in Las Vegas is familiar territory. For a summary and review of the sources, see Rothman, "Colony, Capital, and Casino," 309–18. Also see Farrell and Case, *The Black Book and the Mob.*

38. All the ellipses within sentences are Wolfe's. T. Wolfe, *Kandy-Kolored Tangerine-Flake Streamline Baby,* xvi–xvii.

39. Moehring and Green, *Las Vegas: A Centennial History,* 111.

40. Hess, "Styling the Strip."

41. *Los Angeles Times,* "G. V. Russell: Award Winner in Architecture."

42. Russell, "Interview." Also see Patrick, *An Interview with William J. Moore.* Unfortunately, the self-published book on Russell's architecture provides neither texts nor images of either Ciro's or the Flamingo. Russell, *George Vernon Russell, FAIA and Associates.*

43. *Los Angeles Times,* "George Claude, Neon Lights Scientist, Dies."

44. Lang, "Blackjack and Flashes," 104–5.

45. *Statesville Daily Record,* "Miss Atomic Blast."

46. This legislation had only been passed in 1955. Because the law made corporate investments in gaming illegal, the law only increased the dependence of casinos on questionable sources of investment. Rothman, "Colony, Capital, and Casino," 321.

47. For the intimacies between the first of the great entrepreneurs of the Strip, Howard Hughes, and mob figures, see Barlett and Steele, *Howard Hughes,* 281–95.

48. Venturi, Brown, and Izenour, *Learning from Las Vegas.*

49. The discrepancy between the Vegas described in Venturi, Brown, and Izenour's *Learning from Las Vegas* and its present condition is oddly ignored in discussions of the text such as that of Vinegar and Golec, *Relearning from Las Vegas.* That book is about a book, not about a city.

50. For a full definition of the postmodern as the term is used here, see Jameson, *Postmodernism,* chap. 1.

51. Barlett and Steele, *Howard Hughes,* 296–316.

52. *Las Vegas Review-Journal,* "Hughes Announces New Resort Hotel."

53. Wharton, *Building the Cold War,* 186–89.

54. Goulding, *Grand Hotel.* On the subject of Las Vegas as kitsch, see Irazábal, "Kitsch Is Dead, Long Live Kitsch." For the dangers of making fantasy out of history, see N. M. Klein, "Scripting Las Vegas."

55. Several of these 1990s casinos also introduced theme-park rides, some of which still survive. For an active list, see Vegas.com, "Behind the Scenes with Las Vegas' Top Thrills." I recommend the Big Apple Coaster at New York New York.

56. For a delightful description of making authentic fakes, see Curtis, "Belle Epoxy."

57. *New York Times,* "A Falling Hotel Vies with a Dropping Ball."

58. Debord, *Society of the Spectacle,* 24.

59. For a fuller characterization of the posthuman, see Hayles, *How We Became Posthuman.*

60. All buildings are now potentially panopticons.

61. Las Vegas Convention and Visitors Authority, "Visitor Statistics."

62. Funzug.com, "Top 20 Largest Hotels in the World."

63. And Disneyland Paris draws twice as many visitors as the Louvre. Riewoldt, *New Hotel Design,* 9–10.

64. Fagel, *Street Talk.*

65. *Las Vegas Sun,* "Nevada No. 4 in U.S. for Pedestrian Fatalities."

66. Packer, "Pedestrian Bridge Proposal Heads to County Commission."

67. Perhaps most famously exemplified in the competition for the domination of the New York skyline in 1930–31 between Walter Chrysler with his Chrysler Building and Jakob Raskob with his Empire State Building. Pierpont, "The Silver Spire."

68. The pronoun "who" is deliberately used here (and throughout this text) as an ironic reaction to the appalling identification in 2010 of corporations as persons by the Supreme Court of the United States, in Citizens United v. Federal Election Commission, 558 U.S. 08-205 (2010).

69. Bullivant, "The Most Expensive Development in US History Tries to Redefine Junk-space Urbanism on the Strip."

70. Women, who are preponderantly slot machine players, are an increasingly important source of casinos' profit. For the place of gender in gaming, see Schüll, "Video Poker."

71. There is, indeed, medical evidence of an "addiction" to tanning. Harrington et al., "Addictive-like Behaviors to Ultraviolet Light Among Frequent Indoor Tanners." For a relevant discussion of a pathology of shopping malls, see Davidson, "The World Was Getting Smaller. . . ."

72. This reading is a variation on that of Eco, *Semiotics and the Philosophy of Language,* 81–82.

73. B. Friedman, *Designing Casinos to Dominate the Competition,* 64.

74. For a powerful rendering of fictional deaths attributed to Las Vegas, see Puzo, *Fools Die.* Another example is "The Black Friar," in Kranes, *Low Tide in the Desert.* This fine collection of short stories offers a powerful antidote to Las Vegas glitz. Both Puzo's and Kranes's portrayals of the casino as surreal entanglement rather than as glamorous escape are much more compelling than over-the-top evocations such as that of Thompson, *Fear and Loathing in Las Vegas.*

75. For criticisms of that science and its uses, see Schüll, *Addiction by Design*; Strickland, "Gambling with Science." For an overview of the evolution of the interior of the casino, see Jaschke, "Casinos Inside Out."

76. Mehrabian and Russell, "Basic Emotional Impact of Environments"; Booms and Bitner, "Marketing Services by Managing the Environment"; Bitner, "Servicescapes"; Wakefield and Blodgett, "Importance of Servicescapes in Leisure Service Settings."

77. For example, see Lio and Rody, "Emotional Impact of Casino Servicescape"; Lucas and Dunn, "Estimating the Effects of Micro-Location Variables and Game Characteristics on Slot Machine Volume"; Lucas, "Determinants and Effects of Slot Servicescape Satisfaction in a Las Vegas Hotel Casino"; Johnson, Mayer, and Champaner, "Casino Atmospherics from a Customer's Perspective."

78. Friedman's italics. B. Friedman, *Designing Casinos to Dominate the Competition,* 5. Friedman formerly taught casino management at the University of Nevada–Las Vegas and now heads the Friedman Management Group, Consultants in Casino Marketing, Design and Operations. He laments the absence of innovation now in casino design. Bill Friedman, telephone interview with author, January 4, 2011.

79. B. Friedman, *Designing Casinos to Dominate the Competition,* 14–17.

80. Sara Gorgon, interview with author at the Vdara, Las Vegas, June 24, 2011.

81. Though not all, it seems. In 1984 it was claimed that a hotel conspired to get guests into its casino by not heating its swimming pool, providing TVs without cable or film-showing capacity, and lighting its guest rooms so dimly as to make reading impossible. Margolick, "Under Las Vegas's Neon Beats a Heart of Denim."

82. Buhler, "The Man Behind Casinos' Scent Science."

83. Roger Thomas, interview with author at the offices of Wynn Design and Development, Las Vegas, June 27, 2011.

84. For a useful review of the Wynn at its opening, see Yancey, "Won Over by Wynn."

85. Noseworthy and Finlay, "A Comparison of Ambient Casino Sound and Music."

86. Dixon et al., "Losses Disguised as Wins in Modern Multi-line Video Slot Machines."

87. GoingToVegas, "Gambling Guide"; Eadington, "Vegas Stripped."

88. Randy Adams of Anchor Gaming, quoted in Schüll, "Digital Gambling," 70.

89. For a popular version of the science involved, see Lehrer, "Your Brain on Gambling."

90. Lears, *Something for Nothing,* 1.

91. Schüll, "Video Poker," 168.

92. Ibid. Also see Scheri, *Casino's Most Valuable Chip*; Turdean, "Casinos and the Digitization of the Slot Machine."

93. IGT, "IGT to Showcase Revenue-Driving Games, Machines and Systems."

94. For an engaging discussion of the technology, see Bienn, "REELdepth™."

6. Digital Play

1. Those who cite Huizinga's classic text without recognizing its politics have missed its point. The book begins and ends with bitter comments on the authoritarian regimes of his day. For the author, play in the 1930s had been usurped and transformed into ideology. "The spectacle of a society rapidly goose-stepping into helotry is, for some, the dawn of the millennium. We believe them to be in error." Huizinga, *Homo Ludens,* 206.

2. Ibid., 10.

3. For the persuasive rhetoric of game code, see Bogost, *Persuasive Games.*

4. For the complex history of video game development, see Kent, *Ultimate History of Video Games.*

5. Silverman, Silverman, and Gerasimov, "Spacewar!" Conceived in 1961 by Martin Graetz, Stephen Russell, and Wayne Wiitanen and first realized on the PDP-1 in 1962 by Stephen Russell, Peter Samson, Dan Edwards, and Martin Graetz, together with Alan Kotok, Steve Piner, and Robert A. Saunders, the game is at the time of writing playable on the web. The PDP-1 emulator for this afterlife was produced by Brian Silverman, Barry Silverman, and Vadim Gerasimov in 1997.

6. For a discussion of "identity," see below.

7. Violence and profit are familiar bedfellows. For a cutting critique of the social violence of the video game industry, see Dyer-Witheford and de Peuter, *Games of Empire.* For the role of violence in the new corporatism, see N. Klein, *Shock Doctrine.*

8. Takahashi, "Video Game Industry to Hit $70 Billion by 2015, but Growth Will Slow."

9. For a recent discussion of video game ethics, see G. Young, *Ethics in the Virtual World.*

10. California State Assembly, Assembly Bill 1179 (2005).

11. Ibid., 2.

12. From the syllabus of Brown v. Entertainment Merchants Association, 564 U.S. 08-1448 (2011).

13. For the classic description of rape in cyberspace, see Dibbell, *My Tiny Life*, 11–32.

14. Exemplifying the naive understanding of illusionism's contribution to immersion, see Lindstrand, "Viva Piñata," 354. For an overview and critique of illusionism in gaming, see Wolf, "Abstraction in the Video Game."

15. Götz, "Load and Support," 137. For an opposing plea to attend more carefully to the aesthetics of games, see Kirkpatrick, *Aesthetic Theory and the Video Game*.

16. I am grateful to Corey May, lead writer of *Assassin's Creed* for Ubisoft, for sending me the complete story export for *Assassin's Creed*. For a fuller introduction to the narrative, see the comments of the game's producer, Jade Raymond, "Assassin's Creed Developer's Diary: Storyline."

17. Daftary, *Assassin Legends*.

18. The bibliography on the Templars is massive. One good historical introduction is offered by Forey, *Military Orders*.

19. On the manipulation of the player through affect, see Shaw and Warf, "Worlds of Affect."

20. Désilets, "Assassin's Creed Developer's Diary: Freedom."

21. Ibid.

22. For a smart introduction to the picturesque and its shifting aesthetic status, see Macarthur, *The Picturesque*.

23. Allen, "'Money and Little Red Books'"; Gage, "Turner and the Picturesque."

24. Gilpin, *Three Essays*.

25. Picturesque elements within the cities of *Assassin's Creed* could also be identified. By the nineteenth century the conventions for a picturesque viewing of the urban condition were well established. For an excellent introduction to the urban picturesque and its politics, see Andrews, "The Metropolitan Picturesque."

26. For the popularity of the panoramas of Jerusalem and for an introduction to the lithographic project of David Roberts, see Wharton, *Selling Jerusalem*, 145–88.

27. For Roberts and for bibliographies of earlier studies, see Bendiner, "David Roberts in the Near East"; Clark, "Renderings of an Early Master—David Roberts"; Guiterman, "Travels of David Roberts"; Solon, "Suggestions and Models for Architectural Rendering"; Bourbon, *Life, Works and Travels of David Roberts*; Mancoff, *David Roberts*; Guiterman, "David Roberts, R. A. (1796–1864), part I."

28. Roberts and Croly, *The Holy Land, Syria, Idumea, Arabia, Egypt, and Nubia*.

29. Ruskin, *Works*, 262.

30. Finden, Finden, and Horne, *Landscape Illustrations of the Bible*; Mayer, *Views in Egypt, Palestine, and Other Parts of the Ottoman Empire*.

31. This is, of course, an oversimplified account of lithography. For a full description and history of the technique, see Twyman, *Lithography, 1800–1850*.

32. Particularly at the end of the twentieth century, interest in Roberts's works revived. The three-volume set of lithographs has also been recently reproduced in its entirety by two different publishers, Duke Press and Rizzoli, and exhibitions of the prints are popular. Bourbon, *Life, Works and Travels of David Roberts*; Mezzatesta, *Jerusalem and the Holy Land Rediscovered*.

33. Pirated editions appeared almost immediately in Europe. In response, the original publisher, Moon, participated in a French edition of sixty plates published in Brussels. Octavo editions appeared in the United States in 1855 and 1860 and in England in 1856. Mancoff, *David Roberts*, 115.

34. Wharton, *Selling Jerusalem*, 145–88.

35. Ibid., 206–19.

36. Spence D., "Jesper Kyd and Assassin's Creed."

37. For the importance of acoustics to game play and their effectiveness in *Assassin's Creed* specifically, see Kelly, "Where the Artists Are the Superheroes."

38. According to Jade Raymond, producer of the game. Raymond, "Assassin's Creed Developer's Diary: Storyline."

39. For a critique of the politics of video games, see Lee, "I Lose, Therefore I Think."

40. Block, "Issues for *DSM-V*."

41. K. Young, "Understanding Online Gaming Addiction and Treatment Issues for Adolescents."

42. Crockford et al., "Cue-Induced Brain Activity in Pathological Gamblers"; Han et al., "Brain Activity and Desire for Internet Video Game Play."

43. Mighty Gordon, "sl-addiction."

44. Spingarn-Koff, *Life 2.0*; Van Cleave, *Unplugged*; Rickenbacker, "The SLunkie Factor—Part I–III." For an amusing take on *Second Life* addiction, see Your Girlfriend, "Second Life Intervention."

45. A great deal of research has been devoted to *World of Warcraft*. For a bibliography on the game and a narrative account of its experience, see Bainbridge, *Warcraft Civilization*.

46. Blizzard Entertainment, "What Is World of Warcraft?"

47. Barboza, "In China, New Limits on Virtual Currency."

48. Beust, "Order and Chaos in Alterac Valley."

49. Dyer-Witheford and de Peuter, *Games of Empire*, 151.

50. Stephenson, *Snow Crash*, 24–37.

51. Philip Rosedale, the founder of Linden Labs, gives an account of his inspiration by *Snow Crash* in Sydell, "Sci-Fi Inspires Engineers to Build Our Future." For two semi-anthropological, semidocumentary, and semiautobiographical introductions to *Second Life*, see Boellstorff, *Coming of Age in Second Life*; Guest, *Second Lives*. For a serious consideration of Linden Labs, see Malaby, *Making Virtual Worlds*.

52. As described by Sørensen, "Junk Playgrounds." For the broader context of this remarkable text, see Broderson, "Building a Ludic Environment."

53. For a useful discussion of three ways in which users relate to *Second Life*—immersive (handlers who identify with their avatars and fully engage in *Second Life* society), dissociative (handlers, such as griefers, who have no empathy for their avatars or the community), and augmentative (handlers, such as researchers, who treat their avatars and the setting as a means to an end)—see Clift, "State of Being—Avatar Perceptions."

54. In August 2011, the *Journal of Medical Internet Research*, which identifies itself as "the leading peer-reviewed eHealth journal," returned seventy relevant records on a search with the terms "education 'second life.'" The bibliography for *Second Life* is extensive. See Guest, *Second Lives*.

55. I was investigating religious sites early on in my experience of *Second Life* when I noticed that the bonfire around which we were sitting was made up of books. I asked the member of the evangelical community sitting next to me if books were being burned. "Oh, yes," the neatly dressed avatar answered. "Book burning is a good Christian tradition." For a scholarly treatment of religion in digital worlds, see Geraci, *Virtually Sacred*.

56. For the economies of MMOGs, see Castronova, *Synthetic Worlds*.

57. Linden, "The Second Life Economy in Q4 2010." Boellstorff's claims that the economy of *Second Life* is "creationist capitalism" seem to me to misrepresent both creationism and capitalism. Boellstorff, *Coming of Age in Second Life*, 205–36.

58. For an interview with *Second Life*'s first millionaire, see Hof, "My Virtual Life." For a critique of claims like mine about *Second Life*'s social equity, see Flavey, "Reconstructing Power in Second Life."

59. The first name in the citation in the figure caption and those that follow identifies the sixty-eight-square-acre block (sim) occupied by the site. The sim is the basic module of *Second Life.* The numbers plot the location of the site within the sim. For a more complete analysis of the architecture of the campaign, see Wharton, "Shaping the 'Public Sphere' in Second Life."

60. For *Second Life* physics, see dos Santos, "Second Life Physics." For a playful description of originality in *Second Life* architecture, see Lubell, "Original Sim."

61. Ruskin, "Modern Painters."

62. The conversation took place in *Second Life* on March 31, 2011. When I visited "Israel" in *Second Life* next, in September 2013, the Dome of the Rock was gone.

63. Shops and churches are obvious examples. Leone, "Semiotics of Religious Space in Second Life."

64. For *Second Life* as a site for the construction of your own theme park, see Pearce, "Narrative Environments from Disneyland to World of Warcraft."

65. Like the Dome of the Rock in "Israel," it is now gone. See below, Figure C.8.

66. For example, I was the only U.S. citizen in a group of Egyptians, Turks, Saudis, and Palestinians who met to discuss President Obama's speech in Cairo. The conversation was serious and engaging.

67. Attempts have been made by social scientists to assess systematically the appeal of different aspects of video games. For example, Lortie and Guitton, "Social Organization in Virtual Settings Depends on Proximity to Human Visual Aspect." It is not clear to me that such efforts move knowledge beyond the obvious.

68. Schüll, "Machines, Medication, Modulation," 234.

69. For a discussion of identity and role-play, as well as for a working bibliography, see Williams, Kennedy, and Moore, "Behind the Avatar."

70. Nagel, "What Is It Like to Be a Bat?"

71. Cameron, *Avatar.*

72. Pearce and Artemesia, *Communities of Play.*

Conclusion

1. For the definition of "commodity" used in this study, see the Introduction.

2. Lauer, *Le Trésor du Sancta Sanctorum,* 93–95. Lauer introduces his book with the complex and wonderful story of how he gained access to the altar and its contents.

3. Thomas Aquinas, *Summa Theologica,* Third Part, Question 25, Article 6.

4. Kishkovsky, "In Russian Chill, Waiting Hours for a Touch of the Holy."

5. Hopper, "Bottle of Former Pope's Blood to Go on Display."

6. Chicago Tribune, *International Competition for a New Administration Building.*

7. For a fuller bibliography for the Tribune Tower and a more sustained discussion of its fragments, see Wharton, "The Tribune Tower."

8. Sayers and Kahn, *Sabotage!,* 165.

9. Letter from Henry D. Lloyd to Col. Robert R. McCormick, November 20, 1930, Tribune Tower Fragment Collection Correspondence.

10. Letter from John S. Steele to Col. Robert R. McCormick, April 10, 1934, Tribune Tower Fragment Collection Correspondence.

11. Dr. Jeremy Dupertuis Bangs of the American Pilgrims' Museum in Leiden remembers reading the perplexed interdepartmental exchanges at the Regionaal Archief Leiden concerning the Tribune's solicitation for a piece of the home site occupied by Pilgrims before they sailed to America on the Mayflower. He recalls the solution was to send a brick of approximately the correct date from the city's archaeological warehouse. I am grateful for his communication. Jeremy Dupertuis Bangs, communication with author, November 2, 2007.

12. For the true pyramids of Gaza, see Weizman, *Forensic Architecture,* 4–5.

13. Lightfoot and Harmer, "Martyrdom of S. Polycarp," 189–211; Musurillo, *Acts of the Christian Martyrs,* 354–61.

14. Paulinus of Nola, *Epistulae,* 2:125–33.

15. Letter from L. S. Chakales to Keith B. Capron, May 8, 1950, Tribune Tower Fragment Collection Correspondence.

16. Geary, *Furta Sacra.*

17. It is no *Wunderkammer.* See chapter 2, note 2.

18. For a persuasive reading of how the fragmentary remains of the buildings left behind do ideological work for their interpreters, see Upton, "Starting from Baalbek."

19. For a further discussion of the odd manifestations of Protestant anxiety about things, see Wharton, "Relics, Protestants, Things."

20. Calvin, *Treatise on Relics* (1543).

21. Heidegger, "The Thing," 169.

22. Ibid., 173. For the fourfold, see Heidegger, "Building Dwelling Thinking," 351–53; J. Young, "The Fourfold."

23. Heidegger, "The Thing," 174.

24. Ibid., 182.

25. Heidegger, "The Origin of the Work of Art."

26. Schapiro, "Still-Life as a Personal Object"; Schapiro, "Further Notes on Heidegger and van Gogh."

27. B. Brown, "Thing Theory." Republished with few modifications as B. Brown, *Things.*

28. For example, Patricia Cox Miller, a distinguished scholar of late ancient Christianity, begins her recent book with an homage to Brown. P. Miller, *Corporeal Imagination,* 1.

29. Compare Brown's constriction of things through definition with an anthropologist's inclusive understanding of things: "Things, it is suggested, ought not to be delineated in advance of the ethnographic encounters from which they emerge. To pre-empt an ethnographically defined understanding of what constitutes a thing would be to simply offer an alternative *theory* of things." Henare, Holbraad, and Wastell, "Introduction," 5.

30. B. Brown, "Thing Theory," 16.

31. B. Brown, "Bill Brown Interviewed by Austin Allen."

32. Baudrillard, "System of Collecting," 10.

33. See, for example, the discussion of Flaubert in Said, *Orientalism,* 188–90. For an exploration of the eroticization of the harem through a consideration of colonialist postcards from North Africa, see Alloula, *Colonial Harem.*

34. No overview of anthropological treatments of things is offered here. For such summaries, see Hodder, "Human-Thing Entanglement"; Holbraad, "Ontology, Ethnography, Archaeology."

35. The anthropological understanding of objects as agents is already very much in place in Durkheim's discussion of totems. Durkheim, *Elementary Forms of Religious Life,* 230–33.

36. Mauss, *The Gift,* 3.

37. Ibid., 11–13.

38. Baudrillard, *For a Critique of the Political Economy of the Sign,* 37.

39. Appadurai, "Introduction," 3.

40. Ibid., 5. Appadurai's italics.

41. Ibid., 9. Appadurai's italics.

42. Ibid., 24–26. Also see Douglas, "Primitive Rationing."

43. Gell, *Art and Agency,* 4.

44. Ibid., 13.

45. Kruijff, "Peirce's Late Theory of Abduction"; Douven, "Abduction." For a useful compilation of Peirce's definitions of abduction, see Peirce, *Commens Dictionary of Peirce's Terms.*

46. As in Disney's artificial food smells on Main Street.

47. For variations on abduction, see Daston, *Things That Talk*; Tamen, *Friends of Interpretable Objects.*

48. Gell's argument has been criticized by those seriously considering the agency of objects as well as by those who resist the animation of things. See Leach, "Differentiation and Encompassment."

49. Latour, *Reassembling the Social.*

50. Ibid., 10.

51. Ibid., 71–72.

52. Latour, *Pandora's Hope,* 177. The author goes on to characterize this observation as an overstatement, a caricaturization, but it makes the point perfectly.

53. Latour, *Reassembling the Social,* 63–64. Latour has applied ANT to the design of buildings if not their material lives. Latour and Yanevea, "Give Me a Gun and I Will Make All Buildings Move."

54. Soja, *Thirdspace,* 73. Lefebvre's work is committedly un-Heideggerian. Lefebvre, *Social Production of Space,* 121–22.

55. Heidegger, "Building Dwelling Thinking," 151. Also see T. Anderson, "Complicating Heidegger and the Truth of Architecture."

56. Heidegger's italics. Heidegger, "Building Dwelling Thinking," 146.

57. Corrigan, "Spatiality and Religion," 172.

58. J. Smith, *To Take Place.* For later additions to his critique, see J. Smith, *Map Is Not Territory,* 88–103.

59. Eliade, *The Sacred and the Profane.* In November 2012, the book was ranked by Amazon in its Best Sellers list at 17,443 in books in general and 30 in books on comparative religion; by way of comparison, Smith's book was ranked 679,837.

60. Ibid., 44.

61. Ibid., 21.

62. "Hierophany" does not appear in the *Oxford English Dictionary.* See Eliade and Sullivan, "Hierophany."

63. Bachelard's italics. Bachelard, *Poetics of Space,* xxxiii.

64. See, for example, Merleau-Ponty, *Phenomenology of Perception,* vii–xxiv.

65. For a brief historiography and positive description of phenomenological approaches to material culture, see Thomas, "Phenomenology and Material Culture."

66. Bachelard, *Poetics of Space,* xix.

67. Eliade, *Symbolism, the Sacred, and the Arts*, 36–37.

68. For Eliade's commitment to fascism and his anti-Semitism, see Berger, "Mircea Eliade"; Stigliano, "Fascism's Mythologist."

69. Eliade, *Youth without Youth*, v–ix. Although I cannot recommend the novel, Eliade's story is compellingly retold in film by Francis Ford Coppola, *Youth Without Youth*. The text seems to have functioned in an uncannily autobiographical way also for the filmmaker, as he makes clear in his introduction to the 2007 publication of the novella.

70. For an introduction to the politically sensitive question of the meaning of Zion and its location, see Leithart, "Where Was Ancient Zion?"

71. See, for example, Weill, *Cité de David*; Mazar, "Did I Find King David's Palace?"

72. The walls of Jerusalem were flexible, expanding and contracting. In the Byzantine period, the southwest hill was included within the city walls. It was, however, left outside the walls under the Fatimids. The final renewal of the fortifications by the Ottoman sultan Sulieman the Magnificent, between 1537 and 1541, also excluded Zion. These last walls and their gates were restored under the aegis of Ronald Storrs, governor of Jerusalem, during the British Mandate. For a comprehensive and scholarly assessment of the history of the walls of Jerusalem, see Wightman, *Walls of Jerusalem*. The most insightful overview of the archaeology of the site remains that of Tsafrir, "Southwestern Hill of Jerusalem and Its Place in the Urban Development of the City in the Byzantine Period," chap. 2. A recently completed excavation in Jerusalem uncovered sections of the Hasmonean and Byzantine city walls on Zion. See Resig, "Uncovering the Walls of Zion." For the few excavations that have been undertaken on the southwest hill, see Eshel and Prag, *Excavations by K. M. Kenyon in Jerusalem*; Stern, Lewinson-Giboa, and Aviram, *New Encyclopedia of Archaeological Excavations in the Holy Land*, 1814–15.

73. For a fuller discussion of the archaeology and politics of Mount Zion, see Wharton, "Jerusalem's Zions."

74. The sources on Zion from the fourth through the eleventh centuries are conveniently gathered by Baldi and Wilkinson. Baldi, *Enchiridion locorum sanctorum*, 471–96; Wilkinson, *Jerusalem Pilgrims before the Crusades*. For a diligent review of the primary sources and a good secondary source bibliography, see Pringle, *Churches of the Crusader Kingdom of Jerusalem*.

75. West-Pavlov, *Space in Theory*, 111–42.

76. Foucault, "Of Other Spaces," 23–24.

77. Ibid., 22.

78. Buchanan and Lambert, *Deleuze and Space*.

79. See "1440" in Deleuze and Guattari, *A Thousand Plateaus*.

80. De Certeau, *Practice of Everyday Life*, 36–37.

81. Ibid., 92.

82. For a classic statement of spatial power, see Foucault, *Discipline and Punish*, particularly 195–228.

83. For "faciality" not only as ideology but also as economics and power, see Deleuze and Guattari, *A Thousand Plateaus*, 167–91.

84. Habermas, *Structural Transformation of the Public Sphere*. The extent of the impact of Habermas's public sphere is described by Calhoun, *Habermas and the Public Sphere*, Introduction.

85. Lefebvre, *Social Production of Space*. Lefebvre's work has had an enormous impact on spatial thinking. For those who recognize their debt, see, for example, Harvey, *Spaces of Global Capitalism*; Soja, *Thirdspace*. Lefebvre's ideas are evident elsewhere, even when unacknowledged. See, for example, Tilley, *A Phenomenology of Landscape*. Although the first and last

chapters of Tilley's book attribute the interesting work done in its core to phenomenologists, it owes more to materialist readings of topography.

86. Leibniz and Clarke, *Exchange of Papers.*

87. Peirce, *Commens Dictionary of Peirce's Terms.*

88. Quinn, "Herms, Kouroi and the Political Anatomy of Athens."

89. Rojas, *The Great Wall.*

90. For the place of marks in the construction of the animal's *umwelt,* see Agamben, *The Open,* 40–42.

91. For an argument collapsing virtual and actual "reality," see Grosz, *Architecture from the Outside,* especially chap. 5.

92. Tschumi, "Illustrated Index."

93. Excellent models for reconsidering conventional relations between the human and the animal have been provided by Agamben, *The Open*; Derrida, *The Animal That Therefore I Am*; Haraway, *When Species Meet.* In a very different vein, also see Grandin and Johnson, *Animals Make Us Human.*

94. Woo and Rieucau, "From Dummies to Animations."

95. Derrida, *Of Spirit,* 134.

96. C. Wolfe, *Before the Law.*

Bibliography

Abe, Stan. "Rockefeller Home Decorating and Objects from China." In *Collecting China: The World, China, and a Short History of Collecting,* edited by Vimalin Rujivacharakul, 107–23. Newark: University of Delaware Press, 2011.

Abt, Jeffrey. *American Egyptologist: The Life of James Henry Breasted and the Creation of His Oriental Institute.* Chicago: University of Chicago Press, 2011.

______. "The Breasted-Rockefeller Egyptian Museum Project: Philanthropy, Cultural Imperialism, and National Resistance." *Art History* 19, no. 4 (1996): 551–72.

———. "Toward a Historian's Laboratory: The Breasted-Rockefeller Museum Projects in Egypt, Palestine, and America." *Journal of the American Research Center in Egypt* 33 (1996): 173–94.

Abu El-Haj, Nadia. *Facts on the Ground: Archaeological Practice and Territorial Self-Fashioning in Israeli Society.* Chicago: University of Chicago Press, 2001.

Abu-Lughod, Janet. *Cairo: 1001 Years of the City Victorious.* Princeton: Princeton University Press, 1971.

Adorno, Theodor. "Valéry Proust Museum." In *Prisms,* edited by Samuel Weber and Shierry Weber, 175–85. Cambridge, Mass.: MIT Press, 1981.

Agamben, Giorgio. *The Open: Man and Animal.* Stanford: Stanford University Press, 2004.

Albrecht, Stephan. "Der Kreuzgang als Gerichtsstätte." In *Der mittelalterliche Kreuzgang, The Medieval Cloister, Le cloître au moyen âge: Architektur, Funktion und Programm,* edited by Peter K. Klein, 27–29. Regensburg: Schnell & Steiner, 2004.

Albright, William F. "In Memory of Louis Hugues Vincent." *Bulletin of the American Schools of Oriental Research* 164 (December 1961): 1–4.

———. "Selah Merrill 1837–1909." In *Dictionary of American Biography,* edited by Dumas Malone, 564–65. New York: Scribner and the American Council of Learned Societies, 1933.

Allegro, John Marco. *Search in the Desert.* Garden City, N.Y.: Doubleday, 1964.

———. *The Shapira Affair.* Garden City, N.Y.: Doubleday, 1965.

Allen, Esther. "'Money and Little Red Books': Romanticism, Tourism, and the Rise of the Guidebook." *Lit: Literature Interpretation Theory* 7, nos. 2–3 (1996): 213–26.

Alloula, Malek. *The Colonial Harem.* Translated by Myrna Godzich and Wlad Godzich. Edited by Wlad Godzich and Jochen Schulte-Sasse. Theory and History of Literature. Minneapolis: University of Minnesota Press, 1986.

American Colony Collection. Library of Congress, Washington, D.C.

American Psychiatric Association. *Diagnostic and Statistical Manual of Mental Disorders.* 4th ed. Arlington, Va.: American Psychiatric Association, 2000.

———. *Diagnostic and Statistical Manual of Mental Disorders.* 5th ed. American Psychiatric Publishing. http://dsm.psychiatryonline.org/book.aspx?bookid=556.

Amiri, Avner, and Annabel Wharton. "Home in Jerusalem: The American Colony and Palestinian Suburban Architecture." *Post-Medieval Archaeology* 45, no. 1 (2011): 237–65.

Anderson, John Ward. "Israelis Act to Encircle East Jerusalem." *Washington Post,* February 7, 2005, A15.

Anderson, Travis T. "Complicating Heidegger and the Truth of Architecture." *Journal of Aesthetics and Art Criticism* 69, no. 1 (2011): 69–79.

Anderson, William C. *A Dictionary of Law, Consisting of Judicial Definitions and Explanations of Words, Phrases, and Maxims, and an Exposition of the Principles of Law* [1889]. Union, N.J.: Lawbook Exchange, 1996.

Andrews, Malcolm. "The Metropolitan Picturesque." In *The Politics of the Picturesque: Literature, Landscape and Aesthetics Since 1770,* edited by Stephen Copley and Peter Garside, 282–98. Cambridge: Cambridge University Press, 1994.

Appadurai, Arjun. "Introduction: Commodities and the Politics of Value." In *The Social Life of Things: Commodities in Cultural Perspective,* edited by Arjun Appadurai, 3–63. Cambridge: Cambridge University Press, 1986.

Ariel, Yaakov, and Ruth Kark. "Messianism, Holiness, Charisma, and Community: The American-Swedish Colony in Jerusalem, 1881–1933." *Church History* 65, no. 4 (1996): 641–57.

Arnold, Dana, and Joanna Sofaer, eds. *Biographies and Space: Placing the Subject in Art and Architecture.* London: Routledge, 2008.

Arnold, Dennis G. "Corporate Moral Agency." *Midwest Studies in Philosophy* 30 (2006): 279–91.

Asad, Talal. "Agency and Pain: An Exploration." *Culture and Religion* 1, no. 1 (2000): 29–60.

Ashbee, Charles Robert, ed. *Jerusalem, 1918–1922, Being the Records of the Pro-Jerusalem Council during the Period of the British Military Administration.* 2 vols. London: John Murray for the Council of the Pro-Jerusalem Society, 1921–24.

———. *A Palestine Notebook, 1918–1923.* Garden City, N.Y.: Doubleday, 1923.

Augé, Marc. *Non-Places: Introduction to an Anthropology of Supermodernity.* Translated by John Howe. New York: Verso, 1995.

August, Bille. *Jerusalem.* DVD. Stockholm: First Look International, 1996.

Bachelard, Gaston. *The Poetics of Space.* Translated by Maria Jolas. Boston: Beacon Press, 1992.

Bainbridge, William Sims. *The Warcraft Civilization: Social Science in a Virtual World.* Cambridge, Mass.: MIT Press, 2010.

Baldi, Donatus. *Enchiridion locorum sanctorum: Documenta S. Evangelii loca respicientia.* Jerusalem: Typis PP. Franciscanorum, 1955.

Ballard, Sam, and Jane Ballard. *Paradores of Spain: Unique Lodgings in State-Owned Castles, Convents, Mansions and Hotels.* Boston: Harvard Common Press, 1986.

Barboza, David. "In China, New Limits on Virtual Currency." *New York Times,* July 1, 2009.

Bar-El, Yair, Rimona Durst, Gregory Katz, Josef Zislin, Ziva Strauss, and Haim Y. Knobler. "Jerusalem Syndrome." *British Journal of Psychiatry* 176 (2000): 86–90.

Barghouti, Omar. *Boycott, Divestment, Sanctions: The Global Struggle for Palestinian Rights.* Chicago: Haymarket Books, 2011.

Barlett, Donald L., and James B. Steele. *Howard Hughes: His Life and Madness.* New York: W. W. Norton, 2004.

Barnard, George Grey. “Sculptor Tells of Great Loss: Special Cablegram.” *New York Times,* April 21, 1907, C1.

Barnard, George Grey, Papers. Philadelphia Museum of Art Archives.

Barnet, Peter, and Nancy Wu. *The Cloisters: Medieval Art and Architecture.* New York: Metropolitan Museum of Art; New Haven: Yale University Press, 2012.

Basilio, Miriam. “A Pilgrimage to the Alcázar of Toledo: Ritual, Tourism and Propaganda in Franco’s Spain.” In *Architecture and Tourism: Perception, Performance and Place,* edited by D. Medina Lasansky and Brian McLaren, 93–107. Oxford: Berg, 2004.

Bataille, Georges. *The Accursed Share.* New York: Zone Books, 1991.

Bates, William N. “Archaeological News.” *American Journal of Archaeology* 13, no. 3 (1909): 345–86.

Baudrillard, Jean. *For a Critique of the Political Economy of the Sign.* Translated by Charles Levin. New York: Telos Press, 1981.

———. “The System of Collecting.” In *The Cultures of Collecting,* edited by Jas Elsner and Roger Cardinal, 7–24. Cambridge, Mass.: Harvard University Press, 1994.

Becker, Gary S., and Kevin M. Murphy. “A Theory of Rational Addiction.” *Journal of Political Economy* 96, no. 4 (1988): 675–700.

Ben-Arieh, Yehoshua. *Jerusalem in the Nineteenth Century: Emergence of the New City.* 2 vols. New York: St. Martin’s Press, 1986.

Bendiner, Kenneth Paul. “David Roberts in the Near East: Social and Religious Themes.” *Art History* 6, no. 1 (1983): 67–81.

Benedict, Saint. *The Holy Rule of St. Benedict.* Edited by Boniface Verheyen. Atchison, Kans.: St. Benedict’s Abbey, 1949.

Ben Ishai, Shlomi. “Jerusalem Real Estate Guide: A Pick into the Most Desirable Districts of Jerusalem.” Nadlan-Plus Real Estate. http://www.nadlan-plus.com/articles/jerusalem-real-estate-guide.htm. Accessed May 14, 2008.

Bennett, Tony. *Pasts Beyond Memory: Evolution, Museum, Colonialism.* New York: Routledge, 2004.

Bentham, Jeremy. “Panopticon; or The Inspection-House, Containing the Idea of a New Principle of Construction Applicable to Any Sort of Establishment, in which Persons of Any Description Are to be Kept under Inspection; and in Particular to Penitentiary-Houses, Prisons, Houses of Industry, Work-Houses, Lazarettos, Manufactories, Hospitals, Mad-Houses, and Schools: with a Plan of Management Adapted to the Principle: in a Series of Letters, Written in the Year 1787, from Crecheff in White Russia to a Friend in England by Jeremy Bentham, of Lincoln’s Inn.” In *The Panopticon Writings,* edited by Miran Bozovic. London: Verso, 1995.

Berger, Adriana. “Mircea Eliade: Romanian Fascism and the History of Religions in the United States.” In *Tainted Greatness: Antisemitism and Cultural Heroes,* edited by Nancy A. Harrowitz, 51–74. Philadelphia: Temple University Press, 1994.

Berridge, Kent C., and J. Wayne Aldridge. “Decision Utility, Incentive Salience, and Cue-Triggered ‘Wanting.’” In *Oxford Handbook of Human Action,* edited by Ezequiel Morsella, John A. Bargh, and Peter M. Gollwitzer, 509–34. Oxford: Oxford University Press, 2009.

Beust, Cédric. “Order and Chaos in Alterac Valley.” Otaku. July 25, 2006. http://beust.com/weblog/.

Bevan, Robert. *The Destruction of Memory: Architecture at War.* London: Reaktion Books, 2006.

Bienn, Borris. “REELdepth™: The New Dimension in Slot Play.” Gaming Guide: The Casino & Slot Guide for California. February 2009. http://www.thegamingguide.com.

Binnewies, Robert O. *Palisades: 100,000 Acres in 100 Years.* New York: Fordham University Press, 2001.

Bitner, Mary Jo. "Servicescapes: The Impact of Physical Surroundings on Customers and Employees." *Journal of Marketing* 56, no. 2 (1992): 51–71.

Black, Henry Campbell. *Black's Law Dictionary: Definitions of the Terms and Phrases of American and English Jurisprudence, Ancient and Modern.* Edited by Joseph R. Nolan and Jacqueline M. Nolan-Haley. 6th ed. Saint Paul, Minn.: West Publishing, 1990.

Black, John. *Oxford Dictionary of Economics.* Oxford Paperback Reference. Oxford: Oxford University Press, 1997.

Blizzard Entertainment. "What Is World of Warcraft?" Last updated 2014. http://us.battle.net/wow/en.

Block, Jerald J. "Issues for DSM-V: Internet Addiction." *American Journal of Psychiatry* 165, no. 3 (2008): 306–7.

Bloom, Jonathan M., and Sheila S. Blair. *The Grove Encyclopedia of Islamic Art and Architecture.* 3 vols. New York: Oxford University Press, 2009.

Blumenthal, George. "The New Cloisters." *Metropolitan Museum of Art Bulletin* 30, no. 5 (1935): 98–100.

Boellstorff, Tom. *Coming of Age in Second Life: An Anthropologist Explores the Virtually Human.* Princeton: Princeton University Press, 2008.

Bogost, Ian. *Persuasive Games: The Expressive Power of Videogames.* Cambridge, Mass.: MIT Press, 2007.

Bolín, Luis. *Spain: The Vital Years.* Philadelphia: J. B. Lippincott, 1967.

Bond, James. "Monastic Water Management in Great Britain: A Review." In *Monastic Archaeology: Papers on the Study of Medieval Monasteries,* edited by Graham Keevill, Mick Aston, and Teresa Hall, 88–136. Oxford: Oxbow, 2001.

Booms, Bernard H., and Mary Jo Bitner. "Marketing Services by Managing the Environment." *Cornell Hotel & Restaurant Administration Quarterly* 23 (1982): 35–40.

Bostwick, J. Michael, Kathleen A. Hecksel, Susanna R. Stevens, James H. Bower, and J. Eric Ahlskog. "Frequency of New-Onset Pathologic Compulsive Gambling or Hypersexuality After Drug Treatment of Idiopathic Parkinson Disease." *Mayo Clinic Proceedings* 84, no. 4 (2009): 310–16.

Bourbon, Fabio. *The Life, Works, and Travels of David Roberts, R.A.* New York: Rizzoli, 2000.

Bourdieu, Pierre. *Outline of a Theory of Practice.* Cambridge: Cambridge University Press, 1977.

Bourin, André. "Prix Fémina—Myriam Harry." *Nouvelles Littéraires,* 1959, 1–2.

Breasted, Charles. *Pioneer to the Past: The Story of James Henry Breasted, Archaeologist, Told by His Son.* New York: C. Scribner's Sons, 1943.

Breasted, James Henry. *The Oriental Institute.* University of Chicago Survey 12. Chicago: University of Chicago Press, 1933.

Breck, Joseph. "The Opening of the Cloisters." *Metropolitan Museum of Art Bulletin* 21, no. 5 (1926): 114–16.

Bredekamp, Horst. *The Lure of Antiquity and the Cult of the Machine: The Kunstkammer and the Evolution of Nature, Art and Technology.* Translated by Allison Brown. Princeton: Marcus Weiner, 1995.

Breitman, Richard, Barbara McDonald Stewart, and Severin Hochberg. *Refugees and Rescue: The Diaries and Papers of James G. McDonald, 1935–1945.* Bloomington: Indiana University Press, 2009.

Brilliant, Richard, and Dale Kinney, eds. *Reuse Value: Spolia and Appropriation in Art and Architecture, from Constantine to Sherrie Levine.* Aldershot: Ashgate, 2011.

Broderson, Deborah Ketura. "Building a Ludic Environment: The Aesthetics, Ethics, and Economics of Play." PhD thesis, Duke University, 2001.

Brodie, Neil, Morag M. Kersel, Christina Luke, and Katheryn Walker Tubb, eds. *Archaeology, Cultural Heritage, and the Antiquities Trade.* Cultural Heritage Studies. Gainesville: University Press of Florida, 2006.

Brown, Bill. "Bill Brown Interviewed by Austin Allen." http://bigthink.com/users/billbrown. Accessed November 26, 2011.

———, ed. *Things.* Chicago: University of Chicago Press, 2004.

———. "Thing Theory." *Critical Inquiry* 28, no. 1 (2001): 1–22.

Brown, Dan. *The Da Vinci Code.* New York: Doubleday, 2003.

Brown, Judith Anne. *John Marco Allegro: The Maverick of the Dead Sea Scrolls.* Grand Rapids, Mich.: William B. Eerdmans, 2005.

Brownell, Kelly D., and Mark S. Gold. "Food and Addiction: Scientific, Social, Legal, and Legislative Implications." In *Food and Addiction: A Comprehensive Handbook,* edited by Kelly D. Brownell and Mark S. Gold, 439–46. New York: Oxford University Press, 2012.

Browning, Robert. *Poems in English.* Edited by David Daiches. New York: Ronald, 1950.

Bruner, Jerome S. "On Perceptual Readiness." *Psychological Review* 64, no. 2 (1957): 123–52.

Buchanan, Ian, and Gregg Lambert. *Deleuze and Space.* Edinburgh: Edinburgh University Press, 2005.

Buhler, Brendan. "The Man behind Casinos' Scent Science." *Las Vegas Sun,* January 11, 2010.

Bullivant, Lucy. "The Most Expensive Development in US History Tries to Redefine Junk-space Urbanism on the Strip." *Architectural Review* 227, no. 1358 (2010): 29–30.

Bury, J. B. "The Stylistic Term 'Plateresque.'" *Journal of the Warburg and Courtauld Institutes* 39 (1976): 199–230.

Bylin, Susanna, and Sven-Åke Christianson. "Characteristics of Malingered Amnesia: Consequences of Withholding vs. Distorting Information on Later Memory of a Crime Event." *Legal and Criminological Psychology* 7, no. 1 (2002): 45–61.

Cabrera, Miguel A. "Developments in Contemporary Spanish Historiography: From Social History to the New Cultural History." *Journal of Modern History* 77, no. 4 (2005): 988–1023.

Calhoun, Craig, ed. *Habermas and the Public Sphere.* Cambridge, Mass.: MIT Press, 1993.

Calvin, John. *Treatise on Relics* [1543]. Translated by Valeria Krasinski. Edinburgh: Johnstone, Hunter, 1870.

Cameron, James. *Avatar.* DVD. Los Angeles: Fox Searchlight, 2012.

Camille, Michael. "'How New York Stole the Idea of Romanesque Art': Medieval, Modern and Postmodern in Meyer Schapiro." *Oxford Art Journal* 17, no. 1 (1994): 65–75.

Campo, Juan Eduardo. *The Other Sides of Paradise: Explorations into the Religious Meanings of Domestic Space in Islam.* Edited by Frederick M. Denny. Studies in Comparative Religion. Columbia: University of South Carolina Press, 1991.

Carmel, Alex. *Die Siedlungen der württembergischen Templer in Palästina 1868–1918: Ihre lokal-politischen und internationalen Probleme.* Translated from Hebrew by Perez Leshem. Veröffentlichungen der Kommission für Geschichtliche Landeskunde in Baden-Württemberg. Reihe B, Forschungen 77.2. Stuttgart: W. Kohlhammer, 1973.

Carney, William P. "Battlefield Tours Started in Spain." *New York Times,* July 3, 1938.

Carr, Stanley. "Travel Advisory: Nordic Heritage and Western Wagons." *New York Times,* March 28, 1982.

Carreño de Miranda, Juan. *St James the Great in the Battle of Clavijo* (1660, Museum of Fine Arts, Budapest). Web Gallery of Art. http://www.wga.hu/index.html.

Carro Otero, José. "1785: Proyecto para ampliar el 'Gran Hospital' fundado por los Reyes Católicos." *El Correo Gallego,* June 23, 1996.

Carroll, Thomas H. "To the People of Nevada." *Las Vegas Evening Review and Journal,* May 9, 1930.

Carruthers, Mary. "The Poet as Master Builder: Composition and Locational Memory in the Middle Ages." *New Literary History* 24, no. 4 (1993): 881–904.

Castronova, Edward. *Synthetic Worlds: The Business and Culture of Online Games.* Chicago: University of Chicago Press, 2005.

Chicago Tribune. *The International Competition for a New Administration Building for the Chicago Tribune, MCMXXII, Containing All the Designs Submitted in Response to the Chicago Tribune's $100,000 Offer Commemorating Its Seventy-Fifth Anniversary, June 10, 1922.* Chicago: Chicago Tribune Corporation, 1923.

Clark, Kenneth. "Renderings of an Early Master—David Roberts, Parts I and II." *Pencil Points* 7 (1926): 2–18, 171–76.

Clark, Neils, and P. Shavaun Scott. *Game Addiction: The Experience and Effects.* Jefferson, N.C.: McFarland, 2009.

Classic Las Vegas. "Las Vegas Photos: 1960s." Las Vegas History Blog. March 27, 2010. http://classiclasvegas.squarespace.com/classic-las-vegas-blog/2010/3/27/las-vegas-photos-1960s.html.

Clifford, James. "Objects and Selves—an Afterword." In *Objects and Others: Essays on Museums and Material Culture,* edited by George W. Stocking, 236–46. Madison: University of Wisconsin Press, 1985.

Clift, Pamala. "State of Being—Avatar Perceptions." http://www.virtualhandhold.com/State-of-Being.html.

"The Cloisters." *American Architect* 129 (1926): 617–22.

"The Cloisters: Another Technique in Museum Design. Allen Collens and Willis, Architects; Olmsted Brothers, Landscape Architects." *Architectural Record* 83 (June 1938): 48–52.

The Cloisters Papers and Correspondence Files. Cloisters Library and Archive, New York.

Collins, Judith. *Eric Gill: The Sculpture.* Woodstock, N.Y.: Overlook Press, 1998.

Coppola, Francis Ford. *Youth Without Youth.* DVD. Culver City: Sony Pictures Home Entertainment, 2008.

Correyero Ruiz, Beatriz. "La propaganda turística española en los años de aislamiento Internacional." *Historia y Comunicación Social* 8 (2003): 47–61.

Corrigan, John. "Spatiality and Religion." In *The Spatial Turn: Interdisciplinary Perspectives,* edited by Barney Warf and Santa Arias, 157–91. New York: Routledge, 2009.

Crary, Jonathan. *Suspensions of Perception: Attention, Spectacle, and Modern Culture.* Cambridge, Mass.: MIT Press, 1999.

Creelman, James. "The Profanation of the Holy Sepulchre." *New York Times,* October 24, 1909.

Cresswell, Tim. *Place: A Short Introduction.* Oxford: Blackwell, 2004.

Crews, Frederick. *The Memory Wars: Freud's Legacy in Dispute.* New York: Granta Books, 1995.

Crislip, Andrew T. *From Monastery to Hospital: Christian Monasticism and the Transformation of Health Care in Late Antiquity.* Ann Arbor: University of Michigan Press, 2005.

Crockford, David N., Bradley Goodyear, Jodi Edwards, Jeremy Quickfall, and Naby el-Guebaly. "Cue-Induced Brain Activity in Pathological Gamblers." *Biological Psychiatry* 58, no. 10 (2005): 787–95.

Curtis, Wayne. "Belle Epoxy." *Preservation,* May/June 2000.

Daftary, Farhad. *The Assassin Legends: Myths of the Isma'ilis.* London: I. B. Tauris, 1994.

Dahler, Jerauld. "George Grey Barnard's Cloister." *Architecture* 33 (1916): 51–57.

Dale, Thomas E. A. "Monsters, Corporeal Deformities, and Phantasms in the Cloister of St-Michel-de-Cuxa." *Art Bulletin* 83, no. 3 (2001): 402–36.

Daley, Suzanne. "A Fond Past with an Uncertain Future." *New York Times,* March 3, 2013.

Dalman, Gustaf. *Arbeit und Sitte in Palästina.* Vol. 7, *Das Haus, Hühnerzucht, Taubenzucht, Bienenzucht.* Schriften des Deutschen Palästina-Instituts 6. Hildesheim: Georg Olms Verlagsbuchhandlung, 1964.

Daston, Lorraine, ed. *Things That Talk.* New York: Zone Books, 2008.

Davidson, Joyce. "The World Was Getting Smaller. . . ." *Area* 32 (2000): 31–40.

Davis, Camas, and Ira Glass. "Animal Sacrifice, Act Two: Run Rabbit. No, Really, Run!" *This American Life.* November 30, 2012. http://www.thisamericanlife.org.

Davis, Thomas W. *Shifting Sands: The Rise and Fall of Biblical Archaeology.* Oxford: Oxford University Press, 2004.

Davril, Anselme. "Fonctions des cloîtres dans les monastères au Moyen Âge." In *Der mittelalterliche Kreuzgang, The Medieval Cloister, Le cloître au moyen âge: Architektur, Funktion und Programm,* edited by Peter K. Klein, 22–26. Regensburg: Schnell & Steiner, 2004.

Debord, Guy. *The Society of the Spectacle* [1967]. Translated by Donald Nicholson-Smith. New York: Zone Books, 1994.

de Certeau, Michel. *The Practice of Everyday Life.* Translated by Steven F. Rendall. Berkeley: University of California Press, 1984.

del Castillo, Daniel. "Mad for Jerusalem: Scholars Investigate How the City Preys on the Minds of Some Visitors." *Chronicle of Higher Education,* August 17, 2001, A12.

Deleuze, Gilles, and Félix Guattari. *A Thousand Plateaus: Capitalism and Schizophrenia.* Translated by Brian Massumi. Minneapolis: University of Minnesota Press, 1987.

Dennis, Andrew, Peter Foote, and Richard Perkins. *Laws of Early Iceland: The Codex Regius of Grágás.* 2 vols. Winnipeg: University of Manitoba Press, 1980.

Derrida, Jacques. *The Animal That Therefore I Am.* New York: Fordham University Press, 2008.

———. *Of Spirit: Heidegger and the Question.* Chicago: University of Chicago Press, 1989.

Désilets, Patrice. "Assassin's Creed Developer's Diary: Freedom." Ubisoft, http://assassinscreed.uk.ubi.com/assassins-creed-1/home.php—/devdiary/. Accessed March 11, 2009.

Dibbell, Julian. *My Tiny Life: Crime and Passion in a Virtual World.* New York: Holt, 1998.

Dickson, Harold E. *George Grey Barnard, Centenary Exhibition, 1863–1963.* University Park: Pennsylvania State University Library and the Pennsylvania Historical and Museum Commission, 1964.

Diness, Mendel John, Dror Wahrman, E. S. Carney Gavin, and Nitza Rosovsky. *Capturing the Holy Land: M. J. Diness and the Beginnings of Photography in Jerusalem.* Cambridge, Mass.: Harvard Semitic Museum, 1993.

Disraeli, Benjamin. *Tancred or the New Crusade* [1847]. 2nd ed. London: Longmans, Green and Company, 1871.

Dixon, Mike J., Kevin A. Harrigan, Rajwant Sandhu, Karen Collins, and Jonathan A. Fugelsang. "Losses Disguised as Wins in Modern Multi-line Video Slot Machines." *Addiction* 105, no. 10 (2010): 1819–24.

Dodgson, Campbell. "Rare Woodcuts in the Ashmolean Museum—VII." *Burlington Magazine* 73, no. 424 (1938): 4–5, 7–9, 12–14, 17.

Dorland, William Alexander Newman. *Dorland's Illustrated Medical Dictionary.* Philadelphia: Saunders, 2003.
dos Santos, Renato P. "Second Life Physics: Virtual, Real or Surreal?" *Journal of Virtual Worlds Research* 2, no. 1 (2009): 4–21.
Douglas, Mary. "Primitive Rationing: A Study in Controlled Exchange." In *Themes in Economic Anthropology,* edited by Raymond William Firth, 119–47. London: Tavistock, 1967.
Douven, Igor. "Abduction." *Stanford Encyclopedia of Philosophy.* Spring 2011 ed. http://plato.stanford.edu/archives/spr2011.
Duchesne, Louis. "Saint-Jacques à Galice." *Annales du Midi* 12 (1900): 145–79.
Dudman, Helga, and Ruth Kark. *The American Colony: Scenes from a Jerusalem Saga.* Jerusalem: Carta Jerusalem, 1998.
Duméril, Édmond, and Pierre Lespinasse. *Une abbaye cistercienne du Comminges: Bonnefont. Étude archéologique des restes.* Saint-Gaudens: Aradie, 1926.
Durkheim, Émile. *The Elementary Forms of Religious Life* [1915]. Translated by Joseph Ward Swain. New York: Free Press, 1947.
Durliat, Marcel. "La fin du cloître de Saint-Michel de Cuxa." *Les Cahiers de Saint-Michel de Cuxa* 2 (1971): 9–16.
Dyer-Witheford, Nick, and Greig de Peuter. *Games of Empire: Global Capitalism and Video Games.* Edited by N. Katherine Hayles, Mark Poster, and Samuel Weber. Electronic Mediations. Minneapolis: University of Minnesota Press, 2009.
Eadington, Bill. "Vegas Stripped." *Significance* 3, no. 1 (2006): 5–9.
Eco, Umberto. *Semiotics and the Philosophy of Language.* Bloomington: University of Indiana Press, 1984.
———. "Ur-Fascism." *New York Review of Books* 42, no. 11 (1995): 12–15.
Edwards, Brian, Magda Sibley, Peter Land, and Mohamad Hakmi, eds. *Courtyard Housing: Past, Present and Future.* Abingdon: Taylor and Francis, 2006.
Eire, Carlos M. N. *War against the Idols: The Reformation of Worship from Erasmus to Calvin.* Cambridge: Cambridge University Press, 1986.
"El domingo se inaugura la hostería real de Compostela." *ABC* (newspaper), July 22, 1954.
Eliade, Mircea. *The Sacred and the Profane* [1957]. Translated by Willard R. Trask. New York: Harcourt, Brace, 1987.
———. *Symbolism, the Sacred, and the Arts.* New York: Crossroad, 1985.
———. *Youth without Youth* [1976]. Translated by Mac Linscott Ricketts. Edited by Matei Calinescu. Chicago: University of Chicago Press, 2007.
Eliade, Mircea, and Lawrence E. Sullivan. "Hierophany." In *Encyclopedia of Religion,* edited by Lindsay Jones, 3970–74. Detroit: Macmillan Reference, 2005.
Elman, Miriam F. "Jerusalem and the Demise of the Oslo Peace Process." Paper presented at "Jerusalem Across the Disciplines," Arizona State University, February 19–21, 2007.
Erasmus. "Colloquies: A Pilgrimage for Religion's Sake." In *Collected Works of Erasmus,* edited by Craig R. Thompson, 619–74. Toronto: University of Toronto Press, 1997.
———. "Colloquies: Inns." In *Collected Works of Erasmus,* edited by Craig R. Thompson, 368–80. Toronto: University of Toronto Press, 1997.
Escrivá de Balaguer, José María. *The Way: The Essential Classic of Opus Dei's Founder* [1939]. New York: Doubleday, 2006.
Eshel, Itzhak, and Kay Prag. *Excavations by K. M. Kenyon in Jerusalem, 1961–1967.* Vol. 4. Oxford: Oxford University Press for the British School of Archaeology in Jerusalem, 1995.

Eylon, Lilly. "Focus on Israel: Jerusalem—Architecture in the Late Ottoman Period." Israel Ministry of Foreign Affairs. April 1999. http://mfa.gov.il/MFA/MFA-Archive/1999/Pages/Focus on Israel- Jerusalem - Architecture in the l.aspx.

Fagel, Harry. *Street Talk.* Berkeley: Zeitgeist Press, 1999.

Farrell, Ronald A., and Carole Case. *The Black Book and the Mob: The Untold Story of the Control of Nevada's Casinos.* Madison: University of Wisconsin Press, 1995.

Fergusson, Peter. "Medieval Architectural Scholarship in America, 1900–1940: Ralph Adams Cram and Kenneth John Conant." *Studies in the History of Art* 35 (1990): 127–42.

Fernández Catón, José María. *El archivo del Hospital de los Reyes Católicos de Santiago de Compostela: Inventario de fondos.* Monografías de la Universidad de Santiago de Compostela 11. Santiago de Compostela: Universidad de Santiago de Compostela, 1972.

Fernández Fuster, Luis. *Teoría y técnica del turismo.* 2 vols. Madrid: Editora Nacional, 1967.

Fernández-Poyatos, María-Dolores, Ainhoa Aguirregoitia-Martínez, and Belén Boix-Martínez. "The Way of Saint James and the Xacobeo 2010 in the Tourism Websites of the Spanish Autonomous Communities." *Revista Latina de Communicación Social* 67 (2011): 23–46.

Feron, James. "Correspondent's Choice: Stopping at a Pasha's Palace." *New York Times,* November 4, 1984.

Ferrero-Waldner, Benita. "The EU and the Middle East Peace Process." European Union Department of External Relations. http://ec.europa.eu/comm/external_relations/mepp/faq/index.htm. Accessed December 6, 2006.

Fielding, Temple. *Fielding's Travel Guide to Europe: 1971 Edition.* New York: Fielding Publications, 1971.

Fields, Weston W. *Dead Sea Scrolls: A Full History.* Leiden: Brill, 2009.

Filareti. *Treatise on Architecture: Being the Treatise by Antonio di Piero Averlino, known as Filaretti.* Translated by John R. Spencer. 2 vols. New Haven: Yale University Press, 1965.

Finden, William, Edward Francis Finden, and Thomas Hartwell Horne. *Landscape Illustrations of the Bible: Consisting of Views of the Most Remarkable Places Mentioned in the Old and New Testaments, From Original Sketches Taken on the Spot.* London: John Murray, 1836.

Finn, James. *A View from Jerusalem, 1849–1858: The Consular Diary of James and Elizabeth Anne Finn.* Edited by Arnold Blumberg. Ruthford, N.J.: Associated University Presses, 1980.

Flavey, L. D. "Reconstructing Power in Second Life: Controlling the Virtual Mayhem." *Journal for Cultural Research* 15, no. 1 (2011): 55–74.

Flynn, Dennis O., and Arturo Giráldez. "Cycles of Silver: Global Economic Unity through the Mid-Eighteenth Century." *Journal of World History* 13, no. 2 (2002): 391–427.

Ford, Alexander Hume. "Our American Colony at Jerusalem." *Appleton's Magazine* 8, no. 6 (1906): 643–55.

Forey, Alan. *The Military Orders: From the Twelfth to the Early Fourteenth Centuries.* Toronto: University of Toronto Press, 1992.

Forsyth, William H. "Five Crucial People in the Building of the Cloisters." In *The Cloisters: Studies in Honor of the Fiftieth Anniversary,* edited by Elizabeth C. Parker and Mary Shepard, 51–62. New York: Metropolitan Museum of Art, 1992.

Fortunato, Paul. "Opus Dei's Box-Office Triumph." *New York Times,* June 2, 2006, 21.

Fosdick, Raymond B. *Chronicle of a Generation: An Autobiography.* New York: Harper & Brothers, 1958.

———. *John D. Rockefeller, Jr.: A Portrait.* New York: Harper and Brothers, 1956.

Foucault, Michel. *Discipline and Punish: The Birth of the Prison.* Translated by A. Sheridan. New York: Random House, 1979.

———. "Of Other Spaces" [1967]. Translated by Jay Miskowiec. *Diacritics* 16, no. 1 (1986): 22–27.

Francisca de los Apóstoles. *The Inquisition of Francisca* [1574–77]. Edited and translated by Gillian T. W. Ahlgren. Chicago: University of Chicago Press, 2005.

Franco, Francisco, and Gabriel Arias-Salgado y de Cubas. "Ministerio de información y turismo." *Boletín oficial del estado* 55 (February 24, 1952): 851–53.

Frankfurt, Harry G. *On Bullshit.* Princeton: Princeton University Press, 2005.

French, Peter A. "The Corporation as a Moral Person." *American Philosophical Quarterly* 16 (1979): 207–15.

Frey, Hans-Jost. *Interruptions.* Albany: State University of New York Press, 1996.

Friedman, Bill. *Designing Casinos to Dominate the Competition: The Friedman International Standards of Casino Design.* Reno, Nev.: Institute for the Study of Gambling & Commercial Gaming, 2000.

Friedman, Matti. "Monks Brawl at Christian Holy Site in Jerusalem." *ABC News,* November 9, 2008.

Front, Dov. "The Expurgation of Medical Books in Sixteenth-Century Spain." *Bulletin of the History of Medicine* 75 (2001): 290–96.

Fuchs, Ron. "The Palestinian Arab House and the Islamic Primitive Hut." *Muqarnas* 15 (1998): 157–77.

———. "Palestinian Vernacular Architecture: The Ottoman Connection." In *The Ottoman House,* edited by S. Ireland and W. Bechhoefer, 54–73. Bari: ICAR, 1998.

Fuchs, Ron, and Gilbert Herbert. "A Colonial Portrait of Jerusalem." In *Hybrid Urbanism,* edited by Nezar AlSayyad, 81–108. Westpoint, Conn.: Praeger, 2001.

———. "Representing Mandatory Palestine: Austen St. Barbe Harrison and the Representational Buildings of the British Mandate in Palestine, 1922 1937." *Architectural History* 43 (2000): 281–333.

Fuchs, Ron, and M. Meyer-Brodnitz. "The Emergence of the Central Hall House Type in the Context of Nineteenth-Century Palestine." In *Dwellings, Settlements and Tradition,* edited by J.-P. Bourdier and N. AlSayyad, 403–24. Lanham, Md.: University Press of America, 1989.

Fulcher of Chartres. *The First Crusade: The Chronicle of Fulcher of Chartres and Other Source Materials.* Translated by Edward Peters. Edited by Ruth Mazo Karras and Edward Peters. 2nd ed. The Middle Ages Series. Philadelphia: University of Pennsylvania Press, 1998.

Funzug.com. "Top 20 Largest Hotels in the World." February 3, 2011. http://www.funzug.com/index.php/travel/top-20-largest-hotels-in-the-world.html.

Furstenberg, Rochelle, and Leslie Susser. "Future Shock." *Jerusalem Report,* November 9, 1998, 14.

Gage, John. "Turner and the Picturesque." *Burlington Magazine* 107, no. 742 (1965): 16–25.

Gallery Book: Iron Age (Israelite Period) 1200–1000 BC. Jerusalem: Palestine Archaeological Museum, 1940.

Galor, Katharina, Jean-Baptiste Humbert, and Jürgen Zangenberg, eds. *Qumran, the Site of the Dead Sea Scrolls: Archaeological Interpretations and Debates. Proceedings of the Conference Held at Brown University, November 17–19, 2002.* Studies on the Texts of the Desert of Judah 57. Leiden: Brill, 2006.

García Guerra, Delfín. *El Hospital Real de Santiago (1499–1804).* Galicia histórica. La Coruña: Editorial Atlántico, 1983.

García Sanchéz, Miguel. "Santiago de Compostela and Its Parador." Paradores de Turismo de España, S.A. http://www.parador.es/recursos/doc/Fichas_paradores/Descripcion/Ingles/1141533715_392007122152.pdf. Accessed March 31, 2012.

Gauchet, Marcel. *The Disenchantment of the World: A Political History of Religion.* Translated by Oscar Burge. Edited by Thomas Pavel and Mark Lilla. New French Thought. Princeton: Princeton University Press, 1997.

Gavish, Dov. "The American Colony and Its Photographers" [in Hebrew]. In *Zev Vilnay Jubilee Volume: Essays on the History, Archaeology and Lore of the Holy Land* [in Hebrew], edited by Eli Schiller, 127–44. Jerusalem: Ariel Press, 1984.

Geary, Patrick. *Furta Sacra: Thefts of Relics in the Central Middle Ages.* 2nd ed. Princeton: Princeton University Press, 1990.

Geddes, Patrick. "Jerusalem Actual and Possible: A Preliminary Report to the Chief Administrator of Palestine and the Military Governor of Jerusalem on Town Planning and Improvements." File Z4/10.202. Central Zionist Archives, Jerusalem, 1919.

Gell, Alfred. *Art and Agency: An Anthropological Theory.* Oxford: Oxford University Press, 1998.

Geraci, Robert M. *Virtually Sacred: Myth and Meaning in World of Warcraft and Second Life.* New York: Oxford University Press, 2014.

Gibson, Shimon. "British Archeological Institutions in Mandatory Palestine, 1917–1948." *Palestine Exploration Fund Quarterly* 131 (1999): 115–43.

Giesbrecht, Timo, Scott O. Lilienfeld, Steven Jay Lynn, and Harald Merckelbach. "Cognitive Processes in Dissociation: An Analysis of Core Theoretical Assumptions." *Psychological Bulletin* 134, no. 5 (2008): 617–47.

Gill, Eric. *Autobiography.* London: Jonathan Cape, 1940.

Gilpin, William. *Three Essays: On Picturesque Beauty; On Picturesque Travel; and On Sketching Landscape.* London: R. Blamire, 1792.

Gimpel, René. *Diary of an Art Dealer.* Translated by John Rosenberg. London: Hodder and Stoughton, 1966.

———. *Journal d'un collectionneur, marchand de tableaux.* Paris: Calmann-Lévy, 1963.

Gitai, Amos. *House* [Agav Films, 1980] and *A House in Jerusalem* [Agav Films, 1998]. DVD. Chicago: Facets, 2006.

———. *Kadosh.* DVD. New York: Kino International, 2000.

Godish, Thad. *Sick Buildings: Definition, Diagnosis, and Mitigation.* Boca Raton: CRC Press, 1995.

Goehring, James E. "The Dark Side of Landscape: Ideology and Power in the Christian Myth of the Desert." *Journal of Medieval and Early Modern Studies* 33, no. 3 (2003): 437–51.

GoingToVegas. "Gambling Guide." November 22, 2012. http://www.goingtovegas.com/kpv-play.htm.

Golb, Norman. "The Current Controversy over the Dead Sea Scrolls, with Special Reference to the Exhibition at the Field Museum of Chicago." The Oriental Institute of the University of Chicago. July 30, 2007. http://oi.uchicago.edu/research/projects/scr/dss.html.

Goldberger, Paul. "A Public Work That Ennobles As It Serves." *New York Times,* August 13, 1995.

Goldman, Dan. "The Architecture of the Templers in Their Colonies in Eretz-Israel, 1868–1948, and Their Settlements in the United States, 1860–1925." PhD thesis, Union Insititute and University, Cincinnati, 2003.

Goldman, Shalom. "The Holy Land Appropriated: The Careers of Selah Merrill, Nineteenth Century Christian Hebraist, Palestine Explorer, and U.S. Consul in Jerusalem." *American Jewish History* 85, no. 2 (1997): 151–72.

González, Rubén Camilo Lois, and José Somoza Medina. "Cultural Tourism and Urban Management in Northwestern Spain: The Pilgrimage to Santiago de Compostela." *Tourism Geographies* 5, no. 4 (2003): 446–60.

Goodman, Aviel. "Addiction: Definition and Implications." *British Journal of Addiction* 85 (1990): 1403–8.

———. "Neurobiology of Addiction: An Integrative Review." *Biochemical Pharmacology* 75, no. 1 (2007): 266–322.

Goren, Haim. *For the Sake of Jerusalem: Conrad Schick* [in Hebrew]. Variation 130–31. Jerusalem: Ariel Press, 1998.

Gottdiener, Mark, Claudia C. Collins, and David R. Dickens. *Las Vegas: The Social Production of an All-American City.* Malden, Mass.: Blackwell, 1999.

Götz, Ulrich. "Load and Support: Architectural Realism in Video Games." In *Space Time Play. Computer Games, Architecture, and Urbanism: The Next Level,* edited by Friedrich von Borries, Steffen P. Walz, and Matthias Böttger, 134–37. Basel: Birkhäuser Verlag, 2007.

Goulding, Edmond. *Grand Hotel.* DVD. Burbank: Warner Home Video, 2005.

Grandin, Temple, and Catherine Johnson. *Animals Make Us Human.* Boston: Houghton Mifflin, 2009.

Greenberg, Raphael. "Contested Sites: Archaeology and the Battle for Jerusalem." *Jewish Quarterly* 208 (Winter 2007): 1–7.

Gregor, Alison. "A Room for the Night (Not 40 to Life)." *New York Times,* March 18, 2007.

Gröndahl, Mia. *The Dream of Jerusalem: Lewis Larsson and the American Colony Photographers.* Stockholm: Journal, 2005.

Gross, Charles. *Select Cases from the Coroners' Rolls, A.D. 1265–1413: With a Brief Account of the History of the Office of Coroner.* London: B. Quaritch, 1896.

Grosz, Elizabeth. *Architecture from the Outside: Essays on Virtual and Real Space.* Cambridge, Mass.: MIT Press, 2001.

Gruber, Petra. *Biomimetics in Architecture: Architecture of Life and Buildings.* New York: Springer, 2011.

Guest, Tim. *Second Lives: A Journey through Virtual Worlds.* London: Hutchinson, 2007.

Guillerme, André. *The Age of Water: The Urban Environment in the North of France, A.D. 300–1800.* College Station: Texas A & M University Press, 1983.

Guiterman, Helen. "David Roberts, R. A. (1796–1864), part I." *Old Water-Colour Society's Club* 59 (1984): 53–75.

———. "The Travels of David Roberts." *Archaeology* 40, no. 6 (1987): 46–51.

Haag, John. "Myriam Harry." In *Women in World History: A Biographical Encyclopedia,* edited by Anne Commire and Deborah Klezmer, 31–33. Waterford, Conn.: Yorkin Publications, 1999.

Habermas, Jürgen. *The Structural Transformation of the Public Sphere* [1962]. Translated by Thomas Burger and Frederick Lawrence. Cambridge, Mass.: MIT Press, 1989.

Halper, Jeff. *Between Redemption and Revival: The Jewish Yishuv of Jerusalem in the Nineteenth Century.* Boulder, Colo.: Westview Press, 1991.

Hamblin, Dora Jane. "In Nineteen Lands, Instant America." *Life* 55 (August 30, 1963): 67–74.

Han, Doug Hyun, Nicolas Bolo, Melissa A. Daniels, Lynn Arenella, In Kyoon Lyoo, and Perry F. Renshaw. "Brain Activity and Desire for Internet Video Game Play." *Comprehensive Psychiatry* 52, no. 1 (2011): 88–95.

Haraway, Donna J. "A Cyborg Manifesto: Science, Technology, and Socialist-Feminism in the Late Twentieth Century." In *Simians, Cyborgs, and Women: The Reinvention of Nature*, 149–81. New York: Routledge, 1991.

———. *When Species Meet.* Minneapolis: University of Minnesota Press, 2008.

Hardy-Vallée, Benoit. "Decision-Making in the Economy of Nature: Value as Information." In *Information and Living Systems: Essays in Philosophy of Biology*, edited by George Terzis and Robert Arp, 253–88. Cambridge, Mass.: MIT Press, 2011.

Harrington, C. R., T. C. Beswick, J. Leitenberger, A. Minhajuddin, H. T. Jacobe, and B. Adinoff. "Addictive-like Behaviors to Ultraviolet Light Among Frequent Indoor Tanners." *Clinical and Experimental Dermatology* 36, no. 1 (2011): 33–38.

Harris, Neil. *Building Lives: Constructing Rites and Passages.* New Haven: Yale University Press, 1999.

Harry, Myriam [Maria Shapira]. *The Conquest of Jerusalem: A Tale of Today.* Translated by Terence Shiel. Boston: H. B. Turner, 1906.

———. *The Little Daughter of Jerusalem.* Translated by Phoebe Allen. New York: E. P. Dutton, 1919.

Harvey, David. *Spaces of Global Capitalism.* New York: Verso, 2006.

Hayles, N. Katherine. *How We Became Posthuman: Virtual Bodies in Cybernetics, Literature, and Informatics.* Chicago: University of Chicago Press, 1999.

Heidegger, Martin. "Building Dwelling Thinking" [1954]. In *Poetry, Language, Thought*, edited by Albert Hofstadter, 145–61. New York: Harper & Row, 1971.

———. "The Origin of the Work of Art" [1950]. In *Martin Heidegger Basic Writings*, edited by David Farrell Krell, 139–212. New York: Harper Collins, 1993.

———. "The Thing" [1951]. In *Poetry, Language, Thought*, edited by Albert Hofstadter, 163–87. New York: Harper & Row, 1971.

Henare, Amiria, Martin Holbraad, and Sari Wastell. "Introduction: Thinking through Things." In *Thinking through Things: Theorising Artefacts Ethnographically*, edited by Amiria Henare, Martin Holbraad, and Sari Wastell, 1–31. London: Routledge, 2007.

Henderson, John. *The Renaissance Hospital: Healing the Body and Healing the Soul.* New Haven: Yale University Press, 2006.

Herbert, Gilbert, and Ita Heinze Greenberg. "The Anatomy of a Profession: Architects in Palestine during the British Mandate." *Architectura* 22, no. 2 (1992): 149–62.

Herzl, Theodor. *Old New Land* [1902]. Translated by Lotte Levensohn. New York: Markus Wiener, 1997.

Hess, Alan. "Styling the Strip: Car and Roadside Design in the 1950s." In *The Car and the City: The Automobile, the Built Environment, and Daily Urban Life*, edited by Martin Wachs and Margaret Crawford, 167–79. Ann Arbor: University of Michigan Press, 1991.

———. *Viva Las Vegas: After Hours Architecture.* San Francisco: Chronicle Books, 1993.

Hicks, Dan. "From 'Questions that Count' to Stories that 'Matter' in Historical Archaeology." *Antiquity* 78, no. 302 (2004): 934–40.

High Commissioner and Council of Ministers. "Order of Transfer of Ownership of the Museum." *Palestine Gazette* 1663 (1948): 613.

Hilton, Conrad. *Be My Guest* [1957]. Englewood Cliffs, N.J.: Prentice Hall, 1987.

Hiltzik, Michael A. *Colossus: Hoover Dam and the Making of the American Century.* New York: Free Press, 2010.

Hodder, Ian. "Human-Thing Entanglement: Towards an Integrated Archaeological Perspective." *Journal of the Royal Anthropological Institute* 17 (2011): 154–77.

Hof, Robert D. "My Virtual Life: A Journey into a Place in Cyberspace Where Thousands of People Have Imaginary Lives." *Business Week,* May 1, 2006.

Hoffman, Adina. *House of Windows: Portraits from a Jerusalem Neighborhood.* South Royalton, Vt.: Steerforth Press, 2000.

Holbraad, Martin. "Ontology, Ethnography, Archaeology: An Afterword on the Ontography of Things." *Cambridge Archaeological Journal* 19, no. 3 (2009): 431–41.

Holliday, Eunice. *Letters from Jerusalem during the Palestine Mandate.* Edited by John Holliday. London: Radcliffe Press, 1997.

Holguin, Sandie. "'National Spain Invites You': Battlefield Tourism during the Spanish Civil War." *American Historical Review* 110, no. 5 (2005): 1399–1426.

Holmes, David S. "The Evidence for Repression: An Examination of Sixty Years of Research." In *Repression and Dissociation: Implications for Personality Theory, Psychopathology, and Health,* edited by Jerome L. Singer, 85–102. Chicago: University of Chicago Press, 1990.

Hooper, Tobe. *Poltergeist.* DVD. Burbank: Warner Home Video, 2007.

Hope, Sebastian. *Hotel Tiberias: A Tale of Two Grandfathers.* London: Harper Collins, 2004.

Hopper, John. "Bottle of Former Pope's Blood to Go on Display." *Guardian,* April 27, 2011.

Horn, Walter. "On the Origins of the Medieval Cloister." *Gesta* 12, nos. 1/2 (1973): 13–52.

Hoving, Thomas P. F. *King of the Confessors.* New York: Simon and Schuster, 1981.

———. "A Long-Lost Romanesque Annunciation." *Metropolitan Museum of Art Bulletin,* n.s. 20, no. 4 (1961): 117–26.

Howe, Fisher. *Oriental and Sacred Scenes: From Notes of Travel in Greece, Turkey, and Palestine.* New York: M. W. Dodd, 1854.

Huizinga, Johan. *Homo Ludens: A Study of the Play Element in Culture* [1938]. New York: Roy Publishers, 1950.

Hummel, Ruth Victor, and George Hintlian. "The American Colony in Jerusalem." Library of Congress. http://www.loc.gov/exhibits/americancolony/.

Hyman, Steven E. "Addiction: A Disease of Learning and Memory." *American Journal of Psychiatry* 162, no. 8 (2005): 1414–22.

Ibrahim, Fawzi. *West Meets East: The Story of the Rockefeller Museum.* Jerusalem: Israel Museum, 2006.

IGT. "IGT to Showcase Revenue-Driving Games, Machines and Systems at the Oklahoma Indian Gaming Association Tradeshow, August 9–11." Press Release. August 4, 2009. http://phx.corporate-ir.net/phoenix.zhtml?c=119000&p=irol-newsArticle&ID=1316499&highlight=.

Iliffe, John Henry. "The Palestine Archaeological Museum, Jerusalem." *Museums Journal* 38, no. 1 (1938): 1–22.

International Committee of the Red Cross. "Convention for the Protection of Cultural Property in the Event of Armed Conflict, The Hague, May 14, 1954." http://www.icrc.org/ihl.nsf/FULL/400?OpenDocument.

"Introduction to the Cloisters." Metropolitan Museum of Art. http://www.metmuseum.org/Works_of_Art/introduction.asp?dep=7. Accessed January 28, 2007.

Irazábal, Clara. "Kitsch Is Dead, Long Live Kitsch: The Production of Hyperkitsch in Las Vegas." *Journal of Architectural and Planning Research* 24, no. 3 (2007): 199–223.

Israel, Jonathan. "Counter-Reformation, Economic Decline, and the Delayed Impact of the Medical Revolution in Catholic Europe, 1550–1750." In *Health Care and Poor Relief in Counter-Reformation Europe,* edited by Ole Peter Grell, Andrew Cunningham, and Jon Arrizabalaga, 40–55. London: Routledge, 1999.

Israel Museum. "Rockefeller Archaeological Museum." http://www.english.imjnet.org.il/htmls/page_1684.aspx.

———. "West Meets East: The Story of the Rockefeller Museum." 1995. http://www.imj.org.il/rockefeller/eng/index.html.

Iversen, Leslie. *Dopamine Handbook.* Oxford: Oxford University Press, 2009.

Jacobs, Jane. *The Death and Life of Great American Cities* [1961]. New York: Modern Library, 2001.

Jameson, Fredric. *Postmodernism: The Cultural Logic of Late Capitalism.* Durham, N.C.: Duke University Press, 1990.

Jaschke, Karin. "Casinos Inside Out." In *Stripping Las Vegas: A Contextual Review of Casino Resort Architecture,* edited by Karin Jaschke and Silke Ötsch, 109–32. London: Verso, 2003.

Jeffery, George. *A Brief Description of the Holy Sepulchre, Jerusalem, and Other Christian Churches in the Holy City, with Some Account of the Medieval Copies of the Holy Sepulchre Surviving in Europe.* Cambridge: Cambridge University Press, 1919.

Jetter, Dieter. *Das europäische Hospital von der Spätantike bis 1800.* Cologne: DuMont Dokumente, 1986.

———. *Santiago, Toledo, Granada: Drei spanische Kreuzhallenspitäler und ihr Nachhall in aller Welt.* Geschichte des Hospitals 6. Stuttgart: Franz Steiner Verlag, 1987.

Jewish National and University Library, Hebrew University of Jerusalem. "Ancient Maps of Jerusalem." http://jnul.huji.ac.il/dl/maps/jer/.

Johnson, Kimball. "Dissociative Identity Disorder (Multiple Personality Disorder)." WebMD. May 26, 2012. http://www.webmd.com/mental-health/dissociative-identity-disorder-multiple-personality-disorder.

Johnson, Lesley, Karl J. Mayer, and Elena Champaner. "Casino Atmospherics from a Customer's Perspective: A Re-Examination." *UNLV Gaming Research & Review Journal* 8, no. 2 (2004): 1–10.

Julia, Dominique. "Pour une géographie européenne du pèlerinage à l'époque moderne et contemporaine." In *Pèlerins et pèlerinages dans l'Europe moderne: Actes de la table ronde organisée par le Département d'histoire et civilisation de l'Institut universitaire européen de Florence et l'École française de Rome (Rome, 4 5 juin 1993),* edited by Philippe Boutry and Dominique Julia, 3–126. Rome: École française de Rome, 2000.

Kark, Ruth. *American Consuls in the Holy Land: 1832–1914.* Jerusalem: Magnes Press, 1994.

———. *Jaffa: A City in Evolution, 1799–1917.* Translated by Gila Brand. Jerusalem: Yad Izhak Ben-Zvi, 1990.

Kark, Ruth, and S. Landman. "The Establishment of Muslim Neighbourhoods in Jerusalem, Outside the Old City, During the Late Ottoman Period." *Palestine Exploration Fund Quarterly* 112 (1980): 113–35.

Kark, Ruth, and Michal Oren-Nordheim. *Jerusalem and Its Environs: Quarters, Neighborhoods, Villages, 1800–1948.* Detroit: Wayne State University Press, 2001.

Karp, Ivan, ed. *Museum Frictions.* Durham, N.C.: Duke University Press, 2006.

Karp, Ivan, and Steven D. Lavine, eds. *Exhibiting Cultures: The Poetics and Politics of Museum Display.* Washington, D.C.: Smithsonian Institution Press, 1991.

Kavanagh, David J., Jackie Andrade, and Jon May. "Imaginary Relish and Exquisite Torture: The Elaborated Intrusion Theory of Desire." *Psychological Review* 112, no. 2 (2005): 446–67.

Kelly, Caitlin. "Where the Artists Are the Superheroes." *New York Times,* April 27, 2013.

Kent, Steven L. *The Ultimate History of Video Games: From Pong to Pokémon and Beyond—The Story behind the Craze That Touched Our Lives and Changed the World.* New York: Prima Publishing, 2001.

Kershner, Isabel. "Religious-Secular Divide, Tugging at Israel's Heart." *New York Times,* September 2, 2009.

Khasawneh, Diala. *Memoirs Engraved in Stone: Palestinian Urban Mansions.* Ramallah: Riwaq Centre for Architectural Conservation and Institute of Jerusalem Studies, 2001.

Kimbrough, Sara Dodge. *Drawn from Life: The Story of Four American Artists Whose Friendship and Work Began in Paris during the 1880s.* Jackson: University Press of Mississippi, 1976.

Kirkpatrick, Graeme. *Aesthetic Theory and the Video Game.* Manchester: Manchester University Press, 2011.

Kishkovsky, Sophia. "In Russian Chill, Waiting Hours for a Touch of the Holy." *New York Times,* November 24, 2011.

Klein, Naomi. *The Shock Doctrine: The Rise of Disaster Capitalism.* New York: Henry Holt, 2007.

Klein, Norman M. "Scripting Las Vegas: Noir Naïfs, Junking Up, and the New Strip." In *The Grit beneath the Glitter: Tales from the Real Las Vegas,* edited by Hal Rothman and Mike Davis, 17–29. Berkeley: University of California Press, 2002.

Klein, Peter K. "Topographie, fonctions et programmes iconographiques des cloîtres: La galerie attenant à l'église." In *Der mittelalterliche Kreuzgang, The Medieval Cloister, Le cloître au moyen âge: Architektur, Funktion und Programm,* edited by Peter K. Klein, 105–56. Regensburg: Schnell & Steiner, 2004.

———. "Zur Einführung: Der mittelalterliche Kreuzgang: Architektur—Funktion—Programm." In *Der mittelalterliche Kreuzgang, The Medieval Cloister, Le cloître au moyen âge: Architektur, Funktion und Programm,* edited by Peter K. Klein, 9–21. Regensburg: Schnell & Steiner, 2004.

Koerner, Joseph Leo. *The Reformation of the Image.* Chicago: University of Chicago Press, 2004.

Koolhaas, Rem. "A Foundation of Amnesia." *Design Quarterly* 125 (1984): 5–12.

Kopytoff, Igor. "The Cultural Biography of Things: Commodification as Process." In *The Social Life of Things: Commodities in Cultural Perspective,* edited by Arjun Appadurai, 64–91. Cambridge: Cambridge University Press, 1986.

Kranes, David. *Low Tide in the Desert: Nevada Stories.* Reno: University of Nevada Press, 1973.

Kroyanker, David. *Jerusalem Architecture.* London: Tauris Parke Books, 1994.

———. *Jerusalem: The German Colony and Emek Rephaim Street* [in Hebrew]. Jerusalem: Keter, 2008.

Kroyanker, David, and Dror Wahrman. *Jerusalem Architecture: Periods and Styles—The Jewish Quarters and Public Buildings Outside the Old City.* Jerusalem: Jerusalem Institute for Israel Studies and Domino Press, 1983.

Kruijff, Geert-Jan M. "Peirce's Late Theory of Abduction: A Comprehensive Account." *Semiotica* 153, nos. 1/4 (2005): 431–54.

Kubin, Alfred. *The Other Side.* Translated by Michael Mitchell. Sawtry: Dedaelus, 2000.

Kuriyama, Shigehisa. "The Forgotten Fear of Excrement." *Journal of Medieval and Early Modern Studies* 38, no. 3 (2008): 413–42.

Laffi, Domenico. *A Journey to the West: The Diary of a Seventeenth-Century Pilgrim from Bologna to Santiago de Compostela* [1681]. Edited and translated by James Hall. Leiden: Primavera Pers, 1997.

———. *Viaggio in ponente a San Giacomo di Galitia e Finisterrae* [1681]. Edited by Anna Sulai Capponi. Naples: Edizioni Scientifiche Italiane, 1989.

Lagerlöf, Selma. *The Holy City: Jerusalem II* [1902]. Translated by Velma Swanston Howard. Garden City, N.Y.: Doubleday, Page, 1918.

———. *Jerusalem: A Novel* [1901]. Translated by Velma Swanston Howeard. Garden City, N.Y.: Doubleday, Page, 1915.

Lang, Daniel. "Blackjack and Flashes." *New Yorker,* September 20, 1952, 100–111.

Larsson, Theo. *Seven Passports for Palestine: Sixty Years in the Levant.* Longfield: Longfield Publishing, 1995.

Las Vegas Convention and Visitors Authority. "Visitor Statistics." http://www.lvcva.com.

Las Vegas Review-Journal. "Hughes Announces New Resort Hotel." January 25, 1968.

Las Vegas Sun. "Nevada No. 4 in U.S. for Pedestrian Fatalities." April 7, 1999.

Latour, Bruno. *Pandora's Hope: Essays on the Reality of Science Studies.* Cambridge, Mass.: Harvard University Press, 1999.

———. *Reassembling the Social: An Introduction to Actor-Network-Theory.* Clarendon Lectures in Management Studies. Oxford: Oxford University Press, 2005.

Latour, Bruno, and Albena Yanevea. "Give Me a Gun and I Will Make All Buildings Move: An ANT's View of Architecture." In *Explorations in Architecture: Teaching, Design, Research,* edited by Reto Geiser, 80–89. Basel: Birkhäuser, 2008.

Lauer, Philippe. *Le Trésor du Sancta Sanctorum: Monuments et mémoires publiés par l'Académie des inscriptions et belles-lettres, Fondation Eugène Piot.* Académie des inscriptions et belles-lettres 15.1–2. Paris: E. Leroux, 1906.

Law, Jonathan, and Elizabeth A. Martin. *A Dictionary of Law.* 7th ed. Oxford University Press. 2014. http://www.oxfordreference.com.

Leach, James. "Differentiation and Encompassment: A Critique of Alfred Gell's Theory of the Abduction of Creativity." In *Thinking through Things: Theorising Artefacts Ethnographically,* edited by Amiria Henare, Martin Holbraad, and Sari Wastell, 167–88. London: Routledge, 2007.

Lears, Jackson. *Something for Nothing: Luck in America.* New York: Viking Penguin, 2003.

Lee, Shuen-shing. "I Lose, Therefore I Think: A Search for Contemplation amid Wars of Push-Button Glare." *Game Studies* 3, no. 2 (2003). http://www.gamestudies.org/0302/lee/.

Lefebvre, Henri. *The Social Production of Space.* Translated by Donald Nicholson-Smith. Oxford: Blackwells, 1991.

Lehrer, Jonah. "Your Brain on Gambling: Science Shows How Slot Machines Take Over Your Mind." *Boston Globe,* August 19, 2007.

Leibniz, G. W., and Samuel Clarke. *Exchange of Papers between Leibniz and Clark* [1717], ed. Jonathan Bennett, 2007. http://www.earlymoderntexts.com.

Leithart, Peter J. "Where Was Ancient Zion?" *Tyndale Bulletin* 53, no. 2 (2002): 161–75.

Lemon, Jim. "Can We Call Behaviours Addictive?" *Clinical Psychologist* 6, no. 2 (2002): 44–49.

Leone, Massimo. "The Semiotics of Religious Space in Second Life." *Social Semiotics* 21, no. 3 (2011): 337–57.

Leuchak, Mary Rebecca. "'The Old World for the New': Developing the Design for the Cloisters." *Metropolitan Museum Journal* 23 (1988): 257–77.

Levy, Rev. Clifton Harby. "An American Colony: Studying the Simple Life of Christ in the City of Jerusalem." *Dallas Morning News,* March 23, 1902, 18.

Lewis, Paul H. *Latin Fascist Elites: The Mussolini, Franco, and Salazar Regimes.* Westport, Conn.: Greenwood Press, 2002.

Liebs, Chester H. *Main Street to Miracle Mile.* Boston: Little, Brown, 1985.

Lightfoot, J. B., and J. R. Harmer. "The Martyrdom of S. Polycarp." In *The Apostolic Fathers,* 189–211. London: Macmillan, 1907.

Lim, Timothy H., Calum Carmichael, and Hector MacQueen, eds. *On Scrolls, Artefacts, and Intellectual Property.* Journal for the Study of the Pseudepigrapha Supplement Series 38. Sheffield: Sheffield Academic Press, 2001.

Lim, Timothy H., and John J. Collins, eds. *The Oxford Handbook of the Dead Sea Scrolls.* Oxford: Oxford University Press, 2010.

Linden, Nelson. "The Second Life Economy in Q4 2010." *Second Life Blogs,* January 26, 2011. http://community.secondlife.com/t5/Featured-News/bg-p/blog_feature_news.

Lindstrand, Tor. "Viva Piñata: Architecture of the Everyday." In *Space Time Play: Computer Games, Architecture, and Urbanism; The Next Level,* edited by Friedrich von Borries, Steffen P. Walz, and Matthias Böttger, 354–57. Basel: Birkhäuser Verlag, 2007.

Lio, Hei-Lim (Michael), and Raymond Rody. "The Emotional Impact of Casino Servicescape." *UNLV Gaming Research & Review Journal* 13, no. 2 (2009): 17–25.

Lipman, Vivian David. *Americans and the Holy Land through British Eyes, 1820–1917: A Documentary History.* London: V. D. Lipman and the Self Publishing Association, 1989.

Little, Donald P., and A. Üner Turgay. "Documents from the Ottoman Period in the Khālidī Library in Jerusalem." *Die Welt des Islams,* n.s. 20, nos. 1/2 (1980): 44–72.

London Times. "Val Vester: Hotelier." June 17, 2008.

López Ferreiro, Antonio. "Colección Diplomática." *Galicia Histórica* 1 (1901): 1–632.

———. *Historia de la Santa A. M. Iglesia de Santiago de Compostela: Los dos siglos de decadencia.* Vol. 7. Santiago de Compostela: Seminario Conciliar Central, 1904.

Lortie, Catherine L., and Matthieu J. Guitton. "Social Organization in Virtual Settings Depends on Proximity to Human Visual Aspect." *Computers in Human Behavior* 27, no. 3 (2011): 158–61.

Los Angeles Times. "Gambling Bill Wins Approval." March 10, 1931.

Los Angeles Times. "George Claude, Neon Lights Scientist, Dies." May 24, 1960.

Los Angeles Times. "G. V. Russell: Award Winner in Architecture." March 28, 1989, 18.

Loti, Pierre. *Jerusalem* [1895]. Translated by W. P. Baines. New York: Frederick A. Stokes, 1930.

Lubell, Sam. "Original Sim." *New York Times,* December 7, 2008, 154.

Lucas, Anthony F. "The Determinants and Effects of Slot Servicescape Satisfaction in a Las Vegas Hotel Casino." *UNLV Gaming Research & Review Journal* 7, no. 1 (2003): 1–19.

Lucas, Anthony F., and William T. Dunn. "Estimating the Effects of Micro-Location Variables and Game Characteristics on Slot Machine Volume: A Performance-Potential Model." *Journal of Hospitality and Tourism Research* 29, no. 2 (2005): 170–93.

Lyell, James Patrick Ronaldson. *Early Book Illustration in Spain* [1926]. New York: Hacker Art Books, 1976.

Macarthur, John. *The Picturesque: Architecture, Disgust, and Other Irregularities.* London: Routledge, 2007.

Macintyre, Alasdair. "Social Structures and Their Threats to Moral Agency." *Philosophy* 74, no. 289 (1999): 311–29.

Macon Weekly Telegraph. "Explorations in Palestine." June 29, 1875.

Magen, Yizak, and Yuval Peleg. "Back to Qumran: Ten Years of Excavation and Research, 1993–2004." In *Qumran, the Site of the Dead Sea Scrolls: Archaeological Interpretations and Debates.* Proceedings of the conference held at Brown University, November 17–19, 2002, edited by Katharina Galor, Jean-Baptiste Humbert, and Jürgen Zangenberg, 55–113. Leiden: Brill, 2006.

Magness, Jodi. *The Archaeology of Qumran and the Dead Sea Scrolls.* Grand Rapids, Mich.: William B. Eerdmans Publishing, 2002.

Malaby, Thomas M. *Making Virtual Worlds: Linden Lab and Second Life.* Ithaca: Cornell University Press, 2009.

Mallet, Géraldine. *Les cloîtres démontés de Perpignan et du Roussillon (XIIe–XIVe siècles).* Perpignan: Archives communales de Perpignan, 2000.

———. "Dispersion et restauration du cloître de Saint-Michel de Cuxa (XIXe–XXe siècles)." *Les Cahiers de Saint-Michel de Cuxa* 33 (2002): 145–55.

Mancoff, Debra N. *David Roberts: Travels in Egypt and the Holy Land.* San Francisco: Pomegranate, 1999.

Margolick, David. "Under Las Vegas's Neon Beats a Heart of Denim." *New York Times,* February 16, 1984.

Márquez Villanueva, Francisco. *Santiago: Trayectoria de un mito.* Barcelona: Edicions Bellaterra, 2004.

Marten, Michael. "Imperialism and Evangelisation: Scottish Missionary Methods in Late 19th and Early 20th Century Palestine." *Holy Land Studies* 5, no. 2 (2006): 155–86.

Martínez, Carmelo Pellejero. "La empresa pública en el sector turístico español: ENTURSA 1963–1986." *Papers de Turisme* 22 (1997): 6–45.

———. *El Instituto Nacional de Industria en el sector turístico: ATESA (1949–1981) y ENTURSA (1963–1986).* Málaga: Servicio de Publicaciones de la Universidad de Málaga, 2000.

Masterman, E. W. G. "The Important Work of Dr. Conrad Schick." *Biblical World* 20, no. 2 (1902): 146–48.

Matsson, Eric Dinsmore. *The American Colony of Jerusalem: A Brief Historical Outline.* Menton: E. D. Matsson, 1992.

Mauss, Marcel. *The Gift: The Form and Reason for Exchange in Archaic Societies* [1924]. Translated by W. D. Halls. New York: Norton, 1990.

Mayer, Luigi. *Views in Egypt, Palestine, and Other Parts of the Ottoman Empire, from Original Drawings in the Collection of Sir Robert Ainslee and Engraved by Thomas Milton.* London: William Watts, 1801.

Mazar, Eilat. "Did I Find King David's Palace?" *Biblical Archaeology Review* 32, no. 1 (2006): 16–27, 70.

McNeill, Donald, and Kim McNamara. "The Life and Death of Great Hotels: A Building Biography of Sydney's 'The Australia.'" *Transactions of the Institute of British Geographers* 37, no. 1 (2012): 149–63.

McSpadden, J. Walker. *Famous Sculptors of America.* New York: Dodd, Mead, 1927.

Mehrabian, Albert, and J. A. Russell. "The Basic Emotional Impact of Environments." *Perceptual and Motor Skills* 38 (1974): 283–301.

Melcher, Ralph. *Die mittelalterlichen Kanzeln der Toskana.* Worms: Wernersche, 2000.

Mello, Michelle M., Eric B. Rimm, and David M. Studdert. "The McLawsuit: The Fast-Food Industry and Legal Accountability for Obesity." *Health Affairs* 22, no. 6 (2003): 207–16.

Merleau-Ponty, Maurice. *Phenomenology of Perception* [1945]. Translated by Colin Smith. London: Routledge, 2002.

Merrill, Selah. *East of the Jordan: A Record of Travel and Observation in the Countries of Moab, Gilead and Bashan.* London: Richard Bentley and Son, 1881.

———. "Jerusalem." *Old Testament Student* 5, no. 3 (1885): 97–103.

———. "Modern Researches in Palestine." *Journal of the American Geographical Society of New York* 9 (1877): 109–25.

———. "Nazareth the Home of Jesus." *Biblical World* 11, no. 1 (1898): 5–16.

———. *The Site of Calvary.* Jerusalem: A. M. Luncz, 1886.

Meyvaert, Paul. "The Medieval Monastic Claustrum." *Gesta* 12, nos. 1/2 (1973): 53–59.

Mezzatesta, Michael P., ed. *Jerusalem and the Holy Land Rediscovered: The Prints of David Roberts (1796–1846).* Durham, N.C.: Duke University Museum of Art, 1996.

Michener, James A. *Iberia: Spanish Travels and Reflections.* New York: Random House, 1968.

Mighty Gordon. "sl-addiction." http://www.sl-addiction.com/. Accessed July 30, 2011 (not currently maintained).

Miglio, Viola. "Old Norse and Old English Language Contact: Scandinavian Legal Terminology in Anglo-Saxon Laws." *Nordicum-Mediterraneum* 5, no. 1 (2010): 173–89.

Miguel García, Marta. "An Examination of International Promotion in a Spanish Hotel Network: Paradores." Master's thesis, Bournemouth University, 2003.

Mike. "Is Denver's Animal Murder Act Constitutional?" Crime & Federalism. July 23, 2005. http://federalism.typepad.com/crime_federalism/2005/07/is_denvers_anim.html.

Miller, Daniel. "Consumption and Commodities." *Annual Review of Anthropology* 24 (1995): 141–61.

Miller, Patricia Cox. *The Corporeal Imagination: Signifying the Holy in Late Ancient Christianity.* Edited by Daniel Boyarin, Virginia Burras, and Derek Krueger. Diviniations: Rereading Late Ancient Religion. Philadelphia: University of Pennsylvania Press, 2009.

Miller, Thomas Pelham. "The Cloisters: Retrospect and Prospect." *Connoisseur* 172 (1969): 138–47.

Mishima, Yukio. "The Priest of Shiga Temple and His Love." In *Death in Midsummer and Other Stories,* 59–75. New York: New Directions Books, 1966.

Moehring, Eugene P., and Michael S. Green. *Las Vegas: A Centennial History.* Reno: University of Nevada Press, 2005.

Moffatt, Frederick C. "Re-Membering Adam: George Grey Barnard, the John D. Rockefellers, and the Gender of Patronage." *Winterthur Portfolio* 35, no. 1 (2000): 53–80.

Molina, Luis de. *Descripción del reyno de Galizia* [1550]. Colección de los bibliofilos Gallegos 1. Compostela: Bibliofilos Gallegos, 1949.

Molinero, Carme, Margarida Tintó Sala, and Jaume Sobrequés i Callicó. *Una inmensa prisión: Los campos de concentración y las prisiones durante la guerra civil y el franquismo.* Barcelona: Crítica, 2003.

Monk, Daniel. *An Aesthetic Occupation: The Immediacy of Architecture and the Palestine Conflict.* Durham, N.C.: Duke University Press, 2002.

———. "Review of *Bauhaus on the Carmel and the Crossroads of Empire,* by Gilbert Herbert and Silvina Sosnovsky." *AA Files* 28 (1994): 94–99.

Moody, Eric N. "Nevada's Legislation of Casino Gambling in 1931." *Nevada Historical Society Quarterly* 37, no. 2 (1994): 79–100.

Mortensen, Peder, ed. *Bayt al-'Aqqad: The History and Restoration of a House in Old Damascus.* Proceedings of the Danish Institute in Damascus 4. Aarhus: Aarhus Universitetsforlag, 2005.

Mumford, Lewis. "Pax in Urbe." *New Yorker,* May 21, 1938, 76–79.

———. *Sidewalk Critic: Lewis Mumford's Writing on New York.* Edited by Robert Wojtowicz. New York: Princeton Architectural Press, 1998.

Münzer, Jerome. "Viaje por España y Portugal en los años 1494 y 1495." *Boletin de la Real Academia de la Historia* 84, nos. 1–2 (1924): 32–119, 97–279.

Murphy, Michelle. *Sick Building Syndrome and the Problem of Uncertainty: Environmental Politics, Technoscience and Women Workers.* Durham, N.C.: Duke University Press, 2006.

Mussot, Raphaëlle. "Monastères et tourisme: Enjeux d'une mise en tourisme d'un patrimoine specifique." Diplôme d'études supérieures spécialisées, Faculty of Anthropology and Sociology, University of Lyon, 1998.

Musurillo, Herbert. *The Acts of the Christian Martyrs: Introduction, Texts and Translations.* Oxford: Clarendon Press, 1972.

Nagel, Thomas. "What Is It Like to Be a Bat?" *Philosophical Review* 83, no. 4 (1974): 435–50.

Nashif, Taysir. "Palestinian Arab and Jewish Leadership in the Mandate Period." *Journal of Palestine Studies* 6, no. 4 (1977): 113–21.

National Center for Biotechnology Information. "Drugs and Supplements." National Library of Medicine, National Institutes of Health. http://www.ncbi.nlm.nih.gov/pubmedhealth/PMH0001026/. Accessed May 13, 2011.

Nevada Commission on Tourism. "Nevada Weddings." http://travelnevada.com/weddings-laws.aspx. Accessed August 29, 2011.

New York Times. "American Sculptor Is Lauded in Paris. Artist Faced Privation. State Stopped Payments and He Had to Sell Curios." March 16, 1910.

New York Times. "Big Tract Donated by Rockefeller Jr. to Save Palisades." July 12, 1933.

New York Times. "Censorship in Spain." August 9, 1962.

New York Times. "A Falling Hotel Vies with a Dropping Ball." January 1, 1997.

New York Times. "G. G. Barnard Plans Art School Here: Ruins of Prades Abbey Designed to Be Object Lesson for Young Sculptors." May 11, 1913.

New York Times. "Many Killed and Hurt in Palestine Quake." July 12, 1927.

New York Times. "New Sack of Europe—by Americans." May 28, 1922.

New York Times. "News Notes from the Field of Travel: Old West Display." January 28, 1951.

New York Times. "Pennsylvania's New Capitol: Architect, Sculptor and Mural Painter to Work in Harmony—Large Appropriations to Make It the Finest Capitol in America." July 20, 1902.

New York Times. "Rare Relics Kept from America by French Protest." June 15, 1913.

New York Times. "Southern Leaders Decide to Abandon Fight on Wage and Hour Bill." May 8, 1938.

Nicoletta, Julie, and Bret Morgan. *Buildings of Nevada.* Buildings of the United States. New York: Oxford University Press, 2000.

Noseworthy, Theodore J., and Karen Finlay. "A Comparison of Ambient Casino Sound and Music: Effects on Dissociation and on Perceptions of Elapsed Time While Playing Slot Machines." *Journal of Gambling Studies* 24, no. 3 (2009): 331–42.

O'Brian, C. P. "Neuroplasticity in Addictive Disorders." *Dialogues in Clinical Neuroscience* 11, no. 3 (2009): 350–53.

Oriental Institute: Symbolism. Director's Library, Oriental Institute, University of Chicago. 1932.

Ostling, Richard N. "Is Jesus in the Dead Sea Scrolls?" *Time,* September 21, 1992.

Ousterhout, Robert. "Architecture as Relic and the Construction of Sanctity: The Stones of the Holy Sepulchre." *Journal of the Society of Architectural Historians* 62, no. 1 (2003): 4–23.

Oyediran, Joanna. *Plunder, Destruction, and Despoliation: An Analysis of Israel's Violations of the International Law of Cultural Property in the Occupied West Bank and Gaza.* Ramallah: Al-Haq, 1997.

Pack, Sasha D. "Revival of Pilgrimage to Santiago de Compostela: The Politics of Religous, National, and European Patrimony, 1879–1988." *Journal of Modern History* 82, no. 2 (2010): 335–67.

———. "Tourism and Dictatorship: Europe's Peaceful Invasion of Franco's Spain." In *Spain Transformed: The Late Franco Dictatorship, 1959–1975*, edited by Nigel Townson, 47–66. Basingstoke: Palgrave Macmillan, 2007.

Packer, Adrienne. "Pedestrian Bridge Proposal Heads to County Commission." *Las Vegas Sun*, September 17, 2001.

"The Palestine Archaeological Museum, Austen St. B. Harrison, Architect." *Architectural Review* 78 (September 1935): 89–96.

Palestine Archaeological Museum Files. Archive of the Albright Institute of Archaeological Research, Jerusalem.

Parfitt, Tudor. *The Jews in Palestine, 1800–1882*. Royal Historical Society Studies in History 52. Woodbridge: Boydell Press for the Royal Historical Society, 1987.

Patrick, Elizabeth Nelson. *An Interview with William J. Moore*. Edited by Fred M. Anderson, Mary Ellen Glass, and R. T. King. Oral History Project. Reno: University of Nevada, 1985.

Paulinus of Nola. *Epistulae. Letters of St. Paulinus of Nola*. Edited by P. G. Walsh. Ancient Christian Writers 35 and 36. New York: Newman Press, 1966–67.

Pavlov, Ivan P. *Conditioned Reflexes: An Investigation of the Physiological Activity of the Cerebral Cortex*. Translated by G. V. Anrep. Oxford: Oxford University Press, 1927.

Pearce, Celia, and Artemesia. *Communities of Play: Emergent Cultures in Multiplayer Games and Virtual Worlds*. Cambridge, Mass.: MIT Press, 2009.

———. "Narrative Environments from Disneyland to World of Warcraft." In *Space Time Play. Computer Games, Architecture, and Urbanism: The Next Level*, edited by Friedrich von Borries, Steffen P. Walz, and Matthias Böttger, 200–205. Basel: Birkhäuser Verlag, 2007.

Peirce, Charles S. *Commens Dictionary of Peirce's Terms*. Edited by Mats Bergman and Sami Paavola. University of Helsinki. 2003–. http://www.helsinki.fi/science/commens/dictionary.html.

Perrot, Jean. *Le Musée archéologique de Palestine a Jérusalem*. Paris: Geuthner, 1948.

Perry, Nicholas, and Loreto Echeverría. *Under the Heel of Mary*. London: Routledge, 1988.

Pervukhin, Anna. "Deodands: A Study in the Creation of Common Law Rules." *American Journal of Legal History* 47, no. 3 (2005): 237–56.

Petruccioli, Attilio. *After Amnesia: Learning from the Islamic Mediterranean Urban Fabric*. Bari: Grafica & Stampa, 2007.

———. "The Courtyard House: Typological Variations over Time and Space." In *Courtyard Housing: Past, Present, and Future*, edited by Brian Edwards, Magda Sibley, Peter Land, and Mohamad Hakmi, 3–20. Abingdon: Taylor and Francis, 2006.

Pfeiffer, Alice. "Many Genres, One Giant Space." *New York Times*, October 16, 2011.

Pierpont, Claudia Roth. "The Silver Spire: How Two Men's Dreams Changed the Skyline of New York." *New Yorker*, November 18, 2002, 74–81.

Pietz, William. "Death of the Deodand: Accursed Objects and the Money Value of Human Life." *Res* 31 (Spring 1997): 97–108.

Porter, Stephen, Angela R. Birt, John C. Yuille, and Hugues F. Hervé. "Memory for Murder: A Psychological Perspective on Dissociative Amnesia in Legal Contexts." *Law and Psychiatry* 24 (2001): 23–42.

Pressouyre, Léon. "St. Bernard to St. Francis: Monastic Ideals and Iconographic Programs in the Cloister." *Gesta* 12, nos. 1/2 (1973): 71–92.

Previc, Fred H. *The Dopaminergic Mind in Human Evolution and History.* New York: Cambridge University Press, 2009.

Pringle, Denys. *The Churches of the Crusader Kingdom of Jerusalem: A Corpus (Jerusalem).* 3 vols. Cambridge: Cambridge University Press, 2007.

Puzo, Mario. *Fools Die.* New York: G. P. Putnam's Sons, 1978.

Quinn, Josephine Crawley. "Herms, Kouroi and the Political Anatomy of Athens." *Greece and Rome* 54, no. 1 (2007): 82–105.

Ragette, Friedrich. *Architecture in Lebanon: The Lebanese House during the 18th and 19th Centuries.* Beirut: American University of Beirut, 1974.

Rawlings, Helen. *The Spanish Inquisition.* Oxford: Blackwell, 2006.

Raymond, Jade. "Assassin's Creed Developer's Diary: Storyline." Ubisoft. http://assassinscreed.uk.ubi.com/assassins-creed-1/home.php—/devdiary/. Accessed March 11, 2009.

Read, Jan, and Maite Manjon. *Paradores of Spain: Their History, Cooking, and Wines.* New York: Mason/Charter, 1977.

Reed, Stephen A. *The Dead Sea Scrolls Catalogue: Documents, Photographs, and Museum Inventory Numbers.* Edited by Marilyn J. Lundberg and Michael B. Phelps. Resources for Biblical Study 32. Atlanta: Scholars Press, 1994.

———. "Jerusalem Report." *The Folio* 10, no. 3 (1990): 1, 4–5.

Reichs, Kathy. *Cross Bones.* New York: Pocket Star Books, 2005.

Resig, Dorothy. "Uncovering the Walls of Zion." *Biblical Archaeology Review* 34, no. 6 (2008): 18.

Rhodes, D. E. "Further Notes on an Indulgence of Alexander VI." *The Library* 26, no. 1 (1971): 58–60.

Richa, Giuseppe. *Notizie istoriche delle chiese fiorentine, divise ne'suoi quartieri.* Florence: Pietro Gaetano Viviani, 1754–62.

Richardson, Peter. "Towards a Typology of Levantine/Palestinian Houses." *Journal for the Study of the New Testament* 27, no. 1 (2004): 47–68.

Rickenbacker, Dylan. "The SLunkie Factor—Parts I–III." Dylan's Drama: Adventures in Second Life. June 22, 2009. http://drickenbacker.wordpress.com.

Riewoldt, Otto. *New Hotel Design.* London: Watson-Guptill, 2002.

Rives, James. "Magic, Religion, and Law: The Case of the *Lex Cornelia de sicariis et veneficiis.*" In *Religion and Law in Classical and Christian Rome,* edited by Clifford Ando and Jörg Rüpke, 47–67. Stuttgart: Steiner, 2006.

Rivlin, Joseph Joel. *Me'ah she'arim.* Jerusalem: Ha-Histadrut ha-Tsiyonit be-siyu a Mosad ha-rav Kuk, 1947.

Roberts, David, and Rev. George Croly. *The Holy Land, Syria, Idumea, Arabia, Egypt, and Nubia, from Drawings Made on the Spot by David Roberts, R. A., with Historical Descriptions by the Reverend George Croly, L.L.D., Lithographed by Louis Haghe.* London: F. G. Moon, 1842–45.

Robinson, Edward. *Biblical Researches in Palestine and the Adjacent Regions: A Journal of Travels in the Years 1838 and 1852.* 3 vols. London: J. Murray, 1867.

Robinson, George, and Martin Weinberger. *The George Grey Barnard Collection.* New York: Robinson Galleries, 1941.

Roca Roca, Eduardo. *La regulación jurídica del turismo en España.* Almería: Universidad de Almería—Servicio de Publicaciones, 1998.

Rockefeller Foundation Archives Collections Related to the Palestine Archaeological Museum and the Cloisters. Rockefeller Archive Center, Tarrytown, New York.

Roehl, Wesley S., and Carlton S. Van Doren. "Locational Characteristics of American Resort Hotels." *Journal of Cultural Geography* 11, no. 1 (1990): 71–83.

Rogeberg, Ole. "Taking Absurd Theories Seriously: Economics and the Case of Rational Addiction Theories." *Philosophy of Science* 71, no. 3 (2004): 263–85.

Rogers, Richard, ed. *Clinical Assessment of Malingering and Deception.* 3rd ed. New York: Guilford Press, 2008.

Rojas, Carlos. *The Great Wall: A Cultural History.* Cambridge, Mass.: Harvard University Press, 2010.

Rorimer, James J. *The Cloisters: The Building and the Collection of Medieval Art in Fort Tryon Park.* Edited by Margaret B. Freeman. 3rd ed. New York: Metropolitan Museum of Art, 1963.

———. *Medieval Monuments at the Cloisters: As They Were and As They Are.* New York: Metropolitan Museum of Art, 1941.

———. *Medieval Monuments at the Cloisters: As They Were and As They Are.* Rev. ed. Edited by Katherine Serrell Rorimer. New York: Metropolitan Museum of Art, 1972.

Rosenberg, Joel C. *The Copper Scroll.* Carol Stream, Ill.: Tyndale House Publishers, 2006.

Rosenberg, Ox. "Ultra-Orthodox Spitting Attacks on Old City Clergymen Becoming Daily." *Haaretz,* April 11, 2011.

Rosendorf, Neal Moses. "Be El Caudillo's Guest: The Franco Regime's Quest for Rehabilitation and Dollars after World War II via the Promotion of U.S. Tourism to Spain." *Diplomatic History* 30, no. 3 (2006): 367–407.

Rothman, Hal. "Colony, Capital, and Casino: Money in the Real Las Vegas." In *The Grit beneath the Glitter: Tales from the Real Las Vegas,* edited by Hal Rothman and Mike Davis, 307–34. Berkeley: University of California Press, 2002.

Ruskin, John. *"A Joy For Ever" and Its Price in the Market: Two Lectures on the Political Economy of Art Delivered at Manchester, July 10th and 13th, 1857.* London: George Allen, 1904.

———. "Modern Painters" [1846]. Edited by Juliet Sutherland and Marius Borror. New York: National Library Association, 2009.

———. *Modern Painters.* London: Smith, Elder, 1856–60.

———. *The Works of John Ruskin.* Vol. 35, *Praeterita and Dilecta.* Edited by E. T. Cook and A. Wedderburn. London: George Allen, 1908.

Russell, George Vernon. *George Vernon Russell, FAIA and Associates: Architects, Engineers, Planners.* Los Angeles: G. V. Russell and Associates, 1967.

———. "Interview." *Architectural and Engineering News* 10 (February 1968): 74.

Saad, Yusef. *The Palestine Archaeological Museum and the Dead Sea Scrolls.* 5th ed. Jerusalem: Palestine Archaeological Museum, 1965.

Said, Edward W. *Orientalism.* New York: Vintage Books, 1979.

Saint-Jean, Robert. *Saint-Guilhem-le-Désert: La sculpture du cloître de l'abbaye de Gellone.* Maury: Saint-Georges-de-Luzençon, 1990.

Sánchez Sánchez, Esther M. "Turismo, desarrollo e integración internacional de la España franquista." Paper presented at the EBHA Annual Conference, Barcelona, September 16–18, 2004. Available at http://www.econ.upf.edu/ebha2004/papers/7C2.doc.

Sapir, Shaul. "Conrad Schick and His Works for the English Mission of Jerusalem" [in Hebrew]. *Ariel* 130–31 (1998): 73–77.

Sauer, Paul. *The Holy Land Called: The Story of the Temple Society.* Translated by Gunhild Henley. Melbourne: Temple Society Australia, 1991.

Sayers, Michael, and Albert E. Kahn. *Sabotage! The Secret War against America.* New York: Harper and Brothers, 1942.

Scarry, Elaine. *The Body in Pain: The Making and Unmaking of the World.* Oxford: Oxford University Press, 1985.

Schapiro, Meyer. "Further Notes on Heidegger and van Gogh." In *Theory and Philosophy of Art: Style, Artist, and Society,* 143–51. New York: George Braziller, 1994.

———. "On the Aesthetic Attitude in Romanesque Art." In *Art and Thought: Issued in Honor of Dr. Ananda K. Coomaraswamy on the Occasion of His 70th Birthday,* edited by K. Bharatha Iyer, 130–50. London: Luzac, 1947.

———. "The Still-Life as a Personal Object—A Note on Heidegger and van Gogh." In *Theory and Philosophy of Art: Style, Artist, and Society,* 135–42. New York: George Braziller, 1994.

Scheri, Saverio. *The Casino's Most Valuable Chip: How Technology Transformed the Gaming Industry.* Palo Alto, Calif.: Institute for the History of Technology, 2005.

Schiffman, Lawrence H., and James C. VanderKam, eds. *Encyclopedia of the Dead Sea Scrolls.* 2 vols. New York: Oxford University Press, 2000.

Schlosser, Julius von. *Die Kunst- und Wunderkammern der Spätrenaissance: Ein Beitrag zur Geschichte des Sammelwesens.* Leipzig: Klinkhardt and Biermann, 1908.

Schnabel, Julian. *Miral.* DVD. Beverly Hills: Anchor Bay, 2011.

Schrader, J. L. "George Grey Barnard: The Cloisters and the Abbaye." *Metropolitan Museum of Art Bulletin* 37, no. 1 (1979): 2–52.

Schüll, Natasha Dow. *Addiction by Design: Machine Gambling in Las Vegas.* Princeton: Princeton University Press, 2012.

———. "Digital Gambling: The Coincidence of Desire and Design." *Annals of the American Academy of Political and Social Science* 597 (2005): 65–81.

———. "Machines, Medication, Modulation: Circuits of Dependency and Self-Care in Las Vegas." *Culture, Medicine, and Psychiatry* 30, no. 2 (2006): 223–47.

———. "Video Poker." In *The Inner History of Devices,* edited by Sherry Turkle, 153–71. Cambridge, Mass.: MIT Press, 2008.

Schultz, Anne-Catrin. *Ada Karmi-Melamede and Ram Karmi, Supreme Court of Israel, Jerusalem: Opus 71.* Stuttgart: Axel Menges, 2010.

Schultz, Wolfram. "Responses of Monkey Dopamine Neurons to Reward and Conditioned Stimuli during Successive Steps of Learning a Delayed Response Task." *Journal of Neuroscience* 13, no. 3 (1993): 900–913.

Segal, Rafi, and Eyal Weizman. *A Civilian Occupation: The Politics of Israeli Architecture.* London: Verso, 2002.

Seidel, Linda. "Installation as Inspiration: The Passion Cycle from La Daurade." *Gesta* 25, no. 1 (1986): 83–92.

Shahid, Serene Husseini. *Jerusalem Memories.* Beirut: Naufal, 1999.

Shamir, Milette. "'Our Jerusalem': Americans in the Holy Land and Protestant Narratives of National Entitlement." *American Quarterly* 55, no. 1 (2003): 29–60.

Shaw, Ian Graham Ronald, and Barney Warf. "Worlds of Affect: Virtual Geographies of Video Games." *Environment and Planning A* 41, no. 6 (2009): 1332–43.

Sher, George. "Out of Control." *Ethics* 116, no. 2 (2006): 285–301.

Sherman, Lawrence W. "Preventing Homicide through Trial and Error." In *Homicide: Patterns, Prevention, and Control. Proceedings of a Conference Held 12–14 May, 1992,* edited by Heather Strang and Sally-Anne Gerull, 21–34. Canberra: Australian Institute of Criminology, 1993.

Shirley, John. *City Come a Walkin'* [1980]. New York: Four Walls Eight Windows, 2000.

Short, Vicky. "Spanish Troops in Iraq to Wear Christian Badge." *World Socialist Web Site.* August 12, 2003. http://www.wsws.org.

Siegel, Judy. "Psychiatric Hospitals 'Not Fit for Animals,' Knesset Panel Hears." *Jerusalem Post,* February 10, 2010.

Silberman, Neil Asher. "'If I forget thee, O Jerusalem': Archaeology, Religious Commemoration, and Nationalism in a Disputed City, 1801–2001." *Nations and Nationalism* 7, no. 4 (2001): 487–504.

Silverman, Barry, Brian Silverman, and Vadim Gerasimov. "Spacewar!" http://spacewar.over sigma.com/.

Simpson, D. P. *Cassell's New Latin Dictionary.* New York: Funk & Wagnalls, 1968.

Smith, David Woodruff. "Phenomenology." *Stanford Encyclopedia of Philosophy.* Fall 2011 ed. http://plato.stanford.edu/archives/fall2011.

Smith, Elizabeth Bradford. "George Grey Barnard: Artist/Collector/Dealer/Curator." In *Medieval Art in America: Patterns of Collecting, 1800–1940,* edited by Elizabeth Bradford Smith, Kathryn McClintock, R. Aaron Rottner, and Sarah Andrews, 133–42. University Park: Palmer Museum of Art, the Pennsylvania State University, 1996.

Smith, Jonathan Z. *Map Is Not Territory.* Leiden: E. J. Brill, 1978.

———. *To Take Place.* Chicago: University of Chicago Press, 1987.

Smith, Terry E. *The Architecture of Aftermath.* Chicago: University of Chicago Press, 2006.

Soja, Edward W. *Thirdspace: Journeys to Los Angeles and Other Real-and-Imagined Places.* Oxford: Blackwell, 1996.

Solon, Leon V. "Suggestions and Models for Architectural Rendering: The Lithographic Work of David Roberts." *Architectural Record* 46 (September 1919): 211–20.

Sontag, Deborah. "An Undiplomatic Skirmish in a Pasha's Palace in Jerusalem." *New York Times,* October 27, 1999.

Sørensen, Carl Theodor. "Junk Playgrounds." *Danish Outlook* 4, no. 1 (1951): 314.

Southey, Robert. *The Poetical Works.* London: Longman, Brown, Green & Longmans, 1838.

Spence D. "Jesper Kyd and Assassin's Creed: Composer Discusses His Work on Ubisoft's Surreal Action Game." IGN Music. December 11, 2007. http://music.ign.com/articles/840 /840966p1.html.

Spencer, Charles S. "The Israel National Museum." *Studio International* 170 (1965): 64–67.

Spingarn-Koff, Jason. *Life 2.0.* DVD. New York: Virgil Films and Entertainment, 2012.

Starkie, Walter. *The Road to Santiago: Pilgrims of St. James.* New York: E. P. Dutton, 1957.

Statesville Daily Record. "Miss Atomic Blast." May 9, 1952.

Stephenson, Neal. *Snow Crash.* New York: Bantam, 1992.

Stern, Ephraim, Ayelet Lewinson-Giboa, and Joseph Aviram, eds. *The New Encyclopedia of Archaeological Excavations in the Holy Land.* 5 vols. Jerusalem: Israel Exploration Society; Washington, D.C.: Biblical Archaeology Society, 2008.

Stigliano, Tony. "Fascism's Mythologist: Mircea Eliade and the Politics of Myth." *ReVision* 24, no. 3 (2002): 32–38.

Stingley, Jim. "Keeping Their House in Order: Legalized Prostitution in Nevada." *Los Angeles Times,* February 8, 1976.

Stone, Christopher D. *Should Trees Have Standing? Toward Legal Rights for Natural Objects.* Palo Alto, Calif.: Tioga Publishing, 1988.

Strickland, Erica. "Gambling with Science." Salon. June 16, 2008. http://www.salon.com /news/feature/2008/06/16/gambling_science/.

Sudjic, Deyan. *The Edifice Complex: How the Rich and Powerful—and Their Architects—Shape the World.* London: Penguin, 2005.

Sun, Xue, Paawan V. Punjabi, Lucy T. Greenberg, and John G. Seamon. "Does Feigning Amnesia Impair Subsequent Recall?" *Memory and Cognition* 37, no. 1 (2009): 81–89.

Suri, Roland E., and Wolfram Schultz. "Temporal Difference Model Reproduces Anticipatory Neural Activity." *Neural Computation* 13, no. 4 (2001): 841–62.

Sussman, Ayala, and Ronny Reich. "The History of the Rockefeller Museum" [in Hebrew]. In *Zev Vilnay Jubilee Volume: Essays on the History, Archaeology, and Lore of the Holy Land* [in Hebrew], edited by Eli Schiller, 83–91. Jerusalem: Ariel Press, 1987.

Sutton, Teresa. "The Nature of the Early Law of Deodand." *Cambrian Law Review* 30 (1999): 9–20.

Swyngedouw, Erik. "Metabolic Urbanization: The Making of Cyborg Cities." In *In the Nature of Cities: Urban Political Ecology and the Politics of Urban Metabolism,* edited by Nik Heynen, Maria Kaika, and Erik Swyngedouw, 20–39. New York: Routlege, 2006.

Sydell, Laura. "Sci-Fi Inspires Engineers to Build Our Future." *Weekend Edition Saturday.* NPR. August 21, 2010. http://www.npr.org/programs/weekend-edition-saturday/.

Taha, Hamdan. "The History and Role of Museums in Palestine." *International Committee for Museums and Collections of Archaeology and History: Study Series* (2001): 25–27.

Takahashi, Dean. "Video Game Industry to Hit $70 Billion by 2015, but Growth Will Slow." *Games Beat.* May 25, 2010. http://venturebeat.com/2010/05/25/video-game-industry-to-hit-70-billion-by-2015-but-growth-will-slow/.

Tamen, Miguel. *Friends of Interpretable Objects.* Cambridge, Mass.: Harvard University Press, 2005.

Taylor, Robert R. *The Word in Stone: The Role of Architecture in the National Socialist Ideology.* Berkeley: University of California Press, 1974.

Thomas Aquinas. *Summa Theologica.* New York: McGraw-Hill, 1964.

Thomas, Julian. "Phenomenology and Material Culture." In *Handbook of Material Culture,* edited by Christopher Y. Tilley, Webb Keane, Susanne Küchler, Mike Rowlands, and Patricia Spyer, 43–59. London: Sage, 2006.

Thompson, Hunter S. *Fear and Loathing in Las Vegas* [1971]. New York: Vintage, 1998.

Tilley, Christopher Y. *A Phenomenology of Landscape: Places, Paths, and Monuments.* Oxford: Berg, 1994.

Time. "The Oldest Decalogue." September 29, 1958, 49.

Tribune Tower Fragment Collection Correspondence. Tribune Tower Archive, Chicago.

Tripadvisor. "Parador Hostal Dos Reis Catolicos." http://www.tripadvisor.com.

Tsafrir, Yoram. "The Southwestern Hill of Jerusalem and Its Place in the Urban Development of the City in the Byzantine Period" [in Hebrew]. PhD thesis, Hebrew University, 1975.

Tschumi, Bernard. "Illustrated Index: Themes from the Manhattan Transcripts." *AA Files* 4 (1983): 65–74.

———. *Questions of Space: Lectures on Architecture.* London: Architectural Association, 1990.

Turdean, Cristina. "Casinos and the Digitization of the Slot Machine, 1950–1989." *Annals of the History of Computing* 33, no. 2 (2011): 46–59.

Twyman, Michael. *Lithography, 1800–1850: The Techniques of Drawing on Stone in England and France and Their Application to Works of Topography.* London: Oxford University Press, 1970.

Upton, Dell. "Starting from Baalbek: Noah, Solomon, Saladin, and the Fluidity of Architectural History." *Journal of the Society of Architectural Historians* 68, no. 4 (2009): 457–65.

U.S. National Library of Medicine and the National Institutes of Health. "Medline Plus." http://www2.merriam-webster.com/cgi-bin/mwmednlm?book=Medical&va=catalepsy. Accessed January 15, 2007.

Van Cleave, Ryan G. *Unplugged: My Journey into the Dark World of Video Game Addiction.* Deerfield Beach, Fla.: Health Communications, 2010.

Vázquez de Parga, Luis, José María Lacarra, and Juan Uría Ríu. *Las peregrinaciones a Santiago de Compostela.* Madrid: Blass, 1948–49.

Vegas.com. "Behind the Scenes with Las Vegas' Top Thrills." http://www.vegas.com/attractions/thrillrides.html.

Velazquez, Manuel. "Debunking Corporate Moral Responsibility." *Business Ethics Quarterly* 13, no. 4 (2003): 531–61.

Venturi, Robert. *Complexity and Contradiction in Architecture.* New York: Museum of Modern Art, 1966.

Venturi, Robert, Denise Scott Brown, and Steven Izenour. *Learning from Las Vegas.* Cambridge, Mass.: MIT Press, 1972.

Vergara, Camilo José. "Opening the Doors to the Ghettos." *Chronicle of Higher Education,* January 12, 1996, B88.

Vergés, Joaquim. "Why Governments Sell Public Firms: The Spanish Case." *International Advances in Economic Research* 7, no. 1 (2001): 114–32.

Verlager, Alicia Kestrell. "The Prosthetic Eye." In *The Inner History of Devices,* edited by Sherry Turkle, 32–40. Cambridge, Mass.: MIT Press, 2008.

Vester, Bertha Spafford. *Our Jerusalem: An American Family in the Holy City, 1881–1949.* Garden City, N.Y.: Doubleday, 1950.

Vester, Valentine. *The American Colony Family Album.* Jerusalem: American Colony of Jerusalem, 2008.

Vidler, Anthony. *The Architectural Uncanny: Essays in the Modern Unhomely.* Cambridge, Mass.: MIT Press, 1992.

Vila Jato, María Dolores, ed. *Parador de Santiago "Os Reis Católicos": Un hotel con quinientos años, el más antiguo de Europa.* Madrid: Paradores de Turismo de España, 1999.

Vinegar, Aron, and Michael J. Golec, eds. *Relearning from Las Vegas.* Minneapolis: University of Minnesota Press, 2009.

Wakefield, Kirk L., and Jeffrey G. Blodgett. "The Importance of Servicescapes in Leisure Service Settings." *Journal of Services Marketing* 8, no. 3 (1994): 66–76.

Wallace, Edwin Sherman. *Jerusalem the Holy: A Brief History of Ancient Jerusalem; with an Account of the Modern City and Its Conditions, Political, Religious, and Social.* 2nd ed. Edinburgh: Oliphant, Anderson and Ferrier, 1904.

Washington Post. "Peace of the Harem: There Real Freedom Is Found for Women Says Mme. Myriam Harry." July 12, 1908.

Weill, Raymond. *Cité de David: Compte rendu des fouilles exécutées à Jérusalem, sur le site de la ville primitive, campagne de 1913–1914.* 2 vols. Paris: P. Geuthner, 1920.

Weiner, Deborah. "From Victorian Asylum to 'Princess Park Manor.'" In *Architecture as Experience: Radical Change in Spatial Practice,* edited by Dana Arnold and Andrew Ballantyne, 190–209. London: Routledge, 2004.

Weizman, Eyal. *Forensic Architecture: Notes from Fields and Forums.* Documenta: 100 Notes, 100 Thoughts. Berlin: Hatje Cantz, 2012.

Welch, John R. "Corporate Agency and Reduction." *Philosophical Quarterly* 39, no. 157 (1989): 409–24.

Welles, Benjamin. *Spain: The Gentle Anarchy.* New York: Praeger, 1965.

West-Pavlov, Russell. *Space in Theory: Kristeva, Foucault, Deleuze.* Amsterdam: Rodopi, 2009.

Weyer, F. "In memoriam Peter Mühlens." *Zeitschrift für Tropenmedizin und Parasitologie* 5, no. 3 (1954): 273–75.

Wharton, Annabel Jane. *Building the Cold War: Hilton International Hotels and Modern Architecture.* Chicago: University of Chicago Press, 2001.

———. "Jerusalem's Zions." *Material Religion* 9 (2013): 218–42.

———. "Relics, Protestants, Things." *Material Religion* 10 (2014).

———. *Selling Jerusalem: Relics, Replicas, Theme Parks.* Chicago: University of Chicago Press, 2006.

———. "Shaping the 'Public Sphere' in Second Life: Architectures of the 2008 U.S. Presidential Campaign." *Journal of Virtual Worlds Research* 2, no. 2 (2009): 4–14.

———. "The Tribune Tower: Spolia as Despoliation." In *Reuse Value: Spolia and Appropriation in Art and Architecture, from Constantine to Sherrie Levine,* edited by Richard Brilliant and Dale Kinney, 179–97. Aldershot: Ashgate, 2011.

Whitehead, Christiania. *Castles of the Mind: A Study of Medieval Architectural Allegory.* Edited by Denis Renevey and Diane Watt. Religion and Culture in the Middle Ages. Cardiff: University of Wales Press, 2003.

Wightman, G. J. *The Walls of Jerusalem: From the Canaanites to the Mamluks.* Mediterranean Archaeology Supplement 4. Sydney: Meditarch, 1993.

Wilkinson, John. *Jerusalem Pilgrims before the Crusades.* Warminster: Aris and Phillips, 2002.

Wilkinson-Zerner, Catherine. "The Hospital of Cardinal Tavera in Toledo: A Documentary and Stylistic Study of Spanish Architecture in the Mid-Sixteenth Century." PhD dissertation, Yale University, 1969.

Williams, Dmitri, Tracy L. M. Kennedy, and Robert J. Moore. "Behind the Avatar: The Patterns, Practices, and Functions of Role Playing in MMOs." *Games and Culture* 6, no. 2 (2011): 171–200.

Wilson, C. W. "Obituary of Dr. Conrad Schick." *Palestine Exploration Fund Quarterly* 17 (1902): 139–42.

Woess, Friedrich von. "Personalexekution und cessio bonorum im römischen Reichsrecht." *Zeitschrift der Savigny-Stiftung für Rechtsgeschichte / Romanistische Abteilung* 43 (1922): 485–529.

Wolf, Mark J. P. "Abstraction in the Video Game." In *The Video Game Theory Reader,* edited by Mark J. P. Wolf and Bernard Perron, 45–65. New York: Routledge, 2003.

Wolfe, Cary. *Before the Law: Humans and Other Animals in a Biopolitical Frame.* Chicago: University of Chicago Press, 2013.

Wolfe, Tom. *The Kandy-Kolored Tangerine-Flake Streamline Baby.* New York: Farrar, Straus and Giroux, 1965.

Woo, Kevin L., and Guillaume Rieucau. "From Dummies to Animations: A Review of Computer-Animated Stimuli Used in Animal Behavior Studies." *Behavioral Ecology and Sociobiology* 65 (2011): 1671–85.

Wright, Frank Lloyd. *Frank Lloyd Wright: An Autobiography* [1932]. Petaluma, Calif.: Pomegranate Communications, 2005.

Yancey, Kitty Bean. "Won Over by Wynn." *U.S.A. Today,* June 10, 2005.

Yellin, Yehoshua. *Memoirs of a Son of Jerusalem,* 1834–1918 [in Hebrew]. Jerusalem: Zion Press, 1928.

Young, Bonnie. *A Walk through the Cloisters.* New York: Metropolitan Museum of Art, 1979.

Young, Garry. *Ethics in the Virtual World: The Morality and Psychology of Gaming*. Durham: Acumen, 2013.

Young, Julian. "The Fourfold." In *The Cambridge Companion to Heidegger*, edited by Charles B. Guignon, 373–92. Cambridge: Cambridge University Press, 2006.

Young, Kimberly S. "Understanding Online Gaming Addiction and Treatment Issues for Adolescents." *American Journal of Family Therapy* 37 (2009): 355–72.

Young, Mahonri Sharp. "George Grey Barnard and the Cloisters." *Apollo* 106, no. 189 (1977): 332–39.

Your Girlfriend. "Second Life Intervention." Youtube. September 7, 2008. http://www.youtube.com/watch?v=oN-o-kVJs78&feature=related.

Zako, Reem. "The Power of the Veil: Gender Inequality in the Domestic Setting of Traditional Courtyard Houses." In *Courtyard Housing: Past, Present, and Future*, edited by Brian Edwards, Magda Sibley, Peter Land, and Mohamad Hakmi, 65–75. Abingdon: Taylor and Francis, 2006.

Zias, Joseph. "Palestine Archaeological Museum." In *Encyclopedia of the Dead Sea Scrolls*, edited by Lawrence H. Schiffman and James C. VanderKam, 634–35. New York: Oxford University Press, 2000.

Zimmerman, Susan. "The Diseased Body in Premodern Europe: Ideology and Representation." *Journal of Medieval and Early Modern Studies* 38, no. 3 (2008): 403–12.

Zislin, Josef, Gregory Katz, Sergey Raskin, Ziva Strauss, Alexander Teitelbaum, and Rimona Durst. "Male Genital Self-Mutilation in the Context of Religious Belief: The Jerusalem Syndrome." *Transcultural Psychiatry* 39, no. 2 (2002): 257–64.

Zola, Émile. *The Ladies' Paradise* [1883]. Translated by Brian Nelson. Oxford: Oxford University Press, 1995.

———. *Lourdes* [1894]. Translated by Ernest A. Vizetelly. Pocket Classics. Dover, N.H.: Alan Sutton, 1993.

———. *Pot Luck* [1882]. Translated by Brian Nelson. Oxford: Oxford University Press, 1999.

Index

Abu Dis, Palestine, 109
Académie des inscriptions et belles lettres, 46
Acre, Israel, 165
addicts and addiction, 119–20
Adorno, Theodor, 3
agents and agency, xiii–xxii, 211–19
Albright, William F., 99
Alexander VI, Pope, 64–65
Alhambra, Spain. *See* Granada
Allegro, John M., 51
Allen, Austen, 196–97
American Palestine Exploration Society, 98
American Psychiatric Association, 119, 167
American School of Oriental Research, 46
amnesia, 59–61
Appadurai, Arjun, 195, 199, 200
Aquinas, Thomas, 186
Arab Legion, 47
Arias-Salgado, Gabriel, 75
Art Students' League, 23
Ashbee, Charles Robert, 85, 108–9, Plate 1
Assassin's Creed, xxv, 151, 155–59, 164–66, 170, 173, 181, 183, Plates 5–6
Athens, Greece: Acropolis, 210
Augustine, 186

Bachelard, Gaston, 204
Baedeker, Karl, 159
Ballard, Sam and Jane, 78
Bangs, Jeremy Dupertuis, 249n11
Barnard, George Grey, 4–5, 21–27, 226n73
Bartos, Armand Phillip, 54
Baudrillard, Jean, 197, 198
Becket, Welton, 136
Benedict, Saint, 5, 7
Bentham, Jeremy, xix
Bethlehem, Palestine: Grotto of the Nativity, 191–94
Bevan, Robert, xx
Bierce, Ambrose, 185
Bolín, Luis, 76
Bols, Sir Louis, 112
Bonnefont-en-Comminges, France, 24, 27, 28, 30
Borges, Jorge Luis, 205
Breasted, James, 33–45, 55
Breck, Joseph, 10–14
Brown, Bill, 185, 195–97
Brown, Dan, 156
bullshit, 59

Cairo, Egypt: Egyptian Museum, 33, 50; Nile Hilton, 34; Qasr al-Nil, 33; Tahrir Square, 33
Call of Duty, 154
Calvin, John, 194
Cameron, James, 183
Camino (pilgrimage to Santiago), xxiv, 72–73
Canigou, France. *See* Saint-Martin-du-Canigou, France
Capron, Keith B., 192
Carcassonne, France, 14; Saint-Nazaire, 15
Carroll, Thomas, 123

catalepsy, 53
Cenacle, 206, 207
Chakales, L. S., 192–93
Charles V, Holy Roman Emperor, 70
Chicago: Oriental Institute of the University of Chicago, 33, 45, 46; Tribune Tower, xvii, xxv, 187–94, 198–201; Tribune Tower fragments, 189, 190, 191–94, 199
Clark, William, 123
Claude, Georges, 131
Clement V, Pope, 156
Clermont-Ganneau, Charles Simon, 49
cloister, 5–7
Cloisters Museum, New York City, xvi, xvii, xxiii, 7–31, 187; Annunciation panel, 18–21; "Bonnefont" Cloister, 29, 226n72; Cuxa Cloister, 12; Fuentidueña Chapel, 10; Pontaut Chapter House, 25–26. *See also* Saint-Michel-de-Cuxa, France
Collens, Charles, 10–15
commodity, xvii, 199
Conant, Kenneth, 14
Constantine I, Emperor, 86
Cook, Thomas: map of Jerusalem, 37
Coppola, Francis Ford, 251n69
Corrigan, John, 202
Council of Trent, 191
Counter-Reformation, xxiii, 23, 67, 70
Crary, Jonathan, 224n41
Cross, Frank Moore, 51
Crusader Kings (Paradox Interactive), 164
cue, 119–21
Cuxa. *See* Saint-Michel-de-Cuxa, France
cyborg, 121–22

Damascus, Syria, 164–65; Great Mosque, 158
Dead Sea Scrolls, xxiii, 48–54
Debevoise, Thomas M., 35
Debord, Guy, 138
de Certeau, Michel, 210, 211
Deleuze, Gilles, 201, 209–10, 211
deodand, xiv–xv
de Peuter, Greig, 170
Derrida, Jacques, 195, 217–18
Désilets, Patrice, 157
de Vaux, Roland, 51
Deyan, Sudjic, xx
Diaspora Yeshiva, 207, 208
Disney, Walt, 18, 20, 129
Disraeli, Benjamin, 49
Douglas, Mary, 199
Dubai, United Arab Emirates, 149
Dungeons and Dragons, 164
Dyer-Witheford, Nick, 170

Eisenhower, Dwight D., 131
Eliade, Mircea, xix, xxv, 202–7
Ellerhusen, Ulric H., 45
Erasmus, Desiderius, 69
Ergas, Enrique, 64

Fagel, Harry, 139
Ferdinand of Aragon and Isabella of Castile, xxiii, 64–65
Ferris, George A., 123
Fielding, Temple, 81
Filareti (Antonio di Pietro Averlino), xiii
Florence, Italy: San Leonardo in Arcetri, 18; San Piero Scheraggio, 18
Fontfroid Abbey, France, 30
Ford, Alexander Hume, 113
Fosdick, Raymond B., 34–35
Foster, Norman, 142
Foucault, Michel, 201, 209, 211
fragment, 27–30
Franco, Francisco, xxiv, 73–76, 79, 81
Frankfurt, Harry, 59
Frank Lloyd Wright Foundation, 176
Friedman, Bill, 143–46
Fuentidueña, Spain, 10
Fulcher of Chartres, 85

Geddes, Patrick, 40
Gell, Alfred, 185, 199–200
Gill, Eric, 43–45
Gilpin, William, 160, 161
Gimpel, René, 226n73
Gitai, Amos, 96, 106
Godish, Thad, xxi
Goethe, Johann Wolfgang von, 205
Granada, Spain, xxiii, 64; Alhambra, 40
Grand Theft Auto, 154
Gruber, Petra, xxi

Guattari, Félix, 209–10, 211
Guernica, Spain, 76

Habermas, Jürgen, 210, 211
Hague Convention on Cultural Property, 56
Haifa, Israel: Templer Colony, 91, 92
Harding, G. W. L., 47
Harper, William Rainey, 33
Harris, Neil, xx–xxi
Harrison, Austen St. Barbe, 15, 36
Harry, Myriam, 48–49, 90, 105–6
Hashshashin (Assassins), 155–56
Heidegger, Martin, xix, 185, 194–96, 202, 203–4
Henderson, Nevada: Basic Magnesium Plant, 126
Hilton, Conrad, 78
Holliday, Clifford and Eunice, 92
Holmes, Burton, 112
Hoover Dam, Nevada–Arizona, 125–26
Hoving, Thomas, 18–21, 27
Howe, Fisher, 87
Hughes, Howard, 136
Huizinga, Johan, 151–52, 245n1
Husseini, Kamil Mohammed Taher al-, 111, 112
Husseini, Rabbah Effendi al-, xxiv, 103, 107, 110, 115
Husseini, Salim Effendi al-, 103

identity and identification, 182–83
Iliffe, John Henry, 42, 47
Innocent VIII, Pope, 65
Inquisition, xxiii, 64
Institut français d'archéologie orientale, 46
Istanbul, Turkey: Four Seasons Hotel Istanbul at Sultanahmet, 83

Jacobs, Jane, xx
Jaffa, Israel: Neve Zedek, 94
Jahn, Helmut, 142
James the Greater, Saint (Santiago Matamoros), xxiii, 62, 63, 67, 71–72, 79
Jameson, Fredric, 201
Jeffery, George, 96
Jerusalem, xxii, 85–86, 165; Al-Aksa Mosque, 33; American Colony, xviii, xxiv, 101, 102, 105, 106–15, 240–41n102, Plates 2–3; American Psychiatric Association, 119; American School of Oriental Research (Albright Institute), 97; British School of Archaeology, 97; Church of the Dormition of the Virgin, 206; Church of the Holy Sepulchre, 33, 86–87, 98, 99, 158, Plate 1; Citadel, 40; College of St. George, 97; Dar al-Tifel al-Arabi, 114; Dome of the Rock, xvii, 158; École Biblique, 97; German Colony, 90–93; Hebrew University, 49; Husseini neighborhood (Sheikh Jarrah), 101–6; Rabbah Effendi al-Husseini's house, xxiv, 103–5, Plate 2; Israel Museum, 49, 54; Karm el-Sheikh, 35–36; Kfar Shaul Psychiatric Hospital (formerly the suburb of Deir Yassin), 89; Khalidi house, 236n15; Lionel Rothchild School, 107–8; Me'ah She'arim, 93–96, 97; Museum of the History of Jerusalem, 40–42; Museum on the Seam, 240n100; Palestine Archaeological Museum, xvii, xxiii, 15, 32–56, 230n67; Shrine of the Book, 54; Spafford Children's Center, 107, 239n78; Supreme Court, 52, 228n27; walls of, 251n72; Zion, xvi, xvii, xxv, 203–7
Jerusalem Syndrome, 88–89
John Paul II, Pope, 187
Jordan, the Hashemite Kingdom of, 47, 55–56
Josephus, Titus Flavius, 32, 85

Kelso, James L., 47
Kerkorian, Kirk, 136
Khalidi family, 35
Khirbet al-Mafjar, Palestine: palace at, 33
Khoury, Raymond, 156
Kiesler, Frederic, 54
Knights of the Temple: Infernal Crusade (Starbreeze AB), 164
Kraeling, Carl, 31
Kroyanker, David, 93
Kubin, Alfred, 3
Kyd, Jesper, 165–66

labyrinth, 143
Laffi, Domenico, 71

Lagerlöf, Selma, 85, 87–88, 98, 239n85
Lang, Daniel, 131–32
Langon Chapel, 10
Larsson, Theo, 114
Las Vegas, Nevada, xvii, xxii, xxiv, 121–49, 143; Fremont Street, 123, 126; Golden Nugget Casino, 149; Las Vegas High School (now Las Vegas Academy), 123, 125; Las Vegas Bombing and Gunnery Range (now Nellis Air Force Base), 126
Las Vegas Strip (officially Paradise), 126–49; Bellagio, 137; Caesars Palace, 137, 145, 146; CityCenter, 140, 141–42, 146; Circus Circus, 137; Cosmopolitan, 140; Desert Inn, 127–28; Dunes, 127–28, 138; El Rancho, 127–28, 137; Excalibur, 137; Flamingo, 127–28, 130, 131, 132–33, 138; Hacienda, 119, 127, 138; International Hotel (later the Las Vegas Hilton), 136, 137, 138; Last Frontier, 127–29, 137; Las Vegas Boulevard (formerly Los Angeles Boulevard, U.S. Highway 91), 126, 128, 130; Little Church of the West, 128, 129; Luxor, 137; McCarran International Airport, 139; MGM Grand (later Bally's), 136, 137; Mirage, 137, 140; New York New York, 137; Riviera, 127, 136; Sahara, 127–28; Sands, 127–28; Stardust, 127–28; Treasure Island, 137; Tropicana, 127; Venetian, 137, 139, 140–41, 146; Wynn and Encore, 141, 146–47, Plate 4
Latour, Bruno, 200–201, 212
Lefebvre, Henri, 201, 202, 211
León, Spain: Hostal de San Marco, 78–79
Leo XIII, Pope, 72
Levy, Clifton Harby, 241n102
Lewis, C. S., 186
Libeskind, Daniel, 142, 146
Lindbergh, Charles, 190
Lloyd, Henry D., 190, 198–99
Loivy, A., 107
London: British Academy, 46; British Museum, 46; Savoy Hotel, 73
London Society for Promoting Christianity amongst the Jews (London Jews Society), 93, 107
Los Angeles, California: Beverly Hilton, 136; Ciro's, 131; Sunset Strip, 130
Loti, Pierre, 100
Lourdes, France, 72
Luther, Martin, 87

Macau, China, 149
Madrid, Spain: Castellana Hilton, 78
Marshall Plan, 76
Marx, Karl, 198
Mauss, Marcel, 185, 198–200
maze, 143
McAfee, Guy, 130–31
McCormick, Robert R., 190–94, 197, 199
McDonald, James G., 42
McNamara, Kim, xxi
McNeill, Donald, xxi
Medieval II: Total War, 164
Merleau-Ponty, Maurice, xviii, 204
Merrill, Selah, 98–101, 112–13
Mishima, Yukio, xiv
Molina, Luis de, 69
Moore, William, 127, 129
Mondrian, Piet, 28
Monsempron, Saint-Géraud, France, 15
Mother of All Churches, Church of the Apostles, St. Mary's, 207
Muhammad Ali Pasha, 90
Mumford, Lewis, 21
murder, 3–5
Murray, John, III, 159

Nås, Sweden, 101
al-Nashashibi, Raghib, 112
New York City, 137, 138; Cloisters (George Grey Barnard's museum), 21–22; Cloisters Museum, xvi, xvii, xxiii, 7–31, 187, 226n72; Metropolitan Museum of Art, 7, 22; Museum of Modern Art, 28–29, 135; Times Square, 138; World Trade Center, 210
Notre-Dame-de-Pontaut, France, 24, 25–26

Oldenburg, Claes, 136–37, 196
Olmsted Brothers (John Charles Olmsted and Frederick Law Olmsted Jr.), 10

Opus Dei, 74, 234n62
Orlando, Florida: Disney World, 178; Epcot, 137

Palisades Parkway, New Jersey, 10
Pavlov, Ivan, 120
Paradores de Turismo de España, 75, 78
Paris: Le Cent Quatre, 83
Paulinus of Nola, Saint, 191–93
Paya Rico, Miguel, Cardinal, 72
Pearce, Celia, 183
Pederson, Kohn, 142
Peirce, Charles Sanders, 200
Pelli Clark Pelli Architects, 142
Philadelphia: Philadelphia Museum of Art, 21, 22, 24
Philip IV, "the Fair," King of France, 156
picturesque, 159–63
Piquer, Andrés, 71
Plumer, Herbert, Lord, 35
Ponge, Francis, 195
Pontaut. *See* Notre-Dame-de-Pontaut, France
Pope, John Russell, 15
posthuman, 138
postmodern, 135
Primo de Rivera, Miguel, 75

Ramón-Laca, Alfredo de, 79
Ramsey, William, 32
Reformation, 70, 98, 187, 194
relic, 185–87
Richmond, Ernest, xvii
Rives, James, 64
Roberts, David, 160–64, Plate 5
Rockefeller, John D., Jr., xxiii, 7–10, 13, 16–17, 21–22, 31, 33–47, 55
Rockefeller, John D., Sr., 16–17
Rockefeller Museum. *See* Jerusalem: Palestine Archaeological Museum
Rome: Sancta Sanctorum, 186, 187
Roosevelt, Franklin D., 42
Rorimer, James, 14–15, 23–24, 27
Rosedale, Phillip, 171
Rowling, J. K., 168
Ruskin, John, xix–xx, 160–62, 175
Russell, George Vernon, 131
Rutas Nacionales de Guerra (National Routes of War), Spain, 75–76, 77

Saad, Yusef, 49, 51
Saint-Guilhem-le-Désert, France, 10, 27
Saint-Martin-du-Canigou, France, 30
Saint-Michel-de-Cuxa, France, 8, 10, 13, 18, 23–24, 27
Saint-Michel-de-Grandmont, France, 6, 11
San Francisco, California, 121–22
San Juan, Puerto Rico: Caribe Hilton, 136
Sans, Emmanuel, 24
Santiago de Compostela, Spain: Cathedral of St. James, 62–64, 82; Hospital/Hostal de los Reyes Católicos, xviii, xxiii, xxiv, 61, 62–83; Obradoiro, 65
Sartre, Jean-Paul, 202
Scarry, Elaine, xxii
Schick, Conrad, 93
Schnabel, Julian, 112
Schrader, J. L., 23
Schüll, Natasha Dow, 147–48, 183
Scott, Sir Walter, 156
Second Life, xxv, 167, 170–81, 210–11, 214, 216–17; book burning in, 247n55
Shapira, Maria Rosette. *See* Harry, Myriam
Shapira, Moses Wilhelm, 49
Shelton, Bobby, 139
Sherman, Lawrence W., 59
Shirley, John, 121–22
Siegel, Benjamin "Bugsy," 130
Simmel, Georg, 195
Sixtus IV, Pope, 64
Smilansky, Ze'ev, 94
Smith, Terry, xx
Soja, Edward, 202
Soubirous, Bernadette, 71
Spacewar!, 152–53
spatial marks (mass, point, volume, verge, track), 212–13
Spafford, Horatio and Anna, 106–10
Spanish Civil War, 75–76
Spielberg, Stephen, xviii
spolia, xxiii, 31–32, 56, 193
Starkie, Walter, 73
Steele, John S., 190
Stephen, Saint, 186

Stephenson, Neal, xvi–xvii, 170–71, 173
Stern, Martin, 136
Storrs, Sir Ronald, 112
Sulpicius Severus, 191
Supreme Court, U.S., xv, xix, 154

Tanzimât period, 90
Templars, or Knights of the Temple, 155–56
Templers, German Society of, 90–93
Thiering, Barbara, 52
Thomas Aquinas, 186
Titus Flavius Caesar Vespasianus Augustus, 32
Tolkien, J. R. R., 168
"Tomb of David," 206, 207
Tomb Raider, 154
Toro, Oswardo Luis, 136
Tschumi, Bernard, xviii, 214, 215

Ustinov, Plato von, Baron, 113
Ustinov, Peter, 113

Van Gogh, Vincent, 195, 196, 202
Venice, Italy, 137, 139
Venturi, Robert, Steven Izenour, and Denise Scott Brown, xxiv, 134–35
Vergara, Camilo José, 59
Vester, Bertha, 106, 110, 112
Vienna, Austria: Sacher Hotel, 73
Vincent, Louis Hugues, 114, 240n99
Viñoly, Rafael, 142
Viollet-le-Duc, Eugène, 14

Wallace, Edwin Sherman, 87, 96, 113
Warner, Charles, 136
Washington, D.C.: National Gallery of Art, 15
Wickström, Victor Hugo, 240–41n102
Wilde, Oscar, 205
Wolfe, Tom, 130
Woodhouse, George E., 112
World of Warcraft, xxv, 154, 164, 167–70, 181
Wright, Frank Lloyd, 126–27
Wynn, Steve, 138

Yellin, Yehoshua, 102

Zola, Émile, xiii, xiv, xvii–xviii, 49

ANNABEL JANE WHARTON is William B. Hamilton Professor of Art and Art History at Duke University. She is the author of several books, including *Refiguring the Post Classical City*, *Building the Cold War: Hilton International Hotels and Modern Architecture*, and *Selling Jerusalem: Relics, Replicas, Theme Parks.* In 2014 she was the Vincent Scully Visiting Professor of Architectural History at the Yale University School of Architecture.